Doing Business in Poland

Website: http\\www.vpinternational.com
VP International • Hope Street • Chester • CH4 8BU • England
Tel +44 (0)1244 681619 • Fax +44 (0)1244 681617
E-mail <name>@vpinternational.com

Need to know more... ?

GET
IN
TOUCH
WITH

BRITISH POLISH Chamber of Commerce

- Our services: ▪ essential information on doing business in Poland ▪ representation of your company at government level ▪ conferences & workshops ▪ monthly business breakfasts and cocktails
- Our offices: Warsaw, Gdańsk, Kraków, Katowice, Poznań, Wrocław, London
- Our publications:

BPCC HEAD OFFICE:

ul. Zimna 2 m. 1, 00-138 Warszawa, Poland
Tel: (+48 22) 654 59 71-76, Fax: (+48 22) 654 16 75
Mobile: (+48 501) 100 754, (+48 604) 50 50 28
e-mail: bpcc@bpcc.org.pl, http://www.bpcc.org.pl

REGIONAL OFFICES:

CRACOW

c/o Sunley Polska, ul. Św. Anny 9, 31-008 Kraków
Tel: (+48 12) 421 70 30, 421 56 56, (+48 602) 286 087
Fax. (+48 12) 422 42 64, e-mail: bpcc@bci.krakow.pl

GDAŃSK

c/o Honorary British Consul
ul. Grunwaldzka 100/102, 80-224 Gdańsk
Tel/Fax: (+48 58) 341 43 65, e-mail: consul@abcc.com.pl

KATOWICE c/o British Consulate

ul. PCK 10, 40-057 Katowice
Tel (+48 32) 206 98 01, Fax (+48 32) 205 46 46
e-mail: szura@cz.onet.pl

LONDON

55 Prince s Gate Exhibition Road, London SW7 2PG
Tel: (+44 171) 591 00 57, Fax: (+44 171) 591 00 67
e-mail: bpcc@cwcom.net

POZNAŃ

"Orbis" S.A. Hotel Poznań, Pl. W. Andersa 1, 61-896 Poznań
Tel. (+48 61) 833 19 61, Fax. (+48 61) 852 26 31
e-mail: dyr.hpoznan@orbis.pl

WROCŁAW

c/o TGC Polska, ul. Świdnicka 22, 4th Floor, 50-068 Wrocław
Tel/Fax: (+48 71) 342 30 32, Tel. (+48 71) 341 07 73,
e-mail: madej@bccp.org.pl

CONTACT WITH EAGLE EYE

Bi-monthly magazine
Print-run 5,000 copies
Editor: Ewa Filipek
Tel: (+48 22) 654 59 73
mobile: (+48 604) 521 660
e-mail: esf@bpcc.org.pl

Membership Directory 1999/2000

Annual
Print-run 2,000 copies
Editor: Jolanta Czerwińska
Tel: (+48 22) 654 59 72
mobile: (+48 604) 164 404
e-mail: jola@bpcc.org.pl

Inform@tion Centre

Manager: Dorota Kierbiedź
Tel: (+48 22) 654 59 74
mobile: (+48 604) 160 116
e-mail: bpcc@bpcc.org.pl
http://www.bpcc.org.pl

Doing Business in Poland

This book is written on the basis of information constant in 1999.

First published in 1991
Reprinted in 1992
Second edition 1994
Third edition 2000

Kogan Page Limited
120 Pentonville Road
London N1 9JN

© Kogan Page and contributors, 2000

British Library Cataloguing in Publication Data

A CIP record for this book is available from the British Library.

ISBN 0 7494 3153 9

Typeset by Saxon Graphics Ltd, Derby
Printed in England by Thanet Press Ltd, Margate, Kent

Hearing improves vision.

Solutions that are individually designed to fit your growing needs can only come from people who listen better. And see farther. Together, we can think and do more. Let's talk.
www.ey.com.pl

For more information contact us. Tel.: +48 (22) 528 77 77, Ernst.Young@ey.com.pl

CONSULTING · TAX · ASSURANCE

ERNST & YOUNG

FROM THOUGHT TO FINISH.™

KPMG

KPMG is a leading global professional advisory firm. With more than 100,000 people collaborating worldwide, the firm provides services in the area of assurance, tax, legal, financial advisory and consulting from 830 locations in 160 countries.

With over 600 qualified international and local Polish staff, KPMG Poland offers a complete range of business and advisory services to Polish companies and multinational companies operating in Poland including:

- financial reviews and operational due diligence
- audits of financial statements to meet Polish and international requirements
- assessment of the quality of operational procedures or bank loan portfolios
- advice on banks' acquisitions and mergers
- assistance to banks in licensing proceedings
- corporate income tax, value added tax
- customs duty and excise tax
- personal income tax
- corporate law
- bankruptcy law
- labour and employment law
- property law, intellectual property
- antitrust and trade law
- commercial litigation and arbitration
- transactions structuring, including deal management and negotiations
- prospectus planning and preparation, advisory services concerning public offerings
- business operations improvement: World-Class Finance, World-Class IT, Customer Value Management, Supply Chain Management, Process Improvement, Project Management, Activity Based Management
- packaged solutions (e.g. SAP)
- systems integration: data warehousing, systems architecture, electronic commerce, year 2000

In order to obtain more information please contact our office in Warsaw:

Greg Doyle
KPMG Polska Sp. z o.o.
ul. Chłodna 51, XVI floor, 00-867 Warsaw,
Tel: +48 (22) 582 1000 Fax: +48 (22) 582 1009
E-mail: contact_us@kpmg.pl

Contents

Part 1: The Business Context

Part 2: Market Potential

Part 3: Business Development

Part 4: Building an Organisation

Appendices

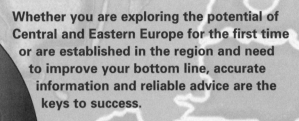
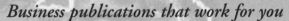

The Contributors

Agro Business Consult (ABC) Poland Ltd is a Polish registered consultancy formed in 1994. The company developed during the period of economic transition and has become a leading international agricultural consultancy operating in Poland, Central and Eastern Europe, the European Union and as far afield as South Africa.

Working alongside the international donor agencies, government agencies and private clients, ABC has managed a series of large projects. The company has ongoing work in the flood affected regions of South Western Poland for the World Bank, projects funded by the British Know How Fund in the grain and arable sectors, a business-to-business development programme for the Danish Department of Trade and Industry and privatisation advisory work for the Greater Municipal Council of Johannesburg in South Africa.

Thom Barnhardt has been a resident of Warsaw for the last four years and is the founder of the *Warsaw Business Journal* and of *Voyage*, a monthly Polish-language travel magazine.

BRE Bank SA is a universal bank with a leading position in corporate and investment banking, as well as private banking, asset management and para-banking services such as leasing, factoring and consumer banking.

The corporate banking focus of BRE Bank is on large and medium sized domestic and multinational corporates for whom the bank provides a full range of commercial and investment banking services.

Lesley Brett joined BOC Distribution Services (BOCDS) Polska in 1995, having previously worked for the Pilkington Group, and was appointed General Director of BOCDS Polska on 1st October 1998. Following a period in Operational Management, Lesley was involved in a major start-up project for Marks & Spencer in the UK and completed a successful contract in the Philippines. She gained her BSc Management & Organisation Degree from the University of Lancaster and has had extensive experience in both manufacturing and distribution.Lesley takes responsibility for all BOCDS activities in Poland and growth in Western and Central Europe.

The **British Embassy's Commercial Section** is ready to assist companies from Britain which are either doing business in Poland or wish to explore business opportunities there. The Embassy provides a range of services, including advice on opportunities, details of potential contacts such as agents and distributors, and tailor-made reports on the likely market for specific products.

Stephen Pattison is Director of Trade Promotion and Consul General at the British Embassy in Warsaw. After studying at the universities of Oxford and Cambridge, he entered the British Diplomatic Service in 1982 and has served at the British High Commission in Nicosia, Cyprus, and the British Embassies of Washington DC and Warsaw. He has represented the British Government at international meetings at the UN in New York, the EU in Brussels, international conferences in Paris and the Hague, and has chaired international negotiations on disarmament in Geneva. He is currently working to encourage British companies to do more business in Poland.

British Polish Chamber of Commerce (BPCC) was established in 1992 and now has over 400 corporate members. The majority of members represent British and international companies and a growing number of Polish companies are joining the Chamber.

The Chamber is active throughout Poland and in the UK, with branch offices and a regular programme of events in Gdansk, Katowice, Krakow, Poznan, Warsaw, Wroclaw and London. Events, ranging from conferences, workshops and seminars to business drinks, breakfast briefings and dinner discussions, provide members with a forum to exchange ideas, make new contacts and meet prominent politicians and officials of British, Polish and European governments, as well as other opinion leaders. It produces two invaluable publications: an annual bi-lingual Membership Directory and a bi-monthly newsletter, *Contact*.

Its close co-operation with other business development organisations, including British Chambers of Commerce Europe-wide, the British Embassy, the Forum of EU Chambers, British Trade International and the Polish Embassy in the UK, gives its members a formidable infrastructure within which to succeed and grow.

Business Management & Finance SA (BMF) was created in 1991 and provides high quality services in corporate finance with special focus on mergers and acquisitions and management consultancy.

BMF has been involved in devising several policy documents for the government in areas such as the automotive industry, railway sector and motorway policy.

In eight years of activity, BMF has completed M&A and financial restructuring assignments with total value of over \$3 billion. With its revenues reaching over US\$6 million per annum and with over 80 employees, BMF has for the last two years, according to Warsaw Business Journal's ranking of management consulting firms, been ranked the number one advisory company operating on the Polish market.

Dr Richard Chmielowiec works for International Apparel Consultancy and specialises in consulting and in lecturing on production systems and quality management, apparel technology and product development. He is registered with UNIDO, ITC, FAO-INF, TI, IAF, EU (Phare), PIF, SWP, BPCC and LCFS.

Dr Chmielowiec has industrial, R&D and academic experience as an international consultant in Poland, the UK, South Africa and Hong Kong. He has worked for UNIDO and other international organisations in Africa, the Middle

East and Far East and recently in Poland (where he has many associates in the field of consulting, manufacturing and trading). Benefiting from extensive world-wide contacts, he also writes for various international apparel and textile journals on issues relating to the apparel industry.

CMS Cameron McKenna is an international commercial law firm advising businesses, financial institutions, governments and public sector bodies. It is a founding member of CMS – the transnational legal services organisation. CMS law firms provide clients with access to integrated pan-European legal services. The organisation currently employs in excess of 1400 lawyers, with a total staff of 3000 in 19 jurisdictions.

With offices and associated offices in various regions throughout the world including the UK, Central Europe, the CIS, Asia and North America, CMS Cameron McKenna advises clients on a wide range of transactions and projects both in the UK and internationally. It provides specialist expertise in areas such as finance and financial services; corporate; utilities and natural resources; real estate and environment; insurance and reinsurance; cross-border investment; technology, life sciences and intellectual property; infrastructure and projects; human resources and pensions; competition and European law; arbitration and litigation.

CMS Cameron McKenna has been advising clients in Poland and Central Europe since 1989.

Korn/Ferry International specialises in providing consulting services for the Human Resources sector. With over 30 years of experience worldwide and seven years in Poland, it helps client companies select high-calibre leaders in local, regional and international markets.

Dorota Czarnota is Managing Partner of Korn/Ferry International's Warsaw office and is responsible for the management of a wide range of assignments for several multinational clients. Before joining Korn/Ferry in 1996 Ms. Czarnota was a Partner with another international executive search firm with responsibility for sales, marketing and public relations in Poland. She has eight years experience in executive search and has successfully executed senior searches in the financial services, pharmaceutical and fast moving consumer goods sectors in Poland and the rest of Central and Eastern Europe.

Katarzyna Bienkowska is a Consultant at Korn/Ferry International in Warsaw, where she has worked since 1994. She is responsible for the management of a wide range of assignments for multinational clients and has five years of experience in senior-level executive search and recruitment. Before joining Korn/Ferry Ms. Bienkowska held the position of Managing Director with a management consulting firm.

Katarzyna Grajda joined Korn/Ferry International in January 1997. Since then she has been responsible for successful management of a wide range of assignments for numerous clients in the Polish market, focusing mainly on industrial and FMCG blue chip companies. Prior to her current position Ms. Grajda was the head of the human resources advertised selection department in another consulting firm.

Dorota Serwinska joined Korn/Ferry International in Warsaw in June 1997. Since then she has contributed to the success of a wide range of search assignments for numerous multinational clients, her primary focus being Advance Technology related products and the Media and Entertainment sector. Before joining Korn/Ferry International Ms. Serwinska held the position of HR Manager at Lucent Technologies Polska (formerly AT&T).

Joanna Szczepanik-Klein joined Korn/Ferry International in August 1996, first working as Office Manager, then, since 1997, as Research Associate. She has recently joined the team of Korn/Ferry consultants and has already successfully completed several assignments. Prior to joining Korn/Ferry International Ms. Szczepanik-Klein had several years experience in customer services and sales.

Each national firm of **Ernst & Young** is a member of Ernst & Young International. Nearly 85,000 professionals operate across 670 offices spanning 132 countries. They deliver demonstrable value to a diverse range of global clients, contributing towards the firm's world-wide revenues of $10.9 billion.

Ernst & Young was established in Poland in January 1990 in response to the growing demand for professional advisory and audit services. Since then the firm has developed a strong presence and employs 700 people in 7 offices in Warsaw, Gdansk, Katowice, Lodz, Poznan, Szczecin and Wroclaw.

The **European Bank for Reconstruction and Development (EBRD)** was established in 1991 and has its headquarters in London. It is a multilateral development bank which fosters the transition towards open market-oriented economies and promotes private and entrepreneurial initiative in 26 countries of central and Eastern Europe and the Commonwealth of Independent States (CIS).

Healey & Baker is an international partnership, established in 1820, providing international real estate consultancy and agency advice. It specialises in all types of commercial property and acts for a range of prominent clients across the corporate, public and private sectors. Healey & Baker operates throughout Europe, the Middle East and Africa. Since September 1998, H&B has been a member of Cushman & Wakefield, delivering a global service through 7800 staff in 130 offices.

Séan Briggs joined Healey & Baker in 1986, working in professional services and subsequently in the Office Agency & Development Department. In January 1995 he joined the Warsaw Office and in 1996 he set up the Retail Department, which now totals eight surveyors.

He has been involved with the development of a number of the largest shopping centres in Poland and is currently working on the leasing of the Galeria Mokotow shopping centre in Warsaw and the Tesco hypermarket malls around Poland. He is also advising ING Real Estate International on the retail element of several of their projects.

Jan J Kluk, OBE is President of ICL Poland and Chairman of the British Polish Chamber of Commerce. ICL is a global supplier of IT systems and services for the government, telecommunications, utilities, banking, retail and travel sectors, and has operated in Poland for over 30 years. Jan has been doing business in central Europe for 25 years, living in Warsaw since 1979, and has a keen interest in cross-cultural management development.

KPMG has offices in 15 countries across the Central and Eastern European region, employing around 2000 people.

In May 1990 an office was opened in Warsaw and today KPMG Polska is a strong national practice with offices in Warsaw, Krakow and Poznan. KPMG Polska employs around 700 staff members specialising in professional advisory services of all disciplines and provides a wide range of advisory services to Polish companies and multinational companies doing business in Poland, including taxation services, audit (in accordance with Polish statutory requirements and international standards), management and IT consultancy, legal advice and financial advisory services.

Krys Szczotka is a Partner at KPMG Polska. Formerly a district inspector with the UK Inland Revenue, Krys has been working in the tax department at KPMG Polska since 1994. He speaks fluent English and Polish, and specialises in cross border investment and corporate structuring.

Eva Doyle is a UK qualified tax advisor and chartered accountant. She came to KPMG Polska in 1996 following almost 3 years in Prague. She specialises in international corporate tax with a special emphasis on mergers and acquisitions, and holds the position of Senior Manager.

Oliver Sinton had a background in commercial management in a UK based multinational when he joined KPMG Polska in 1995. He is a Manager and specialises in transfer pricing. He speaks fluent English and Polish.

Arkadiusz Michonski is head of unit in the Office of the Committee for European Integration in Warsaw. He has been involved in the programming of the EU membership adjustment processes in Poland as well as managing, on behalf of the Office, important trade disputes in bilateral EU–Poland trade relations. His academic contributions include writing about adjustment processes in the area of the free movement of goods and of industrial restructuring.

Dr Andrew Murray is Assistant Director of the British Council in Warsaw. The British Council promotes British culture and education and runs centres throughout Poland. It is the leading English language tuition provider in Poland.

Danuta Pliecka is a consultant specialising in the Polish pharmaceutical industry and healthcare system reform. She has worked for numerous international pharmaceutical companies, advising them on the Polish market and has written and lectured extensively on both the pharmaceutical industry and on healthcare economics. She has acted in an advisory capacity to several government and regional health authorities and she is the author and editor of the bulletin *Forum of Health Service Reforms* as well as other pharmaceutical and healthcare publications.

Joe Senft is Managing Director of Brandstorm International, an independent advertising agency in Warsaw. He has worked at advertising agencies in New York and Warsaw for clients such as Unilever, Nestlé, Citibank, Alima-Gerber, General Motors, and Nabisco.

Kevin R Smith is a partner of AWS Corporate Finance & Consultancy and is currently on secondment to British Trade International as Export Promoter – Finance, Central Europe & Baltic States. AWS acts as an advisor to companies on most financing and accounting matters including raising trade and project finance, debt and equity but has particular expertise in Central and Eastern Europe and the Former Soviet Union.

Richard Thurlow is a director of Ove Arup and Partners and the Managing Director of Ove Arup and Partners Sp.z.o.o. Arup is a leading international firm of multi-disciplinary consulting engineers and planners, having over 5000 staff and operating from over 60 permanent offices throughout the world. The firm has worked in Poland since 1995, and offers a full civil, transport, structural, mechanical and electrical design service.

VP International is the UK's leading supplier of Central and Eastern European business information and is one of the most experienced research agencies specialising in the region. Headquartered in the UK, it has offices in Prague and Warsaw from where it offers a range of complementary services aimed at organisations extending into Central Europe as well as those already active but requiring external support. VP International provides accurate information and reliable advice, the key to successful development in any Central European industry sector.

Nick Sljivic is a Director of VP International and is responsible for the company's Polish activities. He has worked across a wide range of industries and has particular expertise in the automotive, FMCG, medical and packaging sectors.

WS Atkins Polska is a member company of WS Atkins plc, one of Europe's largest, multi-disciplinary consultancies, with over 9500 staff world-wide. It has been active in Poland since the 1980s, and is a registered Polish Company since 1993.

The main focus of activity is technical and engineering consulting, although Atkins is also a key player in the Polish consultancy market – notably with respect to environmental liability audits and site assessments.

Robert Adamczyk is the head of the Environmental Department of WS Atkins Polska. He has worked in Poland since 1993 and has gained a broad range of experience of conducting audit work (Phase I and Phase II) in Poland, UK, Estonia, Romania, Russia and Hungary, including EBRD funded projects. He is a registered EIA expert witness of the Ministry of the Environment and a UK EARA registered auditor. He has conducted over 100 audits of various facilities in Poland ranging from Phase I US ASTM (E1527) type audits to supervision of Phase II intrusive investigations.

Foreword

Ten years ago Poland began on the road of radical political and economical change. In a relatively short time our country has achieved a lot. We have established democratic procedures and political stability. We have created institutional guarantees for civil liberties and for the rule of law. We have successfully developed self-government.

Consecutive governments have, with great consistency, instituted a programme of economic and social reform. Its aim is to maintain economic growth, reduce inflation and fundamentally change ownership structures in the economy, in which a wider and larger role is played by the private sector, based on competitive rules and openness. We have pursued a tough monetary policy and bank privatisation is rapidly progressing. We have built a stock exchange and financial instruments from scratch. Huge investments in infrastructure have recently been made, mostly in telecommunications and work has begun in the transportation sector, more particularly in the construction of motorways and high-speed railways.

The success achieved in Poland can be measured by the country's rapid process of economic internationalisation. We owe this to a stable currency, high levels of investment and systematic privatisation of state-owned enterprises. This carefully calculated and effective policy will be continued. There are of course areas where there remains much to be done. In the 1990s, we are making an effort to restructure heavy industry, including mining, steel and the defence industry. The changes can't be made overnight. Many of the difficulties in these sectors have been struggled with for decades by societies in Western countries.

Polish foreign trade turnover is growing from year to year. About 70 per cent of our trade is with countries of the European Union, with whom we are negotiating over the issue of our future membership. So far we have managed to complete discussions on seven subjects. Before us lie negotiations on the most complex issues such as agriculture, heavy industry, fishery and the protection of the environment, free flow of people and capital, and budget and regional policy.

I hope that we will be able to conclude all negotiations by 2001. However, we must speed our legislative work in the process of adapting our laws to those of the Union.

An important step in the transformation process of Poland was recently taken with the introduction of administrative reform. It created a new division of the country into large and independently strong counties. Strengthening provincial self-government will be conducive to the more efficient performance of public administration. Foreign investors will also benefit from these reforms. It is very important for us to open up the Polish economy and include it in the natural flow of the world economy. We are therefore delighted with the inflow of foreign capital and especially of long-term and stable investment. It is satisfying to note that we have the highest levels of inward investment of all Central and East European countries.

Although Poland may not yet head the list of the world's most attractive investment locations, we are steadily climbing in the rankings. Poland's strength and greatest advantage is its desire and ability to change and improve. That is why I was delighted to hear of the publication of *Doing Business in Poland*. I am sure that reading this publication will bring British business people closer to the modern Poland – a hospitable and dynamic country – and will also encourage them to benefit from this opportunity to do good business in the land of the Vistula.

Aleksander Kwasniewski
President of the Republic of Poland

Foreword

Poland is speeding up the process of becoming an effective member state of the EU. The publication of this book therefore comes at an opportune time as it is designed for those who are seeking more information about the tremendous opportunities presented by the Polish market, both now and in the future. Poland has been described as a country of political, economic and social paradoxes but, as history has shown, it also has an incredible capability for survival. To quote a recent headline, 'Tigerish growth has made Poland the toast of Central Europe'.

The euphoria of EU accession is gradually changing into the pragmatic action needed to conform to EU standards and regulations. The attractiveness of Poland as a place for business development has increased competition, which in turn demands greater discipline to reduce operating costs, and preserve profit margins. The requirement for Polish enterprises to become more effective, in both home and export markets, increases the appetite for strategic alliances with Western partners. This opportunity also demands greater effort by Western shareholders to take an active role in transferring knowledge and skills – while working in partnership with very capable Polish people.

We see a real will by the Polish government to boost the economy through the privatisation process, especially as Poland must open its market in line with the EU's liberalisation policy. This in turn helps develop the country's infrastructure, and produces opportunities for the development of small and medium-sized enterprises, which are the backbone of any strong, privatised economy. An important area that needs to be addressed, in parallel, is social regeneration, which means retraining and redeploying people who will be without jobs as a result of economic reform. The business sector has an important role to play, by stimulating interest in life-long learning and helping to prevent social exclusion.

With over 450 members in the UK and Poland, the British Polish Chamber of Commerce's vision for the future takes into account the kaleidoscopic times for business in Europe. We work in close co-operation with the British Embassy's Commercial Section and the British Council, and we encourage you, both members and prospective members, to share ideas for attractive projects to help Poland on its way into the EU.

Jan J Kluk OBE
Chairman
British Polish Chamber of Commerce

Preface

In the past few years Poland has shown itself to be a star among emerging markets. It has a vigorous entrepreneurial culture and has maintained a strong growth rate, withstanding the crises which have afflicted some developing markets in Europe and elsewhere. It remains a favourite destination for multi-national investment, which now totals over US$30 billion. Since the end of communism, many major European, US and Korean companies have built up a strong presence in Poland in a wide variety of sectors including food processing, automotive, utilities and construction. It is a market with huge potential, on track to become a full member of the EU in the early years of the next millennium.

Successive Polish governments have been committed to economic reform. The current government is pressing forward with privatisation in those few sectors that remain under state control, such as energy and coal. The government has also promoted a major reform of local government and health care, and has started the privatisation of key Polish companies such as the LOT national airline and the state insurance company.

I believe there are huge opportunities for British companies in Poland, whether they are exporters, potential investors or service providers. For exporters, the reduction and eventual abolition of duties on most products and the increasing sophistication of the distribution and retail network offer access to an attractive marketplace. For investors, the British experience of privatisation, public–private partnership, and sophisticated management and marketing techniques give British companies strong advantages in competing for business here.

But Poland is a competitive market. British companies need to seize the opportunities quickly. The British Embassy in Warsaw and the BTI (British Trade International) are ready to help.

It is also a fast-changing market. Analysis produced even a few years ago is quickly overtaken by events. I am confident that this new edition of *Doing Business in Poland* will make an important contribution to companies' success in this signficant market.

John M Macgregor
HM Ambassador to Warsaw

Preface

Poland has been at the forefront of change in Central and Eastern Europe, enacting a peaceful and successful transition from a command to a market economy. The country has enjoyed seven consecutive years of economic growth and its impending membership of the European Union (planned for 2002) places it on a par with other developed European nations.

The outlook for Poland is positive. The country benefits from a favourable geographic location, being at the heart of Central Europe, and plays a pivotal role in facilitating trade between its neighbours. It has a growing market, catering to approximately 40 million customers who enjoy a rising standard of living and higher disposable incomes. The legal framework encourages business activity and the restructuring and privatisation programmes are beginning to bear fruit.

Poland has attracted much foreign direct investment into the manufacturing and services sectors and FDI continues to grow, reflecting the international business community's confidence in the country. It is in the spirit of strengthening business links with Poland that this book has been designed. It aims to provide companies with practical advice on how best to identify and follow up opportunities in the country.

The CBI has been fortunate to draw on the wide range of experience and expertise of the book's contributors. Major international contributors include: CMS Cameron McKenna, KPMG, BMF, BRE Bank, the EBRD, the EU, the BTI (British Trade International), VP International and the British Polish Chamber of Commerce. These contributors have provided a thorough briefing on the investment climate in Poland and, with the benefit of their experience, give us useful advice on how best to take advantage of business opportunities in this large and developed market.

Adair Turner
Director General
Confederation of British Industry

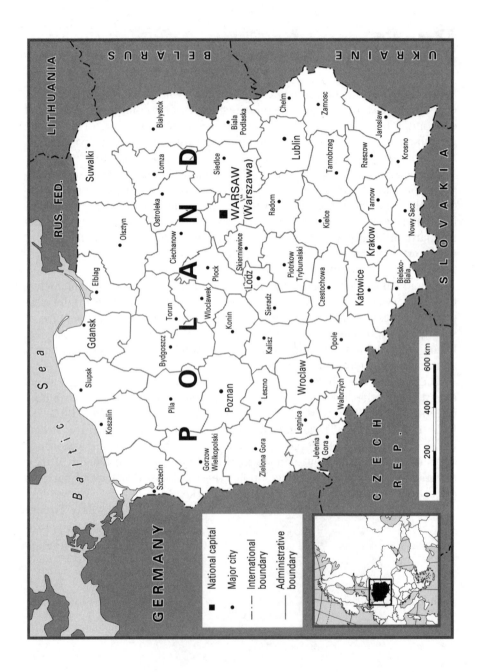

Map 1: Poland and its neighbours

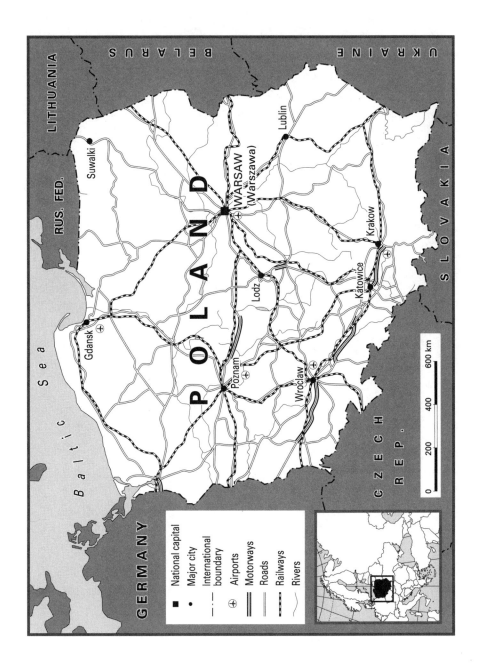

Map 2: Infrastructure in Poland

Part 1

The Business Context

1

Political Environment

Stephen Pattison, British Embassy, Warsaw

Introduction

In 1989, Poland was the first country in Central Europe to end communist rule, after 40 years. This followed a struggle between the trade union Solidarity and the Communist government that captured the world's attention throughout the 1980s.

Post-communist Poland

The first free elections were held in 1989 and resulted in the overthrow of the communist government. The Communist Party collapsed shortly thereafter. Its successor, the SLD, is a broadly Social Democratic party. A key figure in promoting the rapid transformation of Poland in the early 1990s was the deputy prime minister and finance minister, Leszek Balcerowicz. He served under the first two post-communist governments and forced through a tough austerity programme, with rapid liberalisation of prices.

The years 1991–95 saw a rapid succession of governments, including the appointment of Poland's first woman prime minister, Hanna Suchocka, in 1992–93. However, the broad commitment to transformation remained, despite differences over speed and priorities.

The president, Lech Walesa (the leader of Solidarity in the 1980s), played an important role that sometimes brought him into conflict with parliament, with tensions peaking in 1995, when relations between him and Prime Minister Pawlak deteriorated badly. Walesa's refusal to sign legislation raising personal income tax led to a constitutional court ruling that he had acted unconstitutionally. In the bitterly contested presidential elections Walesa was defeated by the SLD candidate, Kwasniewski, who is still president and enjoys an outstanding 78 per cent approval rating. In the same year, the SLD leader Cimoszewicz became prime minister and Polish politics entered a more settled phase.

In the 1997 elections power passed to the opposition, a coalition comprising the heirs of the old Solidarity trade union (AWS), the Freedom

Union party (UW), a pro-reform centre right party. AWS is the larger party. The UW leader, Balcerowicz, returned to his former posts as finance minister and deputy prime minister. Both parties are committed to reform, although AWS is anxious to ensure that Polish trade unionists do not get left behind.

Electoral system

Poland has a bicameral legislature, elected by proportional representation. The head of government is chosen on the basis of the strength of the parties in the lower house. Government ministers do not have to be members of parliament, and there are in government a number of technocrats and politicians from outside parliament.

The president is head of state and has the power to dissolve parliament and to nominate the prime minister. The next presidential elections are due in 2000.

Current political overview

The current composition of the Sejm (lower house of the parliament) is as follows:

- AWS 200;
- UW 60;
- SLD 164;
- Others 36.

When, following the 1997 elections, AWS and UW were invited to form a coalition government, there was much horse-trading over the appointment of ministers. UW secured the finance, foreign affairs, defence, transport, culture and justice portfolios, with the rest going to AWS. (In a subsequent reshuffle, Culture has gone to AWS.) The principle is that, whichever party has the top post in a ministry, the deputy to that post must be a member of the other party in the coalition.

The prime minister is Jerzy Buzek of AWS, a former chemistry professor. The deputy prime minister is Tomaszewski, also of AWS. The leader of UW, Balcerowicz, is finance minister and second deputy prime minister.

Other key ministers include: Wasacz (AWS), minister of the state treasury, responsible for privatising Poland's remaining state-owned assets; Steinhoff (AWS), minister of the economy, responsible for industrial policy, including the reform of the coal and steel sectors; and Geremek (UW), foreign minister.

Local government reform

At the beginning of 1999, the government introduced wide-ranging reform of local government, dividing Poland into 16 new administrative regions (*voivodships*) instead of the previous 49 regions. A new layer of boroughs (*poviats*) was created between these regions and the small town or parish councils (*gminas*).

The reform of the structure was accompanied by measures designed to devolve power to the regions. Each *voivodship* has its own parliament and its own leader of the parliament (marshal) responsible for administering the local budget. This newly created post of marshal is an important one: marshals will be responsible for much of the day-to-day administration and will also play an increasingly important role in developing trade and investment in their regions.

Current political issues

Neither the internal relations between members of the governing coalition nor the government's relationship with the president have always been easy but the coalition is likely to remain in office until the next elections.

The government's reform agenda is ambitious. At the beginning of 1999, in addition to the local government reforms described earlier, it introduced fundamental reforms in health care, education and pensions. The government has been criticised for introducing so many reforms at the same time, an approach many Poles found difficult to digest. The health care reform provoked strikes from workers in the sector. The pension reform, however, has attracted international praise. It requires Polish employees to register with one of several licensed pension funds run by private companies, including many foreign companies. Poland is now one of only two countries in the world to have introduced an obligation to register with a privately run pension fund.

The government is also pressing ahead with privatisation. Much of the Polish economy is already in private hands. The companies that are still under state control are in the heavy industries sector, such as steel and coal, and these pose the biggest political and economic problems. The government has reached agreement with the unions on an ambitious restructuring programme for the coal industry that envisages 100,000 redundancies over the next four years.

Other privatisation objectives for 1999 include finding a strategic partner for LOT, the state-owned airline, and privatising most of the remaining banks, the state insurance company, the state telecommunications company and several electricity generating and distribution plants.

For the past few years the government and the National Bank of Poland (Central Bank) have followed an austere fiscal and monetary policy, introduced in 1997 to avoid economic overheating, and a repeat of the crises that have hit other emerging markets. The policy has been successful and Poland's prudent macro-economic management has won wide international approval and support, though the government's determination to keep to strict budgetary constraints has led to demonstrations by some of the country's hardest hit groups, such as farmers, miners and nurses.

Foreign policy

Poland became a full member of NATO in March 1999, thus fulfilling its long held ambition of joining the Western Alliance. The Polish government is committed to Poland's early membership of the EU and detailed negotiations are under way. The Polish government has said that it intends to be ready for membership by the end of 2002. New legislation will need to be implemented in many areas to bring Poland's laws into line with the EU's *acquis communautaire* (its legal heritage). The most difficult areas are likely to include agriculture and the environment.

2

Investment Climate

European Bank for Reconstruction and Development (EBRD)

Introduction

Since 1991, Poland has been one of the leading countries in Central and Eastern Europe in attracting foreign direct investment (FDI). Having enjoyed seven consecutive years of economic growth resulting in higher incomes, consumer spending and levels of employment, Poland has become an increasingly attractive destination for foreign investors from around the world. Foremost among these are companies from Germany, the USA, France and Italy, with the biggest investments being made in the manufacturing sector.

Western confidence in Poland is likely to become even stronger over the next few years as the country makes further progress on accession to the EU. Poland is now well on track for membership of the EU and is one of the five countries that began accession negotiations in March 1998. The country is rapidly converging with EU standards and aims to be ready for accession by the end of 2002. Polish trade has already pursued new markets, moving away from Russia and other former Soviet republics towards EU countries. By 1997, 65 per cent of Polish exports were destined for the EU, compared with 31 per cent eight years earlier.

Like other countries in the region, Poland was affected by the Russian financial crisis in August 1998, but not severely. Having already developed trade links with Western European economies, Poland was not as dependent on Eastern European markets as many other neighbouring countries. In the long term the crisis is unlikely to have a significant effect.

Economic background

Poland has made rapid headway in its transition to a market economy, recording considerable progress in liberalisation, privatisation, restructuring and financial sector reform. In recent years emphasis has shifted away from industry and towards services, with considerable growth in the private sector. Each year since 1990 the private sector has grown by an average of 15 per cent. By 1997 it accounted for 65 per cent of production, compared with only 29 per cent in 1989.

Positive growth in GDP has been recorded every year since 1992, reaching a peak of 6.9 per cent in 1997. Even in 1998, it remained healthy, at 4.8 per cent, despite the financial crisis in the region, and in 1999 it is predicted to remain positive at around 3 per cent. Inflation has declined from 44.3 per cent in 1992 to approximately 8.5 per cent in 1998.

Foreign direct investment

FDI inflows have risen every year since 1991, reaching a total of some US$ 15 billion of investment over the past eight years, according to the National Bank of Poland. This figure rises to US$30 billion if reinvestments and investments in kind are included. One of the main areas of growth has been investment in equipment and machinery, which accounted for half of all investments in 1997. In spite of difficulties in the financial markets, FDI into Poland has continued to grow, reaching an estimated peak of US$6.6 billion in 1998. This total reflected increased levels of investment from firms already present in the Polish market, as well as commitments from new investors.

According to the Polish Agency for Foreign Investment (PAIZ), foremost among foreign investors are the Italian car producer Fiat, whose investments exceed US$1 billion, and the Korean-based Daewoo, which has also invested over US$1 billion in the automotive, electronics and construction sectors. Other leading investors include the German financial institution Bayerische Hypo und Vereinsbank. The leading new investor is the Russian gas company RAO Gazprom, which invested US$938 million in 1998 in the construction of a gas pipeline.

As of the end of 1998, most foreign capital had been invested in manufacturing – a total of US$15.9 billion – including investments in food processing, transport equipment and other non-metallic products. The second most significant sector for FDI is the area of financial services, which amounted to a total of US$4.8 billion by the end of 1998. Other sectors attracting significant levels of foreign investment include wholesale and retail trade, construction, transport and communications, and hotels and restaurants.

By the end of 1998 a total of 714 foreign companies from 34 countries had invested in Poland, up from 585 a year earlier. For the first time in five years, German companies represented the largest source of investment, committing over US$5.1 billion (18.8 per cent of total FDI), just ahead of US companies, which have invested a total of US$4.9 billion. Almost 89 per cent of FDI into Poland originated in OECD countries, which have invested a total of US$24.3 billion.

Polish Agency for Foreign Investment (PAIZ)

PAIZ was established by the State Treasury in 1992 to increase foreign investment in Poland. Its main aim is to organise and promote activities that attract foreign capital to Poland. These include:

- providing direct assistance to foreign investors in the execution of investment projects;
- publishing information on investment opportunities in Poland;
- consulting with Polish authorities to create favourable conditions for foreign investments in Poland;
- marketing Poland abroad as an attractive investment option.

The agency assists in negotiations between foreign investors and Polish partners, helping to find the best solutions for both parties and to bring projects to a successful conclusion. It produces a wide range of useful publications on the investment climate, investment regulations, opportunities in particular sectors and the results of its regular surveys of foreign investors' experience in Poland. All its services are free of charge (Website: www.paiz.gov.pl).

New legislation for foreign investors

Investment procedures for foreign companies have been simplified through a new law enacted in October 1998, which brings Polish legislation closer to EU and OECD regulations. Under the new legislation, foreign firms are no longer restricted to operating as limited liability or joint-stock companies, but can take the form of any business organisation permitted by Polish law.

The number of sectors requiring concessions has been reduced from 28 to 6: surveying and mining of minerals, weapons manufacturing and trade, manufacturing and processing of liquid fuels and energy, air transport, security services and construction of toll motorways. Licences are obligatory for those operating in 14 sectors, including alcohol and tobacco production and international transportation, but have disappeared for 11 sectors, including the metal and precious stone trade and freshwater fishery.

Reasons to invest in Poland

A growing market

Poland has a rapidly expanding market economy of 40 million consumers. Under the government's economic programme for 1999–2001, the main objective is to ensure long-term growth at an annual rate of at least 6 per cent, combined with consistent job creation. Accession to the EU will expand the country's potential market even further.

Favourable geographic position

Located in the heart of Central Europe, Poland forms a bridge between East and West, and enjoys good relations and practical co-operation with all of its neighbours.

Macro-economic stability

Poland's economy has grown rapidly in recent years and its economic performance is set to remain strong in 1999 and beyond.

A modern legal framework for investment

Comprehensive legislation exists in the area of commercial law. Company laws contain provisions for corporate governance and the protection of shareholders' rights. Bankruptcy law includes detailed provisions for reorganisation and liquidation.

Developed business infrastructure

Poland has made substantial progress in price liberalisation and has taken steps to reduce abuse of market power and to promote a competitive environment, including the substantial reduction of entry restrictions. Substantial progress has been made in establishing bank solvency and a framework for supervision and regulation. There is significant lending to private enterprises and a large number of private banks. More than 25 per cent of large-scale enterprise assets are in private hands or in the process of being privatised.

Integration in the international community

Poland is a member of the Organisation for Economic Cooperation and Development (OECD), the European Free Trade Association (EFTA), the World Trade Organisation (WTO) and in March 1999 joined NATO. In November 1998 substantive negotiations for EU accession got under way, which will provide an impetus for continued structural reform.

Major privatisation programme

The privatisation of major assets, accompanied by industrial restructuring, will provide significant investment opportunities for foreign investors.

Under the government's privatisation programme, unveiled in May 1998, the target is to sell most of the state's remaining 3000 enterprises by 2001 – about three quarters of the top Polish companies ranked by turnover are still state-owned. Priority sales will be large state-owned assets in infrastructure, heavy industry, mining and finance.

Investment opportunities by sector

With Polish economic performance set to remain strong in 1999, there are ample opportunities for foreign companies to invest in a variety of sectors. Some of the most dynamic areas are outlined below.

Car industry

Over the past few years, car sales in Poland have risen rapidly, reaching over half a million in 1998. Leading foreign investors include Fiat (Italy), Daewoo (South Korea) and General Motors (USA). To meet the rising demand for cars in Poland and elsewhere in the region, all three companies have invested heavily in new capacity. Several foreign investors are also involved in the manufacture of car parts in Poland. As the market for cars continues to increase, further opportunities will open up for large-scale investment in this sector.

Financial sector

Major changes have taken place in the Polish banking system in recent years, with a gradual increase in the number of bank privatisations. Foreign banks have acted quickly to take advantage of the opportunities in this sector. Out of Poland's 83 banks, 29 were foreign-owned at the end of 1997. Some foreign banks operate through subsidiaries established in their own name, such as Deutsche Bank and ABN Amro, while others have established strategic partnerships. In addition, there are a large number of minority foreign shareholders. The strategic approach of the authorities has been to restructure and recapitalise banks prior to privatisation. Further progress in this area is expected in 1999 and beyond.

Food processing

Food processing is a rapidly expanding sector, with a significant level of foreign investment and potential for much more. It is the largest manufacturing industry in Poland and contributes 6 per cent of GDP. EU accession requirements are likely to lead to greater investment possibilities over the next few years.

Investment opportunities are widespread in the grain and potato processing sector, where increasing demand for potato products has led to the creation of new privately owned factories making crisps and chips. Bread consumption is also high, and large foreign investments are expected. In the sugar industry new regulations allow sugar companies to generate profit and more foreign investment is expected as a result.

Brewing

Beer production is growing faster in Poland than anywhere else in the world. Great technological progress has been achieved through rapid privatisation of the largest breweries and high levels of investment. Western investors include Carlsberg (Denmark), Heineken (Netherlands) and South African Breweries. With growth estimated at 10 per cent a year, there is significant potential for further investment.

Retailing

Retailing has grown at remarkable speed in Poland and remains an area of great potential. A huge new market of consumers has a growing disposable income and is eager to take advantage of the new range of products available. About US$2.2 billion has been invested in the retail and wholesale trade by foreign companies, the largest of which is Metro (Germany). The company has spent almost US$600 million investing in a chain of hypermarkets and plans to invest a further US$650 million.

Chemicals and pharmaceuticals

Full privatisation of the chemical industry is being undertaken in Poland, with completion expected by 2001. The pharmaceutical industry is experiencing rapid growth, with demand expected to grow by 25–30 per cent over the next few years. Sales are forecast to reach approximately US$4 billion by 2005, accounting for over 40 per cent of pharmaceuticals sold in Central and Eastern Europe.

Paper and pulp

The paper and pulp industry has attracted significant foreign investment since undergoing widespread privatisation. Between 1996 and 1997 investments in the industry rose by 138 per cent and quality has improved. The most dynamic areas include newsprint and printing, and writing and copying paper. American and Swedish companies have been the main source of foreign investment.

Construction and property

The construction market continues to show rapid growth, of about 20 per cent each year. Most of this involves commercial and industrial facilities but residential construction projects are also on the increase. A wide range of opportunities exists for investment in all aspects of construction as Poland improves its infrastructure to prepare for accession to the EU.

Tourism

Poland has established a good tourist infrastructure, including hotels of all classes. In 1997 it attracted over 87 million visitors, making it the eighth most visited country in the world. By mid-1998 foreign investments in tourism totalled about US$340 million, with the largest investment being made in the hotel sector by Bau Holding AG (Austria). Expansion over the next two years of the Polish National Tourist Office network is set to maintain rising tourist income. In 2000 Krakow will feature as a European cultural capital and is already recognised as a World Heritage Site.

Heavy industry

Poland's heavy industry giants have not yet attracted much interest from foreign investors. The ongoing privatisation of the steel industry will, however, help to increase investment opportunities significantly. Poland is a major steel producer, operating more than half of the 40 steel mills in Central Europe. Since the start of the decade, 11 of the state-owned steel mills have been sold through privatisation, and plans are in place to privatise some of the largest steel mills by 2001. At the same time a restructuring programme aims to help Polish steel mills become competitive in the EU market over the next four years.

Telecommunications

Extensive reforms have recently been enacted to create major opportunities for private investment in Poland's infrastructure. In telecommunications, the country continues to liberalise and improve its services prior to EU accession. In 1998 the government sold 15 per cent of Telekomunikacja Polska (TPSA), the national telecommunications operator, and plans to sell an additional 25–35 per cent stake to a strategic investor in 1999–2000. Greater private sector participation will help TPSA to meet the huge demand for phone lines in Poland and to reduce the queue of 2 million still waiting for phones. It is forecast that the telecommunications sector will grow at about 25 per cent per year and will be worth US$5 billion by 2000.

Transport

The government has made extensive plans for the development of roads, railways, inland waterways, airports and seaports up to 2015, which will create a number of investment possibilities for foreign companies. In the road sector the plan calls for the existing network to be upgraded to EU standards, which would cost some US$26 billion. Funding proposals under discussion include public–private partnerships, with the state providing up to 50 per cent of construction costs.

A major restructuring programme is under way for PKP, the state railway firm, which is to be divided into two enterprises. These will ultimately be transformed into joint-stock companies and partially privatised in 2000–02. In 1998 the government awarded the first licences for nationwide railway services to independent operators.

Airport privatisation is due to get under way with the sale of Gdansk's Rebiechowo airport in 1999. It is hoped that the sale will act as a pilot project for further airport sales.

Energy

Energy legislation passed in December 1997 has reduced obstacles to foreign investment and has already resulted in an increase in private and foreign involvement in the sector. For example, Enron (USA) has begun construction of a US$120 million gas-fired combined heat and power plant at Nowa Sarzyna. Further investment opportunities will be created through a privatisation strategy for the power sector adopted by the government in July 1998.

3

Poland and the European Union

Arkadiusz Michonski, Office of the Committee for European Integration

Introduction

Poland has been a leader in the process of transformation from socialist command economies to free markets. Poland's radical programme of reforms, introduced in 1989, established not only the foundations for a market economy and a democratic system but also turned out to be a success story. Poland's progress in adjusting its economy and creating stable democratic institutions was formally recognised by its acceptance as a member of the Organisation for Economic Cooperation and Development (OECD) in 1996 and of NATO in 1999. Additionally, since 26 November 1991 Poland has been a member of the Council of Europe. It is also an active participant of sub-regional multi-lateral initiatives such as the Visegrad Group, the Central European Free Trade Organisation (CEFTA), the Central European Initiative (Hexagonale) and the Council of Baltic Sea Countries.

Association with the EU

Poland aspires to fulfil one more ambition with respect to its foreign policy: full membership of the EU. Two agreements paved the way to the realisation of this ambition. The first agreement was a Trade and Economic Co-operation Agreement, signed in December 1989. It was followed by the signing of the Europe Agreement (EA) on 16 December 1991. The EA established an association between Poland and the EU, the most advanced status that a third country can enjoy in relation to the EU. Trade-related measures of the EA entered into force on 1 March 1992 in the form of an Interim Agreement. The remaining provisions became effective on 1 February 1994.

The most common criticism of the EA stems from the fact that it did not mention Poland's membership of the EU as a mutually shared goal of

the signatories. The Preamble to the EA only contained a one-sided declaration that 'the final objective of Poland is to become a member of the
Union and that this association, in the view of the Parties, will help to
achieve this objective'. Moreover, in respect of trade provisions, the
requests of the Polish negotiators, namely to achieve deeper trade concessions in the area of agricultural products, were not met. The scope of
the provisions relating to the freedom of flow of the workforce was also
very limited. Under the Agreement, most Polish industrial products
enjoyed free access to the EU market as from 1996 (with the exception of
textiles, for which quantitative restrictions were abolished only in 1998).
The process of creation of a free trade area between the EU and Poland
for industrial products is almost complete. The last step of duty reduction
will take place for EU steel products, imported into Poland, in 2000 and
for EU-produced cars imported into Poland in 2002.

EU membership criteria

Poland's aspirations towards EU membership were formally, and for the
first time, expressed through the submission of an application for membership on 8 April 1994. As mentioned above, full membership of the EU
was not guaranteed by the EA and that agreement only contained provisions which indirectly served the purpose of supporting preparations
towards achievement of such status. A breakthrough in this respect took
place during the Copenhagen Summit of the European Council, held in
June 1993, during which it was decided that the countries of Central and
Eastern Europe could seek full membership in the EU subject to certain
conditions, including:

- **political criteria:** a respect for the principles of democracy and the
  rule of law, observance of human rights, the full protection of the rights
  of minorities;

- **economic criteria:** a functioning market economy, the business sector's ability to face competitive pressures and free market forces within
  the EU single market;

- **formal criteria:** the ability to manage the responsibilities associated
  with membership – this is understood to mean the implementation of
  the *acquis communautaire* (the legal heritage of the EU);

- **'safe-guard clause' criteria:** refer to the EU's ability to see through
  enlargement – this is understood to mean the possible deferring of
  enlargement should essential internal reforms within the EU not yet be
  implemented.

Preparation for EU membership

Invitation for EU membership was soon facilitated by the issuing of a White Paper setting out guidelines for the legal harmonisation process. Although this document listed the most important legislative measures of the internal market, it did not cover two of the most relevant areas for Poland: agriculture and free movement of workers. Moreover, it was criticised for its one-sided approach as it did not provide for any adjustment of policies by the EU in order to facilitate enlargement. Also, the document did not give a timetable for harmonisation other than the general two-tier sequencing process (immediate and medium-term measures). In response, the Polish government issued its own White Paper Harmonogram (timetable), a detailed blueprint for the adjustment process, which was approved in July 1997. This document distributed harmonisation tasks among ministries and provided for the monitoring of adjustment measures by following an established timetable of harmonisation. The White Paper led to the implementation of a substantial part of the *acquis communautaire* into the Polish legal system. Implementation of the White Paper was accompanied by a new instrument of legal appraisal designed to assess the drafts of legislative acts with respect to their conformity to the *acquis communautaire*. This has become an important instrument of stimulation for ministries and governmental bodies in the process of law adjustment.

Adjustment process

Poland's membership of the EU requires a broad adjustment of its economic and social systems. Many of these indispensable changes have already been realised on the basis of the provisions of the EA. There has been considerable discussion, however, concerning the prioritisation and sequencing of the pre-accession process, some arguing that only those regulations necessary to the proper functioning of the internal market should be implemented immediately. Therefore, it is suggested, regulations that generate additional requirements in order to ensure high social and environmental standards but can hamper economic growth could be deferred and possibly taken on, after accession, with necesssary support from the EU.

In 1997 the 'National Strategy for Integration' policy document was published. It summarised the integration measures implemented to date and formulated adjustment tasks for the period directly preceding accession. A timetable of implementation measures and a division of responsibilities were outlined in order to facilitate the execution of these tasks.

An important stimulus for the adjustment process in Poland was the positive Opinion (the so-called *Avis*) on Polish application for EU membership that was issued by the European Commission on 16 July 1997.

This Opinion opened the way to accession negotiations with Poland. In it, the European Commission (EC) stated that:

- Poland is a democratic state with stable institutions that guarantee the rule of law, human rights and respect for the rights of ethnic minorities;

- Poland could be regarded as having a functioning market economy, and in the medium term it would be able to deal with the pressures of competition and market forces within the EU;

- if Poland continued its efforts towards the adoption of the EU legal heritage, the *acquis communautaire*, in particular with respect to the single market, and intensified work on its implementation, it should, in the medium term, become fully capable of full participation in the EU single market. It was stressed that special effort and substantial investment would be indispensable in sectors such as agriculture, environmental protection and transport.

Subsequent documents issued by the EU outlined recommendations and timetables for Poland's short- and medium-term adjustment policy, highlighting the following priority areas:

- establishment of medium-term economic policy priorities and acceleration of privatisation procedures;

- adoption of a steel industry restructuring programme;

- upgrading of administrative capacity in such fields as customs, state aid, financial control, phytosanitary (crop disease) control and taxation;

- further alignment of internal market regulations concerning industrial property, public procurement and liberalisation of capital movements;

- development of more effective border control;

- establishment of a coherent rural development agricultural policy and upgrading of certain food processing plants;

- establishment of detailed environmental protection programmes.

Following assessment by the European Commission of the medium-term objectives of the adjustment processes, Poland set a deadline of 31 December 2002 for its compliance with EU membership requirements.

What remains to be done?

Democracy and the rule of law

Major efforts are being directed towards a reform of the courts, with the aim of making them more efficient. This involves, in particular, the elimination of such shortcomings as overly lengthy proceedings and the difficulty of enforcing judgements. New organisational units of courts of law are being established, such as lower divisions of larger district courts.

Civil service

The new law on the civil service came into force on 1 July 1999 and implementation of its provisions has started. The law's main provisions include: ensuring all citizens equal and fair access to employment in state administration agencies; providing for open, public and competitive recruitment procedures for the civil service; and subjecting all elements of the recruitment process to independent control.

Internal market

In the area of public procurement, EC contracting rules for public utility companies will be introduced. As far as industrial property is concerned, Poland will have to align patent protection along the lines of EC legislation by extending the time coverage of the existing protection regulations.

Functioning of market economy and structural changes

Poland has embarked on the ambitious task of restructuring its heavy industry sector before the achievement of accession. Therefore, reform of the mining and steel sectors will have to be completed in 2001. After that date, no further state involvement in those sectors can be expected as Poland has committed to ending privatisation procedures by then. The 'Programme of Privatisation until the Year 2001' provides for the intensification of privatisation processes in such key areas as telecommunications, energy, iron and steel industries, hard coal and lignite mines, insurance, pharmaceuticals, sugar refining and distilling. Only a few individual enterprises are to remain in the State Treasury's hands – these include Poczta Polska SA (Poland's postal authority), sea- and airports, power grids and the railway and inland waterway infrastructure.

Free movement of goods

The adjustment policy involves changes in third-party certification and the introduction of a conformity assessment system based on producers' liability – these changes are predicted for 2000–1. Moreover, the implementation of specific safety regulations concerning pharmaceuticals, food, automobiles etc is planned by the end of 2002.

Free movement of capital

The influx of foreign direct investment is of utmost importance to the growth and modernisation of the Polish economy. Hence the liberalisation of capital flows in mutual dealings is a very important element of Poland's integration with the EU. Certain provisional exclusions may be sought in relation to the purchase of second homes (subject to accession negotiations).

Competition

In order for Polish anti-trust regulations to achieve full compliance with EU legislation, it is necessary to implement provisions allowing for individual and block exemptions from the ban on competition-restricting agreements. Furthermore, in order to eliminate the time- and resource-consuming notification of mergers having no or insignificant impact on competition, the threshold requirements for notification will have to be raised.

In the area of state aid, a monitoring agency that would fulfil tasks of notification and reporting on state aids will be established.

Broadcasting

Recent legal harmonisation efforts had to take into account contradictory measures stemming from Poland's need to fulfil its OECD membership requirements and its commitments relating to EU accession, namely the application of EC provisions establishing obligatory content of European TV production.

Economic and monetary union

Poland has committed itself to co-ordinate its economic policy with EU member countries upon accession to the EU. Currently, it is able to fulfil two of the convergence criteria: those relating to budget deficit and level of public debt. The 'internal' nature of the common currency regulations implies that, at its present stage of European integration, Poland remains a third country.

Taxation

Tax system reform provides for a further elimination of differences between the Polish and EU systems. Plans include the gradual introduction of VAT in agriculture, the establishment of a system of tax warehouses, the reduction in the discrepancies arising in the levying of taxes on goods and services on different categories of taxpayers, and the changing of the system of real estate taxation.

Agriculture

The policy objectives for the agricultural sector include the implementation of structural and rural development instruments that will solve the structural problems of Polish agriculture. Implementation of veterinary and phy-tosanitary regulations consistent with EU standards is foreseen, backed by the upgrading of veterinary and phytosanitary control services. Institu-tional reform will include reinforcement of administrative structures so that these become able to implement all common agricultural policy regu-lations effectively. All the changes will have to take into account environ-mental issues, with efforts instituted to maintain biological diversity.

Regional policy

The adjustment toward regional development should concentrate on the creation of an efficient and effective system in which, on the regional level, local government and administration would replace the national government in its control over the use of Structural Funds.

4

Legal Framework

Janusz Adamkowski, CMS Cameron McKenna

Historical background

The history of the Polish legal system is intricately linked with Poland's history as a nation. The natural development of the law was interrupted at the end of 18th century, when, after three consecutive partitions of the country, Poland lost its independence for more than one hundred years. As a result, different parts of Poland developed under the influence of the Austrian, Prussian or Russian legal systems, and of the Napoleonic Code in the sphere of civil law.

When Poland regained its independence in 1918, its legal system was extremely complicated and since then there have been many efforts towards unification and codification. These led to the drafting of two codes, the Code on Obligations of 1933 and the Commercial Code of 1934. A number of laws were also enacted concerning, *inter alia*, those on co-operative societies, on copyright, on inventions and industrial designs, on bills of exchange and promissory notes, and on cheques.

Many other legislative proposals were prepared just before 1939, and later served as a basis for the unification of civil law carried out after 1945. Some of these laws are still in existence, such as the Act on Acquisition of Real Estate by Foreigners of 1920 and the Commercial Code of 1934.

The situation changed after World War II, though not immediately. In the late 1940s, unification of civil legislation was continued and completed, and other efforts were made to continue the work stopped in 1939.

A new Constitution defining the political, social and economic structure of the Polish People's Republic was instituted in 1952. The era of socialist law began and, from that time, legislative acts were instituted to fulfil the needs emanating from political, structural and socio-economic changes. Notwithstanding the flavour of the socialist era, many fundamental legal acts such as the Civil Code, the Civil Procedure Code, the Penal Code and the Labour Code were drawn up in the 1960s and 1970s. The level of private business activity was very low in that period but the legal system, unusually, offered separate legal regimes for state-owned and for private entities.

At that time, there was also an explosion of so-called 'xerox laws' or hidden laws, when ministers and other governmental authorities would issue thousands of circulars, letters and orders, quite often marked as confidential, and which were never publicly announced.

Despite numerous and frequent changes in the legal regulations, including significant replacements made in 1981 and 1982, the legal framework remained unchanged until the early 1990s.

Present legal system

The Polish legal system is a Continental one, *par excellence*. It is based on statutory law, made by the parliament. Regulations supplementary to law are issued by the Council of Ministers or by ministers, within the scope of the authority provided by legal acts. The Constitutional Tribunal verifies the conformity of legal acts to the Constitution. Court decisions carry a legal meaning to a certain degree, but Poland has no case law system and court precedents do not play a significant role.

The legal system that now exists in Poland is a result of continuous economic and structural reforms, started at the beginning of the 1990s. At a very early stage, Poland's Association Agreement with the EU forced changes in Polish legal regulations and, during these years, many areas of law, such as that on foreign exchange, were completely revised.

The development and progress of economic reform has also triggered substantial changes in areas such as privatisation, securities law, investment funds, and regulations concerning these areas have been substantially amended to adjust them to the changing environment. The legal system in Poland is still in a very dynamic situation, as the system evolves to match European standards.

Future of the legal system

Changes to Polish law will continue to be made regularly. The market is always creating new products or new types of activity, and civil law needs to recognise these. A new Companies Act is being drafted to replace the now quite dated Commercial Code. The developing business environment and Poland's impending accession to the EU will also encourage change in the Polish legal system.

5

Privatisation

Business Management & Finance (BMF)

Introduction

Privatisation in Poland began in 1990. It formed part of a larger programme to transform the country from a centrally planned to a market
economy.

Privatisation, along with the liberalisation of prices, the freedom to
conduct any commercial activity and the removal of central planning,
were among the most evident and spectacular elements of this transformation. The creator of the transformation programme, Leszek
Balcerowicz, has stated on numerous occasions that market mechanisms will not force efficient behaviour if adopted in an economy where
the dominant role is played by state-owned enterprises (SOEs). The
reasoning behind this is that SOEs will not react sufficiently strongly to
changes in prices and that they will not go bankrupt when proven ineffective. Therefore, the faster the thousands of SOEs find new, private
owners, the faster they will begin to operate according to the logic of
the market economy.

At the end of 1990, there were 8453 SOEs (excluding agricultural
enterprises). At that time these businesses accounted for 88 per cent of
total sales in industry and employed 86 per cent of all employees.

The macroeconomic effects of the privatisation process between 1990
and 1997 were as follows. The number of SOEs fell by two thirds to 2498.
Since a good number of these remaining companies are currently in liquidation, bankruptcy or under administration, at the end of 1997 there were
1364 normally functioning SOEs, ie 16 per cent of the total number in
1990. In 1997, the state sector accounted for only 27 per cent of total
sales and employed 32 per cent of all employees.

Looking back upon almost nine years of the privatisation process, it
should be noted that, despite being run by various governments over that
period, from the strongly right-wing to the firmly left-wing, the process
continued throughout the whole period and its basic aims and principles
were never questioned.

Methods of privatisation

The general strategic guiding principle of the privatisation process adopted in 1990 and carried out, although not always consistently, to this day is that of equivalence. This means that the transfer of state assets is carried out through a sale preceded by a valuation at market value.

National Investment Fund programme

Non-equivalent privatisation was introduced in Poland on a relatively large scale only in 1995. It was then that 15 National Investment Funds (NIFs) were created, to which 512 companies were transferred in order to be managed and restructured. At the same time, all citizens received free mass privatisation share certificates (PSUs). Free trading of these certificates was permitted, which led to a relatively rapid concentration of ownership. Approximately 30–40 per cent of owners sold their certificates almost immediately after receiving them. Since the introduction of the 15 NIFs onto the Warsaw Stock Exchange in 1997, the PSU certificate allows its owner to receive one share in each of the NIFs.

The NIFs were created as active bodies, similar to some venture capital funds, which were to restructure and increase the value of the companies in their possession, and ultimately find active investors for them. At the time of creation, half the companies owned by the NIFs were not generating a profit. By 1999, the majority were in profit and had increased their net profitability. Three years after the start of the NIF programme almost half the participating companies have found strategic or financial investors.

In the case of **equivalent privatisation**, the following methods have been and continue to be used:

1. indirect privatisation (capital privatisation);

2. direct privatisation (winding-up privatisation);

3. privatisation through liquidation, similar to bankruptcy proceedings.

Indirect privatisation

Indirect privatisation is carried out in two phases. At first the SOE is transformed into a State Treasury-owned joint-stock company (JSC) and then the shares of this newly created company are sold by tender. This process is centralised at the level of the State Treasury.

From 1990 to the end of 1999, approximately 1400 SOEs have been transformed and shares in 252 SOEs have been sold. The sale can be conducted through an initial public offering (IPO) directed towards a wide range of small investors (although sometimes there is the possibility of selling larger tranches of shares to large strategic or financial investors) or solely by way of a sale to a strategic or financial investor.

Indirect privatisation is used for the privatisation of the largest companies that have the highest value and generate the majority of the State Treasury's earnings (see 'Some Figures on Privatisation' below).

Some elements characteristic to transactions involving the sale of JSCs are negotiations on job guarantees, social packages and investment commitments, including investments in environment protection. In general, it is impossible to obtain safeguards from the State Treasury against possible financial and legal claims from third parties, which may only come to light after completion of the transaction.

The procedure for selling shares in JSCs owned by the State Treasury usually follows a similar pattern. The vast majority of merger and acquisition (M&A) services connected with the sale are performed by advisors acting on behalf and under the supervision of the State Treasury. These advisors, selected on a tender basis, include investment banks and M&A divisions of large consulting companies.

Direct privatisation

Direct privatisation mainly relates to small and medium-sized SOEs: only 14 per cent of SOEs covered by this form of privatisation were companies employing over 500 people. Direct privatisation is used for companies in good financial condition.

There are three basic methods used in direct privatisation:

1. sale of the whole company to a strategic investor;

2. contribution in kind of an SOE to another company;

3. management and/or employees' buy-out using lease-to-buy and leveraged-buy-out techniques as a way of transferring the ownership from the state to employees.

Liquidation of SOEs

SOEs in poor financial condition, for which there is no point in adopting the methods of privatisation described above, are liquidated and their assets are sold. The procedure is similar to bankruptcy proceedings in force in Poland, with the sole difference being that it is carried out by a liquidator appointed by the founding bodies (local government authorities, provincial authorities and ministries other than the State Treasury) and not by a receiver appointed by the court.

Participation of employees in the privatisation process

Employees of privatised State Treasury companies and SOEs have the right to free participation in the financial benefits of the privatisation.

In the case of indirect privatisation, employees have the right to receive up to 15 per cent of the shares owned by the State Treasury free of charge. The total book value of the free shares for employees cannot, however, exceed the equivalent of 18 or 24 months' average wages in the company's sector of the economy multiplied by the number of employees in the company. Note that the number of shares available to employees is calculated according to their book value and not their market price.

In the case of direct privatisation, if the company is sold, up to 15 per cent of the negotiated price of the company must be transferred by the buyer to the social fund of the company, intended for financing services for employees. The amount transferred to the fund cannot, however, exceed the equivalent of 18 months' average wages in the company's sector of the economy multiplied by the number of employees in the company.

If the company is transferred by the State Treasury to a different company as a contribution in kind, the employees are authorised to receive up to 15 per cent of the shares owned by the State Treasury free of charge. The same upper limit is applied as in the case of indirect privatisation.

Some figures on privatisation

Indirect privatisation

Up to the end of the first quarter of 1999, approximately 1400 SOEs have been transformed. Shares in 252 companies have been sold and shares in 512 companies transferred to the 15 NIFs.

In 43 JSCs owned by the State Treasury, the sale of shares was carried out by way of an IPO, in 38 companies by way of a public tender and in 184 companies as a result of negotiations resulting from a public invitation.

Strategic investors have purchased shares in 222 companies, including Polish investors in 119 companies, foreign investors in 87 companies and Polish-foreign consortia of investors in 16 companies.

Of the foreign investors, the largest group included investors from Germany, the USA, Netherlands, Sweden and France. These investors accounted for 34 per cent of all strategic investors. Foreign investors clearly preferred manufacturing companies, and showed the least interest in construction, trade and services.

Of the 252 companies privatised using the indirect method, the majority came from the following sectors:

- food processing   42
- machine industry   32
- construction   30
- mineral industry   29
- electrical engineering   21
- electrical machine   19
- *Total*   173 (ie 69 per cent of the total)

The income to the State Budget from indirect privatisation (earnings plus receivables from instalments) between 1990 and 1997 totalled Zl 13,003 million at constant 1997 prices (US$4250.4 million), excluding income from the privatisation of banks. The income generated in specific years is given in Table 5.1.

Table 5.1   Budget income from indirect privatisation

Year	1990/91	1992	1993	1994	1995	1996	1997	Total
No. of companies	30	22	46	36	25	25	41	225
Budget income (Zl millions)	755	1044	1101	1615	2440	2255	3793	13,003
Income per company (Zl millions)	24	45	22	42	94	93	92	

At constant 1997 prices. Bank privatisation excluded

Although the number of domestic investors exceeded that of foreign investors, the latter had a significantly greater effect on the State Budget's income, especially in recent years. In 1996, the income from foreign investors was over double that from domestic investors, and almost five times higher in 1997. The structure of budgetary income from indirect privatisation is shown in Table 5.2.

Table 5.2   Budget income from indirect privatisation, by origin (%)

Origin of income	1995	1996	1997
Public offering	11.4	9.8	51.0
Domestic investors	33.5	29.1	8.6
Foreign investors	55.1	61.1	40.4

Bank privatisation excluded

The difference between foreign and domestic income is due to the fact that the average value of a company taken over through indirect privatisation by a foreign investor was seven times higher in 1996, and almost 12 times higher in 1997, than that of a company acquired by a domestic investor.

Almost all transactions were accompanied by commitments by the strategic investor to conduct specific investments in the future. The size and structure of these commitments is presented in Table 5.3.

Table 5.3   Investment commitments accompanying indirect privatisation transactions

Investment commitments	1991	1992	1993	1994	1995	1996	1997
Total (Zl million)	872	1635	2785	1107	2185	1516	1578
Domestic							
Total (Zl million)	27	59	745	258	485	758	303
No. companies	11	6	17	17	13	16	25
Per company (Zl million)	2.5	9.5	43.8	15.2	37.3	47.4	12.2
Foreign							
Total (Zl million)	845	1576	2040	874	1700	758	1275
No. companies	7	15	27	13	9	7	11
Per company (Zl million)	121	105	76	67	189	108	116

At constant 1997 prices. Bank privatisation excluded

Direct privatisation and the liquidation of SOEs

In the period from 1991 to the end of the first quarter 1999, 1735 SOEs were dealt with by direct privatisation. The following methods were used:

	SOEs
• sale of the assets of the SOE	365
• contribution of assets to a different company	151
• management and/or employees' buy-out	1152
• mixed solutions	67

The income to the Budget from direct privatisation between 1990 and 1997 amounted to Zl 2860 million at constant 1997 prices.

Permanently unprofitable SOEs are liquidated and their assets sold. In the first phase of Polish economic transformation, this form of privatisation was used quite frequently. As time went by, the number of SOE liquidations has systematically fallen: from 517 in 1991 to 44 in 1998. In total, from 1991 to the end of the first quarter 1999, 1602 liquidation processes had been started, of which 782 were complete, 208 were in progress and 610 were SOEs declared bankrupt.

Privatisation in 1999: main aims

Over 70 State Treasury JSCs are to undergo indirect privatisation. Companies from the power industry (three power stations, six central heating plants), the steel industry, the coal industry (certain mines), the spirits industry and the sugar sector are being or will be privatised. The privatisation process is continuing for Polish Telecom (Telekomunikacja Polska SA) and PLL LOT SA, the Polish airline.

The Polish refining industry and fuel distribution system are also being privatised, with Petrochemia Plock, Petrochemia Gdansk and the largest network of petrol stations – CPN – going through the process.

Privatisation of the banking and insurance sectors is under way. The privatisations of Bank Zachodni SA and the PKO SA banking group have already been completed. Work is being conducted on producing a restructuring and privatisation strategy for Bank Gospodarki Zywnosciowej SA (Food Economy Bank) and preparations are being made for the privatisation of the largest Polish retail bank, Bank PKO BP. In relation to the largest insurance group, PZU SA, a privatisation strategy is being prepared together with a capital infusion.

This chapter is primarily based on: Dynamika przekształceńwłsnościowych, no. 40/1999, MSP; M. Bałtowski Prywatyzacja przedsiębiorstw państwowych, Warsaw 1998.

6

Financial Sector

Carolin Killmer, BRE Bank

Introduction

Poland's financial sector is largely dominated by banks. Due to recent reforms, however, insurance companies, mortgage banks and other non-bank financial institutions will become more notable players in the financial sector. In line with increased economic activity and rising GDP, there is demand for a wider variety and for more sophisticated financial services. New forms of intermediaries are developing rapidly to meet this demand. Nevertheless, most of these services are being set up with the involvement of banks.

Banking system

Poland can be characterised as still 'under-banked' in terms of capital, products and customers. The banking sector as a whole is growing considerably faster than the Polish economy, with assets rising by 27 per cent in 1998 to Zl 334 billion. Banks' own capital increased from Zl 13.5 billion in 1997 to Zl 24.7 billion in 1998. While performing well in this respect, net profits simultaneously fell by 36 per cent. The deterioration of banks' results during 1998 was caused by the following factors:

- substantial provisioning due to the Russian crisis;

- slower overall growth of the Polish economy;

- outlays for the expansion of branch networks and the modernisation of banking technology;

- falling net interest margins;

- high mandatory reserve requirements.

Consolidation

The banking sector as a whole is still very fragmented. In 1998, 84 commercial banks and 1265 co-operative banks were operating in Poland. In comparison to Western banks, the size of Polish banks is small: if all Polish banking entities were merged into one single bank, the resulting financial institution would still have relatively small capital, ranking outside the top 50 banks in the world in terms of capital and outside the top 100 in terms of balance sheet total. Other figures also indicate the relative size of the Polish banking system. The ratio of banks' total assets to GDP amounts to 60 per cent in Poland, compared to about 160 per cent in the Czech Republic and 250 per cent in Germany. Loans extended by Polish banks represent 24 per cent of GDP, compared to 75 per cent in the Czech Republic and about 150 per cent in Germany. In light of Poland's aspiration to join the EU, consolidation will be necessary for the banking sector to become efficient by international standards and to provide the basis for a competitive domestic banking environment.

A poll carried out among the presidents of the largest Polish banks in mid-1998 revealed that they expect between four and seven large banks to be operating in Poland by the year 2003. Analysts predict that, due to further mergers and acquisitions, the system will be left with two or three dominant universal banks shortly thereafter.

The consolidation of Polish banks has been conducted differently for separate groups of banks. The largest Polish banks have been most active in the process so far. The merger and integration of three regional banks into the Pekao group resulted in the formation of the country's largest banking institution, with a balance sheet total of Zl 150 billion, capital exceeding Zl 13 billion, a 16 per cent market share of loans and a 21 per cent share of deposits. Other transactions in the process of consolidation to date include:

- take-over of the privatised Bank Gdanski by Bank Inicjatyw Gospodarczych;

- take-over of Polski Bank Inwestycyjny by Kredyt Bank;

- acquisition of Polski Bank Rozwoju by BRE Bank;

- acquisition of Pierwszy Komercyjny Bank by Powszechny Bank Kredytowy.

The consolidation activities of the larger banks also impose competitive pressure on small and medium-sized banks. In addition, some of the smaller banks have further problems: not meeting minimum capital requirements; a limited role in the market due to legal lending limits; and high cost/income ratios. Small and medium-sized banks cope with these restrictions by merging with other smaller banks or related entities such as credit agencies. The reaction of a few other smaller banks seeking closer co-operation and a stronger market position has been to set up a new banking association. The association's objectives are close integration and co-operation in management and branding among the banks involved and the consideration of joint holdings or other capital links in the future.

Another group of banks facing consolidation is the co-operative sector. Their organisation and ownership structure is complicated. As only 19.5 per cent of the existing co-operative banks currently fulfil the National Bank of Poland's minimum capital requirement, the majority will be forced to merge. Through mergers, their number is expected to be reduced by half by the end of 1999.

Privatisation and foreign investment

From recent privatisation initiatives in the Polish banking sector it has become clear that the government's privatisation plans involve more than just the strengthening of the national banking system and the provision of a competitive market. Its objectives also include the securing of the highest possible revenues for the banks to be privatised in order to stimulate economic growth and to finance and support fundamental reforms.

Domination by a single bank or investor should be avoided, while the foundations for capital concentration should be provided. The State Treasury also wishes investors to purchase shares with their own capital, rather than with borrowed funds. The general framework for bank privatisation was laid down in the 'Guidelines on privatisation of banks involving State Treasury equity to the year 2000'.

At present, 15 banks are listed on the Warsaw Stock Exchange and almost all of these have foreign shareholders. The State Treasury's dominant stake is now retained only in three large banks (PKO BP, BGZ and BGK) and a smaller unit (Budbank). After the recent privatisation of two large institutions (Pekao SA and Bank Zachodni) the state banks' share of the sector's total assets has dropped to 26 per cent.

In 1998, an important step in the process of privatising the banking sector was taken with the partial privatisation of Bank Pekao SA, in the course of which 15 per cent of shares were sold by way of a public offer. The further privatisation of the group, ie the sale of a 51 per cent stake to a consortium of Unicredito Italiano and Allianz, was completed in mid-1999. At the same time the privatisation process for Bank Zachodni was completed, Allied Irish Bank being the chosen strategic investor. Among a number of privatisation transactions in 1998, Bayerische HypoVereinsbank's acquisition of 36.7 per cent of shares of Bank Przemyslowo-Handlowy for Zl 2.1 billion from the State Treasury was the largest.

The last major banks to be privatised are the still wholly state-owned PKO BP and BGZ, together accounting for almost a quarter of the total assets of the Polish banking industry. Their privatisation has been postponed until at least the year 2003 due to the need to restructure their organisation and balance sheets, which would burden a potential investor and make PKO BP and BGZ unattractive investments.

PKO BP was, under the communist regime, the main state retail bank which collected deposits and served as a means for many people to pay tax and utility bills. It still has the largest share of deposits, with nearly 40 per cent, and boasts 15.9 million savings accounts. However, with more than 1000 outlets and 40,000 staff it is one of the least efficient.

Aggressive offers in recent bidding processes have illustrated the fact that for many domestic banks the current privatisations are the last chance to grow other than organically and that for many foreign banks this is the last chance to enter a market promising great potential.

Other than participating in privatisations and acquiring larger stake-holdings in Polish banks, foreign banks have invested in the Polish banking sector through the setting up of branches, establishing wholly owned subsidiaries under the Polish Banking Law or forming joint ventures with Polish banks. Due to Polish membership in the OECD, foreign players have had largely unrestricted access to the Polish banking industry from the beginning of 1999.

Foreign capital is invested in 44 banks, with 31 of these banks being majority-owned by foreign investors. In 1998, their share of total banking equity amounted to around 46 per cent. The largest investments have been made by American and German banks, followed by Dutch, French and Austrian investors.

Trends and outlook

One area where banks see enormous potential and try to win significant market share is retail banking, as it remains relatively undeveloped. Only 27 per cent of Poles keep current accounts in banks and 50 per cent do not use banking services at all. Key services, including consumer finance, credit cards and home loans, are in their infancy. In 1998, debit cards were used by 15 per cent of bank clients, credit cards by 5 per cent; usage in 1999 is expected to increase to 29 per cent and 25 per cent respectively. The number of automatic teller machines is expected to rise from 600 early in 1998 to 3500 by the end of the year 2000. This comparatively late start in offering private clients standardised products via a large network of micro-branches, telephone and internet banking should theoretically enable banks to leapfrog Western banks in terms of technology, product sophistication and network design.

One major reason for banks to engage in retail banking is the prospect of cheap funding. If achieved at reasonable infrastructure cost, retail deposits are considered a less costly long-term source of funding than at high margins through the inter-bank market.

As far as the range of banking activity is concerned, the market has enforced banks' accelerated evolution towards universal banking. Banks with foreign shareholding are now strong universal entities, offering retail and corporate banking services. This trend, however, does not imply the end of specialist banks. In the field of investment banking, entities such as brokerage houses and consultancies with thorough knowledge of the local market and high flexibility retain a competitive advantage. There is also room for specialist banks operating in selected niches, such as in the energy sector, environmental protection, regional business, etc. Needless to say, large universal banks will exercise control over some of the specialised financial institutions.

The president of the National Bank of Poland, H. Gronkiewicz-Waltz, predicts that the advent of the euro and the prospect of Poland's admission to the EU could trigger an open price war between Polish banks and other banks operating in Poland. So far, foreign banks have largely not competed on price with established domestic operators, accepting prices prevailing on the local market as these offered higher profits than prices in their home markets.

As for profits, Polish banks must become accustomed to the fact that base interest rates are falling in step with inflation. The success in limiting inflation has led to the narrowing of the gap between interest on deposits and on loans, which translates into lower profits for the banks. Consequently, the only way for Polish banks to compensate for pressure on the income side and to generate substantial profits in the future is to focus on the expense side and begin controlling costs.

Non-bank financial institutions

Insurance companies

The Polish insurance market is largely dominated by the still wholly state-owned insurance company Powszechny Zaklad Ubezpieczen (PZU) SA. PZU holds about 60 per cent of market share but is in dire need of capital and foreign expertise in order to streamline operations. Therefore, the State Treasury has invited bids for a 30 per cent stake to be sold to a strategic investor. Some of Europe's largest insurers such as Eureko, the pan-European financial services alliance, are said to be interested in PZU. Foreign insurance companies such as Commercial Union, AIG and Nationale Nederlanden have already begun to erode PZU's dominant market position both in the life and non-life sectors – often with the support of local banks and smaller Polish insurance companies. Estimates predict that PZU's share of the market will shrink to 50 per cent in 2000, though spending on insurance will increase by 70 per cent by 2005.

Mortgage banks

In the past, mortgages in Poland were rare because of the high interest rates customers had to pay and of the high risk banks had to bear because of the long-term character of mortgages in relation to short-term funding.

A new Law on Mortgage Bonds and Mortgage Banks has been introduced and mortgage banks are now allowed to fund their lending through mortgage bonds with longer maturities. Several domestic and foreign banks applied to the Banking Supervision Commission for mortgage bank licences in 1998. The first one to receive such a licence, in March 1999, was the mortgage bank jointly established by BRE Bank and RHEINHYP Rheinische Hypothekenbank.

Pension funds

Following extensive social security reform in Poland over the last year, close to 20 pension fund companies have received operating licences, though experts believe that there is room for only ten funds on the Polish market. The pension fund companies will manage the assets of open-ended pension funds, collected as part of social security contributions from the working population. The remainder of employees' contributions will go to the social insurance authority ZUS, operating according to the traditional 'pay-as-you-go' rules.

The potential of the pension fund market is estimated at about 5.5 million participants, who will make cumulated annual contributions of around Zl 8 billion to the pension fund companies. In the future, the funds are expected to manage capital of Zl 100–150 billion, forming the second largest financial sector after banks. One positive effect of the pension reform will be an increased savings rate in Poland, now at less than 20 per cent. Capital will flow to the Warsaw Stock Exchange, to well-managed companies and to mortgage banks, contributing to a lasting reduction of interest rates and to the expansion of housing construction.

Brokerage houses

In the past, most brokerage houses were an integral part of commercial banks but now they must operate as separate legal entities. Brokerage houses generate the largest part of their earnings by trading in securities that they own. Another large portion comes from commission from brokerage services and fees for consulting services. In 1998, they ran more than 1.3 million investment accounts. The vast majority (99.6 per cent) of these were owned by private persons, but the value of securities in these accounts amounted to only 26 per cent of all the stocks and securities on the market, while the rest was in the hands of institutional investors.

7

Capital Markets

Pawel Lipinski, BRE Bank

Introduction

After several years of strong economic growth, which fostered the development of the Polish capital market, the Warsaw Stock Exchange (WSE) is widely considered the most reputable exchange in Central Eastern Europe. This chapter describes the main elements of the Polish capital market, the WSE, the over-the-counter market and the fixed income market.

Warsaw Stock Exchange

After lying dormant for more than fifty years, the WSE was reopened in 1991. After eight years, market capitalisation has reached Zl 90 billion, i.e. the equivalent of US$22 billion (equal to 15 per cent of GDP), with more than 200 companies being quoted on the exchange. Compared to Western Europe, where market capitalisation reaches levels of 60–80 per cent of GDP, the capitalisation on the WSE is low. Trading on the WSE includes stocks, Treasury bonds, warrants, futures and pre-emptive share rights. Additionally, in the context of the Mass Privatisation Programme, Common Participation Certificates were traded on the WSE between 1996 and 1998. Foreign investors are said to contribute about 40 per cent of the WSE turnover, which equals the share of domestic retail investors, while the remaining turnover is generated by Polish institutional investors.

The WSE is regarded as an efficient securities market that meets international standards with fully computerised trading, rolling settlements and a central securities depository. The international financial community appreciates the strictness of the Polish capital market regulations and its organisational efficiency. The WSE is a member of the International Federation of Stock Exchanges (FIBV) and enjoys the status of a designated off-shore securities market as granted by the US Securities and Exchange Commission.

The organisation of the WSE is modelled on the structure of the Lyon Stock Exchange. Companies approved for public trading by the Polish Securities and Exchange Commission must publish periodic reports of their financial conditions on a monthly (until July 1999), quarterly, semi-annual and annual basis. In addition, they must disclose any event that could materially influence the price or value of securities. The Exchange Supervisory Board grants permission for the admission of shares on the so-called main market of the WSE, provided that the company fulfils certain requirements, concerning minimum book value, minimum share capital, the value of shares to be listed, number of shareholders, minimum profits, etc.

Since 1993 the WSE has also operated a **parallel market**, which allows smaller companies with a shorter track record to raise capital through an official regulated market, where initial listing requirements are easier to meet.

The so-called **free market** is the third market segment on the WSE, where listing requirements are even less difficult to meet than on the parallel market.

The WSE features two trading systems: the single-price auction and continuous trading. Large blocks of securities can also be traded off-session. The process of accounting, settlement and registration is fully computerised. Each investor has to have a securities account with a broker. In turn, every brokerage house holds a securities account with the National Depository of Securities.

An investor who, as a result of a purchase of shares in a given company, is entitled to 5 per cent or 10 per cent of the votes at the company's shareholders' meeting must notify the Securities and Exchange Commission, the Antimonopoly Office and the company concerned within seven days of such a purchase. The same provision concerns any change in the number of shares exceeding the 2 per cent limit for investors already owning more than 10 per cent of the company's votes. An investor wishing to purchase shares entitling him/her to 25 per cent, 33 per cent or 50 per cent of votes at a shareholders' meeting must give prior notification to the Securities and Exchange Commission and the WSE, and obtain permission.

By the end of 1998, the number of investment accounts in Poland had reached 1.25 million. Only 5 per cent of the Polish adult population were investors, far fewer than in Western European countries with more developed capital markets. At the beginning of 1999 the average daily equity turnover amounted to Zl 170 million, with an average of 35,000–40,000 orders. More than 40 brokerage firms are registered as WSE members.

Latest developments

In recent years, the WSE has expanded rapidly (Figure 7.1). In 1998 alone, the WSE market capitalisation rose by 76 per cent. The privatisation of TPSA significantly altered the structure of the market's capitalisation: the share of industrial companies decreased from 43.6 per cent at

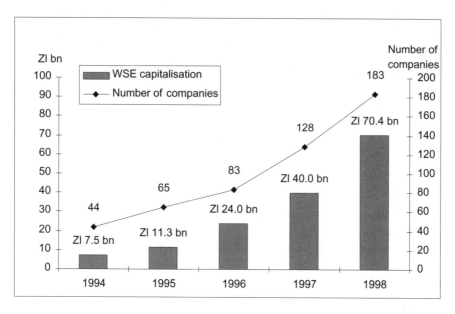

Figure 7.1 WSE capitalisation and number of companies on the WSE

the year-end 1997 to 15.7 per cent at year-end 1998, while the share of the services industry (excluding banks and financial services) increased from 20.3 per cent to 52.4 per cent respectively. By year-end 1998, 183 companies were listed on the WSE.

During 1998, derivatives were introduced to public trading on the WSE. In January futures on the WIG 20 were launched, in March warrants on Elektrim shares and on the NIF index and in September futures for the US$ exchange rate. In December the Finance Ministry abolished the income tax on transactions in derivatives. The Securities Commission also allowed the introduction of pre-emptive share rights for public trading, which facilitates the listing of shares issued during equity increases.

Over-the counter market

The Polish over-the-counter market (CTO) offers all companies, especially small and medium-sized companies, the opportunity to enter the Polish capital market regardless of their size, share capital or number of share-holders. CTO-listed companies do not have to issue a full prospectus but a shorter memorandum only, and the listing and disclosure requirements are less restrictive. Over-the-counter trading is decentralised as transactions are concluded directly between the CTO members (brokerage houses). Foreign investors can use the same brokers for CTO and WSE operations. Clearing and settlement procedures are generally the same for the CTO market as for the WSE. However, there is a possibility of buying and selling securities repeatedly in the same day on the CTO market, which is impossible on the WSE. The CTO market now hosts shares of 24 companies, municipal, corporate and Treasury bonds, as well as warrants. At the end of 1998, the capitalisation on the CTO market reached Zl 500 million, albeit at a low turnover.

Fixed-income

The fixed-income segment of the Polish capital market is still in a nascent stage of development, particularly in comparison with Western European capital markets. The market is dominated by government securities. Commercial debt is growing, but so far constitutes a small part of the market only. Figure 7.2 shows the structure of Poland's fixed-income capital market.

Government securities

Treasury bills
Treasury Bills are the most important source of funding of Poland's public debt. The Treasury issues T-bills of Zl 10,000 in a dematerialised form with maturities of 8, 13, 26, 39 and 52 weeks. Banks are the most important investors, but a number of Polish and foreign investors also buy in

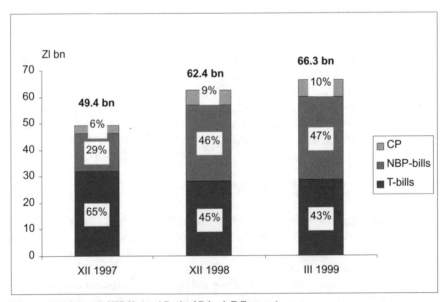

(CP, commercial papers; NBP, National Bank of Poland; T, Treasury)

Figure 7.2 Structure of Poland's fixed-income capital market

fixed income securities. T-bills are sold weekly through a bidding procedure. Every Monday, the National Bank of Poland (NBP) organises tenders for these instruments on behalf of the Finance Ministry. The NBP also maintains the Central Depository, where T-bills are registered. Additionally, the Central Bank (NBP) issues its own bills with maturities up to 273 days, similar to T-bills, though only Polish banks are allowed to purchase these securities. T-bills, especially those with 52-week maturity, provide a benchmark for the Polish financial market. They allow for liquidity management by use of high-yielding, highly liquid securities. They also enable the building of investment portfolios with the use of risk-free securities of diversified maturity and they convey market expectations regarding future levels of inflation and interest rates. Secondary trading in T-bills is conducted on the inter-bank market. Most banks publish the yields at which they are prepared to buy or sell T-bills with a given maturity, and several brokerage houses (including some outside Poland) intermediate. The secondary T-bill market is one of the most liquid segments of the Polish financial market. The yields of T-bills depend on four major interrelated factors:

- the NBP's interest rate policy;

- expectations of interest rate developments;

- T-bill supply;

- foreign capital inflows.

The policy of high real interest rates, pursued by the NBP since 1997, affected the real return of T-bills, which reached 10 per cent towards the end of 1997 and even 16 per cent in the first quarter of 1998. In April 1999, the real return on T-bills was 5 per cent.

Treasury Bonds

Government bonds are either fixed- or floating-rate securities with maturities ranging from one to ten years. In the primary market they are sold by way of tender, subscription or public sale. Fixed-rate bonds are auctioned every month. Floating-rate bonds with a one- or three-year tenor are auctioned every three months and those with a ten-year tenor every two months. Secondary trading is divided into two segments: the stock exchange market and the inter-bank market. WSE transactions are executed either via the single-price quotation system or during continuous trading with blocks of 10 or 100 bonds offered in individual transactions at the agreed price.

Non-government securities

Municipal bonds are issued via private placement or through a public offering. Most municipal bonds issued so far have been private placements in which they have been placed with a small number of institutional investors.

Commercial Papers (CPs) are securities with a maturity of one, two, three or six months and interest rates based on WIBOR (Warsaw interbank offered rate). CPs are issued in the form of promissory notes, short-term bonds or as 'securities in terms of the Civil Code'. At the end of 1998, the value of CPs issued amounted to Zl 5.7 billion. Dealers acting as market makers created a secondary market for CPs, thus providing liquidity to the CP market, albeit at a fairly low level. Investors usually hold the purchased CPs until maturity.

Foreign portfolio investment in Poland

Foreign portfolio capital, ie capital invested on the securities market excluding foreign direct investments, is very sensitive to internal and external economic conditions. Financial perturbations in emerging markets during 1998, particularly the Russian crisis, scared Western investors away from Poland: it is estimated that about US$1.8 billion has been withdrawn from the Polish capital market in the wake of the Russian crisis. Despite this outflow, the capital market situation in Poland remained fairly stable. At the end of 1998, the total value of foreign portfolio capital invested in debt securities and on the stock exchange constituted only 29 per cent of Poland's foreign currency reserves. In comparison, this indicator reached 300 per cent in Russia in 1998 before the crisis, 300 per cent in South Korea in 1997 and 160 per cent in Indonesia.

Non-resident purchases of Polish public securities have been considerably liberalised. The Law on Public Trading of Securities guarantees foreign investors free access to the Polish capital market. Foreign investors are allowed to repatriate profits earned from shares of listed companies and from government securities.

The biggest foreign portfolio investments are concentrated on the stock market and in T-bills and T-bonds. At the end of 1998, the share of foreign capital in WSE capitalisation was estimated at US$6 billion, ie 30 per cent. The value of T-bills held by foreign investors amounted to US$0.35 billion and the value of T-bonds reached US$1.38 billion. Poland is also present on the Euromarkets. In 1995, US$250 million Eurobonds were issued and in 1997 the State Treasury went to the market with issues of US$500 million of 10- and 20-year bonds.

Prospects for the Polish capital markets

The launch of privately managed pension funds on 1 April 1999 under the ambitious pension system reform could provide a boost to the capital market in Poland. Pension funds are allowed to invest 40 per cent of assets in equities, but they are likely to limit share purchases initially in order to limit their performance risk. In the beginning, pension funds are expected to invest mainly in safe securities such as T-bills and T-bonds. Mortgage banks, which will fund their lending through mortgage bonds, are likely to become another source of supply of long-term debt securities. Another area of rapid development is mutual and investment funds. Although Pioneer still has a market share of more than 50 per cent, new competitors, particularly Skarbiec, DWS, Eurofundusz and Korona note above average growth rates of their assets under management.

8

Business Culture

Anna Gebicka, Business Management & Finance (BMF)

Introduction

Any understanding of current business culture in Poland requires an appreciation of the tremendous changes that the system and its structures are now undergoing. The opportunities offered by the Polish economy today stem from the political changes introduced in 1989 and the widespread economic reforms begun in 1990. The Polish economy then suffered from hyper-inflation and shortages of basic products, a non-convertible currency and low foreign currency reserves, large hidden unemployment, severe inefficiencies resulting from state subsidies equivalent to 15 per cent of GDP and a state-owned sector producing more than 75 per cent of GDP.

Reforms successfully increased production levels, oriented both to exports and to domestic consumption, significantly reduced inflation, made the zloty convertible and increased foreign currency reserves. They also liberalised most prices, obtained a reduction of foreign debt from creditors, reduced the dependence on the public sector in general and encouraged the growth of the private sector.

Poland – a leader on the road to private enterprise

The creation of new enterprises and the success of the privatisation process have given the private sector more than a 40 per cent share of industrial production, an 86 per cent share of the construction sector, a 43 per cent share of transport and a more than 90 per cent share in total trade turnover. Over 65 per cent of the labour force works for the private sector and produces more than 65 per cent of GDP. Since 1990, the number of state-owned enterprises has been reduced by more than 60 per cent and the continued privatisation programme, supervised by the Ministry of Treasury, continues to provide investment opportunities.

Changing attitudes

The most important aspect of the transformation, however, does not appear in these statistics. Over the last seven years Polish companies and their managers have fully espoused the principles of the free market. Both private and state-owned entities understand the importance of profit and shareholder value and, with only a few exceptions, have learned to fend for themselves without government help. Corporate governance structures, modelled on the German system, are functioning no less efficiently than they do in Western Europe. The concept of corporate citizenship is being rediscovered and, as employees began to realise that the success of their company and their job security lay in their own hands, a new work ethic emerged.

Corporate citizenship

New opportunities for business and citizens

The dramatic political and economic changes that have swept across Poland over the past decade have brought new opportunities and unfamiliar challenges. Democratic reforms and the shift to a market-driven economy have in a short space of time ensured better prospects for security and long-term prosperity within a wider Europe. Underpinning this has been the rebuilding of a civil society where citizens participate actively in civic affairs and in their own organisations, and where companies are expected to build safe, ethical and commercially sustainable businesses, which meet the interests of local communities.

Achievements – but some disillusionment

Overall, the change has been remarkable and success stories continue. Although economic and social progress has not been uniform, transformations in attitudes, expectations and behaviour have brought both gains and losses. The new problems facing government, business, citizens and the international community include rising unemployment, rapidly changing values, economic insecurity, the collapse of physical infrastructure, the erosion of social infrastructure and threats to public safety from increasing crime. Problems such as this lead to disillusionment, suspicion of private business, and alienation of the young and others affected by social change and political instability.

Among the key challenges in this respect are the preservation of a social safety net, the rebuilding of civil society, the establishment of legitimate services for law and order and public protection, and ensuring that groups adversely affected by the transition are not excluded from economic life.

Contribution of competition

In this context, international and national business already seem to have responded to rapidly changing and unfamiliar circumstances. With the emergence of new entrepreneurs and the restructuring of many companies, the primary contribution of business has been in industrial restructuring to meet competitive international standards in the development of human resources, in the creation of new markets and in the introduction of more efficient and clean technologies. In this way, business has contributed to sustainable prosperity through improved wages, local procurement and tax revenues.

Business investment in market and social development

However, businesses are also expected to contribute to the development of the market and of society through public-private partnerships that must not only provide infrastructure and essential services but also invest in skills and resources, and encourage employee action. Many business leaders understand this but only few play an active part in promoting such thought.

There are many examples 'proving' the 'business rationale' for company involvement in educational, social, non-governmental and local government infrastructure. The concept of a 'good corporate citizen' is gaining popularity, especially as it builds business reputations, improves employee relations and skills, wins acceptance in the community and contributes to improved links with suppliers, local government and other institutions whose support is necessary for long-term business success.

Local workforce

Traditionally, the Polish workforce has been well educated, productive and resourceful. There had been very little concern for quality, however, and teamwork was non-existent. Old organisations were extremely centralised and there were no differences in pay, some supervisors even earning less than their operatives. Management skills were strong in production and design, while marketing, financial management and accounting systems were typically the weakest areas.

Upward mobility

Competent, flexible managers aged 40 or over are very scarce in Poland: finding such talent is an intriguing but vexing issue for potential employers. And outside big centres like Warsaw, Poznan and Katowice, the problem becomes more acute. Obviously, this issue concerns not only international companies but Polish ones as well. Polish firms have a better chance of penetrating the local labour market, however, and often accept candidates recommended by current employees or friends.

Poles are still less mobile than other, especially Western, populations, but mobility works differently according to demographics. It is easier to persuade a young, single person to move by offering him/her, after a short period of training, a position with a high level of independence and responsibility. Shortening the training period seems to be a great motivating factor and Western companies are therefore hiring younger managers for top positions. This shifts the normal relationship between seniority and age and can create problems in filling middle management positions. Senior Polish managers (most of them still under 30) are now earning hefty compensation packages. Companies are understandably unwilling to have pay scales filter down the organisation but, as a result, salaries can treble or quadruple between junior and senior management, increasing the temptation for ambitious and talented managers to jump ship rather than wait for internal promotion. Pay scales for middle-level and junior management may also vary two- or even threefold between comparable firms in the same sector, making it very hard for top management to work out what to pay to whom. Turnover at all levels is far higher than in the West: it is quite normal to spend only one or two years in a job, thanks to the twin pressures of rapid promotion and intensive poaching.

Benefits packages

Benefits packages are becoming increasingly complex and expensive. A year-end '13th month salary' bonus is now expected in almost all white-collar positions. Performance-based pay is also becoming increasingly common, especially in sales and marketing, and for financial sector employees. Most companies give their employees computers and notebooks for home use. Increasingly, company benefits also include free medical care (sometimes for the whole family), life insurance, additional old age pension insurance and preferential prices for company shares. Some packages are even more tempting and may include, for example, low-interest loans, different types of insurance, stock options and help in developing professional qualifications.

Keeping employees sweet: modern-day perks

Perks are not recent additions to working life in Poland. They existed in the communist era, when, according to some estimates, there were well over 50 or maybe even 100 types of perks. The famous coal quotas were a right for all employees, while cars and apartments were bonuses reserved for Communist Party members. However, modern-day perks are a true revolution in motivating people.

The modern-day perk appeared in Poland with the influx of foreign companies, though domestic business is learning fast and now is not far behind. A company car and a mobile phone are now almost standard. At least half of Poland's middle managers use company cars and all of these use them on weekends and holidays. Driving is pleasant and economical since the company covers the cost of gas, repairs, insurance and even parking fees. At least three quarters of these managers have mobile phones provided by the company – which some call the employees' leash.

Carnival balls for the whole company have become a must. For example, this year the annual IKEA ball in Warsaw was attended by 300 employees and their families. Another good team-building tool is a picnic that can be attended by everyone from salespeople, cleaning and security staff to the company president.

Incentive travel has been a hit on the list of perks lately – the farther away the better. A few years ago ambitious companies would reward their employees with trips to Majorca, Cyprus or the Canary Islands. Today, employees and their families are sent to the Caribbean, Bali or Mauritius.

Summary

Poland is now recognised as the most lucrative market in Central and Eastern Europe, and it is rapidly developing sound economic policies, stable politics and an 'open arms' attitude to foreign investment. In the last three years, Poland has achieved one of the highest rates of economic growth of any European country. It has Central Europe's largest economy and is strategically placed as a commercial link between East and West. With its successful reorientation towards a Western-style approach to business culture, Poland is a real land of opportunity for those investors who understand the corporate responsibilities of their companies and are ready to address the question of staff motivation.

Part 2
Market Potential

9

Advertising

Joe Senft, Brandstorm International

Introduction

After years in New York, I found myself in Warsaw debating with an Englishman the merits of an advertising campaign that I wanted him to approve and produce. This client did not like the execution of the campaign I was proposing: as the marketing director for a multinational foods group, he applied his experience to challenge my recommendation.

Still, the core idea of the campaign was distinctive and motivating. The execution could be changed, but the brand idea was worth pushing for. After several minutes, the client finally threw up his hands. 'Look,' he said dryly, 'this is an intellectual discussion – and you are from a coffee culture, not a tea culture.'

Most people would not immediately define a culture by its choice of beverage. However, such a comparison reminds us that, in successful marketing, we must define user segments and we must offer a relevant and motivating proposition within these segments. Some companies operate in Poland without doing these things. I can only suppose that they have more money than sense.

Advertising media expenditures in Poland will top US$2 billion this year and have grown in real terms by an average of 37 per cent during each of the last three years. No less than 12 individual hypermarket chains are now operating or breaking ground across the nation. If you want to build great brands in Poland's rapidly evolving economy, marketing will need your special attention. The good news is that this extra effort is actually a lot of fun. Ask me and I'll tell you how, over a cup of … coffee or tea?

Define your brand in Polish terms

Of course you already know what your brand offers and all about that 'brand values' rubbish that overeager advertising people stuff into their overhead presentations. But does the Polish consumer know? Cussons,

Carrefour and Citibank all mean different things to Poles than they do to consumers in their domestic markets. Also, today's Polish consumer does not gravitate to brands simply because they might be Western. Your average Jan Kowalski gives high marks to domestic labels in many categories, including dairy products, confectionery, packaged soups and sauces, insurance and ready-to-drink beverages.

'It would actually damage perceptions of the Polish brand,' a client once told me after conducting research for a new package design. His multinational firm had purchased a Polish brand and wanted to add the Western parent name to the pack. Intended as a guarantor of quality, this second brand would have had the opposite effect among Poles.

Moreover, the distinction between Western and Polish is increasingly blurred as smart marketers exploit opportunities to leverage the best of both worlds. Frugo is a wildly successful youth beverage created in Poland by Alima-Gerber. Unilever developed a value-priced tea called Saga, which not only trades well in Poland's large economy tea segment (where Unilever is typically absent), but which provided a model for similar brands in Russia and elsewhere. Meanwhile, domestic juice marketer Tymbark looks like an international brand with new single-serve cartons, impulse-driven distribution and a wide range of flavours.

Good opportunities to develop a world class brand with a Polish face exist in several categories. International brands should ply their international credentials, but what is important is not always the most obvious.

Start with robust research

To define your brand in Polish terms, go to the Polish consumer. Major research agencies run long-term, quantitative testing for a variety of product and service categories (eg juices or banking). You can easily afford a report on the latest trends in consumer attitudes and usage. If no off-the-shelf research exists, you can commission some, but this will cost more.

If you're in a preliminary stage of planning, you can place a handful of questions into an omnibus survey. Major research agencies run these regularly and they include questions from a variety of marketers. There are also research products that define consumer psychographics, or lifestyle segments. The major research shops in Poland will be keen to inform you of their quantitative products and how these are meant to illuminate strategy and increase your chances of success.

Qualitative testing such as focus groups can help you identify major themes of the category and responses to product or advertising concepts. This is no substitute for quantitative research, but it can be useful to probe hypotheses and to evaluate elements of your advertising. When buying qualitative programmes, be sure to meet the moderator beforehand. Some smaller research shops have excellent people in this position.

Media research on all major vehicles is available in Poland, as it is throughout Europe and America, with outdoor billboards being the only exception.

In all research, ask questions about the methodology. Are your target users included? What about consumers who may have tried and rejected certain brands? What about substitute categories (eg, beverages can be refreshment, but also a snack food). Does the sample include smaller towns and rural areas? Warsaw and Krakow are not representative of Poland.

The advertising you make will only be as good as the positioning you identify for your brand. Here, you must be sufficiently brave to declare not only what your brand stands for, but also what it will not stand for.

Define your target audience

Polish consumers exhibit heterogeneous patterns of lifestyle and consumption. Brands enjoy far richer opportunities for volume and segmentation than elsewhere in Central and Eastern Europe, where oligarchies and high barriers to entry can prevail. For example, the coffee category in Poland has two leading brands, but another dozen competitors comprise more than half of volume sold. Moreover, half the Polish population is under the age of 35 and open to new brand relationships with each successive life stage.

Although the Polish female homemaker has traditional duties, the majority of these women also work at least part time. Therefore a woman will not only shop for her family, but will also have some disposable income with which to indulge herself. Also, we know that Polish homemakers tend to manage the complete family budget, including income earned by the husband. Call her a juggler – she shoulders the responsibility for quality of life at home while looking for diversions from the banality of domestic and part-time work. Variety and value for money are key.

Marketing to independent urban and suburban women is one of the most overlooked areas in Poland. Major opportunities remain in underdeveloped or traditionally male categories such as financial services, cars, and alcoholic beverages.

Across both sexes, you will want to establish levels of adoption. Is your target group risk averse and partial to traditional brands? Or does it prefer to try something new, perhaps foreign? Is it introverted and focused on family, or is it extroverted and keen to win the acceptance and approval of peers? One may explain Mercedes ownership because 'it is a reliable car', but really enjoy the prestige of driving such a brand. Across consumer segments, Poles are many times more likely to equate brand names with status than their Western cousins. There are, nevertheless, some interesting exceptions.

Occasionally, it is popular to assume that Polish consumers over-emphasize price, but this is not true. Most categories do not have a single standard for quality, and there is value for money at every price point. The old proverb 'I'm too poor to buy anything cheap' is echoed by the burgeoning number of middle-class Poles. Nevertheless, the ones who do buy on price can become extremely loyal users if we add supporting emotional values to the mix. This is what Unilever has done with Saga tea, and consumers are 'trading over' within the economy segment.

You must define your target user beyond the usual criteria of income and place of residence. With the right consumer insight, your advertising will give the brand a role to play in the life of the target audience.

Conquer by word-of-mouth

The Polish consumer has been bombarded with new and different products and the associated advertising, sampling, promotions and public relations. Television breaks run eight minutes or more. Ranks of billboards jostle for attention around major intersections. Across the marketing mix, the Polish consumer has experienced in a decade what Western consumers achieved over half a century.

Maybe that's why word-of-mouth recommendations can be important for brand selection in Poland. A friend or family member helps sort things when there's too much, too soon. Although word-of-mouth varies by product category, one can see it at work with both high- and low-involvement brands.

It is time for advertising to harness its true power: the power to earn a recommendation. Most advertising in Poland is rapidly forgotten and probably deserves to be. Your advertising must be noticed and remembered, so that it can be recommended. Of course, you have already briefed the agency on your brand's benefit to consumers and the attributes that make this possible.

Request better ideas, ones that are simple and unexpected. If you want to get the most from your agency ask them how their recommended campaign is simple and unexpected. 'Simple' they may justify. 'Unexpected'? Probably not. But 'unexpected' is precisely what attracts attention in the rapid pace of an emerging market. Tell your agency you want to see an idea that is at once consistent with the personality of your brand and unexpected for its category.

Word-of-mouth is the greatest honour advertising can achieve and is proof of your campaign's effectiveness. It gives your brand additional value for your marketing investment. You can accomplish this with a simple and unexpected idea, or you can do it with excessive media spending. The choice is yours.

Summary

Advertising practice in Poland is not unlike that in other countries. Where marketers sometimes err, it is usually because they make incorrect assumptions about the Polish consumer or they have failed to make their case in a distinctive way. Be sure to extract the maximum value from your marketing activity in Poland. I can assure you that some of your competitors won't – and you will be that much farther ahead.

- Define what your brand is *and what it isn't*: these can be different in Poland than in the brand's home market.

- Start with research: it is a cliché, but lots of money gets wasted without robust understanding of the Polish market and consumer motivations.

- Define your users: what unique role will your brand play in their lives?

- Conquer by word-of-mouth: unexpected advertising gets noticed and gets consumers talking about your brand.

10

Agricultural Sector

Simon Gill, Agro Business Consult

Introduction

Polish geographical statistics can be summarised as follows:

- total land area 31.2 million hectares;

- farmland area 18.6 million hectares, of which 8.7 million hectares is in cereal production: 31 per cent winter wheat, 34 per cent rye and 35 per cent other;

- 8.9 million hectares of forestry;

- 505,000 hectares of protected National Park (a large percentage of which is closed to the general public);

- 803,000 hectares of freshwater lakes.

Poland, with 18.6 million hectares of agricultural land, is a potent European farming and horticultural economy. Aided by a continental climate, Poland is already a major producer of some important commodity crops, including wheat, rye, potatoes, onions, soft fruit and apples.

Primary agricultural production

Poland's land resource is currently owned by some 2.1 million individuals. This gives a countrywide farm size average (7.8 hectares) that belies the current situation and infrastructure of Polish farming. Note that statistics confuse land ownership with being a farmer. It has been suggested by some eminent Polish agricultural economists that in practice there are approximately 600,000 commercial farmers in Poland. The problem is that there is a growing number of what, in the EU, would be termed 'hobby farmers', whose principal source of income is not agricultural and whose socio-economic position is rapidly deteriorating.

'Large farm' sector

Unlike many other transitional and aspiring EU candidate countries in Central and Eastern Europe, where restitution of land has led to a fragmented farming sector, Poland has maintained its 'large farms' (more than 50 hectares). It is this 'large farms' sector that now dominates agricultural markets in Poland, providing more than 70 per cent of all marketed agricultural produce.

Poland resisted the collectivisation of its farmlands during the late 1940s and early 1950s, with the result that in 1989, at the moment of transition, 85 per cent of agricultural land was still under private ownership. The former state farming sector is now largely under private commercial control. The preferred system of 'privatisation' has been a system of providing tenancies of up to 30 years. From an original 'large farm' land resource that peaked at 5.2 million hectares (or 22 per cent of all agricultural land) there are now more than 5500 large farms with an average size of approximately 490 hectares for lease; 13 per cent are between 200 and 500 hectares, while 23 per cent are larger than 1000 hectares. Also, some 669 estates, with an average area of 372 hectares, have been sold. To date there has been no restitution of agricultural property to former owners. Of the total 'large farm' land area, 64 per cent is now leased, 79 per cent of these tenancies held by former employees of the communist state system. Of the remaining 21 per cent, the typical profile is that of a new tenant who is 'young, highly qualified, acquainted with rural issues and experienced in agriculture. Often trained or with experience from abroad and often having a foreign investment partner'.[1]

Economic aspects of farming

In Poland the return on capital in farming is generally higher than in the EU, with no income taxes and lower rents on land. This has made Polish agriculture attractive to foreign farming investment and it is thought that there is significant investment by foreign investors, especially in these former state farmlands. A number of foreign business entities also hold leases in their own right.

Despite having such a large agricultural sector, Poland is not a predominately agrarian economy. This is now contributing to a growing gap between the fortunes of the urban and the rural populations. One in five Poles now live below the subjective poverty line and a large proportion

---

[1] Pyrgies, Fedyszak Radziejowska, Lapinska-Tyszka (1997). *The New Masters of State Farms*. Institute of Rural and Agricultural Development. Polish Academy of Sciences, Warsaw. Reported World Bank EU Accession Conference, Warsaw, June 1999.

of these people are under-educated, are young women or are rural 'landowners' attempting to make a living on farms of less than five hectares. Unemployment in Poland is highly regionalised. In most of the urbanised provinces unemployment is below 10 per cent. In the predominantly rural provinces unemployment still remains high, even reaching 21.6 per cent in the north-east of Poland. Of all Polish households, 33 per cent are located in 'rural' areas with an average household size of 3.6 inhabitants (an average urban household has less than three inhabitants).

The Polish economy has now started to slow after spectacular results during the 'catch up' period of early transition. GDP growth has for now 'bottomed out' at around 4 per cent, although many analysts believe it will have grown again by the year 2000 to around 6 per cent. The *Polish Market Review* reports the slowdown in the economy as being the consequence of a 'slackening in the growth of domestic consumption, combined with a continuing low growth rate in exports'. This was complicated by the multiplier effects of the shock in the second half of 1998 of the Russian crisis and of the economic slowdown in the EU, two large economies with which Poland is inextricably linked. The consequence for the agricultural sector is that traditional export markets to the East will remain sluggish in the short term. However, foreign direct investment in Poland's food industry sector continues and at present there appears to be latent capacity in developing the sophistication of the Polish retail markets in semi-processed and processed food.

Arable farming

The characteristics of Polish traditional farming mean that between 67 per cent and 72 per cent of any farmer's available land area is typically arable. There will also be a grassland area of between 13 and 22 per cent of the total available land area and the small remainder will be used for market gardening, orchard or forestry.

The latest Agricultural Census, in 1996, suggests that up to 42 per cent of the arable area is used for cereals (8.7 million hectares), 31 per cent for winter wheat and 34 per cent for rye. Potatoes, a major Polish crop, are grown on an estimated 1.3 million hectares (7 per cent of all farmland).

Crop yields in recent years have been unseasonably variable due to freak meteorological events, including harsh winters and heavy rains in late spring/early summer.

Since transition began with regard to food markets in January 1990, total cereal yields have fluctuated between 19.9 million tonnes (1992) and 27.8 million tonnes (1991). The total cereal yield for 1997 was estimated at 25.3 million tonnes. Average cereal yields are stated as 3.6 tonnes/hectare; however, large farms now yield more than this average and more than half of the cereals supplied to the market come from these larger units.

The significant change in the Polish market is the quantity of 'visible' trade in cereals, which has grown from 15 per cent of total national yield in 1992 to more than 45 per cent for the 1998 harvest.

Market prices have been higher than those on many world commodity markets, as a result of border protection and the price intervention policies of the Polish government. This is due in great part to the strong Polish agricultural lobby. Higher prices have led to higher demand for better uniformity and quality in marketed grains. These factors discriminate against and worsen the position of the large number of smaller farmers, while positively favouring large farm producers. This may in part explain the relative attractiveness for foreign investors of primary arable production on former state farms throughout Poland, where returns on investment are often significantly higher than those obtainable on similar large arable units in the UK, Germany or the Netherlands.

Livestock farming

The fortunes of livestock farmers have been poor in comparison. Since 1989, the livestock count has fallen dramatically. Total head of cattle has dropped from 8.8 million in 1991 to 7.3 million in 1997. The number of breeding sheep has fallen from over 7 million to less than 400,000 and pig numbers have become some 3 million lower over the same period.

Although there have been declines in total livestock numbers, production efficiency in many sectors has increased through better use of animal feeds and improved husbandry practices. Dairy cows are an example, where total raw milk production has reattained its pre-transition level despite there being some 1.1 million fewer milking cows, indicating a significant yield increase per lactation. Small farm yields, in particular, have increased from an average of less than 3000 litres per lactation in 1991 to current levels of 3400 litres.

The meat markets in Poland have been shown to be vulnerable to external market pressures. This is especially true of pig and poultry meat. Despite this, considerable interest has been shown by foreign investors in meat processing in Poland, including a hostile buy-out, on the Warsaw Stock Exchange, of one of Poland's former largest state companies, Animex, by the Smithfield Corporation (USA).

Horticultural crop and orchard production

Field-scale vegetable production plays an important role in Polish agricultural production. Poland is the second largest producer of onions and cabbages in Europe. Orchard production, though highly regionalised, is also a significant enterprise for many smaller and more specialised Polish producers. There are extensive apple orchard areas located south of Warsaw, making Poland one of Europe's largest apple producers and the world's largest exporter of apple concentrate. Poland is also noted for its large production of soft fruit, which includes strawberries, raspberries, black-currants and redcurrants.

The fruit and vegetable processing market is largely dominated by two companies: Agros Holdings and Hortex. These companies have extensive procurement systems for the purchase of raw processing materials and col-lectively control as much as 50 per cent of the markets for selective semi-processed and processed fruit and vegetable production (including frozen).

Agricultural supply industries

Poland, like many transition economies, suffered from a collapse in its agricultural supply industries as a result of decentralisation and of the removal of subsidies to largely state-controlled industries. The problems facing Polish agricultural supply still remain, with poor levels of distribu-tion for seed, fertilisers and crop chemicals, and a rapidly ageing machin-ery park that smaller farmers cannot afford to replace.

Poland has some 1.3 million tractors in use in agriculture; these have probably reached their terminal age in that the average age of Polish trac-tors is now 19 years. The replacement level is very low and, as the aver-age age remains 19 years, this implies a diminishing tractor population and a demechanisation of Polish agriculture.

Polish agriculture and accession to the EU

Large-scale production in Poland is attractive but the capital resources required are already at a level comparable with any other agri-sector in Europe. Investors must be careful to note that the Polish market is now linked into world markets. A good example of this came in 1995–96 with the transmission of the volatility of world grain prices to Polish grain prices, which rose to nearly twice those of 1994. Large farms typically use more capital and less labour per unit output than the smaller farmer and, as a consequence, are more exposed to distortions and instability than are input markets.[2]

There is not a very favourable outlook for the small farmer with or with-out the prospect of EU accession. Animal production still dominates on

[2]Information for the following paragraphs was taken from: Safin M and Guba W. Agricultural Price Policy Impacts in Poland. ECSSD Rural Development and Envi-ronment Sector Working Paper no 7.

smaller farms where policy has been specifically targeted so that price support for animal products benefits small-scale operations and not larger ones.

The large farms, characterised by a high share of crop production in their total output, benefit most from the agricultural price support policies of the Polish Ministry of Agriculture and, as a result, accumulate most of the market transfers. They also have better access to finance resources (either their own or credit). They have lower unit transaction costs in purchasing inputs and selling outputs. Importantly, in an enlarged Europe Poland's large farmers have already proved themselves capable of producing extensive quantities of agricultural commodities of reasonable quality and with high homogeneity, which is already reflected in higher farm gate prices for the larger farms. This is despite restricting competition from imports and distorting signals on quality requirements. With a more sophisticated downstream processing and retailing sector, and growth in the general wealth of the country, product price differentiation based on quality will continue to grow.

11

Automotive Industry

Nick Sljivic, VP International

Introduction

Nothing symbolises the successful transformation of Poland's economy more effectively than the remarkable developments that have been witnessed in its automotive industry.

At the start of the decade, the Polish automotive industry lagged far behind that of the rest of the world in all aspects: marketing, technology, manufacturing, design and productivity. In less than a decade, automotive manufacturing has seen a renaissance, due largely to the commitments made by Fiat, Daewoo, General Motors and VW, acting as powerful magnets in drawing international first- and second-tier suppliers into Poland.

Numerous leading vehicle manufacturers and international component companies have become established in Poland. According to PAIZ, the inward investment agency, by the end of 1998, over US$8 billion of the total US$30 billion of foreign investment into Poland was into the automotive industry. The investment will have been mainly as a result of the huge commitments made by the four major car manufacturers noted above.

The Polish government has also adopted aggressive measures in its endeavour to attract inward investment. The terms offered to investors have been very generous, most notably within the Special Economic Zones. These were created to attract manufacturing investment in regions where the demise of traditional heavy industries has led to high unemployment levels. The bulk of the investment in the automotive industry has been in these zones.

Market overview

Sales of new cars have increased steadily since the start of the decade. The market is now comparable in size to that of Belgium and the Netherlands. Sales of new cars in 1998 were up 8 per cent on 1997 levels to 515,000 units (Table 11.1 shows projected passenger vehicle production for 2000). Domestically produced vehicles accounted for 375,000 units, or nearly three quarters of all new car sales. In 1998, Fiat sold 149,000 new cars in Poland. In terms of market share, Daewoo is rapidly catching up with Fiat and the latest figures indicate that Daewoo is within 2 per cent of Fiat's 30 per cent market share.

As of the end of 1997, an estimated 10 million vehicles were on Polish roads: 1.5 million commercial vehicles and 8.5 million passenger cars. The car park is very aged (the average vehicle is over nine years old) and ownership still remains low by European levels estimated in 1997 at around 221 cars per '000 population (compared with 373 in the UK).

Table 11.1 Forecast production of passenger vehicles for 2000

Manufacturer	Forecast production for 2000	Location
Fiat	350,000	Bielsko Biala Tychy
Daewoo-FSO/DMP	350,000	Warsaw Lublin
GM Opel	75,000	Gliwice
VW/Skoda	80,000	Poznan
Others	20,000	
Total	875,000	

Source: VP International

Fiat

Fiat has had a very long involvement in the Polish automotive industry and has been present in Poland since the beginning of the 20th century. Until the second half of the 1990s, virtually all cars produced in Poland were of Fiat design, these having been made at the local FSO and FSM plants.

Fiat acquired the Polish car manufacturer FSM in 1993 and inherited a highly vertically integrated company with extensive in-house component operations. Since then, Fiat has actively divested many of these to its own or other international component suppliers. Fiat still retains an extensive component manufacturing capability, in addition to that of its own sub-sidiaries that followed it into Poland. In 1998, the company produced 336,665 vehicles from its plants in Bielsko Biala and Tychy.

Daewoo

Daewoo acquired the former state-owned car manufacturer FSO and the light commercial vehicle manufacturer FSL in 1996. In 1998, the company acquired diesel engine manufacturer Andoria.

The company states that it will have committed US$2.2 billion in investment to its Polish operations by the year 2001. Its aim is to produce over 500,000 vehicles by the year 2002 and, of this number, 390,000 will be exported.

Daewoo has two vehicle manufacturing sites in Poland (Daewoo-FSO in Warsaw and Daewoo Motor Polska in Lublin). In addition to its vehicle manufacturing operations, Daewoo has an extensive number of subsidiary component companies into which it has been actively seeking to attract investment by international component manufacturers. In mid-1996, Daewoo announced a whole raft of joint ventures between its subsidiaries and Korean companies and, in 1998, Daewoo FSO announced a joint venture with Dana to produce rear axles and driveshafts.

Looking ahead, Daewoo has ambitious automotive manufacturing plans, not only for Poland, but also for its other operations across Central and Eastern Europe (including Czech Republic, Romania, Uzbekistan and Ukraine). As a consequence, its Polish supplier companies will become significant component suppliers within the next few years.

In addition to its light commercial vehicle output, Daewoo Motor Polska is one of Poland's largest component companies, supplying an extensive range of castings, forgings, wheels, fasteners, springs and coils for the Polish automotive industry as a whole.

General Motors

GM opened an assembly plant in Warsaw in 1992, where it commenced low-volume Astra production. In 1997, GM committed to opening a new plant in Gliwice, in southern Poland. The state-of-the-art Gliwice plant opened in October 1998 and will initially be producing 70,000 Astra Classics annually for both the Polish market and other Central and Eastern European countries.

In 2000, there are plans to begin production of a new compact car (designed jointly with Japan's Suzuki). With this new model, total output is expected to reach 150,000 units by the year 2001.

VW/Skoda

VW's first commitment to Poland was in 1992, with wire harness production in Poznan. Since then, the company has moved into the assembly of Skoda cars and Transporter T4 vans. Engine production is due to commence in 1999 with the opening of a US$190 million investment in Legnica, which will supply VW plants around the world.

Ford

Ford has a low-volume CKD assembly operation in Plonsk for Transit vans and Escorts.

Commercial vehicle manufacture

Commercial vehicle manufacture in Poland consists of the three, long-established domestic manufacturers (Star, Jelcz and Autosan), now owned by Grupa Zasada, as well as assembly operations established by international heavy vehicle manufacturers. International commercial vehicle groups in Poland are as follows:

Company	Location
MAN	Poznan
Volvo	Wroclaw
Scania	Slupsk
Neoplan	Poznan

The largest commitment has come from Volvo, which has committed US$50 million to create a new manufacturing plant outside Wroclaw.

Grupa Zasada is a holding company of Poland's domestic manufacturers of commercial vehicles. In the group are Star (trucks), Autosan (coaches and buses) and Jelzcz (trucks). Altogether these companies employ nearly 11,000 people and have extensive in-house commercial vehicle component manufacturing capability. The company has a series of co-operative arrangements with Mercedes and MAN.

Component manufacture

In response to the investment by international vehicle manufacturers, Poland has seen enormous investment by international first- and second-tier component manufacturers. As vehicle output of both passenger cars and commercial vehicles is set to continue increasing for the next few years, this will create a growing demand for component manufacture.

Within a decade, Poland's automotive component manufacturing base has been transformed from being isolated, under-invested, technologically backward and having poor quality production, to being an increasingly important European manufacturing centre. It now supplies both domestic and international automotive manufacturers. International component companies have transformed the technologically backward domestic component industry that existed at the start of the 1990s. Domestic companies have had to raise manufacturing standards, productivity and service levels to meet the demands set by international customers.

In addition to the subsidiaries and companies closely linked to Fiat and Daewoo, other automotive component groups present include Delphi, Visteon and Piast. GM-owned Delphi has made a series of acquisitions and greenfield investments to supply both the GM plant in Gliwice and also other automotive groups in Poland. Delphi is one of the few international automotive companies committing to R&D in Central Europe, with its planned investment of US$30 million by the end of 1999 in a technical centre in Kracow. Delphi-owned operations in Poland are:

Product group	Location
Heat exchangers	Ostrow Wielkopolski
Wire harnesses	Jelesnia
Seats	Warsaw
Seats	Gliwice
Shock absorbers	Krosno
Steering systems	Tychy

Visteon acquired the automotive component manufacturing operations of Polmot Holdings in 1998.

International component manufacturers in Poland are listed in Table 11.2.

Table 11.2 International component manufacturers in Poland

Manufacturer	Product	Location
Allied Signal	Brakes	Twardogora
Autoliv	Seat belts and airbags	Wroclaw
British Vita	Foam	Brzeg Dolny
Dana	Filters	Gostyn
Delphi	Air conditioning	Ostrow Wielkopolski
	Car seats	Warsaw, Gliwice
	Wire harnesses	Jelesnia
	Shock absorbers	Krosno
	Steering systems	Tychy
Eaton	Engine valves	Bielsko Biala
Eaton	Gearboxes	Gdansk
Exide-CEAC	Batteries	Poznan
Fichtel & Sachs	Clutches	Trnava
Findlay Industries Mazowiecki	Car seats	Tomaszow
Gestind Poland	Steering wheels	Wapienica
	Headrests	
Gilardini	Exhaust pipes	Dabrowa Gornicza
	Mirrors	
GKN	Driveshafts	Twardogora
Goodyear Tires	Tyres	Debica
Isuzu	Diesel engines	Tychy
Lucas SEI	Wiring systems	Leszno
Magnetti Marelli	Instrument panels	Sosnowiec
	Lights	
	Heating systems	
Mazzer	Metal and plastic parts	Zywiec

Table 11.2 *continued*

Manufacturer	Product	Location
Mercedes Benz		
Lenkungen	Steering systems	Miedzyrzecze
Michelin	Tyres	Olsztyn
Ovatex	Sound insulation and interior panels	Bielsko Biala
Pilkington	Windows Glass products	Sandomierz
Sestind Manifattura		
Di Bruzdo	Steering wheels Headrests Hubcaps	Wapienica
St Gobain	Windows	Zary
Teksid	Iron and aluminium castings	Bielsko Biala Skoczow
Teksid	Aluminium and zinc castings	Skoczow, Bielsko Biala
Tenneco	Exhaust pipes	Rybnik
Tenneco Automotive	Exhaust pipes	Rybnik
Timken	Bearings	Sosnowiec
TVAB	Wire harnesses	Lodz
UTA	Wire harnesses	Mielec
Visteon	Brakes Motors	Prazka

Source: VP International

The future

The overall future for Poland's automotive industry should be viewed with optimism. Over the next few years, the country will see its significance as a major European producer of vehicles and parts continue to increase, based on the ever growing levels of investment and manufacturing output.

The existing passenger and vehicle manufacturers all have ambitious expansion plans, while many of the component groups that are already established have commitments to increase investment and output levels. In addition to those already present, many other international groups are actively looking at establishing operations in Poland in order to supply both the domestic and export markets. This is graphically illustrated by Toyota's announcement in mid-1999 that it was to commit $300 million to establishing a transmission plant that will start production in 2002.

12

Construction

Richard J Thurlow, Ove Arup

Introduction

Poland now constitutes one of the largest and most dynamic markets in Central and Eastern Europe, which is reflected in its construction industry. In most major cities cranes litter the skyline. Warsaw, in particular, is seeing a construction boom without precedent.

Since 1992, Poland has enjoyed continuous economic growth of over 5 per cent per year. Growth for 1999 is expected to be 4 per cent and foreign direct investment now totals over US$30 billion. Increased industrial production and a rising standard of living have all contributed to the growth of the Polish construction market, which in 1998 increased by 17 per cent over that of the previous year.

Government policies are designed to encourage this growth, through laws and tax incentives, as well as through the creation of Special Economic Zones.

The advent of Poland's accession to the EU will attract further growth in the construction sector. This will be due to the inflow of pre-accession funds for the upgrading of infrastructure and for the establishment of industries created to employ workers released by the restructuring of the agricultural, mining, railway and steel industries.

A growth industry

Poland started from a very low base of quality facilities: most building and infrastructure stock was poor, industry was undeveloped for the production of modern consumer goods and large areas were suitable for redevelopment.

Over the past few years, the construction industry has grown at an enormous rate, totalling over US$20 billion in 1999 and forecast to grow to over US$50 billion by 2010. Construction growth was over 17 per cent in 1997 and 1998, and is predicted to be in double digits for the next five years, with growth still increasing at over 4 per cent until the end of the next decade. As an example of this, cement consumption rose by 20 per cent in 1998.

If the construction industry's target is to be able to provide facilities to match the standard of those in Western Europe, the following will be needed:

Sector	Area (million m²)	Cost (US$ billion)
Over 3 million houses	250	125
Offices	15	10
Hotels	4	5
Retail	8	4
Motorways	2500	2
Total		146

This demand will be fed by continuing foreign direct investment (now the highest in Europe). Foreign companies are continuing to invest in Poland, attracted by its relatively low labour costs, its educated workforce and by the growth fostered by an expanding middle class with high expectations and a rising disposable income.

Whether or not all this will be achieved, only time will tell. However, if only a part of these objectives are met in the near future, then economic growth will stimulate a continuing major construction need.

Law and incentives

In the mid-1990s, the government realised that planning processes needed to be simplified and that incentives were needed to stimulate construction growth. A number of measures were adopted as a result.

In 1995 building regulations were changed to allow for an easier and more straightforward planning and development process. Previous to this, construction was a nightmare, with numerous permits having to be obtained from a variety of sources. Now, although the process is not perfect, a more precise methodology is in place, placing the onus on the authorities to act within a set period of time from the date of application. Decision points have, in theory, been reduced to two: the Development Conditions and the Building Permit, with the period in between the two being taken up by obtaining agreements from interested parties. Once granted, a Building Permit is valid for two years. After construction, a permit to 'use the building' must be obtained. Although the procedure is now more straightforward, bureaucratic attitudes take longer to change and the process is still highly political and highly personal.

Taxes were also reduced for investors, in the housing industry in particular, and subsidies were granted for public investment in areas of high unemployment. These have had some effect on the residential sector but private individuals have not always found it easy to raise funds, thus keeping the housing market relatively depressed.

Finally, the government created the first Special Economic Zones (SEZs); there are now 17 of these. The benefits vary from zone to zone, but generally they include:

- tax exemption for ten years, with a lower rate for the next ten;

- property tax exemptions;

- reduced stamp duties.

These exemptions are given provided the investment exceeds €2 million (depending on the zone). However, impending EU accession and competition rules have meant that the government has had to announce that most SEZs can only accept new investment until the end of 2000, except in certain very special cases.

Participants in the industry

The Polish construction industry has had a long and respectable history of working both inside and outside Poland, the latter particularly in the 1970s and 1980s. Polish engineers are highly trained and competent and the standard of trade workmanship is high, though sometimes requiring external supervision and management planning.

Many foreign contractors, particularly German and Austrian, have successfully established themselves in Poland, sometimes buying into Polish firms and providing management and programming skills. The presence of British contractors is low and, despite construction growth, opportunities for them to enter this highly competitive market now appear limited.

The professional design, architecture and engineering business is very fragmented, with most of the engineering firms in particular being small and single-disciplinary. The Polish architect remains a key individual in the planning and approvals process. A great deal of the foreign-funded work is done by a combination of foreign and Polish designers, thus achieving a combination of lower fees and local knowledge.

Many of the old state design institutes are living on the glories of past times and have not come to terms with modern design techniques or competition. A few have done so and are competing successfully, but much of the engineering design work is undertaken by small, single-discipline firms or individuals working in isolation. There is a lack of true multi-disciplinary designers.

The areas that do have a large British presence are real estate, cost consulting and project management, and most of the big British players are represented here. These firms filled a gap in the market as their skills were previously unknown in Poland.

Industrial construction

Industrial construction reached very high growth rates of over 17 per cent in 1997 and 1998, and a growth rate of 15 per cent is predicted for 1999. Significant foreign investment, as well as high and increasing investment from Polish sources, is responsible for this. Investors are often companies wishing to consolidate their position in the market and those who are anxious not to miss the boat.

Large investments have been made in fast-moving consumer and white goods production, and there has been and continues to be huge investment in the automotive industry, with leaders Daewoo and Fiat battling for market share. Most foreign investment tends to associate itself with greenfield sites, even allowing for the large costs of providing infrastructure of all types.

Warehousing and business parks are a growth area, with a number of collection, warehousing and distribution facilities being built on the outskirts of many major cities.

Continued growth is expected in the following areas of industrial construction:

- automotive and automotive products;
- food industry;
- energy sector privatisation;
- pharmaceuticals;
- printing and publishing;
- construction materials.

Residential construction

The relatively low level of housing construction (88,000 new starts are predicted in 1999, mostly apartment blocks) is heavily influenced by the paucity of mortgage facilities. However, the sector is doing considerably better than in the early 1990s, when there was a year-by-year decrease.

The lack of availability of mortgages, and high lending rates, mean that cash plays a significant part in the funding of current residential construction. However, government legislation is now in place to enable a system of housing finance for people with average incomes. This should include the establishment of housing and loan savings schemes, and the inflow of funds from newly established building societies should greatly stimulate the market from 2000 onwards.

Little of this will help the renovation of the huge stock of sub-standard flats that exists throughout Poland, and for which there is as yet no apparent solution.

Office construction

The boom in office construction continues, particularly in Warsaw, where more than 65 per cent of such construction takes place. This expansion is now spreading to other major cities such as Lodz, Krakow and Poznan.

These offices are superseding the run-down and sub-standard offices built in former times. There is little rehabilitation and, because of the large number of vacant lots in city centres, it is cheaper (and usually more straightforward given land ownership uncertainties) to build new rather than to renovate the existing stock of offices with their poor layouts, construction and quality.

It is said that Class A is not to the same standard as elsewhere in Western Europe, but rents remain high for this standard in Warsaw, although they are now down from the earlier figures of US\$40–50/month/m^2. This high yield will ensure the continued construction of new offices as demand still outstrips supply. New offices of a lower standard will appear, as there is great demand, particularly among Polish firms, for reasonable quality accommodation at a lower price.

Retail construction

Out-of-town and suburban retail centres are being built at a frenetic pace, with most major cities having several centres planned or in existence. Over the last couple of years, the shopping pattern has been transformed, particularly so in Warsaw. Several large French chains, such as Géant, Leclerc and Carrefour, are seizing the growth opportunity provided by the young Polish middle class with rising disposable incomes.

The major growth is in food retailing, DIY and gardening. 1998 saw a 90 per cent increase over the previous year, and there will probably be a 20 per cent growth in the provision of such space in 1999, with 10 per cent expected in the years thereafter.

Hotel construction

A number of four star hotels already exist in the major cities, and several more are planned. The real opportunities are in the construction and operation of three star hotels for businessmen.

Civil engineering

Railways

The railways need restructuring and slimming down but this process will be politically difficult as the railway company PKP is the largest employer in the country. Major improvements will continue to be on the E20 line, running east–west through Poland (the Berlin–Warsaw–Moscow route), and the line running south–east (the Berlin–Wroclaw–Kiev route). These lines will be improved along their existing alignment so that passenger trains will be able to travel at a speed of 160 kph and goods at 120 kph.

The Government plans to privatise PKP in due course, perhaps along the British model, but in the meantime improvements are being funded by the EU and EIB, and funding for reorganisation and improvements by the issue of Bonds.

Roads

Polish roads are in a poor state: the majority are sub-standard in alignment, width and riding quality. New and rehabilitated roads are desperately needed. Unfortunately, the motorway programme has got off to a poor start. Poland declared that the vast majority of its motorway construction programme of 2500 km was to be funded privately. However, it became clear that the traffic figures were not high enough to make private projects viable and the result has been stasis for over a year on the two concessions so far awarded, the A2 Swieko to Strykow and the A1 Gdansk to Torun. The government is considering changes to the laws that would allow public finance to contribute to the construction of motorway projects and, if passed, this would enable construction to start in 2000.

Other smaller sections of motorways (mainly bypasses) are being funded by grants from the EU and the World Bank is funding the improvement of sections of national highways.

Harbours

The World Bank is funding improvements to the port and surrounding infrastructure of Gdansk and Gdynia. The European Bank for Reconstruction and Development (EBRD) is supporting various terminal developments in the area and there are several private new facilities planned.

Airports

A second terminal is being planned at Warsaw and is likely to be tendered in 1999. In the long term, another airport to the north of Warsaw is foreseen as the present facilities will become overloaded during the next decade. Other airports also have planned developments ranging from new terminals to the extension of runways.

Environment

A great deal of money has already gone into the improvement of environmental facilities, mainly water supply and waste-water treatment, to bring these up to the standard of Western Europe. These investments have been mainly funded by the EU. Significant funds will continue to be spent in the field of environmental improvement.

Privatisation of the water supply and treatment works of various cities is also being planned. Poznan is well advanced and other cities contemplating this type of improvement are Bydgoszcz and Wroclaw. These will give considerable opportunities to water firms in the UK, although competition from French firms will be intense.

Conclusion

This brief résumé of the construction sector in Poland can only be superficial. There is plenty happening, however, and the only way to find out about it is to be in Poland. Being accepted will take some time and it helps considerably to have a Polish speaker as an integral part of your team. Lucky are the firms that have senior personnel on their staff who speak Polish!

The author wishes to thank European Construction Research for supplying many of the facts in this article.

13

Distribution

Lesley Brett, BOC Distribution Services Polska

Market trends

Since BOC entered the Polish market some six years ago with the acquisition of a company providing international temperature-controlled distribution, the international movements market has been eroded by a number of factors.

Poland's balance of payments has reflected higher imports and a sharp decline in exports year on year, which suggests that neighbouring countries are sending their vehicles into Poland laden with goods and offering cheap movements out of Poland to fill their empty mileage. The 1998 collapse of the Russian stock market and its subsequent economic crisis made many European countries react cautiously about doing business in Poland, even though Poland's economy had become stable enough to deflect any fallout. The Russian crisis did however result in a surge of sub-standard transportation from Russia searching for work of any kind. This further undermined prices and many operators found it difficult to maintain viable rates.

Customs

Customs delays are still a major concern among Western multinationals operating in Central and Eastern Europe. A survey conducted by DHL (1999) polled the views of 500 companies, of which 62 per cent stated that they still experienced customs difficulties through rules and regulations changing too regularly, over-zealous application of the rules, bureaucracy in general and corruption. All of this paints a poor picture for the professional international mover and customers who would not normally accept such poor levels of service are drawn to the low rates.

EU requirements

Whereas local manufacturers have traditionally selected transport according to price, it had been anticipated that Western multinational corporations would select their service providers on the basis of quality and the ability to meet existing and future EU legislation. This trend has been slower to evolve than anticipated but we are now seeing many producers who require a more tailored service. This will have a significant impact on Poland's logistics market, as small operators unable to meet the high levels of investment required are likely to feel the pressure most. They will be forced to either amalgamate or go out of business as vehicle legislation falls in line with EU operational requirements. The speed of this transition relates directly to Poland's ambitions to become a fully fledged member of the EU by 2002 and its success in achieving this goal.

Road network

Further barriers to the development of a more sophisticated supply chain offering is the current state of Poland's road network, which requires massive investment in order to improve its infrastructure. Also detrimental to the move towards cost-effective bulk movement is the network of wholesaler/retail outlets, which provides a wide spread of delivery points while offering no critical mass. This is considered to be the least cost-effective method of moving goods from point of production to point of sale. The last 30 years in the UK have seen the role of the wholesaler almost completely eroded by the growth and market domination of the supermarket chains. The UK currently has two main wholesale distributors, the USA 12 and Poland some 12,000. The situation in Poland is therefore bound to change.

Opportunities

Professional logistics suppliers who understand the complexities of working in Poland and have a track record with key clients have great potential to expand their customer base as new opportunities present themselves. Potential clients who realise the benefits of out-sourcing their logistics will, over the long term, have a distinct advantage over their competitors. Integrity of goods, minimal stock-outs and cost-effective movements will give them a competitive edge – but this does require front-end investment.

The pattern of demand in Poland has changed dramatically over the last ten years. Today we see rampant consumerism, increased expectations and a requirement for a range of goods that were not previously available. Everything from designer T-shirts to frozen food now has a common place in Poland's purchasing profile. This has led to the development of a number of large outlets such as hypermarkets that are struggling to keep pace with demand. Over the next five years, demand will be increasingly met by such outlets, which will require Western-style logistics services. Development of efficient distribution schedules (Just-in-Time deliveries), modern warehousing and the specialisation required for temperature regimes, fragile goods and short-life products will be a feature of logistics offerings.

14

Energy

Tomasz Minkievicz, CMS Cameron McKenna

Introduction

Polish infrastructure sectors, due to insufficient investment over the last two decades, lag behind the overall development of the economy and threaten to become bottlenecks to further growth unless they can attract the substantial capital they require for modernisation, refurbishment and new facilities. A large number of major players in the various infrastructure sectors have entered Poland, though the size of their investment may have been below some expectations, largely as a result of slow administrative processes (including preparation of and implementation of privatisation projects) and an inadequate legal environment. This chapter presents basic facts and legal regulations pertaining to the electricity and heating sectors.

Basic facts

Poland's power system, with an installed capacity of approximately 33,000 MW, is the largest in Central Europe.

Electricity generation

Electricity generation is concentrated in 20 large power stations, accounting for approximately 85 per cent of installed capacity, and in several large combined heat and power (CHP) stations, dispatched by the national system operator. The overwhelming majority of the power generated in Poland is produced in facilities fired by lignite (approximately 60 per cent of power produced) and hard coal (34 per cent). The share of hydro-generation and other energy sources, including gas, is almost insignificant. There are no nuclear power plants in operation or under construction. Although the government has declared diversification of the fuel base, including the significantly increased role of natural gas, to be one its strategic goals, there exist important considerations that may affect the implementation of this strategy, such as the need to support the restructuring of the coal mining industry.

Transmission system

The transmission system consists of approximately 5,000 km of 400 kV high voltage lines and 8,000 km of 220 kV lines, all of which are owned and operated by Polskie Sieci Elektroenergetyczne SA (Polish Power Grid Company or PPGC). PPGC is a wholly state-owned company that is responsible for the overall security and reliability of the electrical system and that provides peaking power capacity for stabilisation of the grid. PPGC is also the major purchaser of electricity from generators, with approximately 65 per cent of the capacity contracted based on medium- and long-term power purchase agreements.

Distribution system

The distribution system in Poland consists of approximately 37,000 km of 110 kV lines, some of which directly supply large industrial customers and parts of the railway network. There are an additional 270,000 km of 15 kV and 20 kV medium-voltage lines, linking into low-voltage lines, and also directly supplying industrial customers, railways and municipal customers. The distribution and supply sub-sector of the electricity industry is covered by 33 regional state-owned distribution companies. Traditionally, the distribution companies purchased most of their electricity from PPGC. Recently, however, they have become more active in acquiring electricity directly from the generators or from trading companies (the latter having recently emerged as an entirely new phenomenon in the sector), for the purposes of which the distributors often form regional consortia.

Heat supply

The heat supply sector, in addition to the several large state-owned CHP plants, includes a large number of smaller municipal and industrial heat or co-generation facilities. The majority of these are owned by municipalities, by distribution companies or by their industrial customers and many of them require modernisation or refurbishment to achieve acceptable pollution and efficiency levels. The heat distribution networks, some of which (such as the Warsaw district heating system) rank among the largest in Europe, are typically operated by municipal-owned distribution companies or by heat generators.

Opportunities and developments

Despite its current over-capacity, the Polish power generation sector requires urgent modernisation. Over 38 per cent of the plants are over 25 years old, with over 22 per cent being over 35 years old. Only a few of those plants have been modernised and benefited from lifetime extension programmes. About 40 per cent of plants can be described as relatively modern, ie with an age below 20 years. The modernisation problem apart, the Polish power stations require significant efficiency improvements and environmental investment in order to match Western European standards.

Developments in the power sector (and the heat sector with regard to heat co-generated with electricity) have probably attracted more of investors' and public attention that any other utility sector in Poland over the last two to three years. This is partly due to the enactment of an entirely new regulatory regime and also to developments in the privatisation process. The most remarkable of the legislative developments was undoubtedly the enactment of the Energy Law of 10 April 1997, and of its secondary legislation. These regulations govern such vital areas as licences for conducting activity in the energy sector, setting of tariffs, third-party access and the maintenance of fuel reserves by power and heat producers.

The Energy Law

Energy Regulatory Authority

Pursuant to the Energy Law, a central governmental agency called the Energy Regulatory Authority (ERA) was created for the purposes of regulating the activities of energy enterprises. Its objective was to balance the interests of such enterprises, enabling these to operate profitably in a stable environment, with the interests of final consumers of electricity, gas and heat, protecting these against the abuse of the suppliers' monopolistic position. The president of the ERA is appointed by the prime minister for a term of five years. He is not a member of the government and cannot be removed from his position prior to the expiration of his term of office, except in specified, limited circumstances. This enables him to remain immune from short-term political pressures. The president of the ERA operates through its office, which is composed of its headquarters and of eight regional branches.

Key responsibilities of the president of the ERA include:

- issuance and withdrawal of licences for production, transmission, distribution and trading in energy and fuels;

- approval of prices for lignite and tariffs for gaseous fuels, electricity and heat;

- control of the quality of supply and customer service standards with respect to trade in gaseous fuels and electricity;

- resolution of certain disputes within the ERA's jurisdiction;

- verification of the qualifications of persons operating the grid, energy installations and equipment.

Decisions of the president of the ERA may be appealed against to the Anti-monopoly Court in Warsaw.

Licensing of energy activity

The Energy Law, for the first time, introduced licensing requirements with respect to all enterprises engaged, over a certain level, in the generation, transformation, storage, transmission, distribution and trade of energy or liquid or gaseous fuels. The Energy Law provides that licences will be issued for periods not shorter than ten years and not longer than 50 years. In practice, almost all (if not all) licences issued so far have been issued for a period of ten years. Licences may be issued only to enterprises that are registered in Poland, demonstrate availability of sufficient funds and technical capabilities and ensure employment of properly qualified personnel. With respect to facilities not yet completed, these enterprises must have obtained administrative approval for the development of the site on which the particular project will be located. Additionally, members of the executive authorities of the enterprise cannot have been convicted for criminal offences committed in connection with energy-related activity.

The licensing procedures are relatively straightforward and expeditious, provided that the applicant presents all information and documentation required by the ERA. Consultation with the relevant self-government authorities (the result of which is non-binding but is usually reflected in the decision of the ERA) at the provincial (voivodship) level is required prior to issuing any licence or amendment thereto. As the self-government authority is given only 14 days to respond, the consultation does not significantly delay the process. Initially, the president of the ERA concentrated his efforts on issuing licences to the enterprises already engaged, at 4 June 1997 (the date of promulgation of the Energy Law), in the activity subject to licensing; these were eligible, *ex officio*, for licences. Subsequently, more licences for new entrants have been granted. In total, the president of the ERA had issued more than 2500 licences by mid-1999.

Issuing licences pursuant to the Energy Law is not subject to any up-front payment but all licensed enterprises are subject to an annual licensing fee. The levels and the methods of calculation of such licensing fees are defined in the secondary legislation, and are in proportion to the revenues of the enterprise in the preceding year. However, the fee may not be less than Zl 1000 or more than Zl 500,000 annually.

Tariffs

The Energy Law provides that all licensed energy enterprises must prepare and submit tariffs regarding electricity, heat and gaseous fuels for approval by the president of the ERA. The Energy Law contains only very general guidelines regarding the level of tariffs established by energy enterprises. Such tariffs should cover justified costs incurred by energy enterprises, including costs associated with modernisation, development and environmental protection, and protect consumers against unjustified price levels.

More precise guidelines regarding the calculation of tariffs are contained in two ordinances issued by the Minister of Economy, separately with respect to electricity and heat. No gas tariffs ordinance has been issued as yet, as gas prices will continue to be set by the Minister of Finance until at least December 1999. The guidelines apply both to energy sale tariffs (on the level of generators and distributors) and to inter-connection and transmission tariffs. Although these ordinances are lengthy and detailed, they are widely criticised within the industry. The main criticisms are that they are unclear, inflexible, suited to the needs of distribution companies and not of the generating companies, and that they do not take into account the specific requirements of project financing under long-term power and/or heat purchase agreements. Finally, they are deemed outdated as they build on the 'RPI – X' (ie retail price index minus efficiency factor) formula, already abandoned in other countries.

Approved tariffs are subject to publication in the official bulletin of the ERA or, with respect to heat tariffs, in the provincial official gazette, which is a pre-condition to their effectiveness.

The president of the ERA may exempt the energy enterprise from tariff approval if he is satisfied that the enterprise 'operates in a competitive market'. The exemption may be withdrawn at any time. It is expected that the competitive market exemption will be used with respect to the power generation sector for the purposes of creating an electricity exchange or pool market, anticipated to be organised in the year 2000.

Third-party access

The Energy Law provides that all energy enterprises engaged in the transmission or distribution of energy or fuel must transmit and distribute, subject to technical and economic feasibility, energy or fuel produced in Poland, on terms contractually agreed by the parties. However, secondary legislation provides for a gradual implementation of the third-party access (TPA) principle. This enables various groups of power, heat and gas consumers to gain access to the grid over specified periods, depending on their annual purchases of energy, gas or heat (the larger the annual consumption, the sooner TPA will apply). TPA will not be fully applicable prior to 5 December 2005 with respect to power and gas, and 1 January 2003 with respect to heat.

Privatisation

The energy sector remains one of the few industries that still await privatisation, though the process has already begun. One large CHP plant (EC Krakow) and a 2200 MW group of three large lignite-fired power plants (PAK) have been sold to strategic investors and there has been a public offering of one smaller CHP plant. Another company comprising six CHP plants (EC Warsaw) and a power plant (Polaniec) is expected to be privatised in 1999 or early in 2000. More transactions are expected in the near future, ultimately leading to the State Treasury passing the control of all the companies involved in the sector (except for PPGC) to private investors by the end of 2002. Privatisation of the energy sector will be governed by the same rules and will be effected via similar procedures as in other sectors, it is expected with the following specific features:

- distribution companies, except for the two largest, will be sold in packages of four to seven companies;

- policy or even legal safeguards against concentration of market power and vertical integration beyond certain limits will be implemented.

As currently perceived, the success of privatisation will depend on the resolution of some industry-specific issues. These include existing long-term power purchase agreements, implementation of the power pool/exchange market, environmental liability for past pollution, and employment and social issues, which also occur in many other sectors.

15

Health Care

Nick Sljivic, VP International, and Danuta Pilecka

Introduction

1 January 1999 was the date when the long-proposed and heatedly debated reforms to the Polish health care system became a reality. The key aspects of this new system were the division of health care into fund-holders and service providers and a move away from the centralised control of health care provision.

Poland is not unique in the problems that face its health care system; the issues mirror those of countries the world over. The four key and often conflicting issues are: inefficiency in the use of scarce resources, increasing consumer expectations, spiralling costs of health care and the lack of adequate funding.

It is the final point that is the most significant in Poland. According to 1997 OECD figures, Poland, of all Central European countries, spends the lowest proportion of GDP on health care. For the last three to four years this has been below 5 per cent, compared to 6.5 per cent in the Czech Republic. Polish expenditure is around half of what much wealthier Western European nations spend (nearly 9 per cent in the UK and over 10 per cent in Germany). For 1999, expenditure on health care was estimated at Zl 25.8 billion (US$6.66 billion) or 4.32 per cent of estimated GNP of Zl 596 billion.

This low level of state expenditure, however, does not cover expenditure by patients. At present it is estimated that about 33 per cent of all health care costs are paid directly by patients to health care institutions for services not covered by insurance, or are paid to the private sector. With this expenditure taken into account, it is estimated that in fact approximately 6.5–7 per cent of Polish GNP is spent on health care. It must also be noted that an estimated 20–25 per cent of the population cannot afford the higher levels of health care services that require co-payment. Table 15.1 gives an overview of health care statistics.

Table 15.1 Health care statistics

Demographic statistics 1997		
Deaths per 1000 population		9.7
Live births per 1000 population		10.5
Infant mortality rate per 1000 live births		10.7
Male life expectancy (years)		68.5
Female life expectancy (years)		77.0
Medical statistics		
Category	*Total no.*	*No. per 10,000 population*
Doctors	911,000	23.6
Dentists	17,600	4.6
Out-patient clinics	6,264	
Pharmacists	20,700	5.3
Nurses	217,200	56.2
Hospital beds	209,961	54.3
Pharmacies	7,342	
Visitation statistics		
Average hospitalisation (days)		10.4
Total no. of visits for medical treatment ('000)		240,428
– visits to general practitioner ('000)		151,729
– visits to consultant ('000)		81,499
– other ('000)		7,200
Visits to doctor per person per year		6.2
– medical		5.3
– dental		0.9

Life expectancy

In 1995 life expectancy at birth for men was 68.5 years and 77.0 years for women. This is considerably lower than the European average: in member states of the EU the figures were 72.9 years and 79.5 years respectively. The main causes for this disparity are attributed to a poor diet and excessive cigarette and alcohol consumption.

The health care system: pre-1 January 1999

The Polish health care system underwent drastic reform as of 1 January 1999, with the aim of decentralising funding and administration.

The Polish Constitution states that citizens have the right to equal access to health services financed by the state, including free primary and specialist out-patient care, in-patient care and emergency care. The overseeing body responsible for all matters pertaining to the nation's health care provision was the Ministry of Health and Social Welfare (MHSW).

Health care in Poland was financed from the Central Budget and administered by central and local governments. Under the state-run national social insurance system (ZUS), a 48 per cent tax was paid by the employer for health care and pensions; these contributions went straight to the central budget. The Sejm (the lower house of the parliament) determined the health care budget and this was then distributed by the Ministry of Health to the 49 voivodships (provinces) for the financing of health care in their localities. The voivodships were responsible for the financing of hospitals in their areas. The Ministry of Health remained directly responsible for the financing of medical academies, the national health policy, R&D programmes and certain hospitals.

The Polish health care system provided services through three tiers of a highly structured network, corresponding to the administrative organisation of the country. The three tiers were as follows:

- **central**: Ministry of Health;

- **voivodship**: 49 local governmental administrative units;

- **ZOZs** (Zespol Opieki Zdrowotnej): 400 locally integrated health care management units serving populations of 30,000–150,000 people.

At the central level, the Ministry of Health was directly responsible for national health policy programmes, national regulations and policy, medical safety issues, university medical schools, medical research institutes, national research centres and national post-graduate education centres.

Every one of the 49 voivodships had a health department responsible for health and social services in its region. These were further divided into local-level, integrated health care management units (ZOZs). There were between 3 and 33 ZOZs in each voivodship. Each ZOZ provided a full range of integrated primary- and secondary-level health services. Each ZOZ was supposed to have at least one hospital, several out-patient care facilities, as well as other specialised health care services such as paediatrics, gynaecology, obstetrics and dental care.

Private health care emerged in the 1980s, largely involving payment to doctors in single or co-operative practices and normally on an occasional basis. Most individuals cannot afford to pay the full cost of treatment by private doctors or of care in the few private clinics and hospitals.

Health care reforms: post-1 January 1999

The health care system in Poland has been undergoing continuous and gradual reform since 1990, culminating in the Health Insurance Act, which came into force on 1 January 1999.

Essentially, the Health Care Reform Act adopted in 1997 was designed to decentralise the highly centralised national care system in a move to curtail spiralling costs and improve what was regarded as a highly inefficient system. The main aims of the Act are to:

- decentralise health care provision;

- improve financial control;

- give patients greater say in the choice of health care providers;

- strengthen the role of primary health care;

- increase the autonomy of local health care providers.

This new system brings Poland very much into line with many of the health care reforms seen across Europe. Key elements of the reform are:

- **Decentralisation:** Responsibility for all aspects of administration (financial and operational) is largely to be devolved to voivodships and large cities, and the role of the centralised Ministry of Health will dwindle.

- **Introduction of a mixed insurance-budget model of health care financing:** The system is decentralised by the regional collection and allocation of subscriptions. In the new system, in addition to regional subscription insurance funds, a second source of financing is via the State Budget and local government authorities. Sixteen regional insurance funds will be created, overseen by a National Fund Union. The mandatory, tax-deductible health insurance premium amounts to a 7.5 per cent tax on an individual's income. The State Budget will cover individuals who do not earn wages, including students and the unemployed. The basic organisational structure will be the Regional Health Insurance Fund. Each region will consist of several voivodships and have 1.2–5.0 million inhabitants. The National Social Insurance Fund (ZUS) collects health insurance premiums from employers and transfers them to the Regional Funds.

- **Contract basis:** A form of market was introduced. Contracts are drawn up between funds and health care providers (hospitals, clinics and individual doctors). Funds are free to determine where contracts are placed.

- **Focus on primary care:** The emphasis will switch from specialist treatment to family doctors and community nurses in a primary care role. It is estimated that 70 per cent of doctors are currently acting as specialists and the intention is to reduce this proportion drastically. Patients will have the ability to choose their physician independently. The aim is for the family doctor to act as a gate-keeper to other medical specialists as per requirement.

- **Self-management by health care providers:** Each provider (clinic, hospital or doctor) will become an autonomous operational unit with responsibility for its own financial management and for the drawing up of contracts with health insurance funds.

The estimated cost for the programme of health care reform is estimated at around Zl 1.5 billion (around US$425 million).

In reality, the decentralisation of funding is an illusion due to 'national health insurance', which is obligatory and applies universally. In addition, this insurance is monopolistic because this system is the only insurance company (and will probably continue to be until 2002) and because it is the only purchaser of health care services, as private insurance remains virtually non-existent in Poland.

National health programmes

Health care expenditure is determined by the priorities set by the Ministry of Health under its National Health Programme. The decade-long National Health Programme that started in 1996 promotes preventative medicine in the major disease categories and also focuses on the treatment of these major diseases, which include:

- heart protection;
- cancer diagnosis and treatment;
- intensive care units for accident victims;
- stroke prevention and treatment;
- improving pre-natal care;
- care of mental patients;
- hearing difficulties;
- dialysis.

Key categories for medical device manufacturers of kidney dialysis, cardiology and cancer are:

- **Heart protection:** Health education programmes are being implemented to reduce coronary disease and the consequential number of deaths. The aim is also to improve the diagnosis and treatment of heart disease and improve patient access to specialist centres. The objectives for this programme to achieve by the year 2000 include that of reducing the number of patients suffering from coronary disease by up to 10 per cent. The number of specialist diagnoses and treatment facilities is planned to be doubled and there is a planned increase in the overall number of cardiology units across Poland. The 1996–2000 expenditure on this programme was budgeted at around US$150 million.

● **Cancer:** An education programme to reduce the level of lung cancer due to smoking was adopted. Improvements in the early diagnosis of tumours as well as greater access to treatment are also planned. On an administrative level, epidemiological data collection will be improved in order to monitor the success of the programme and how effective cancer care programmes are across the country. The 1996–2000 expenditure on this programme was budgeted at around US$300 million.

● **Dialysis:** The objective by the year 2000 is that all patients suffering from chronic kidney disease will be able to have dialysis. In order to achieve this, Poland will by then have 171 dialysis centres (up from 120 in 1995) and 1289 dialysis machines (up from 1001 in 1995). In the year 2000, 7445 patients will be able to receive treatment, up from 4835 in 1996. There will also be an increase in the number of patients treated by dialysis in out-patient clinics, up from 400 in 1995 to 1000 in 2000. The 1996–2000 expenditure on this programme was budgeted at around US$140 million.

● **Intensive care units for accident victims:** This programme is for the establishment of regional intensive care units across Poland, aimed at reducing the level of mortality from traumas by 15 per cent.

Future of the health care system

The precise long-term implications of the health care reforms remain uncertain as the various health care providers and the health care fund adjust to their respective new roles and responsibilities. The 7.5 per cent tax rate for health care is regarded as completely unrealistic as no insurance-based system can function on such a low premium. To increase this amount, taxes or co-payment by the patients will need to be increased. Both solutions are highly politically contentious at the moment.

Operationally, the administration of the collection of social insurance is seeing significant shortfalls, with only about 60–70 per cent of expected revenue making its way to the coffers. Contracts with providers were based on the assumption that all taxation revenue targets would be met, so there is a significant and growing cash-flow problem within the system.

Initial indications are that there is severe dissatisfaction among both the providers and the recipients of health care services. Health care workers are becoming increasingly militant with regard to pay and service levels, with the threats of closure of many hospital units and of redundancy adding to the lowering of morale. With all this confusion and uncertainty, it is not surprising that there should also be general dissatisfaction among the public as to what benefits have emerged from the reforms.

Whether the long-awaited (and long-discussed) health care reforms will eventually bring about more efficient use of resources and better standards of health care provision with what are still inadequate levels of funding remains to be seen; initial indications are not promising.

16

Heavy Industries: Mining, Steel and Shipbuilding

Leszek Filipowicz, Business Management & Finance (BMF)

Introduction

The three industries described in this chapter traditionally constituted the core of Polish heavy industry. Their role in the economy as a whole has been significant in terms of both their contributions to GDP and number of jobs they provided. In the political perspective, it is important to note that workers in mines, steel mills and shipyards were the social base for the 'Solidarity' movement, which was the driving force behind the Polish political and economic transformation.

For these three industries, transition proved to be painful. In the new market-driven economy it turned out that demand for products supplied by the mining, steel and shipbuilding industries was not sufficient to utilise the production capacities built in earlier times. The volume-oriented investment decisions of the past led to the creation of a production apparatus that was unprepared to serve the new market adequately.

Over the past few years, all three industries have been going through a restructuring process aimed at modernisation, cutting excessive capacity and employment, and increasing productivity. So far, only in the case of shipbuilding has restructuring been successful. It seems the steel and mining industries still have a way to go.

Mining

Coal has traditionally been the most important raw material in Poland. Its strategic significance was based on its dominant share of the Polish primary energy mix. Although this share declined from 64 per cent in 1990 to 55 per cent in 1998, it remains well above the average of European countries.

Coal mining in Poland is important not only for economic but also for social and political reasons. Most of the coal industry is located in Silesia, in the south of Poland, and for many years Silesia was the most industrialised region of the country. Historically, in the centrally planned economy, coal was regarded as a strategic raw material and as the basis for the country's development. The only target for mines was to excavate more; demand seemed to be unlimited and cost was never an issue. Miners' work was crucial to that system and the communist government therefore treated them as the highly regarded élite of the working class. They were relatively well paid and benefited from additional privileges such as the right to purchase scarce consumer goods in special 'miners only' shops.

This special treatment did not secure the miners' loyalty to the communist system: in fact, miners participated in all the protests against it. They were also strong supporters of 'Solidarity' – the labour union and freedom movement that ultimately brought the communist regime down at the end of the 1980s. A few hundred thousand miners entered the economic transition period with a sense of victory, a victory to which they contributed much. Unfortunately, as it soon turned out, the results of changes in the economic system proved to be very different from expected.

The restructuring of the coal industry started in April 1990, when individual mines were reorganised as independent, commercially oriented state-owned enterprises. It was expected that competition would improve their efficiency and that they would be able to restructure rapidly. Unfortunately, market conditions at the time were extremely unfavourable. Coal prices were still regulated and deep recession caused a dramatic decline in demand. In these circumstances, initial attempts at restructuring failed. The industry's financial position deteriorated fast and the government decided to work out a new restructuring programme.

The first step was to consolidate the industry. In 1993 most of the existing mines were grouped into seven joint-stock corporations, fully owned by the state:

- Bytomska Spólka Weglowa SA   (11 mines)

- Rudzka Spólka Weglowa SA   (6 mines)

- Gliwicka Spólka Weglowa SA   (7 mines)

- Nadwislanska Spólka Weglowa SA   (8 mines)

- Rybnicka Spólka Weglowa SA   (5 mines)

- Jastrzebska Spólka Weglowa SA   (6 mines)

- Katowicki Holding Weglowy SA   (10 mines)

In addition, 10 mines were left as independent companies.

The aim of consolidation was to improve the management structure of the industry and facilitate the government's supervision of its restructuring. Individual mines owned by the seven corporations were to remain independent economic entities, which would help to measure their performance and economic efficiency. The seven corporations and all individual mines were asked to prepare full business plans based on real accounting information. The most inefficient mines with the highest costs of excavation were to be closed, employment was to be cut back and non-core assets disposed of.

The programme was not successful and coal mining continued to incur heavy losses. The policy of successive governments was, for political and social reasons, to avoid announcing the insolvency of mines. High social security and tax liabilities were tolerated and some of the debts were simply written off. Mines were financing themselves by delaying payments to suppliers and exports became a source of liquidity. In 1998 the industry's total loss was of Zl 3.1 billion (approximately US$0.8 billion) and total debt was Zl 15.2 billion.

The financial problems in the Polish coal mining industry are caused by two factors: excessive production capacity and excessive employment. Despite the fact that mines are making losses, miners are still the best-paid group of workers. Wages constitute 50–60 per cent of the costs of production and any attempt to bring these down is resisted by the strong labour unions.

Demand in the domestic market continues to decrease. In 1998 alone, consumption declined by 20 per cent. This is due, among other factors, to the increasing use of alternative sources of energy and to the more efficient use of coal. Imports of cheaper coal from Russia, Australia and other countries increase the pressure on prices, which in 1998 declined by 6.6 per cent in real terms. The situation in the exports markets is no better. Average prices declined by US$5.5 per tonne and the increase in domestic railway transportation costs made Polish coal even less competitive.

The process of cutting production capacities and employment is relatively slow. The update of the restructuring programme, prepared in 1998, defines the following aims:

- coal corporations should be profitable at the operational level by the year 2000;

- after 2000, corporations should start to repay their financial liabilities;

- the production of coal should decrease by 25 million tonnes by the year 2002 and then by a further 31.5 million tonnes by 2010;

- the workforce should be cut back to 138,400 employees by the end of 2002;

- new jobs (outside mining) should be created in the traditional mining areas.

The current government's plans assume full liquidation of 15 mines between now and 2004. Additionally, some mines will be partially liquidated. These processes should allow for limiting production and cutting the labour force by close to 76,000 workers. Among the other instruments used to stimulate departures of miners from the industry are: retraining programmes, early retirement programmes, loans for establishing small businesses and, most of all, special lump sum payments available for miners who are willing to leave their jobs permanently. It is expected that by the year 2002 almost 80,000 miners will benefit from this form of support. Current employment targets set by the government are 190,000 for 1999, 166,000 for 2000, 151,000 for 2001 and 138,000 for 2002.

It is estimated that the total cost of the programme of cutting production and employment levels will reach Zl 7.2 billion by 2006, approximately US$1.8 billion. The World Bank will provide part of the necessary financial resources in the form of a long-term loan.

Steel

Reconstruction of Poland after World War II created huge demand for steel products. Steel was regarded as a strategic material and Poland – as any other communist country – was investing heavily in the development of its own steel industry. To central planners, it was essentially the volume of steel produced that mattered. As a result, the investment process focused on capacity expansion, with much less attention given to product quality or improvements. The crisis in the communist economy in the 1980s and the economy's subsequent liberalisation in the 1990s had a profound impact on the steel industry. Falling domestic demand, increased international competition and the social and organisational burden of the communist past put most plants in a difficult position. The need for deep restructuring became obvious.

The Polish steel industry today consists of 25 companies with a combined production of around 10 million tonnes of raw steel. The industry remains important to the country's economy. It accounts for 5 per cent of sales of Polish industry and 6 per cent of its exports. In June 1998, it employed 82,000 workers directly and employment in steel-related sectors was estimated to be around 250,000. However, despite the restructuring efforts undertaken in the mid-1990s, the industry is in crisis.

The only bright factor is the continuous growth in domestic demand for steel products. In the last five years, domestic consumption increased from approximately 4.5 million tonnes in 1993 to 6.6 million tonnes in 1998. It is expected that by the year 2010 demand will grow by 50 per cent to 9.5 million tonnes. Demand is driven by the growth of the economy as a whole and by the relatively low level of annual steel consumption – currently 160kg per capita in Poland, compared to 300 kg in the European Union.

It is uncertain whether the Polish steel industry will be able to benefit from these positive developments on the demand side. Its technology is to a large extent obsolete: the average age of the machinery is 40 years and the depreciation ratio for fixed assets exceeds 85 per cent. In fact, more than 35 per cent of fixed assets are fully depreciated. Production and exports are in decline and the industry faces the increasing pressure of competition from foreign producers. All this is reflected by the weak financial position of the industry: most of the steel companies are losing money and some are dangerously close to insolvency. Among the reasons for their financial problems are shrinking market share (sales), high financial costs caused by past investment programmes and slow restructuring.

The market position of Polish steel companies is deteriorating. This is caused by the fact that the structure of their production is not well adjusted to the structure of demand. Poland's fast-growing economy needs more technologically advanced products that fulfil high quality requirements. As in any other developed markets, the demand for high value added flat products (used in the car industry, white goods production, packaging etc.) is growing faster than demand for long products used mostly in construction. Flat products constitute 45.6 per cent of Polish demand for steel but only 32 per cent of its steel companies' production. As a result, the level of import penetration of the Polish market in the flat products segment (the ratio of imports to domestic consumption) rose from 22 per cent in 1996 to 36 per cent in 1998.

The inadequate reaction of steel companies to changes in demand is caused by a number of factors, including the structure of investments in the past, their weak capital base and slow restructuring. The Polish steel industry is fragmented by too many and too small independent companies. Most of these, including the two largest mills, Huta Katowice and Huta T. Sendzimira, are still in state hands. In the first half of the 1990s, most of these companies undertook ambitious investment programmes, based on an assumption of independent development for all these individual companies. Given the consolidation processes in the global and European steel industries and the scarce financial resources available to Polish mills, this miscalculation is clearly at the root of current problems.

Most of the companies that were trying to pursue their own independent development programmes tried to transform themselves into integrated producers with a full production cycle. Accordingly, they began by investing in upstream production facilities such as the production of coke, blast furnaces and continuous casting technology. These investments, although important and needed, have consumed most of the financial resources available and overshadowed investments in the downstream, where most of the added value in the current steel industry comes from. As a result, as of the end of the 1990s, Polish companies face increasing problems with supplying their customers with products that have the dimensional and quality characteristics they need.

Recognising the difficult situation of the steel industry, the Polish government, with the support of EU consultants, worked out and adopted, in June 1998, a special Restructuring Programme of the Polish Steel Industry. The main tasks defined in the programme are to:

- increase the economic efficiency of individual plants;

- complete the transformation of ownership;

- modernise technologies;

- cut production capacity and employment.

According to some estimates, the total cost of implementation of the programme may reach Zl 12 billion (around US$3 billion), of which most was planned to be spent in 1998–2001.

Given the current financial problems of the steel companies and the government's tight budget policy, the financing of such an ambitious programme would not be possible without privatisation. The government expects that by the end of 2000 at least the most important plants, including Huta Katowice and Huta T. Sendzimira, will find private owners. If this does not happen, the crisis in the Polish steel industry is likely to continue.

Shipbuilding

The Polish shipbuilding industry consists of three large yards (Stocznia Gdynia, Stocznia Gdanska, Stocznia Szczecinska), a medium-sized yard (Stocznia Polnocna) and a small yard (Stocznia Ustka). In addition to yards that build ships, there are a number of repair yards, of which the largest are Gdanska Stocznia Remontowa, Stocznia Remontowa 'Nauta', Morska Stocznia Remontowa, Stocznia Remontowa 'Gryfia'. Some of the ship repair yards, like Gdanska Stocznia Remontowa, are also capable of building ships. Finally, the construction of hulls and superstructures is also performed by a number of small companies, which usually do not even own any fixed assets.

The history of the industry in the last ten years is a remarkable example of transformation from an inefficient, state-owned sector to a competitive and market-oriented industry. Shipbuilding was deeply affected by the economic transformation of 1989–90. In just a few months, the old system of cheap financing and subsidies for shipyards disappeared. At the same time, the Soviet market, which used to provide 60 per cent of orders, collapsed. Shipyards entered the following years of transition overburdened with non-core assets, excessive employment and no state support. The economic consequences of this situation appeared very soon: the ratio of net loss to sales for all shipyards amounted to 50 per cent in 1991, 34 per cent in 1992 and 36 per cent in 1993. Total debt exceeded the value of sales by 75 per cent in 1991, 37 per cent in 1992 and 45 per cent in 1993. The poor economic performance of shipyards inevitably worsened the situation of suppliers, sub-contractors and creditors.

By 1992 it became obvious that solving the shipyards' debt problem was a precondition for further restructuring and production growth. Shipyards themselves initiated debt relief negotiations with banks, suppliers and the state. Special legal procedures were used and as a result most of the ship-yards benefited from debt write-offs, debt rescheduling and debt-for-equity swaps. In exchange for debt relief, shipyards had to commit to implement-ing internal restructuring programmes that were aimed at increasing pro-duction and improving productivity. In one case debt restructuring proved to be an insufficient measure. Stocznia Gdanska, which is famous for being the cradle of the 'Solidarity' movement, was unable to secure financing for further operations and was declared bankrupt in 1996.

Debt restructuring brought about changes in shipyards' ownership structure. By the end of 1995, due to the debt for equity swaps the state was no longer the exclusive owner and private institutions' stakes varied from 40 per cent to 74 per cent. The first privatised yard was Stocznia Szczecinska, which completed its debt restructuring procedures in 1993, with some commercial banks and management taking equity positions. The largest and most modern, Stocznia Gdynia, initially went in the same direction. Two banks obtained a controlling stake in exchange for past debts. In the next step, banks sold their stake to the company created by Stocznia Gdynia's management and employees.

One of the results of privatisation was the initiation of a consolidation process within the industry. Stocznia Szczecinska has built its own capital group taking over, among others, the majority stake in smaller Stocznia Ustka and the producer of cranes – Towimor. Stocznia Gdynia, after the successful completion of its management buy-out, acquired the assets of the bankrupt Stocznia Gdanska and started expansion into the construc-tion business. Finally, Gdanska Stocznia Remontowa – the largest and most successful repair yard – purchased a controlling stake of Stocznia Polnocna and is planning further expansion by purchasing one of the ship repair yards on the west coast of the Baltic.

The current situation of the shipbuilding industry in terms of produc-tion and sales proves that tough restructuring measures undertaken in the past brought good results. In 1998, Polish shipyards built 37 ships with total capacity of 673,000 GT (gross tonnage) and value of around US$1 billion. These included 26 container ships, 5 bulk carriers, 2 chem-ical cargo carriers, 1 ferry and 1 fishing boat. Poland is the sixth largest world producer, with a 3.1 per cent share of world output. The Polish shipbuilding industry as a whole reported a positive net margin of 1.42 per cent compared with a negative 11.3 per cent only two years before. The evolution of production and sales, since the beginning of decade, is shown in Table 16.1.

Table 16.1 Shipbuilding production and value of sales

Year	Tonnage (CGT '000)	Value (US$ million)
1991	200	278
1992	306	423
1993	324	507
1994	440	811
1995	490	885
1996	504	880
1997	485	916
1998	517	1040

At the end of 1998, Polish shipyards had a combined order book of 54 ships with a capacity of 770,000 CGT. Ships ordered included 15 container ships, 9 bulk carriers, 8 general cargo vessels, 11 chemical cargo carriers, 7 ferries, 2 gas product carriers and 1 vehicle carrier. Their total value was approximately US$1.6 billion. The two shipyards that secured most of the orders were Stocznia Szczecinska and Stocznia Gdynia. The former plans to achieve sales levels of more than US$500 million in 1999 and is ranked among the top ten shipbuilders in the world.

Polish ship repair yards have also recorded good results in 1998. Their income from repair work reached US$158 million, with 65 per cent of that being contributed by Gdanska Stocznia Remontowa. The latter is an especially interesting example of the successful adoption of a new business strategy based on diversifying from repair works only into building ships and off-shore constructions.

Looking back to the beginning of the transition period it would be justifiable to say that the Polish shipbuilding industry has made much progress on its way to the top of the world league. Now, its future depends on its ability to increase productivity, enter new markets of greater value and consolidate further (and/or diversify) to utilise possible synergies.

17

Information Technology

Jan J Kluk OBE, ICL Poland

From an interesting history, a promising future

The first experiments with 'electronic brains' in Poland date as far back as 1948, when a group of mathematicians founded The Group (the Institute) of Mathematical Machines at the Polish Academy of Sciences. Their pioneering experiments slowed in the 1950s, but in the 1960s and 1970s production started with the co-operation of ICL, which provided the operating system 'George'. Odra mainframe computers were born in the Elwro Electronics Enterprise in Wroclaw, while Mera mini-computers were made in Warsaw. The development of both architectures (Odra was compatible with ICL's 1900 series, under an agreement with ICL) was abruptly stopped at the beginning of the 1980s due to 'state piracy', ie when COMECON countries began copying IBM 360/370 and DEC PDP-8 machines (Riad and SM series computers). Thus, Poland's computer production programme collapsed even before the collapse of the old regime and economy.

Rucksack imports – the new era begins

The tough beginning of the 1980s saw the emergence of IT entrepreneurs in Poland – young people, mostly from technical universities, bringing both parts and whole PCs direct from the Far East. COCOM regulations resulted in official imports from the USA and other NATO members becoming almost impossible. As various scientific programmes were launched, many scientists took fellowships at American and European universities, returning with the habit of using computers in their work, and of keeping in touch with other scientists (via the Internet). This was the main driving factor of the first Polish connection to the Internet, which took place via the University of Copenhagen in 1992.

In the years 1992–95, a new market emerged – the private IT sector. It consisted of approximately five thousand, mainly small, companies (sometimes one-man entities) selling PCs and peripherals, writing and selling software, some of them even assembling the computers from imported parts. Very few state-owned companies from the previous era survived, but among these were Elzab (today a manufacturer of fiscal cash registers), some computer centres (COIG – in the mining industry, CIE – in energy) and the network of state-owned computing service companies (ZETO). The survivors subsequently went through changes of ownership. At the same time, the most powerful Polish IT companies emerged: Optimus, JTT Computers, Prokom and Softbank, an ICL joint venture.

During these years, almost all the international hardware and software manufacturers and distributors appeared on the Polish market, most of them by means of Polish partners, but several companies chose to establish Polish subsidiaries. Some renewed their former presence, like IBM, which appeared in Poland for the first time in 1923, then left and came back, while ICL has been continuously present since 1962. Many foreign companies had, and some still have, production facilities (Motorola, Oli-com, Mod-Tap, ICL-Furnel, and software production by Lucent Technologies and Alcatel). Polish subsidiaries of CHS (ABC Data) and Computer 2000 are the top distributors competing with growing local players (Tech-mex, Action, ST Group).

Microsoft, which has numerous Polish partners, is hoping to build on the success of its localised personal productivity software, in the arena of operating systems for small and medium-sized enterprises (SMEs). It is trying to win a substantial market share for Windows NT from Novell NetWare, which has traditionally been very strong in Poland.

The success of Polish versions of Windows 3.x/95/98/NT 4.0, Office and Internet Explorer supported Microsoft's policy of launching Polish versions within three months of the main languages. Most competitors have been swept away (WordPerfect/Corel and Lotus suites, and personal productivity tools created by local software houses). Microsoft's Polish subsidiary, together with the popularity of its software, played a substantial role in reducing the rate of piracy following the introduction of Poland's new Intellectual Property Protection Act for the protection of software. In 1999, a joint ICL-Microsoft Solutions Centre was set up in Katowice as part of a Global Alliance.

Polish IT companies vs international giants

As the pioneers' era of 1000 per cent margins came to an end, Polish IT companies had to find markets for themselves, and the means to survive and develop their activities – while facing growing competition from inter-national players.

The largest Polish IT companies – Optimus, ComputerLand, Prokom and Softbank, the ICL joint venture company – have been floated on the Warsaw Stock Exchange (Prokom and Softbank also in international financial markets), and have been lucky enough to benefit from an initial 'high season'. They were followed on secondary and over-the-counter markets by medium-sized integrators and software houses (eg Apexim, MacroSoft, Ster-Projekt, Simple). However, the Far Eastern and Russian financial crises had an impact on the Warsaw Stock Exchange, slowing float preparations by some others (Techmex, ST Group, JTT Computer).

The situation with Polish IT companies has changed under pressure from international players. As mentioned above, although Polish software houses left the arena of personal productivity tools, their position is very strong in business applications for Polish SMEs, mainly in the area of simple accounting programs. Some Polish software companies have gained international recognition with their niche products (Young Digital Poland – educational software; Logotec Engineering – document management; and InterDesign – CAD/GIS).

The largest Polish PC assemblers (Optimus, JTT, NTT) have lost some of their dominant market share, yet over 50 per cent of PCs sold in Poland continue to be assembled locally. The big international players (Compaq, Dell, Fujitsu, IBM, HP) are selling mainly to large accounts and are slowly increasing their market share. The losers in the last two years are the Polish assemblers from the middle group, ie those selling 5000–10,000 units per year. An interesting phenomenon is the significant presence of very small assemblers (up to 1000 units per year). Many are acting not only as hardware suppliers but also as 'micro-integrators' for close neighbours – principally small trading companies and shopkeepers. They are supplying two to five networked PCs, setting up software, training staff, providing maintenance and upgrading systems. PCs sold by these very small companies are estimated at 70,000–100,000 units per year.

Tables 17.1 to 17.5 provide basic statistical information on the Polish IT market.

Table 17.1 Poland – the region's biggest IT market

	GDP (nominal, 1998), US$ billion
Poland	150.0
Czech Republic	56.8
Hungary	46.5
Slovak Republic	21.5
Slovenia	19.0

Source: Business Central Europe

Table 17.2 IT expenditure, 1997

	US$ billion	US$/capita	IT as % of GDP
Czech Republic	1.41	137	2.67
Hungary	0.86	84	1.91
Poland	1.91	48	1.36
Slovak Republic	0.39	72	2.00
Western countries			
Greece	1.02	96	0.88
Ireland	1.29	363	2.08
Portugal	1.45	147	1.42
Germany	48.37	578	2.15
USA	328.93	1082	4.29

Source: Teleinfo, EITO'98

Table 17.3 PC sales in Poland

	1996	1997	1998*	1999*	2000*
PCs – total	368.3	469.4	580	670	750
Desktop	346.1	442.7	545	625	640
Portable	22.2	26.7	35	45	60

* prognosis
Source: EITO'99, Teleinfo

Table 17.4 IT penetration: PCs per 100 white collar workers, 1996

Poland	23	Portugal	34
Czech Republic	30	Greece	36
Hungary	38	Ireland	78
USA	103	Norway	91

Source: EITO'98

Table 17.5 Largest players in the Polish IT market (1998 preliminary results)

Polish companies	Sales (US$ million)	International vendors (subsidiaries)	Sales (US$ million)
Optimus (group)	259	HP Polska/HP*	237
Prokom	131	CHS/ABC Data	148
JTT Computer	126	Siemens ICP/SBS	126
Action	121	Computer 2000 Poland	110
Techmex	117	IBM Polska/IBM*	110
ComputerLand Poland	106	Dell Computer Poland	52
Softbank	77	ICL Poland/ICL*	49

Source: Teleinfo 500

* Estimated combined sales – Polish subsidiary and sales in Poland through international channels

Solutions market

As is the case worldwide, in Poland the future lies in the solutions market, especially in those areas in great need of integrated MIS (Management Information Systems) and ERP (Enterprise Resource Planning) systems: banking, financial services, telecommunications, public administration, health services. The strong growth expected in these areas has already attracted international players, IT and consulting companies alike (Andersen Consulting, PriceWaterhouseCoopers, Ernst & Young, EDS, IBM, ICL, HP, SAP, Oracle, Baan, etc). They are all present in Poland, building the strength of their teams and developing networks of local partners. Usually starting with a base of global agreements, with Polish subsidiaries of multi-national corporations in manufacturing and retail, they offer services for Polish companies that are particularly aware of international competition.

This is especially true for the banking sector, which in the next few years will have to extend its portfolio. At present, only 30 per cent of the Polish population have a bank account, and there are only 3.6 million credit cards in circulation (for a population of some 38 million).

The strong growth of telecommunications, which is expected as a result of deregulation, will result in an extensive deployment of IT solutions by the new operators of new services, as well as intelligent networks and network management.

In preparation for Poland's accession to the EU, public administration will be raising the level of IT solutions (tax, customs, police, defence), and the same applies to social security and health service systems. All are currently undergoing reforms.

Local government, which is more active in introducing IT, is in need of even more sophisticated systems – such as GIS – to support local investments, the construction industry and the collection of property taxes.

Despite some slowdown in a dynamic IT market in 1998, the rate of growth of the IT industry in the next few years is estimated at 20 per cent (with services growing at 30 per cent), up from US$1.91 billion in 1997.

Internet, wide area networks, e-commerce

Although it has a low population density (20/100) and poor service provision from the basic telephone network, Poland does have a very modern backbone and a WAN (wide area network) built in ATM/Frame Relay technology. Originally built for the scientific and academic community by the Scientific Research Commission, it is now widely used by businesses – banks, companies with networked manufacturing facilities, supermarket chains etc. There are strong Polish operators of the backbone networks (CST TP SA, Telbank, Tel-Energo, POL34/155), giving a good base for a fast increase in the number and quality of services.

Despite the low telephone density, low penetration of PCs in households and high prices compared to average incomes, the Global Information Society is developing in Poland. Most interesting is the 'Internet for Schools' programme, with over 2500 schools currently connected. This social initiative by academic circles was followed by central government investment of US$27 million. Most recent is the ICL 'Cybergmina' project, partly funded by the British Know How Fund, and co-ordinated by the British Polish Chamber of Commerce.

As the number of Internet users is only about 1.5 million (of a 38 million population), e-commerce is still in its infancy. Total revenues of e-commerce in Poland in 1998 were estimated at US$25 million, business-to-business activities included. Looking at the revenue growth of Polish Internet service providers (average 100 per cent on a 1998/1997 basis), this will be the fastest-growing IT sector in the next few years.

Thanks are expressed to Tomasz Kulisiewicz of Teleinfo, and Aleksander Frydrych, vice-president of the Polish Chamber of IT and Telecommunications, for their contributions to this article.

18

Insurance

Beata Balas-Noszczyk, Katarzyna Malinowska and Anna Tarasiuk, CMS Cameron McKenna

Introduction

The insurance market has been one of the most rapidly developing markets in Poland over the last few years. Insurance activity is conducted on the basis of the Insurance Activity Act of 28 July 1990 (the 'Act'), the Commercial Code, the Civil Code and other executive legislation. The Act has been amended many times, and changes have been made to provide more profitable space for foreign investment on the insurance market.

Insurance companies

According to the Act, insurance activity may be conducted in the form of a joint-stock company or of a mutual insurance company, although the only form available to foreign entities conducting insurance activity in Poland is a joint-stock company and a branch office. Otherwise, companies with foreign participation that undertake and carry out insurance activity within Poland are subject to the same requirements as Polish companies.

Mutual insurance company

A mutual insurance company (MIC) conducts its activity by insuring its members on a reciprocal basis. Generally, membership of a MIC must be tied to an insurance contract and loss of membership follows the expiry of that insurance relationship.

MICs do not play a significant role on the Polish insurance market, as they are not profit-making entities.

Following changes in the Act in 1995, the statutes of a MIC may contain provisions allowing for the insurance of persons who are not members of that MIC. However, the number of these persons must be restricted so that the contributions provided by non-members do not exceed 10 per cent of all contributions collected by the MIC.

A more popular and useful form for conducting insurance activity is a joint-stock company.

Joint-stock company

A joint-stock company is governed by the Commercial Code. However, there are several provisions introduced by the Act that impose specific requirements upon joint-stock companies conducting insurance activity.

An important restriction concerns the amount of the share capital; this may not be lower than the highest minimum amount of the guarantee capital required for the insurance groups in which the insurer operates. The minimum guarantee capital is defined in an ordinance issued by the Minister of Finance. At present, it represents the zloty equivalent of €200,000–800,000. The amount of the guarantee capital depends on the groups of insurance, covered by the company's activity. Moreover, the share capital may not be contributed in the form of in-kind contributions, but only in the form of cash contributions, and must be paid in full before the company is registered. Therefore it is not possible to pay only a quarter of the nominal value of the share capital before the company is registered. The statute and any amendments to it are regulated and must be approved by the Minister of Finance.

Another limitation introduced by the legislator is the restriction on trading in shares or the rights arising from shares of insurance companies. The purchaser of the shares or rights arising from shares must notify the Minister of Finance about the acquisition, if the total amount of shares held allows the purchaser to have more than 10 per cent of the total number of votes at its general meeting. The approval of the Minister of Finance is required for the purchase of shares or rights arising from shares if holding such shares would allow the purchaser to exceed 25, 33, 50, 66, 75 per cent of votes at the general meeting of the insurance company. Should the purchaser infringe the above-mentioned requirements, he/she may not exercise any voting rights to the shares. Any resolution of the general meeting adopted contrary to these provisions of the Act would be null and void.

Branch office

From 1 January 1999, foreign insurance companies may undertake and carry out insurance activity within Poland not only by establishing an insurance subsidiary but also through their main branch offices.

A main branch operates on the basis of its own articles of association provided by the foreign insurance company and in accordance with Polish law. The articles of association and all amendments to them are subject to the approval of the Minister of Finance. The provisions of the Act generally apply to main branches of foreign insurance companies, unless expressly stated otherwise.

A vital condition for commencing insurance activity by a main branch office is to obtain a permit from the Minister of Finance. Such a permit is issued after the State Office of Insurance Supervision (PUNU) expresses its opinion upon the application of the foreign insurance company. A permit may be granted to the interested party only if the foreign insurance company already operates in the form of a joint-stock company or mutual insurance company in the country where its registered seat is located.

Although a main branch does not have the status of a legal entity, it may acquire rights, undertake obligations, sue and be sued. A foreign insurance company is subject to unlimited personal liability for the obligations of a main branch.

According to the draft Act, a director is in charge of the main branch. He/she is required to have a permanent place of residence in Poland, keep all documents referring to the activity conducted by the branch in Poland and possess adequate qualifications. He/she is authorised to represent the main branch. Irrespective of this, the main branch may be represented by two deputy directors jointly, or the headquarters of the foreign insurance company may appoint any other representative. The activities undertaken by a representative are effective only after that representative is entered into the register.

A foreign insurance company must have, within Poland, sufficient financial means to meet the margin of solvency requirement. Apart from this, a foreign insurance company must also provide technical underwriting reserves to cover present and future obligations that may arise from insurance contracts concluded through the main branch. The minimum guarantee capital required for the main branch amounts to 50 per cent of the minimum guarantee capital determined by the Minister of Finance for each kind of insurance. A main branch must invest insurance funds under the same principles as an insurance company.

Permit to conduct insurance activity

In both cases, whether the insurance activity is undertaken as a mutual or as a joint-stock company, it will require a permit, granted by the Minister of Finance after consultation with the State Office of Insurance Supervision (PUNU). In order to obtain such a permit, the interested party should submit an application containing, *inter alia*, the following information:

- name, seat, and territorial and objective scope of activity of the insurance company;

- amount of share capital;

- form of insurance activity;

- details of the founders of the insurance activity;

- names of the persons intended to be members of governing bodies of the insurance company;

- amount of the organisational fund intended for the establishment and organisation of a network of representations.

The following documents must be attached to the application:

- **business plan,** which should show, among other information, the method of calculating technical and underwriting reserves, the maximum amount of risk subscribed and the manner of its determination, solicitation costs, administrative costs and the calculation method of premiums. The business plan should also include financial projections for the first three calendar years of activity (both a best-case and a worst-case version) and include an abridged profit and loss account and a balance sheet. The simulations should also provide the following data: a forecast amount for collected premiums, level of indemnity, amount of technical and underwriting reserves, damage ratio, margin of solvency and company means;

- **document** confirming that the applicants have their **own funds** to cover the amount corresponding to the share capital and organisational fund (these resources being free from any encumbrances), and a declaration as to the allocation of those funds to cover the share capital and organisational fund;

- particulars relating to the **qualifications** of persons to be members of the management board, supervisory board and actuaries: their curricula vitae along with any documents confirming their qualifications and experience in the field of insurance;

- the **statutes (articles of association)** of the insurer;

- general **terms and conditions** of insurance.

The Minister of Finance may refuse to issue a permit for conducting insurance activities if the application and the documents referred to above do not meet the requirements specified in the Act. A permit may also be refused if the persons (at least two) designated for the positions of members of the management board do not have the experience and qualifications necessary to manage an insurance company, or have been convicted for intentional offences relating to documentation or for penal-fiscal offences. The latter also applies to the founders of an insurance company. A permit may also be refused for the following reasons:

- there is no guarantee that the founders will conduct insurance activities properly;

- the applicants fail to present evidence that the insurer has the required capital referred to above;

- the applicants fail to ensure (in the business plan) the permanent capability of the insurance company to carry out its obligations;

- the proposed activities pose a threat to an important economic interest of the state.

The Minister of Finance will issue a permit if all requirements are met according to the Act. However, it should be noted that the amount of share capital required to obtain a permit is at the discretionary power of the Ministry of Finance. A permit is granted for groups or classes of insurance specified in the appendix to the Act.

An insurer may not directly pursue a business activity other than an insurance activity and an activity related thereto. An insurance company may not simultaneously conduct activity within both the class of life insurance and the class of non-life insurance. This means that two separate companies must be established for life and non-life insurance activity. The process of obtaining a permit takes about one year.

Pursuant to the Act, during its whole period of activity, an insurance company must possess financial means at least equal to the margin of solvency. The amount of the required minimal solvency margin depends on the scope of the activity conducted by the insurance company and must be approved by the supervisory authority. Should the insurance company not meet that requirement, the supervisory body will ask to see a financial plan showing how the situation will be corrected.

Similar requirements apply when the financial means of the insurance company are lower than the required guarantee capital (the guarantee capital is one third of the margin of solvency). In such a case, the insurance company must submit a short-term solvency plan to the supervisory body for approval.

If the insurance company has not prepared a short-term solvency plan, if the submitted plan does not guarantee solvency or if the plan proves to be ineffective, the supervisory body may appoint a trustee receiver for a period of between six months and a year. The appointed trustee receiver will take over decision-making and the management board of the insurance company will be dissolved. The appointment of a trustee receiver is subject to registration in the commercial register.

The Act provides wide powers for the Minister of Finance regarding the withdrawal of a permit to conduct insurance activity. This may happen in the following circumstances:

- the insurance company conducts activity that violates the provisions of the law;

- the insurance company no longer meets its regulatory requirements;
- the insurance company fails to submit, within a specified time limit, a viable short-term solvency plan;
- the management of the assets and/or of the business of the insurance company is endangering the interests of the insured.

A permit for the foreign insurance company to conduct or extend the scope of insurance activity within Poland may not be granted if one or more of the circumstances listed below arise:

- the application and supporting documents do not meet the requirements specified in the Act;
- the director of the main branch office and one or more deputies do not have the qualifications and professional experience necessary to manage insurance activity;
- the foreign insurance company does not provide an extended warranty of proper conduct of insurance activity;
- the foreign insurance company cannot prove that it possesses sufficient funds to guarantee its solvency;
- the application runs counter to interests of state;
- the business plan and financial projections for the main branch in Poland cannot ensure the foreign insurance company's ability to perform its obligations.

A foreign insurer will be granted a permit to conduct insurance activity if it pays a deposit securing the future obligations of the company. The deposit is 50 per cent of the minimum amount of guaranteed capital needed. The security deposit is maintained during the whole period of activity in Poland. It is included in the company's funds and is placed with a domestic bank in an interest-bearing account. The security deposit is not subject to collection, and satisfaction from it may only take place in a process of liquidation of a main branch. The security deposit is returned along with interest only after all claims arising out of insurance contracts concluded through a main branch in Poland are satisfied.

A foreign insurance company may obtain a permit to conduct insurance activity within Poland in the field of one or more classes of insurance, or one or more types of insurance as listed in the schedule to the Act. It must begin insurance activity within a year of being granted a permit, failing which the permit will expire.

Insurance intermediary activities

According to the Act, insurance intermediary activities are the conduct of factual or legal acts involved in the conclusion or the performance of insurance and reinsurance contracts. Insurance companies may use the services of such intermediaries only as insurance agents or insurance and reinsurance brokers. Reinsurance intermediary activities can only be performed by reinsurance brokers.

Insurance agent

An insurance agent is an entity (a natural person or legal entity, or a business entity that does not have the status of a legal entity) acting for and on behalf of an insurance company. An insurance agent may be a natural or legal person authorised by an insurance company to conclude insurance contracts on a permanent basis in the name and for the benefit of that company or to act as an intermediary at the conclusion of contract.

The performance of an insurance agent's activities requires a permit from the supervisory authority. That permit is granted if the natural person:

- resides in Poland;

- has never been convicted for an intentional offence against property, documentation or for a fiscal offence;

- has completed the training organised by the insurance company and passed a final examination;

- has full contractual capacity.

The insurance company is responsible for the actions of an authorised agent. This liability cannot be limited by any provision of law.

Insurance broker

An insurance broker, directly or as an intermediary, concludes insurance contracts in the name of the insured. A broker's activity may only be undertaken by a natural or legal person, with a permit from the supervisory authority. A broker may not remain in an employment relationship with an insurance company, be a member of its governing body or be a party to an agency contract.

A permit to conduct brokerage activity is granted by the supervisory authority upon the request of a natural or legal person. That person must meet the following conditions:

- have his/her residence or registered seat in Poland;

- have full contractual capacity;

- have members of his/her management board give a guarantee of the proper conduct of his/her activity;

- have never been convicted for an intentional offence against property, documentation or for a fiscal criminal offence;

- have passed the examination for insurance and reinsurance brokers.

The supervisory authority

The specific character of the insurance industry requires a supervisory authority that can protect the interests of insured persons and prevent a situation in which the insurer is not able to pay a due benefit to the insured. The supervision of insurance activities is carried out by the State Office of Insurance Supervision (PUNU), a central state administrative authority. Its decisions are final, though appeals against them may be made to the Supreme Administrative Court. The function of the authority includes:

- assuring the proper functioning of the insurance market and the protection of the insured;

- issuing permits for broker and agency activities;

- supervising the activities of insurers and brokers.

The supervisory authority may at any time conduct an inspection of the activity and financial position of an insurance company.

It should be noted that supervision of insurance companies is compliant with European standards and is only of a financial nature.

19

Oil and Gas: Market and Industry

Leszek Filipowicz and Jacek Kwaśniewski,
Business Management & Finance (BMF)

Introduction

The Polish energy market is the largest in Central and Eastern Europe. Demand for energy is close to 100 million tonnes of oil equivalent, which is two and a half times more than in the Czech Republic and four times more than in Hungary. In terms of sources of energy, coal remains by far the most important fuel. In the structure of the Polish primary energy mix in 1998, coal accounted for 55 per cent, while the respective shares for oil and gas were 17 and 10 per cent. Given Poland's growing environmental awareness, the declining cost competitiveness of coal and the explosive growth of car use, it is expected that the relative importance of oil and gas in the Polish energy mix will grow.

Sources of supply

Poland depends heavily on imports of both crude oil and natural gas. Domestic production of crude oil satisfies no more than 2 per cent of domestic demand. In 1998, Poland imported 15.7 million tonnes of crude, of which more than 83 per cent came from Russia and the Commonwealth of Independent States (CIS). The dominance of Russia in the structure of imports is due to a number of factors. These include the lower cost of Russian crude, the efficiency of its transportation via the 'Friendship' pipeline and the technical capability of the two largest Polish refineries to process large amounts of the more sulphurous Russian grades.

In contrast to crude oil, Polish natural gas reserves are believed to be fairly significant. Proven reserves are estimated at around 146 billion m^3 and probable reserves at 640–900 billion m^3. Identified gas fields are located mainly in the southwestern and central part of Poland; new sites have also been discovered in the Baltic Sea shelf. In 1998 domestic production of natural gas amounted to 3.7 billion m³ and satisfied around 30 per cent of domestic consumption. It is expected that, by the year 2010, Polish production will reach 4.6 billion m³.

Similarly to crude oil, most of the natural gas imported comes from Russia (nearly 80 per cent), with smaller amounts coming from Ukraine (18 per cent), Germany and the Czech Republic. It is estimated that gas imported from Russia is 20–30 per cent cheaper than from other sources.

Transportation logistics

The key elements of the logistics needed for crude oil transportation include pipelines and port facilities. Relatively small amounts of crude are transported via rail to the five small refineries in the south of the country. Russian crude is transported via the 'Friendship' pipeline, which crosses Poland from east to west. This pipeline consists of two branches: one that goes from the eastern border to the Plebanka terminal near the Plock refinery and the other which supplies crude from Plebanka to German refineries in Leuna and Schwedt. The capacity of the first branch is estimated to be around 37 million tonnes per year and of the second branch about 27 million tonnes. Apart from 'Friendship', there is also the 'Pomerania' pipeline with a capacity of 21 million tonnes, transporting crude from Plebanka to Gdansk on the Baltic coast. The whole crude oil pipeline system (as well as the product pipelines) is managed by the 100 per cent state-owned PERN company.

Supply of crude oil from the sea is possible through the Gdansk Northern Port and 'Naftoport', also located in Gdansk. Total capacity of the two ports is around 33 million tonnes and in the near future will be expanded to 36 million tonnes. Given the capacities of pipelines and port facilities, the Polish refining industry should be regarded as well secured in terms of stability and flexibility of crude oil supplies.

Natural gas is transported from Russia via gas pipelines. A new development in this area is the construction of the Yamal-Europe pipeline, which will cross the central part of Poland. The Yamal contract provides for Poland to import 250 billion m³ of gas from Russia over the next 25 years.

Demand for oil products

The rapid development of the Polish refining and marketing industry in the last few years reflects the dynamic growth in the demand for oil products. In 1998, Poland used approximately 5.5 million tonnes of gasoline and 5.6 million tonnes of diesel. In the five-year period from 1992 to 1997, the average growth rate of demand for gasoline was almost 7 per cent but, according to some experts' predictions, this rate will stabilise at a level of 3–4 per cent in the period up to 2005. Demand for diesel in the period 1992–97 has also been rising, but at a lower rate of approximately 2.6 per cent.

Fast growth of the economy (on average 5.6 per cent in the last five years) is the main factor stimulating demand for oil products. With a population of around 38 million, Poland remains one of the fastest-growing markets for new cars. There are currently almost 10 million cars registered in Poland, which is approximately twice as many as ten years ago. The number of new cars sold each year exceeds 0.5 million.

It is important to note that, in the last few years, demand for oil products in Poland has been substantially higher than the available supply of domestic production. In 1998, Polish refineries supplied approximately 69 per cent of the gasoline and 80 per cent of the diesel consumed in the country. Despite recent expansion programmes at Polish refineries, it is expected that Poland will remain a net importer of oil products for the foreseeable future.

Prices of oil products in Poland were deregulated in 1997. Since then, domestic prices generally have followed import parity prices, thus reflecting price changes in world markets. The fiscal component is currently around 64 per cent of the total price, which is lower than the European Union average of 74 per cent. Net prices in Poland are also lower than in the rest of Europe. It is expected that the price level will gradually increase with the development of the market and with integration with the EU.

Demand for gas

Independent analysts and sector specialists predict that the level of consumption of natural gas in Poland in 2010 will reach 17 billion m^3. There is a consensus that demand for gas will grow significantly, possibly by 15–20 per cent per annum over the next decade. This growth will be driven by both residential usage and power generation needs.

Power generation creates the most important opportunity for the development of the gas industry. It is expected that the impact of environmental regulations will undermine the viability of coal-fired power production. In particular, older coal plants that do not have long-term power purchase agreements will not be able to fund necessary upgrading investments. At the same time, the rising transportation cost of coal to plants that are located far from mines will erode their competitiveness. Given the lack of alternative energy sources to gas (nuclear or hydro), gas-fuelled electricity generation has a number of competitive advantages:

- gas-fuelled power plants cost half of a new coal-fuelled plant;

- gas-fuelled power plants are about 20 per cent more efficient than coal plants;

- gas-fuelled power plants have lower maintenance costs and shorter construction time than coal-fuelled power plants;

- gas-fuelled power plants are environmentally friendlier.

Gas prices are currently subject to government controls. At present, the price does not cover the total cost of supplying gas, particularly to household consumers. The difference has been made up by tax exemptions and subsidies. In accordance with government policy, the market is to be partially liberated and prices will be adjusted to Western European levels. As a result of the new Polish Energy Law, the government will cease to control gas prices on 4 December 1999.

Refining and marketing

There are seven oil refineries operating in Poland, with a combined crude processing capacity of 17.4 million tonnes. Two of them, in Plock and Gdansk, are the most modern and important, with capacities respectively of 12.6 and 3.5 million tonnes. The remaining five are small refineries located in the south of Poland: Czechowice (0.5 million tonnes capacity), Trzebinia (0.4 million), Glimar (0.17 million), Jedlicze (0.14 million) and Jaslo (0.12 million).

The joint share of the Plock and Gdansk refineries in domestic production is approximately 90 per cent. In the last few years both refineries have been going through extensive upgrading programmes. By the end of 1999, capital expenditure in Plock is expected to reach US$2 billion and in Gdansk US$450 million. This modernisation programme, which is now nearly complete, will make Plock and Gdansk members of the élite 'top ten' league of the most modern refineries in Europe by the year 2000.

Plock refinery is the unquestionable leader of the industry. Located in central Poland, 100 km from Warsaw and near the 'Friendship' pipeline, Plock is well positioned to supply the Polish market. It is the largest and most modern refinery in the country. Given the country's weak transportation infrastructure, Plock's competitive advantage is strengthened further by the fact that it is the only refinery with direct access to product pipelines. One of these pipelines runs from Plock to the Warsaw area; the other links Plock with the western part of Poland (Rejowiec near Poznan) and the last travels south, to Boronowo, which is located close to the industrialised region of Silesia. The extension of this southern link further in the direction of Silesia is planned in the near future. This will improve Plock's ability to supply, via pipeline, the most populous, southern part of Poland.

Petrochemia Plock is also a dominant supplier of petrochemical products to the domestic market. Its market share ranges from 72 per cent for ethylene, 68 per cent for polyethylene, 52 per cent for polypropylene and

47 per cent for phenol. Given the strong demand for chemical products in Poland, the production of petrochemicals can be regarded as a promising direction for future development.

Retail marketing of oil products in Poland is dominated by Polski Koncern Naftowy (PKN), the company created in 1999 by the merger of Petrochemia Plock and Centrala Produktow Naftowych (CPN). Until the early 1990s, CPN had been the state monopoly responsible for the distribution of oil products. Although its market share in the last decade has decreased significantly, it has managed to maintain its dominant position in the retail market.

There are currently 6324 retail sites in the country, out of which 1896 (30 per cent) are controlled by PKN. Independent private owners control almost 58 per cent of sites, multi-national companies like BP Amoco, Shell or Statoil own 8 per cent, and 4 per cent belong to Gdansk and other refineries. In terms of volumes sold, it is estimated that PKN's share of the retail market at the end of 1998 was about 40 per cent.

PKN's strong position in the Polish market is due to its large number of outlets, to good access to transportation and storage facilities, and to benefits from integration with refining. Other players in the market, especially multi-nationals, are aggressively challenging this position. PKN's sites are of varying quality. Many are located in rural areas with low population density and, as a result, 70 per cent have collectively throughput of less than 3 million tonnes of fuel per year. Most of the PKN's stations have no shops, bars or car washes. This is in contrast with stations owned by multi-nationals, which are typically large, well located and benefit from additional revenues from shops, bars and other services.

Structure of the gas industry

The Polish gas industry is organized in the form of the Polish Oil & Gas Co (PGNiG), which it is a vertically integrated company established in 1982 by the merger of previously separate upstream and downstream activities. PGNiG has 49 branches, which include oil and gas exploration and production, transmission, storage and distribution of gas to end users, drilling, pipe construction and repair. It also owns a 48 per cent stake in Europol Gaz, a Polish-Russian joint venture, which is the owner and operator of the Polish section of the Yamal pipeline, currently under construction. PGNiG is the only producer of gas in Poland and one of the two producers of crude oil.

The total length of the gas transmission system lines is around 17,100 km. The system is operated by six Regional Transmission Companies and supplies industrial consumers (2400) and city gates (3900, of which 520 towns) through gas pressure reduction and measurement stations (1630). The system has three international inter-connections with the

German gas transmission system and two main receiving terminals for gas from Belarus and Ukraine. A strong point of the system is that it covers almost the whole national territory. A weak point is its technical characteristics: working pressures for old pipelines are generally low (55 bar) and this can create bottlenecks in the gas grid and constitute an impediment to upgrading.

The distribution system consists of 24 distribution companies operating under the PGNiG umbrella. Distribution networks supply around 6.7 million residential, commercial and small and medium-sized industrial customers, of which approximately 6 million are in urban areas. The total length of lines is around 87,500 km. Each year the length is increased by 2000–3000 km. Working pressure is from 25 mbar (low pressure) to 4 bar (medium pressure).

The storage system in Poland is very well endowed with depleted gas fields that can be used for Euro-Storage. The potential working volume is of around 27 billion m^3 with good locations: close to the German border (Zuchlow – 13 billion m^3; Zalecze – 9 billion m^3) and the Transgas pipeline in Slovakia. There are currently six underground gas storage (UGS) facilities operating in Poland, with working volume of around 1 billion m^3. Two of them, Mogilno and Wierzchowice, are in the development phase. After completion of their construction (in 2000 and 2010 respectively) they will have a combined working volume of around 4.8 billion m^3.

There are other players in the Polish gas market, apart from PGNiG. These are either companies active in gas trading (Bartimpex, GAS Trading) or holders of concessions for gas exploration and development. In this latter category are, among others: Petrobaltic (owner of exclusive rights for exploration in the Baltic shelf), Apache, FX Energy, Calgas and Texaco.

Restructuring and privatisation of the oil industry

Since the early1990s, the government of Poland has undertaken a number of steps aimed at restructuring the oil sector in order to prepare it for privatisation. One of the important elements of the initial restructuring and privatisation programme adopted in 1996 was the transfer of most of the oil sector's assets to the newly created Nafta Polska, a state-controlled holding company. The main task of Nafta Polska, which took over control of seven refineries and CPN, was to supervise the restructuring of its holding companies and prepare for their privatisation.

The amendment to the restructuring and privatisation programme that was adopted by the Council of Ministers in May 1998 set out a new framework for the sector's privatisation. The basic assumption was that two integrated marketing and refining centres would be created around the Plock and Gdansk refineries and then be privatised. Plock refinery would be merged with CPN to create Polski Koncern Naftowy (PKN), the Polish 'national champion' in the oil industry. Gdansk refinery's position would be strengthened by the acquisition of close to 200 retail sites from CPN. The government envisaged different methods of privatisation of individual companies. PKN was to be privatised through the sale of initially up to 30 per cent of shares through an Initial Public Offering (IPO) in the Polish and international markets, while the majority stake of the Gdansk Refinery was to be offered to strategic investors. The five 'southern' refineries were to be restructured and privatised according to individual programmes.

The government programme envisaged that the State would retain control for the near future over the most important elements of the sector's logistics: the PERN pipeline company (direct control by the State Treasury), the Naftobazy storage company and the DEC rail transportation company (both 100 per cent owned by Nafta Polska).

The implementation of the privatisation programme began in 1998 and it is expected to be completed by the end of 2000. Its main element, the IPO of PKN, is planned to take place in the autumn of 1999.

Restructuring and privatisation of the gas industry

In December 1997 the Polish government passed a new Energy Law. The Law established a process for restructuring the energy industry and set out a regulatory framework with the intention of attracting foreign investors to selected areas of the energy industry, specifically to upstream natural gas and electric power generation. The Energy Law addressed two principal issues:

- **Guaranteed third-party access:** guaranteed access to the natural gas and electricity grids provided that the third parties are producers of energy within Poland and have met certain contractual and governmental obligations. The 'domestic producer' limitation limits competition to domestic players and fulfils government promises to allow foreign companies that have entered the upstream in Poland to sell gas to third parties; it also serves to protect the dominant imports monopoly of PGNiG. According to detailed regulation, from December 2000 access to the gas grid will be given to buyers who purchase not less than 25 million m^3 of gas annually. This group includes the largest industrial gas users, with a total consumption of 34 per cent of total Polish natural gas consumption. From 2004, this access will be given to the buyers of at least 15 million m^3 annually. After 2005, smaller buyers will also be given access to the gas grid.

- **An independent energy regulator:** the authority (Urzad Regulacji Energetyki – URE) was established in December 1997 and reports directly to the prime minister. The regulator issues licences required for energy companies and also monitors and approves gas prices based on the cost of service and including 'reasonable returns on investments'. The regulator is obliged to take into account government policy decisions.

The State Treasury, which is responsible for PGNiG's restructuring and privatisation, has so far selected an advisor to conduct the necessary analyses. These analyses must look beyond the gas sector itself: natural gas is an integral part of the whole Polish energy sector and its development cannot be planned in isolation. Gas is a part of the energy balance and any significant increase in its use will have an important impact on other parts of the energy industry.

Any reasonable programme for the Polish gas sector must go beyond the simple tactics of just getting the companies privatised. The aim should be to build a sustainable gas industry that bears comparison with industries elsewhere in Europe. In developing such an industry one cannot ignore specific factors affecting Poland, such as the dominant role of hard coal in the energy balance and Poland's position as the gateway to Western Europe for Russian gas.

PGNiG has long benefited from its monopolistic position, avoiding pressure from customers, markets and successive governments. Its adjustment to the changing market environment may be difficult and painful. Nevertheless, organisational and ownership changes for PGNiG are inevitable and indispensable. There are a number of ideas being floated as to how the company should be restructured and privatised. The near future will show which of these will earn government approval.

20

Oil and Gas: Regulatory and Legal Framework

Tomasz Minkiewicz, CMS Cameron McKenna

Despite the fact that Poland's oil and gas industry dates back to the mid-19th century, it is perceived as an area of high development potential, both on the production and consumption side, particularly with respect to natural gas. Estimated total undiscovered reserves of natural gas range between 640 and 1200 billion m^3 (BCM), and discovered recoverable reserves are estimated at approximately 195 BCM. Oil reserves are assessed at between 110 and 350 million tonnes onshore and 21–27 off-shore. More than two thirds of the gas consumed in Poland is imported, and almost 100 per cent of the imports come from Russia. More than 90 per cent of crude oil used by the Polish petrochemical industry is imported from diverse geographical locations.

Gas represents only about 8 per cent of the country's total consumption of primary energy, much below West European average, with nearly 50 per cent of total gas burned by household consumers and no material quantities of gas used for power generation. A number of new gas-fired, mostly co-generation facilities are, however, at various stages of development. The gas supply network is relatively well developed, but the grid is asymmetrical, with large areas of the country insufficiently covered.

The structure of the Polish gas sector is characterised by the dominant position of the state-owned Polish Oil and Gas Company (POGC). POGC owns the entire gas transmission and distribution network and is virtually the only domestic producer of natural gas, and the largest producer of crude oil. During the years of its operation, POGC, through its regional divisions, has accumulated an abundance of geological data and an understanding of local conditions. Two years ago, the government initiated a programme of restructuring and privatisation of that company, which should eventually lead to the demonopolisation of the Polish gas sector.

Since the early 1990s Poland has made steps towards attracting foreign investment in the upstream petroleum business. Following legislative changes in 1991, a few bidding rounds for natural gas and coalbed methane exploration areas were organised. Many of the world's largest petroleum companies participated in the bidding, but no significant geological work programmes were implemented as a result of this, partly due to the global situation in the petroleum industry and partly as a result of further changes of the Polish legal environment. Consequently, the first petroleum exploration concessions were issued to Western companies in late 1995 and early 1996. Since then, a few dozen exploration or combined exploration and exploitation concessions have been granted to foreign investors, both American and European, and substantial data reprocessing, seismic acquisition and drilling programmes have been realised, with promising results but no significant discoveries thus far. Further work programmes have been announced, including exploration and/or development activities conducted in collaboration with POGC.

Introduction

Poland does not have a distinct body of petroleum legislation. Instead, activity in upstream oil and gas business is regulated by legal acts concerning geology and mining, and conducting business activity in general. The most relevant pieces of legislation include:

- Geological and Mining Law dated 2 February 1994, as subsequently amended (the 'Mining Law');

- Energy Law dated 10 April 1997, as amended (the 'Energy Law');

- Law on Companies with Foreign Participation dated 14 June 1991, as amended (the 'Foreign Investment Law').

Ownership of minerals and mining usufruct

Mineral deposits located within the Polish territory, including the territorial sea, are owned by the State Treasury, except for those shallow accumulations of minerals (eg sand, clay, stone) that are considered part of the surface and are therefore owned by the owner of the relevant plot of land. The State Treasury may grant third parties (including state-owned entities) the right to explore for and/or extract minerals by instituting a so-called mining usufruct. A mining usufruct is established by a commercial agreement with the representative of the State Treasury, called the concession authority, who is generally the Minister of Environmental Protection, Natural Resources and Forestry (the 'Environmental Minister'), in the case of oil and gas. A mining usufruct can also be granted by the relevant local administrator, the *wojewoda* or *starosta*, depending on the size of the area covered or the expected volume of production. The holder of the mining usufruct is entitled to conduct the activity specified in the mining usufruct agreement, within the area and subject to the possible additional requirements specified therein. The geological data obtained and minerals extracted as a result of the activity are owned by the holder of the mining usufruct.

Whereas any entity authorised to conduct business in Poland can obtain mining usufruct, oil and gas mining usufructs are normally granted to companies (either joint-stock or limited liability) or to registered ('commercial') partnerships. The concession authority may, but is under no obligation to do so, grant mining usufruct following tender procedures. According to the current policy of the Environmental Minister, mining usufruct regarding oil and gas should generally be granted by open tender.

The main elements typically found in mining usufruct agreements regarding oil and gas include the specification of the mineral concerned, the territory covered, duration of the usufruct and obligations of the entrepreneur regarding exploration work, fees and reporting. Exploration mining usufructs are usually granted for a period of three to six years, whereas exploitation usufructs are often much longer. Mining usufruct is transferable but, in order to conduct mining operations based on the usufruct, the purchaser must obtain a concession from the concession authority, pursuant to the procedures ordinarily required for granting concessions.

Disputes arising from mining usufruct agreements are subject to resolution by common courts, unless the agreement provides for arbitration. The latter is typically the case of mining usufruct agreements with foreign-owned companies. Although various arbitration arrangements are possible from a legal point of view (although arbitration between two Polish entities must be held in Poland), the Environmental Minister is currently reluctant to agree to any other than institutional Polish arbitration, such as by the Arbitration Court of the Polish Chamber of Commerce (see Chapter 48 on Dispute Resolution).

Mining concessions

A mining concession constitutes a permit to conduct certain types of geological or mining activity and its obtainment is necessary for the mining usufruct to become effective. Concessions are required for:

- exploration of minerals;

- extraction of minerals from natural deposits;

- underground storage;

- exploration and extraction of minerals from mining wastes.

Although concessions are generally granted separately for different types of mining activity, it is possible to obtain a concession covering both exploration and exploitation (so-called 'joint concessions'). If a joint concession is granted, the entrepreneur, prior to entering into the exploitation phase, must obtain an additional decision from the concession authority regarding the detailed terms of exploitation, which is issued based on approved geological documentation of the discovery.

Concessions are granted for specific periods, but the law does not specify any maximum periods permitted. In practice, the concession covers the whole period of the mining usufruct.

The party submitting a concession application must present an environmental impact assessment regarding the planned activity, prepared by a certified Polish expert. An applicant for an exploitation concession must demonstrate its legal title to officially approved geological documentation regarding the discovery concerned.

In addition to the decision of the concession authority, the process of concession granting involves consultation with the local authorities (*gminas*) on whose territory the activity is to be conducted. The results of the consultation are non-binding with respect to exploration or joint concessions but the concession authority cannot issue an exploitation concession or a decision regarding the detailed terms of exploitation unless the local authority approves it. Any refusal of acceptance by the local authority must be based on the local development plan (eg if the plan designates certain areas as recreational, this could be a good reason for the refusal) and can be appealed against to the second-tier authority and then to the Administrative Court.

In the past, the process of consultation with respect to exploration or joint concessions, which usually cover a relatively large area (the maximum permitted is 1200 km^2) involving several *gminas*, was often very time consuming. In 1998, the Mining Law was amended to give the local authorities 14 days to respond to the request for consultation, following which the lack of a response is deemed to signify consent. Nevertheless, bearing in mind the importance of good overall relationships with local authorities, it is advisable to follow the example of some investors who try to organise informal meetings with local authorities while submitting a concession application. Such an approach enables officials to become familiar with applicants' intentions and for potential benefits to the local communities to be put forward.

In addition to specifying the scope and term of the permitted activity, an exploration or joint concession typically specifies the work programme that the concession holder has agreed to implement, the amount of concession fees and the requirements regarding environmental protection.

Concessions issued pursuant to the Mining Law are non-transferable.

Fees charged to mining entrepreneurs

Depending on the circumstances, a party engaged in petroleum mining operations may be required to pay the following fees:

- a mining usufruct fee;

- a concession fee;

- an exploitation fee (royalty).

The mining usufruct fee is a purely contractual fee payable to the State Treasury and based on the mining usufruct agreement. The total amount of the fee is negotiated by the parties and its amount usually depends on the size of the area concerned, the prospects of finding commercial discoveries and the expected geological conditions, such as the depth of the basement strata. Although the parties to the mining usufruct agreement usually agree on a specified amount for the fee, other fee arrangements, such as a fee expressed as a percentage of the value of the petroleum discovered, is also possible. The fee can be payable up-front or in instalments but at least a part of the mining usufruct fee is usually payable upon receipt of the concession.

The concession fee is charged upon the issuance of an exploration or joint concession. The amounts are not set by the statutes, but the Environmental Minister has established certain policy rules, which set ranges within which the concession fees should be calculated, based on the acreage and geological conditions. Sixty per cent of the concession fee is payable directly to the local authorities on whose territory the activity is to be conducted, proportionally to the acreage, and the remaining part is transferred to the National Environmental Fund.

Exploitation fees (royalties) are paid with respect to minerals extracted, as a percentage of their value. The percentages applicable to various types of minerals are established by secondary legislation to the Mining Law (within a statutory upper limit of 10 per cent), and are currently set at 6 per cent with respect to oil and gas. The concession authority has discretion to increase or decrease the percentage, by no more than 50 per cent of the percentage rate set by the secondary legislation, if the geological conditions are exceptionally favourable or difficult. The royalties are paid to the local authorities and to the National Environmental Fund, similarly to the concession fees.

Ownership of geological data

Pursuant to the Mining Law, data obtained as a result of geological work are owned by the party that paid the costs of such work. Although the above rule is straightforward, in practice the ownership status of a number of items of geological documentation prepared in the past is unclear, since the source of their financing is difficult to identify. Ownership rights to geological data owned by the State Treasury are exercised by the Minister of the State Treasury.

Ownership of geological data is transferable, subject to the consent of the Environmental Minister. The State Treasury has, by operation of law, a call option to acquire geological data at a fair price. In addition, the geological administration is entitled to receive, free of charge, copies of all geological data but these copies cannot be used for commercial purposes.

Surface rights

Mining usufruct and concessions do not grant the entrepreneur any rights to the surface that may be needed for mining operations. Such surface rights (eg ownership, perpetual usufruct, leasehold etc.) must be obtained from the landowners on a commercial basis. However, in the event that no agreement with the owners can be reached, the entrepreneur may obtain the rights to the plots of land 'indispensable for the activity regulated by the Mining Law' through court proceedings. Whereas this route may not be practical in exploration activities, due to the slowness of court proceedings and to the difficulty in proving the indispensability of a particular plot of land, it may prove useful at the stage of development and exploitation.

Liability

Subject to one exception, liability for damages that may arise as a result of upstream petroleum operations is governed by the generally applicable rules of contractual and tort (including environmental) liability. The particular feature of liability of mining entrepreneurs is that they may become liable for damages not caused by themselves or their agents. If the party who caused the damage resulting from mining activity cannot be identified, the damage must be redressed by the entrepreneur who has the right to exploit minerals in the area concerned at the time the damage was discovered. The liability of the entrepreneur is joint and several with that of his professional contractors who performed the mining works.

Equipment used in mining operations

Approval from the Polish mining supervision authorities must be obtained for all major equipment used in mining operations, in addition to any other technical certificates otherwise required. In practice, this requirement does not constitute a major obstacle for foreign investors, as they normally employ Polish contractors to perform all seismic and drilling work. Many of these contractors possess state-of-the-art equipment and qualified personnel to meet the expectations of international petroleum companies.

Access to the gas grid

Since construction of pipelines is costly and may be extremely time consuming due to permitting issues, access to the gas grid would be essential for any entrepreneur who has a gas discovery. Such access must be negotiated with the grid owner, ie the Polish Oil and Gas Company (POGC). With the recent entry into force of the Energy Law, Polish law now reflects the so-called TPA (third-party access) principle. According to this principle, the gas grid operator (similarly to the electric and heat grid operators) is obliged to render transmission services with respect to all gas produced in Poland, subject to the technical and economic feasibility of the inter-connection to the grid and transmission. However, the TPA principle will not become fully operative with respect to gas until 5 December 2005. Initially, as of July 2000, only gas transmitted to the largest customers, consuming more than 25 million m^3 annually, will be eligible. Potential disputes regarding access to the grid are resolved by the president of the Energy Regulatory Authority, whose decisions can be appealed to the Antimonopoly Court in Warsaw.

Proposed amendments to mining legislation

The government is currently preparing an extensive amendment to the Mining Law which, if enacted (possibly by the end of 1999), would affect the legal environment for oil and gas activity. The most important changes include the implementation of mandatory tender procedures in granting mining usufruct regarding oil and gas, the abandonment of joint exploration/exploitation concessions and the introduction of transferability of concessions. As a whole, the proposed changes should be favourable to oil and gas companies, though they do not address all of the areas of concern communicated in the past to the Environmental Minister by various industry representatives.

21

Pharmaceuticals

Nick Sljivic, VP International, and Danuta Pilecka

Introduction

Continued market growth, wholesale privatisation of domestic companies, investment by leading international groups, consolidation in the distribution channels and major restructuring of the funding of the Polish health care system – these factors all add up to Poland being one of Europe's most dynamic and challenging environments for pharmaceutical companies.

A growth market

Though by Western European standards pharmaceutical consumption is low, the trend has been towards increasing total consumption in terms of both volume and value. According to a 1999 ING Barings report, the Polish pharmaceutical market had total sales of US$1.72 billion in 1998, up nearly 11 per cent on 1997 sales of US$1.55 billion. This report predicts that, fuelled by the growing number of elderly people, per capita expenditure on medicines will continue to increase at a rapid rate in Poland. In 1998, the average Pole spent US$45 on medicine, up from US$40. (This is still low in European terms. In France, for example, per capita consumption was over US$300.) In 1999 Polish per capita expenditure is expected to increase to over US$50, and by 2001 reach US$65. At this level, the market will be worth over US$2.6 billion. Industry forecasts suggest that, to 2005, the value of medicine sales in Poland will rise at a rate of 10–15 per cent annually.

The largest increase is expected to be in over-the-counter (OTC) medicines, which, according to industry estimates, are expected to expand by over 50 per cent in the next three years, due to a combination of increased availability of OTC products, marketing by pharmaceutical companies and growing consumer affluence.

Higher-value imports

As with all the countries of Central and Eastern Europe, there is a huge disparity between the prices charged for domestically manufactured drugs and prices for imports.

Virtually ever major international pharmaceutical company has a presence in Poland that includes representative offices and a sales force; most were established in the early 1990s when import restrictions were lifted. Sales for domestic products by volume account for circa 80 per cent of total sales, whereas by value these sales account for only 40 per cent, reflecting the huge disparity between the price of domestically produced and imported medicines.

About 2000 types of medication are produced in Poland. In terms of product range, Polish factories satisfy 65–70 per cent of domestic demand. As with virtually all East European plants producing pharmaceuticals, most domestic production consists of generic versions of foreign drugs.

Government action to control health care spending

The full implications for the pharmaceutical industry of the restructuring of the Polish health care system (1 Jan 1999) have yet to be fully determined. It is currently unclear whether the measures that are designed to separate the cost of funding and the provision of medical services, in order to establish a form of internal market, will have any major effect on the total drugs bill or any specific component of it.

There are over 20,000 medicines registered in Poland but less than half are commonly used. To control the spiralling drugs bill the government has introduced three reimbursement levels for medicines:

- cost totally refunded by the State;

- the patient pays 30 per cent;

- 50 per cent co-payment structure.

Distribution

Pre-1990, distribution of all pharmaceuticals was undertaken by the state-owned CEFARM. This state monolith has now been split up and largely privatised (on a regional basis) but still dominates the sector, with CEFARM companies having over 30 per cent of the distribution market.

There are over 1000 listed distributors of pharmaceuticals but, of these, there are only an estimated 200–300 that are active. Throughout the decade, numerous smaller distributors, including companies such as

Prosper, Farmakol, Cormay, Medicines and Carbo, emerged. None of these has more than an estimated 5 per cent market share. Consolidation is however occurring with a growing number of mergers and acquisitions amongst the distributors.

The total number of pharmacies in Poland has increased throughout the decade, as entrepreneurial pharmacists started up their own retail units. In 1998 the total number of pharmacies was an estimated 7500, of which over 90 per cent were privately owned.

Companies

There are over 300 Polish pharmaceutical companies, the vast majority being small firms, with less than 50 of them having over 50 employees. The largest company in terms of sales is Glaxo, which entered the market via the acquisition of Polfa Poznan. Table 21.1 lists the leading pharmaceutical firms in Poland.

The industry is still dominated by the traditional Polfa companies, which had a state-owned monopoly position pre-1989. However, the government is committed to privatising these companies and, so far, 6 of the 14 Polfa companies have been privatised. Polfa Jelfa went public in 1994 and Polfa Kutno in 1995. These are now listed on the Warsaw Stock Exchange.

In 1997, a further three Polfa companies were privatised, Polfa Lodz, Polfa Rzeszow (ICN Pharmaceuticals) and Polfa Krakow (sold to the Croatian company Pliva). In January 1998, Polfa Poznan was purchased by Glaxo Wellcome. It is expected that Polfa Starogard and Polfa Tarchomin will also go public in the near future.

The Ministry of Industry and Trade estimates that, by the year 2000, more than US$1 billion will be required to modernise Polish pharmaceutical plants. One key requirement is the implementation of Good Manufacturing Practice (GMP) in Polish plants. Polish companies are trying to achieve GMP accreditation in order to be able to maintain, or develop, export markets.

Table 21.1 Poland's leading pharmaceutical companies

Company	Revenues (Zl million)		
	1997	**1996**	**1995**
Glaxo Wellcome Poznan	332.1	267.8	192.8
Kutnowskie Zaklady Farmaceutyczne Polfa	214.5	171.2	148.1
Krakowskie Zaklady Farmaceutyczne Polfa	214.3	177.1	107.5
Przedsiebiorstwo Farmaceutyczne Jelfa	200.3	151.6	128.8
Glaxo Wellcome Polska	183.5	131.5	n/a
Pabianickie Zaklady Farmaceutyczne Polfa	173.5	133.8	100.7
Servier Polska	170.4	115.0	54.3
Grodziskie Zaklady Farmaceutyczne	156.1	116.0	89.1
ICN Polfa Rzeszów	140.5	111.8	87.3
Sanofi-Biocom	119.0	75.1	n/a

Source: PAIZ

International investment

Table 21.2 shows major foreign direct investment in the pharmaceutical sector in Poland. The largest single investment has come from Glaxo Wellcome, when it bought an 80 per cent share in Polfa Poznan for US$220 million in 1998. ICN pharmaceuticals acquired a majority shareholding in Polfa Rzeszow. Polfa-Krakow was acquired by Croatian producer Pliva, which bought 60 per cent of the company for US$85.7 million.

Table 21.2 Foreign direct investment in Poland's pharmaceutical sector

Investor	Current investment (US$ million)	Planned investment (US$ (million)	Origin	Entry route
Glaxo Wellcome	230.4	0.0	UK	Polfa Poznan acquisition
Pliva	100.0	70.0	Croatia	Polfa-Kraków
Solco Basel	41.2	0.0	Switzerland	Greenfield in Warsaw
Krka	15.0	–	Slovenia	Greenfield in Warsaw
ICN	33.7	33.3	USA	Polfa-Rzeszów SA
Gerresheimer	8.0	4.0	Germany	Fabryka Materialow Medycznych Polfa in Boleslawiec
Lek-Ljubljana	6.0	0.0	Slovenia	Greenfield in Pruszków

Source: PAIZ

22

Publishing and Media

Thom Barnhardt, Warsaw Business Journal

Introduction

Poland's media and advertising market is growing at a rapid pace, driven by an economy in its sixth year of fast growth and continued foreign direct investment. Advertising spend in 1998 was more than 30 per cent higher than the previous year, much of which growth was channelled into television advertising.

Magazines

The market is following a development pattern easily recognised in most developing countries, in which the initial major investments are into fast-moving consumer goods and products targeted at young women, consequently driving the growth of women's glossy magazines. Standard, licensed titles such as *Cosmopolitan* and *Marie Claire* are present alongside Polish titles with a similar format but more local appeal (*Pani, Uroda, Twój Styl*).

Continued growth of the economy has spurred more investment in the media business, as advertisers look for more efficient and specialised ways of reaching their target audiences. New print titles are continuously being launched, keeping pressure on existing print titles' operating margins, and further reinforcing the value of consolidation in the sector. Specialised titles have largely been the domain of smaller Polish publishing start-ups but the sector has recently attracted international investment attention as focus shifts towards the less developed trade publishing segment.

The publishing landscape is in the very early stages of consolidation, as smaller publishing houses continue to get squeezed by the larger players. Though many major German and Swiss publishers (Axel Springer, Gruner+Jahr, Marquard) are present on the market with such titles as *Cosmopolitan*, American and British publishing groups lack a major presence. Several Polish-owned publishing groups are emerging as critical players: for example VIPress, a joint venture publisher of the licensed *Playboy* magazine and *Twój Styl*, a women's title that successfully pre-empted most Western women's magazines and has carefully carved out an image as Polish born and raised. Scandinavians have had mixed success, with Orkla of Norway owning a major Polish daily, and Bonnier's (of Sweden) launch three years ago of its daily business paper, *Puls Biznesu* (reportedly a US$9 million investment to date).

The top-selling magazines are as follows:

- *Magazin Gazeta Wyborcza* – general interest;

- *Wprost* – general interest;

- *Twój Styl* – for women;

- *Polityka* – politics and current affairs;

- *Claudia* – for women;

- *Murator* – building and decorating;

- *Pani Domu* – general interest;

- *Elle* – for women.

Newspapers

The newspaper market has grown rapidly, with revenue growth of 29 per cent in 1998 and 20 per cent in 1997, further reflecting the nature of this emerging market. The largest newspapers are *Gazeta Wyborcza*, *Rzeczpospolita* and *Super Express*, a tabloid majority owned by a Swedish group.

Television and radio

Television is the dominant single medium, taking advantage of Poles' unusually high TV viewing habits (a trait emblematic of the lack of alternative entertainment available). Major foreign investment has flowed into this sector, including substantial investment from AtEntertainment (American) and CanalPlus. Yet Polsat, mostly Polish-owned and operated, continues to beat the 'big boys' at their own game. Meanwhile, the growing strength and strategic position of Agora, which owns Poland's dominant daily *Gazeta Wyborcza* and recently went public on the Warsaw Stock Exchange, adds a new element to the radio market, and is further supported by its minority investor Cox Communications of the USA.

Other media sectors

Poland's media sector is beginning to attract the attention of major telecom and software investors as well, as the much-heralded concept of convergence takes hold. Optimus, a leading computer hardware manufacturer, is eyeing investments in the Internet area, while Elektrim, TPSA and Netia (all big telecom competitors) are also searching for partnerships and alliances in the media sector.

23

Retailing

Séan Briggs, Healey & Baker

The retail revolution

Like many sectors in Poland, the retail market is still in its infancy, although changing quickly. It is not easily apparent why the retail market took so long to develop following the country's economic reforms, especially compared to the Czech Republic and Hungary. While Poland was once economically behind its Central European neighbours, this is no longer the case, with the Czech Republic's economy going through a turbulent time and some of Poland's tough reforms now paying dividends.

The first entrants to the market were the fast food operators, followed closely by the cash and carry, supermarket and large convenience stores. Of the operators on the market, Tricon have a good business with Pizza Hut and KFC, and there are now over 100 McDonald's in Poland, seemingly covering most of the country. Macro Cash and Carry has a thriving operation, with five stores nationwide. The supermarket chain Billa has not capitalised on its entry to the market but the smaller discount stores of Rema 1000 and Globi have solid businesses, although it is likely that trade has been adversely affected by the expanding hypermarkets.

The initial difficulties encountered by retailers and developers alike were the uncertainty of land and property ownership, the difficult and long drawn-out process of purchasing property and securing the necessary permits (arguably still the case today), unreliable statistics (still also problematic due to the unaccountability of the grey market) and, for some retailers, a shortage of suitable franchisees or joint venture partners. Some of these hurdles are still present, but the market is getting easier and there is now some good professional advice on hand to assist potential investors.

Much of this is now in the past, with retailers and developers alike appreciating the potential of the Polish market. This can be summarised as a country of about 38 million inhabitants, a relatively young population (with nearly half the population under the age of 36), a stable political environment, a strong economy and a well-educated workforce. Much of retailing is about market awareness and economies of scale. Poland has seven cities or conurbations with populations of more than 450,000 and a further 13 cities and towns of more than 200,000. Certainly, all the main cities have established retail markets of varying degrees.

Retailers

Taking a closer look at the retailers, there are a number of areas to consider. The market can be split into local, national, international (or 'cross-border') retailers, who in turn can be divided into in-town and out-of-town retailers. There is an increasing number of very capable local and national retailers willing to take on the larger cross-border retailers, in some cases having done so successfully. Multiple retailers of note include Royal Collection, Americanos, Gabriel, Euro and a number of jeans retailers.

Cross-border retailers

Many cross-border retailers wish to enter the market by way of a franchise, typically with a local company. Examples of franchises include McDonald's, Burger King, TGI Friday's, Hugo Boss, Versace, Bhs, Mothercare, Intersport, Esprit, Levi's and Jaeger. Recently granted franchises include the Arcadia brands (Top Shop, Dorothy Perkins, Principles and Burtons), Marks & Spencer (due to open in September 1999), Zara, River Island and Celio. There are too many active cross-border retailers to mention in full but household names include Benetton, Carli Gry, Carpetland, Cortefiel, Deichmann Schuhe, Extrapol, Fnac, Giacomelli Sport, Part II and Martinique (InWear), KappAhl, La Halle, Mango, Orsay, Sephora and Vision Express.

Hypermarkets

The food retailers are a category on their own. The market is now being dominated by hypermarkets that offer a mixture of food and non-food products, typically in sales area of more than 10,000 m^2. Due to their size and high car parking requirements they tend to be located in the suburbs and, as the detrimental effect they are having on the smaller local food shops is causing some concern, there is now some political lobbying to restrict their development. Despite this, hypermarkets are proving to be the most effective anchors for the first generation of shopping centres and are popular with the consumer. Active players include Ahold, Auchan, Carrefour, E. Leclerc, Géant, Hit, Jeronimo Martins, Real and Tesco. The home improvement sector is also active but with fewer players. Operators in the market include Castorama (which, along with the local operator Nomi, were recently purchased by Kingfisher), Leroy Merlin, Obi and Praktiker.

Free-standing hypermarkets have encouraged the rise of hypermarket-anchored shopping centres. Initially these were relatively small and limited to a 'check-out' mall. However, a typical centre will now have between 5000 and 12,000 m² of additional retail space, which equates to 30–70 shop units. The rental levels for these units clearly depend upon location, use and size. However, for a 125 m² fashion shop in a good centre with a good location in Warsaw, the rent would be in the region of US$37.50 m²/month, excluding VAT and service charge.

While the development of these centres is rapidly continuing and indeed creating a danger of over-development in some cities/areas, the next generation of shopping centres is on the drawing board and, in one case, already under construction. These centres are the larger ones where the emphasis is more on 'comparison' shopping and leisure rather than on groceries, although a supermarket would generally be included in the tenant mix. The first such centre is the 50,000 m² Galeria Mokotów in Warsaw. Developed by GTC, the centre is currently under construction and is due to be opened in May 2000. Other projects at various stages of design include ING Real Estate International's 180,000 m² Zlota Centre in Warsaw (not all retail); Chelverton International's 70,000 m² Nowy Centrum in Katowice and Tishman Speyer's 230,000 m² Nowy Miasto in Krakow (also not all retail).

Leisure

The leisure sector is now flavour of the month but frequently full of hype. A casual observer may be mistaken for thinking there are dozens of leisure complexes open in Poland. In fact there is one purpose-built multiplex in Poznan and four more under construction. The most active operators are Multikino (a joint venture between UCI and the local company ITI) and Ster Century from South Africa. However, there are a number of other players in the market, including Ciniplex Odeon, Greater Union (through a joint venture), Israeli Theatres and Decatron. Leisure is not limited to multiplexes and there are family entertainment centre operators active such as New Park and Atomic Entertainment, which are also introducing bowling to the Polish market.

City centres

Not all retail activity is in the suburbs. City centres are starting to see more activity with the relative increase in the availability of shop units. Poland's cities and towns do have an advantage over many other European countries in so far as most are densely populated and are not pushing residential districts out to the suburbs. This has helped maintain strong and identifiable high streets, although Warsaw is probably the least defined. Each city naturally has its own character, but streets of note are Nowe Swiat in Warsaw (prime rent about US$80 m²/month), ul. Florianska in Krakow (US$80), ul. Piotrkowska in Lodz, ul. Swiedniska in Wroclaw and ul. Swientojanska in Gdynia.

Conclusion

With all this activity, one might be mistaken for thinking that the retail market in Poland is saturated and overly competitive. Certainly there is competition and in some sectors, like hypermarkets, it is extremely tough competition. However, there are still many opportunities. The high streets are only just beginning to become available to retailers. It is likely that incumbent retailers will be given the opportunity to purchase their shops. Not only will this lead to more lettings but also to an investment market. There have been no open market investment transactions to date but this will change in due course. There are few urban and city centre developments, primarily due to the difficulty in securing sites. Further out of town, there are also very few retail warehouse parks at present. Though the retailers are in the market, land prices are currently too high to make such speculative development worthwhile. Factory outlet centres are not that established in Continental Europe and, while it is too early for them in Poland, they will arrive eventually.

In summary, while the market is progressing quickly, opportunities do still remain for retailers, developers and investors.

24

Shipping

Business Management & Finance (BMF)

Introduction

The peak period in the growth of Polish shipping was in the 1970s and 1980s. The development and maintenance of a large commercial fleet was encouraged for a number of reasons:

- it brought the country desperately needed hard currency;
- it was conducive to the development of Poland's commercial relations with the rest of the world;
- it allowed Polish importers and exporters to maintain transport capability;
- it created demand for production and related services (shipbuilding, brokerage services, forwarding etc).

The shipping development was directly supported and financed by the State and the purchase of new ships was financed from the State Budget.

The period of economic transformation has been extremely painful for the shipping industry. At first it was expected that shipping, like foreign trade companies operating at the point of transition between a centrally planned and free market economy, would quickly and easily adapt to new conditions. These assumptions turned out to be completely incorrect.

Shipping companies could not operate with ease in their new conditions. All of a sudden faced with the problems of generating and maintaining a profit, maintaining assets (especially the fleet) and financing repairs and new purchases at a time of high inflation, the companies rapidly fell into debt. The preferred methods for dealing with this situation were either the sell-off of assets, the restriction of the scale of operations or getting into even deeper debt. It is telling that, regardless of the method adopted, not one Polish ship owner has to this day regained financial liquidity. The situation was further complicated by the deepest crisis to hit the shipping industry for a number of years. The Baltic Index ratio fell to a level of 800 points, which is a long-unequalled record. Ship owners' expectations concerning recovery of the shipping market at the end of 1997 proved premature against the backdrop of the economic crisis affecting the Far East, Russia, the Commonwealth of Independent States (CIS) countries and Brazil.

There are currently three main ship owners operating in Poland:

- Polska Zegluga Morska SA (PZM), based in Szczecin;

- Polskie Linie Oceaniczne SA (PLO), based in Gdynia;

- Polska Zegluga Baltycka SA (PZB), based in Kolobrzeg.

Apart from the previously mentioned State Treasury companies, there also exists the Baltic Container Line (BCL), based in Gdynia. BCL is jointly owned by the Port of Gdynia, by C. Hartwig Gdynia SA (the leading sea freight forwarder in Poland) and by PLO.

PZM

PZM is the largest Polish ship operator, owning, at the beginning of 1999, 103 ships including 99 bulk carriers and 4 tankers. Of these, 46 operate under the Polish flag, with the remainder – for economic reasons – being reflagged to so-called 'cheap flags of convenience'. PZM is still the largest European carrier of bulk cargo and the fifth largest in the world. Despite such an elevated position, PZM possesses only a 1 per cent share of global bulk cargo transportation, which is testimony to the extremely high degree of concentration of services in this sector and to the strength of the competition.

This State Treasury company provides tramp shipping, mainly transporting bulk goods between continents and around Europe; transportation on the Baltic Sea is insignificant. The main product groups served by PZM ships are grain, liquid fuel, coal, metal ore and chemical raw materials. PZM also operates routes between Polish and overseas ports, as well as routes between foreign ports. Examples of these include such routes as:

- North America and the Caribbean (grain, processed grain products);

- Northern Europe and the Mediterranean (scrap, ore);

- the Mediterranean (grain);

- Europe to the Great American Lakes (steel and steel products);

- Middle East to Europe (liquid fuel).

PZM still conducts its own operating activity, despite creating several dozen service (exploitation) and shipping (owners, set up during the purchase of ships) companies. Despite its extremely complex financial situation and its high level of debt, PZM continues efforts to further modernise its fleet by placing orders for new ships from Polish, Japanese and Indonesian ship-yards. Thanks to these purchases, PZM possesses the newest fleet among Polish ship owners.

At the same time, PZM has started restructuring the company, planning further reflagging of ships, a reduction over two years of 20 per cent of sailing personnel and a 40 per cent reduction of sea personnel. It also plans to dispose of assets on land such as social buildings, plots, commercial property and the massive PAZIM office and commercial complex located in the centre of Szczecin.

PLO

Traditionally, and to this day, PLO has been engaged in liner traffic. It almost exclusively serves general cargo (package freight), including containerised cargoes.

Finding itself in ever-increasing trouble during the period of Poland's economic transformation, State Treasury-owned PLO was put into administration (changed three times). Restructuring actions were based on:

- creation of a holding structure for PLO and the take-over of operational activity by its subsidiaries;

- reflagging the fleet;

- sell-off of part of the company's assets (including vessels);

- employment cuts;

- debt restructuring.

Actions taken by successive management boards did not bring about the desired effects. There are currently 39 ships in the PLO group, of which 23 are owned by PLO and 16 are chartered. Only one ship sails under the Polish flag, while the remainder have been reflagged. The average age of the PLO fleet is 17 years, so it requires quite rapid modernisation. Currently, PLO only carries out ownership supervision and leases out assets. Shipping and support activity is conducted through subsidiaries within the PLO group.

The PLO group currently consists of 40 companies. The most important of these are the following shipping companies:

- Pol-Levant – engaged in shipping on the Mediterranean;

- Pol-America – maintains a service between Europe and South America, the Caribbean and the Gulf of Mexico;

- Pol-Asia Shipping Lines Ltd – created in 1998 from the merger of Pol-Seal and Pol-Asia and provides a service between Europe and East and Southern Africa, South Asia, the Far East and Australia;

- Euroafrica – liner service between Europe and West Africa, ferry service between Poland and Scandinavia, and European services (British, Dutch, Irish and Finnish);

- BCL – as the feeder from Gdynia to Western European ports;

- Pol-Atlantic – company in liquidation, which did not operate ships itself but only operated slots on lines between Europe and North America (operating slots is extremely risky, especially in a time of low demand).

Apart from the above mentioned companies in the PLO group there are also five service companies. Of these, two should be mentioned:

- Pol-Supply – engaged in supplying ships, repairs and conservation, it also possesses significant assets on land;

- Pol-Container – in liquidation, it was engaged in logistics and trading in containers, and was associated with Pol-America.

The remaining companies are off-shore type foreign companies under the complete control of PLO, or PLO companies created in countries that offer cheap flags of convenience.

PLO is preparing to be privatised. Finding an investor or group of investors could help PLO rebuild its position in the ship owners' market.

PZB

PZB, also a State Treasury company, is the smallest Polish ship operator. Its core business is passenger and vehicle ferry shipping on the following routes:

- Swinoujscie–Copenhagen;

- Swinoujscie–Malmo/Ystad;

- Swinoujscie–Ronne;

- Gdansk–Oxelosund;

- Gdansk–Nynashamn.

PZB operates five ferries, including a superfast Boomerang catamaran. PZB owns two ferry ports: in Gdansk and in Swinoujscie. In addition, PZB is engaged in tramp and cabotage shipping on the Baltic Sea, operating seven ships (mainly old and worn) for these operations: five general cargo vessels and two bulk carriers. PZB also possesses the commercial port in Kolobrzeg, with an annual cargo handling capacity reaching 250,000 tonnes per year.

Earnings from ferry operations dominate PZB's total earnings. The liquidation of duty-free zones between EU countries should significantly increase interest in ferry crossings to Poland and as a result dynamically increase earnings from duty-free shops on ferries and ferry ports. These new opportunities will be accompanied by increased competition, as some ferry operators from the EU will start to seek out attractive new areas, in which duty-free zones can still operate. One such direction is unquestionably the Southern and Eastern Baltic.

25

Telecommunications

Business Management & Finance (BMF)

Introduction

The telecommunications sector was, up until the late 1980s, one of the most neglected areas of the Polish economy. During the communist era, the development of this sector was restricted by lack of access to the funds needed for the development of the network (especially hard currency) and problems with access to modern Western technology, which was generally covered by the COCOM embargo.

Going into the last decade of the twentieth century, Poland therefore possessed one of the lowest penetration ratios in Europe of only 8.2 telephone lines per 100 inhabitants. What's more, the quality of telecommunications services left much to be desired, especially in terms of international and long-distance connections.

With the introduction of the free market in Poland, the insufficient development of the telecommunications network became especially painful for thousands of newly opened private companies, for which access to a telephone was often a primary condition of doing business. Problems with telecommunications also created a barrier for Polish companies in their search for foreign investors and commercial partners.

Decisions were taken as early as 1990 with respect to improving the Polish telecommunications system. The development and modernisation of the network first began with international and long-distance connections. This enabled not only an improvement in the quality of services but also created the conditions in which the long-distance network would be able to serve the new traffic that would be generated as a result of the development of the local networks.

Telekomunikacja Polska SA

At the beginning of the 1990s, Telekomunikacja Polska SA (TP SA) was the sole telecom operator in Poland. The company was created at the turn of 1991–92 as a result of the transformation of Poczta Polska, Telefon i

Telegraf, which, as a state monopoly, had for years provided a wide range of communication services.

Between 1992 and 1997 TP SA spent approximately Zl13 billion (equivalent to over US$5 billion) on investments for the development of the network. As a result, the company managed to quite thoroughly modernise the long-distance network, while at the same time increasing the number of local lines from 4 million in 1992 to 7.5 million at the end of 1997 (that figure now already exceeds 8 million). Along with the increased number of lines, there was a significant improvement in the quality of connections, ensuring practically problem-free local and long distance connections, which had only a few years earlier been such a major concern.

Although the situation in large towns and cities has significantly improved, satisfying to a large degree local needs, the penetration rate (line density) in rural areas is still low and this will have to be resolved over the next few years.

Competition

The Polish government took early action aimed at creating the conditions necessary for breaking the monopoly held by TP SA. The legal basis for the demonopolisation of the sector was created by the Telecommunications Bill of November 1990. According to this document, only international communications were to remain the sole preserve of TP SA. In reality, however, the protection from competition granted by the government to TP SA was significantly more comprehensive than the intentions expressed in the Bill. For example, despite the process of granting licences to independent operators being started relatively quickly, the majority of licences for the largest cities (the most attractive for operators) were only awarded in 1998 (by coincidence also the year privatisation of TP SA began). The bidding for licences for long-distance (inter-city) connections is only just being planned for 1999.

In the beginning, the conditions placed on independent operators applying for licences did not create significant barriers to business. For this reason, the number of independent operators who obtained licenses was relatively high. Few of them, however, had a sufficient capital base to start real development of the network in the licensed area. From 1991 to the time the Telecommunications Bill was amended in mid-1995, 141 licences for providing telecommunication services were issued (of these, 65 related to the use of existing company networks). Licences for the less attractive rural areas (giving no guarantee of profitability), combined with the lack of sufficient experience and capital resources, resulted in only a small percentage of licensed operators starting actual operations. However, bids for licences to serve large cities required bidders to indicate their sources of finance for the project and, more importantly, to pay high licence charges. It is assumed that the operator investing in the licence will make moves to recover the initial investment.

Consolidation over the last few years has already identified some early market leaders. The largest independent operator is undoubtedly Netia. This company was built on the foundations of RP Telecom (created in 1990), which gradually took over the licences for new areas, while at the same time broadening its number of shareholders. One of the largest shareholders in Netia is currently Telia – the Swedish national operator. Netia possesses licences for areas with a total of 13 million inhabitants, including such agglomerations as Gdansk, Poznan, Katowice, Krakow and Lublin. Recently Netia completed an IPO on NASDAQ, becoming the first Polish company to be listed in the US.

El-Net has recently become the main competitor to Netia. This company is part of the Elektrim capital group, which is quoted on the stock exchange. It started its operations by obtaining the licence for the city of Bydgoszcz. The winning of the tender for the licence for Warsaw has opened the way for El-Net to become one of the largest telecom operators in Poland.

Other important operators include PTO (covering approximately 8.1 million inhabitants) and Telefonia Lokalna (approximately 5.5 million inhabitants).

At the beginning of 1999, Elektrim announced a take-over of Pilicka Telefonia while simultaneously signing an agreement regarding the purchase of shares in the largest Warsaw cable TV company, AsterCity. In this manner, Elektrim, which already controlled GSM ERA, El-Net and a number of other smaller telecommunications companies, has become one of the main competitors to TP SA.

Mobile telecommunications

The first operator to offer mobile telecommunication services was PTP Centertel, a company created in 1991 as a joint venture between Telekomunikacja Polska SA (with 51 per cent of shares), France Telecom (24.5 per cent) and Ameritech (24.5 per cent). Currently, TP SA owns 66 per cent of the company, with the remaining shares held by France Telecom. PTK Centertel began operations by offering NMT 450 services. Approximately 200,000 subscribers use PTK Centertel services.

At the beginning of 1996, licences were awarded for the construction and operation of GDM 900 digital services. The winners of the bid were:

- PTC (ERA trade mark), whose main shareholders were Elektrim, Kulczyk, Warta, DeTeMobil and US West;

- Polkomtel (Plus trade mark), whose main shareholders are Petrochemia Plock, KGHM, PSE, TeleDenmark, AirTouch, Stalexport and Weglokoks.

GSM operators started in autumn 1996, just six months after obtaining their licences. At first GSM operated only in the largest cities but there are currently over 2 million GSM users throughout Poland (each of the networks has over 1 million subscribers).

In August 1997, PTK Centertel received the licence to provide DCS 1800 standard services. The network started operating under the name 'Idea' in March 1998.

In July 1999, further licences were granted: Centertel received a GSM 900 licence, which was followed by DCS 1800 licences for PTC and Polkomtel.

Privatisation of TP SA

In the autumn of 1998, the long-expected Initial Public Offering (IPO) of shares in TP SA took place, through which investors purchased 15 per cent of shares in the company from the State Treasury. A further 15 per cent of shares was given free of charge to the employees of the company. The IPO was a success, despite it taking place during a very difficult period, following the crisis in the Russian market. After the IPO, TP SA became the largest company listed on the Warsaw Stock Exchange, its capitalisation reaching almost US$10 billion in mid-1999.

As early as September 1998 and before the privatisation of the company, an agreement was signed between the Ministry of Telecommunications and TP SA. The agreement intended to define the relationship between the regulator and the privatised company in the period before the amendment to the Telecommunications Bill. In the first half of 1999, the Minister of the State Treasury began his preparations for the realisation of the second phase of the company's privatisation: the obtaining of a strategic investor for TP SA.

One of the elements of the preparation for full privatisation is the creation of stable regulations, which would form the foundation for the operation of the telecommunications sector in subsequent years. The new Telecommunications Bill will ensure the conditions for far-reaching demonopolisation of the sector and be a significant step in the integration of Poland with the EU.

The future

The future of the Polish telecommunications sector looks very interesting. The full privatisation of TP SA, involving a strategic investor, will guarantee the further development of the company. Meanwhile, consolidation among independent operators enables us to predict that, very shortly, services competing with TP SA will begin to appear in the large conurbations.

This may be especially beneficial to corporate users, who will be among the first potential customers targeted by independent operators. One of the most interesting developments may turn out to be the tender for long-distance (inter-city) licences. There are already a number of companies that have the infrastructure that would allow an immediate start-up for the provision of long-distance services as an alternative to TP SA (eg Kolpak, Telenetgo, Telbank). One should expect that the largest local network operators, Elektrim and Netia, will also bid for these licences. The issuing of licences could result in a rapid increase in competition in this area and accelerate the 'tariff rebalancing' process.

26

Textile and Apparel Industry (Light Industry Sector)

Richard Chmielowiec, International Apparel Consultancy

Introduction

The textile and garment industries in Poland have a very long tradition, going back to the Middle Ages. Their most rapid development, however, occurred at the end of the 19th and the beginning of the 20th century. At that time, the industry became concentrated in three main textile regions: Lodz, Bielsko-Biala and Czestochowa. After World War II other cities such as Bialystok, Torun, Walbrzych and Jelenia Gora also developed as textile/clothing centres, following the construction of new plants.

To understand the current situation, mention must be made of the recent economic history of the country, which, following its calamitous experience as a centrally planned economy during its 45 years under Soviet rule, embarked on a restructuring programme in the aftermath of the political changes of 1989. During that period of economic transformation the textile sectors suffered most, owing to the loss of the large markets of the Soviet Union and to Poland's unpreparedness to compete on the more demanding Western markets. Some companies became bankrupt, while others reconstructed their operations following privatisation and are currently undergoing rapid modernisation.

An integral part of the recent economic transformation of Poland was the opening up of a wide range of contacts with international trade and its various institutional organisations, culminating in March 1998 with the beginning of negotiations for accession to the European Union. Poland became a member of the WTO and the OECD, and recently joined NATO, all of which should reassure Western investors that this is a country safe for long-term investment.

Poland has so far attracted over US$35 billion of foreign direct investment (FDI) from many countries around the world. Its market size of 38 million people and convenient geographical location on the crossroads between Western and Eastern Europe make it a convenient location for future investment.

Now is an opportune time to consider business links with Polish partners in manufacturing and trade. One way of achieving this could be through participation in the twice yearly Poznan Fashion Week, an international fair held in March and September that is a meeting point and melting pot of the textile and apparel industries. There, successful partnerships can be initiated in the form of joint ventures, reciprocal supply chains in the retail sector, etc.

Textiles: the industrial super-sector

The Polish light manufacturing industry stands out in the national economy as an industrial super-sector encompassing three main groups (following a classification by Dariusz Klimek, undersecretary of state in charge of light industry until March 1999):

- **Textiles:** According to the European Classification of Activity (ECA 17), this includes production processes such as preparation processes for spinning and fabric making, textile finishing treatments, knitting processes and the manufacturing of non-woven textiles, technical textiles and geo-textiles.

- **Clothing:** According to ECA 18, this includes the production of garments from fabrics (outerwear, dresses and suits, underwear, sportswear and workwear, as well as fur products).

- **Leather footwear:** According to ECA 19, this embraces the tanning and treatment of skin, the manufacturing of leather (excluding furs and garments) and leather-like accessories, luggage and handbags, saddles and harnesses, as well as the production of shoes, boots, etc.

Basic economic indicators

Basic economic indicators (first seven months of 1998) for the textile industry in Poland are as follows:

- **Number of light industry establishments:** A total number of 1298 economic entities (with more than 50 employees) were registered:

  - 358 textile companies;

  - 722 clothing companies;

  - 218 leather-footwear companies.

- **Employment structure:**
  - Total employment: 293,100;
  - Sectoral breakdown:
    - textiles: 105,200;
    - clothing: 142,900;
    - leather footwear: 45,000.

In addition to the above figures there is a textile and apparel 'grey sector', which is not included in official statistics; some sources estimate this as providing employment to 400,000 persons or more.

- **Exports and imports:**
  - Share of light manufacturing industries in Poland's total exports (for companies of over 50 employees):
    - textiles 3.3 per cent;
    - clothing 11.3 per cent
    - leather footwear 1.5 per cent.
  - Share of light industry in total imports:
    - textiles 3.1 per cent;
    - clothing 6.5 per cent;
    - leather footwear 1.1 per cent.

In addition, it was estimated that in 1996 grey sector 'exports' (via bazaar-type markets) amounted to about US$2.7 billion (60–70 per cent apparel). The 'importers' were so called 'suitcase traders' entering Poland through its eastern and/or western borders. The introduction in 1997 of visas for these people, citizens of Commonwealth of Independent States (CIS) countries, resulted in a 30–40 per cent reduction in the sales of small-sized companies trading in the grey sector, which affected the industry's 1998 economic results. There is the possibility of locating sub-contracting operations in this sub-sector as well.

- **Economic and financial performance:**
  - Total revenues US$2331.6 million (US$ mean annual exchange rate Zl 3.7), including:
    - textiles US$1145.6 million;
    - clothing US$831.1 million;
    - footwear US$354.9 million.

- Net profit (-)US$4.67 million, including:

  • textiles (-)US$3.1 million;

  • clothing US$14.6 million;

  • leather footwear (-)US$16.2 million.

- Gross profitability Zl 1.3 per cent, including:

  • textiles Zl 1.0 per cent;

  • clothing Zl 3.6 per cent;

  • leather footwear: Zl –3.2 per cent.

● **Ownership structure:** There is a diverse ownership structure. The percentages of receipts on sales and average employment in the private and public sectors, respectively, are:

● textile industry 30 and 70 per cent;

● clothing 85 and 15 per cent.

Labour costs and skills

The labour costs in the textile industry are relatively low – about 14 times lower than in Germany and 10 times lower than in Italy. Productivity is expected to double as a result of the wide-ranging modernisation programme planned for this industry in the coming years. Average monthly wages in industrial sectors in 1997 amounted to US$337.4, though workers in the apparel sector earned 35 per cent less than the national average in 1996. Assuming that the same conditions prevailed in 1998, the average wage level in the apparel industry would have been US$220 per month. In some regions with a higher unemployment rate than in the large cities, the wages were even lower for the same skill level.

In the country as a whole, there are 360 apparel schools providing various courses from technician level to vocational craftsmanship. Apart from state educational establishments (technical colleges and vocational schools), there also exists a network of training facilities for the tailoring sector, run by local guilds, where young people can complete an apprenticeship to qualify them for work in the apparel industry. However, the industry frequently undertakes its own on-the-job training activities, thus securing an adequate skill level tailored to its own requirements.

Foreign buyers have a high opinion of the skills of factory middle management in this sector; these skills are due to long-standing co-operation with Western counterparts with respect to modern technology and market requirements.

Sourcing of raw materials

The majority of raw materials are imported (eg cotton, silk, wool and very high-quality linen); there are insufficient quantities of domestically produced man-made fibres. Sewing threads of sufficient quality and accessories such as ribbons, fastenings and embroideries are available from local distributors.

Many clothing manufacturers are sourcing raw materials in Western Europe in order to obtain very high-quality fabrics to match their excellent design and processing capabilities; substantial investment is needed in order to build sufficient dying-and-finishing facilities at local textile mills.

Foreign investment

Statistics published by the IDA (Industrial Development Agency), which registers investment over US$1 million, show that 25 foreign companies have already invested in this sector, while some form of foreign capital participation has been recorded in over 1000 Polish companies.

Customs tariffs

All protective customs tariffs on textile imports from the EU into Poland were abolished on 1 January 1999 and no quota exists for Polish products imported into the EU.

Also noteworthy for foreign buyers is the fact that in 1998 a new Polish Customs Act was implemented, designed according to EU Customs Law, and containing a number of simplified procedures to speed up various administrative formalities. Further proposals are being considered in order to amend this Act and introduce even more favourable conditions for the textile/apparel sector and to encourage foreign investors.

Forms of trade in the clothing industry

OPT

Data for 1997 show that 88.5 per cent of garment export was carried out as OPT (Outward Processing Trade) operations, 8.1 per cent of the country's total exports.

These activities have recently found less favour with the main investment groups, the NIFs (National Investment Funds), which were designed to aid the transfer of state-owned companies to private ownership. The main reason given for the loss of favour of OPT operations is their low profitability. The governing bodies of the NIFs tend to prefer to promote Polish design and brand labels, but this is not proving easy.

Retailing

Some larger enterprises have merged with manufacturers of ancillary products and together opened their own strong chains of retail facilities throughout the country. They warmly welcome foreign investors into production/trade partnerships.

Retailing is carried out in small shops and medium-sized department stores in city centres, and in large hypermarkets in the suburbs, opened in the last few years by Western investors. The quality of service is improving in comparison with the 1980s state-owned shops. All shops in Poland are now in private hands and speciality shops are mushrooming throughout the country.

Machinery in the apparel industry

Large enterprises have an average Western level of sewing machinery units (those processing on a CMT (cut, make and trim) basis in particular). An increase of 55 per cent in investment in modern machinery and technological installations is recorded for the first six months of 1998 (compared with like-period 1997). A good example of production modernisation is noted in Bydgoszcz-based Modus, a company that, along with Vistula, Bytom, Intermoda and Sunset Suits, ranks among the top five menswear manufacturers. Modena, a company based in Poznan and a leading ladies' outerwear producer, recently acquired a Pierre Cardin licence and has also invested heavily in modern CAD/CAM machinery. Its labels rank among those of the highest quality to be found in famous European retail shops.

This chapter is based on the author's comprehensive report on Poland published in 'World Clothing Manufacturer' by World Textile Publications Ltd., Bradford, UK.

27

Tourism

Thom Barnhardt, Warsaw Business Journal

Introduction

Poland is slowly but surely developing its in-bound tourism industry to appeal to international travellers. Western tourists have begun to recognise the unique appeal of the country, stretching from the unpretentious setting of the Baltic Sea to the southern ski slopes of the Carpathian mountains. And Poles themselves are recognising the appeal of building a business around tourism – relying as much on the domestic market as on in-bound foreign tourists.

While the official tourism count (over 18 million visitors in 1998) places Poland as the eighth most visited country in the world, the border trade with Germany and the eastern countries of Belarus and Ukraine accounts for enough traffic to render that statistic fairly meaningless. Even so, in-bound 'real' tourist visits are clearly rising significantly every year. The western part of the country and the northern coast increasingly draw German and Scandinavian tourists, and the southern cities of Krakow and Zakopane draw the most visitors, both Poles and international tourists.

Tourism infrastructure remains poorly developed, a characteristic resented by the country's tourism boosters but appreciated by those Western tourists with a penchant for unusual experiences. The highways don't deserve their appellation, many of the small hotels and inns are functional but without a soul, and service standards are poor. Yet, despite these few shortcomings, Poland's appeal to tourists grows noticeably with every passing year. And the trains run like clockwork.

Short stays

The bed and breakfast industry is blossoming into an identifiable tourism segment, and entrepreneurs, both foreigners and Poles, are offering new cosy destinations – frequented mainly on weekends by resident expatriates, the emerging Polish middle class and, increasingly, foreign visitors; places like the Akiko pension in the southern Polish town of Nowy Sacz, inaccessible to all but a four-wheel vehicle, whose Japanese owner graciously receives a range of guests from around the world. In the same spirit is the Kania Lodge, a bed and breakfast near Gdansk, run by an Australian importer of fine wines. These small businesses are catering to weekend tourism, as well as benefiting from the growing trend of business and training seminars.

Three or four years ago, very few Poles would have left home on a weekend bed and breakfast trip but the concept is rapidly gaining acceptance. This increasing domestic demand is driving further investment interest among Poles, making the short stay tourist industry a rapidly expanding sector. The more popular destinations such as Krakow continue to broaden their appeal to international tourists through better and more numerous restaurants and hotels (as well as through direct flights from London and New York). Meanwhile, the lesser known old towns such as Wroclaw, Torun and Zamosc are also receiving facelifts and are delightful (and often little known) destinations for a weekend.

Places of interest

The following are some of Poland's most appreciated tourist destinations.

Krakow

A trip to Poland would be incomplete without taking in the historic sites of Poland's former capital, where Polish kings reigned for centuries. Graced by one of Europe's largest squares, the city remains the jewel in Poland's tourism industry. And the city has only become more attractive over the last five to seven years, emerging from the cobwebs of communism. A university town, the student population imbues Krakow with energy and vitality and, along with a growing business community, provides a balance to the surge of summer tourists. Though Krakow's hotels are only now providing a range of reasonable accommodation, the restaurant offerings include fine French, Italian (and my favourite Greek diner just off the square), as well as hearty Polish cuisine. Nightlife is centred on the ubiquitous cellar cafés and pubs.

A side-trip from Krakow might include the nearby salt mines, or Oswiecim, more notoriously known by the name of Auschwitz.

Zakopane

This southern town in the Carpathian range has boomed in recent years as Poles have come to appreciate its rustic appeal, charming local culture, the skiing slopes in winter and the hiking trails in summer. Though Zakopane is widely viewed in Poland as the country's most popular winter destination, the town disappoints some Western visitors, who complain about its poor ski and accommodation infrastructure. The city had hopes of attracting the next Winter Olympics, but its extraordinary natural beauty can't overcome its infrastructure deficiencies. The city continues to draw modest amounts of investment into housing, both permanent and for tourism. This area is excellent for hiking and summer cycling.

Mazury Lakes district

In northeastern Poland, a few hours' drive from Warsaw, this vast area of lakes, many inter-connected, provides ample recreational appeal for sailors and swimmers.

Bialowieska forest

This is the last primary forest in Europe, and visitors are likely to see bison as well as a broad range of bird species.

Slowinski National Park

Abutting the Baltic Sea and next to the small summer resort of Leba, Slowinski remains virtually unknown to Western tourists, and unvisited by many Poles. Its shifting sand dunes and large beachfront area make the park idyllic for wandering, walking and feeling quite removed from the rest of Poland. Often used as background for fashion shoots for Poland's new modelling companies, you're more likely to see Polish families on bicycles than scantily clad beauties.

Gdansk

The town of Gdansk is one of the three towns on the northern coast (including Sopot and Gdynia) known as Trojmiasto. Lech Walesa, Poland's most famous electrician, rallied his fellow shipworkers and supporters throughout Poland from his base here in Gdansk. At once a victor over communism and a victim of capitalism (its shipyard recently declared bankruptcy), Gdansk is worth a visit. And its old town, though small, is delightful.

Warsaw

Much maligned, tourists often remark that Warsaw is 'not as bad' as they thought it would be. Its proud populace paid a heavy price for resisting the German war machine, yet toiled after the war to rebuild the Old Town, using pictures and memories to restore the area to its earlier grandeur. The Old Town and the main artery (Nowy Swiat and Krakowskie Przedmiescie) leading into it have heavy tourist traffic (in the spring and summer) as well as Warsaw residents going about their daily chores, or strolling arm-in-arm. The Old Town square, adorned in earthy pastel colours, is crowded and vibrant in summer, joyless in winter. Several excellent restaurants ring the square, yet the restaurants just behind the main square remain unenthusiastic. In one corner of the square is the Warsaw City Museum, offering a fascinating glimpse into this city's character. One should not miss the old black-and-white film of the Warsaw uprising, depicting in agonising detail the destruction of the city in World War II.

The investment opportunities in Warsaw are good, with new restaurants being opened at a rapid pace, catering to the increasingly wealthy business community. The international investment community based in Warsaw is steadily growing, testament to the more than US$30 billion in foreign direct investment that has come into the country. This community is further driving demand for more restaurants, hotels, office space and entertainment outlets.

Castles and fortresses

Historic castles dot the landscape, some not renovated, some decadently so. Probably more than twenty locations are worth visiting, and those that are not may be worth a glance if only to assess their investment potential. The State has sold off many of these old treasures, and is encouraging investors to buy and renovate them. In addition to being used as tourist destinations, many are used by corporations looking for off-site training and seminar locations, providing an important, and often primary, income stream for the owners.

Events

From Warsaw's Summer Jazz Days to music festivals in the beach resort town of Sopot, Poland's events organisers are always finding more innovative ways to entertain. Whether it's a Miss Bikini contest in the coastal town of Miedzyzdroje or the annual jousting tournaments in late July in Gniew, Poland's entrepreneurs are creating events to showcase the country's natural and cultural attributes.

28

Transport Infrastructure

Business Management & Finance (BMF)

Introduction

The 1990s have been years of dynamic change in all transport areas in Poland. The freight structure and the transport geography have been transformed. The railways have lost their dominant position in goods transportation to road transport. This is especially true of the transportation of mass cargoes with the reduced significance of the mineral sector. The declines in mineral extraction (coal, sulphur and metal ore) and in heavy industry (coking plants, steelworks) production have resulted in a reduction in the demand for transportation services relating to the movement of raw materials and products.

Simultaneously, there has been unprecedented growth in minor production and trade. This was very much the result of the privatisation processes of whole sectors of industry and of the influx of foreign investment, which directed capital mainly to the processing industries. These factors generated rapidly growing demand for general road transportation services.

Along with geographical changes to Poland's trade, there was a geographical change in transportation. EU countries became the main trading partners, accounting for over 60 per cent of Poland's trade. Road transport accounts for over two thirds of this trade, although rail transportation still claims a significant proportion of goods transportation, mainly in the trade of raw materials with Eastern Europe.

The 1990s have been a period of unprecedented growth of transit freight, especially in the East–West direction. The highest rate of growth has been registered by road transport. The economic crisis in Russia, the Ukraine and Belarus has temporarily weakened the expansion of this form of transport, although there has been already a slow but gradual increase in transit movement.

Poland's transportation network was and still is unprepared to receive such increased demand for transport services. Over the last few years many ideas and reports have appeared concerning its development. The problem lies in the fact that not many of these plans have reached the realisation phase.

Roads

The main network of road links in Poland consists of national roads with a total length of over 17,000 km, of which 5550 km are international roads on which transit traffic is concentrated. Almost 80 per cent of road traffic is concentrated on the national road network. Poland is among the most rapidly growing countries in Europe in terms of car ownership. Already, the number of passenger vehicles registered in Poland is nearing 9 million, while there are almost 1.5 million heavy goods vehicles. In addition, there are thousands of transit vehicles travelling along Polish roads every day. The Polish road network is not prepared to receive such traffic. Its main flaws include:

- the lack of a motorway network or a system of expressways (dual carriageways);

- poor inter-crossing facilities for different types of traffic;

- most transport routes pass through built-up areas;

- the lack of sufficient bridges;

- the unsuitable geometrical parameters of roads and their insufficient carrying capacity.

According to the latest data, only one quarter of road surfaces are in good condition, while the remainder are either poor or unsatisfactory. Road modernisation work in recent years has concentrated on widening existing roads, constructing bypasses, repairing ruts and increasing the carrying capacity of road surfaces. Resources intended for these investments originate from the State Budget or from World Bank or European Bank for Reconstruction and Development (EBRD) credits.

The Motorway Construction Programme envisages the construction by 2015 of almost 2500 km of motorways running along Poland's main East–West (A-2 and A-4) and North–South (A-1) international transit routes. The motorway system will be supplemented by a network of expressways, which will have similar standards to motorways and have a total length of approximately 3500 km.

It was originally planned that the motorways would be toll roads and would be constructed using private capital in exchange for 25-year licences for the exploitation of specific road sections. The State Treasury was only intended to participate in this project through the purchasing of land for the future motorways. However, these plans were eventually deemed too optimistic. According to the Motorway Construction Agency, it will now be necessary for the State to participate in the construction of motorways through direct joint financing. In return, part of the toll earnings will be paid back to the State.

Railways

The Polish railway network consists mainly of standard-gauge lines with a width of 1435 mm covering almost 21,000 km, 427 km of 1520 mm wide-gauge lines and 1100 km of narrow-gauge lines (from 600–1000 mm). With railway line density of 6.95 km per 100 km², Poland is considered as having a well-developed railway network. Ninety per cent of goods and passenger traffic travels on rail lines with a total length of 12,000 km. Almost half of the standard-gauge lines are electrified. Sixty per cent of railway lines are deemed of national importance, and are financed by the State Budget. The condition of the railway lines is significantly better than that of the roads. This does not, however, mean that the railways do not require investment.

The main aim at present is to increase the speed of Intercity and Euro-city type passenger trains. Currently, these trains service the links between main Polish cities and, on selected sections, travel at speeds of 110–140 km/h. In accordance with AGC and AGTC international agreements, the aim over the next 15 years is to achieve speeds of 160 km/h for passenger trains on main lines and of 120 km/h for freight trains. The modernisation work currently under way on the E-20 route (Berlin–Warsaw–Moscow) should allow the introduction of trains of this speed between Berlin and Warsaw within the next two years.

The railway network in Poland also includes 3700 stations and railway stops, including 155 passenger stations and 2000 passenger stops. For a number of years, serious modernisation has taken place, thanks to which modern stations have been constructed in Czestochowa, Krakow, Gdansk and Lodz. Modernisation of freight stations has also taken place, based on the introduction of an automatic system of forming and unforming trains, automated control of train movement and the construction of modern container terminals and combined transport terminals.

Polish State Railways now faces revolutionary changes in its management. Over the next few years, the government plans to begin the privatisation of the company, although it plans to separate operating activity from the management of the infrastructure.

Airports

There are over 150 airports of various size and usage in Poland, although there are only nine that service regular passenger traffic: Warsaw, Lodz, Krakow, Wroclaw, Poznan, Gdansk, Szczecin, Katowice and Rzeszow. It is estimated that, in the long term, civil aviation will require approximately 30 airports.

The main airport in Poland is Warsaw-Okecie, which handled almost 3.8 million passengers in 1998. This airport's good location and well-developed connections with Western and Eastern Europe are responsible for the high 15 per cent increase in passenger traffic. Warsaw has the opportunity of becoming a regional hub servicing transit traffic from Western Europe and North America to Eastern Europe. The infrastructure of Warsaw-Okecie (runways, ways of manoeuvring, technical equipment etc) allows it to increase traffic by up to 12 million passengers per year. The modern airport building was designed to handle 4.5 million passengers per year. As a result, the construction of a new terminal is planned in 2000–01; it will be capable of handling a further 7 million passengers per year.

There is even more dynamic growth in cargo traffic through Warsaw-Okecie. Currently, it services 44,000 tonnes of cargo per year, increasing this figure by almost 20 per cent per annum. In the longer term, it would appear necessary to build a completely new cargo airport near Warsaw.

Of the other passenger airports, the airports in Krakow and Gdansk have registered the largest amount of traffic. This is due to the gradual opening of these airports to foreign airlines and the increased number of flights by LOT, the Polish airline. Both these airports play the role of reserve airports for Warsaw. Both have newly constructed terminals (in Krakow a second terminal is being built) and a modernised airport infrastructure (a new control tower is being built in Gdansk).

Of the remaining passenger airports currently in operation, new terminals have been built in Wroclaw, Katowice and Poznan. In the spring of 1999, after almost 40 years, the passenger airport in Lodz was reopened and it is to service increasing passenger traffic for this conurbation of over a million inhabitants. The above mentioned airports mainly service domestic traffic, although there is a growing number of regular short-haul international connections.

The state-owned enterprise Polskie Porty Lotnicze is responsible for maintaining passenger airports but local authorities support the growth of civil aviation at local airports. Not all airports are profitable: the relatively low number of regular connections (a few a day) do not provide sufficient revenue. This situation could change substantially after the implementation of an 'open sky' policy. The responsibility for negotiating the frequency and destinations of flights with airlines will be managed by specific airport authorities.

Seaports

Poland has four fully developed commercial seaports: Gdansk and Gdynia, located in the Bay of Gdansk, and Szczecin and Swinoujscie in Western Pomerania. These ports account for 98 per cent of freight turnover:

Port	Annual turnover in 1998 ('000 tonnes)
● Gdansk	20,624
● Gdynia	8,016
● Szczecin	13,736
● Swinoujscie	8,291

Source: Statistical Yearbook for 1999

Cargo handling at these ports is dominated by bulk cargoes such as coal, coke, oil, oil derivatives, minerals, grain, cement and fertilisers. Approximately 22 per cent of cargoes are general cargoes (package freight). Gdansk and Szczecin are mainly bulk cargo ports. Gdynia is the main general cargo port in Poland, possessing a modern container terminal with a handling capacity of 400,000 tonnes. Swinoujscie is also a bulk cargo handling port, although it also handles general cargo transported by ferries from Scandinavia.

The shortcomings of Polish seaports include their peripheral location in relation to main shipping lines as well as the hydrological conditions of the Baltic, which restrict the size of ships entering the Baltic Sea. For this reason, Polish seaports are mainly feeder ports. Many cargoes, especially general cargo (package freight), are transported by 'feeders' to the large European ports, where they are reloaded onto larger ships from where they are sent on trans-ocean lines. Polish ports are also, above all, national ports and transit cargoes account for only a few per cent of cargo handling. Increasing the volume of transit cargoes would mainly depend on the modernisation of transport infrastructure beyond the ports.

The most modern seaport is Port Polnocny in Gdansk. Artificially constructed on the Bay of Gdansk, it can handle the largest ships entering the Baltic. It has three terminals: a coal terminal, an oil and liquid fuel terminal and a mineral terminal. The construction of a grain terminal and a container terminal is also planned. This old Gdansk seaport handles bulk cargoes (fertilisers, timber, cement) and a certain amount of uncontainerised general freight. It is also the location of the ferry terminal.

The port of Gdynia is the main general cargo (package freight) port in Poland and the main container port. The container terminal is currently capable of coping with the country's requirements. The plan to increase the handling of general transit cargo (to and from the Ukraine and Belarus) requires increasing the capacity of the current terminal by an additional 200,000–300,000 tonnes. Gdynia is also the main passenger port servicing ships cruising on the Baltic.

Szczecin and Swinoujscie operate practically as a port group. The location of Szczecin almost 70 km from the sea and the relatively shallow water lanes in the Zalew Szczecinski and the Odra river mean that, before entering into Szczecin, certain ships are 'lightened' in Swinoujscie. The unfavourable hydrological conditions of Szczecin are compensated for by its location on the Odra, the only fully navigable river in Poland, and the proximity of Berlin, for which Szczecin seems to be the natural port. Swinoujscie is mainly a bulk cargo port (coal) and is also the main ferry port in Poland.

Inland waterways

The network of inland waterways in Poland is over 3800 km long, of which only 1530 km are used for transport purposes. It is the least developed mode of transport and has a poor and fragmented infrastructure. Approximately 9.3 million tonnes of cargo per year are transported on inland waterways, the main cargoes being sand, gravel, coal, minerals, metals and steel products.

The main waterway is the Odra river, serviced by the Gliwice canal. However, in the middle of its course there is a narrow bottleneck where there are depths of less than 1.3 m, which makes shipping on this almost 200 km long waterway economically unviable. The Programme for the Development of the Odra Waterway to 2005 envisages adapting the Odra river to achieve the standards of at least a class III waterway, and even class V on certain sections, thus incorporating the Odra river into the European system of waterways. Currently, almost three quarters of inland waterway freight transport is concentrated on the Odra river.

The Vistula river has the status of a class V waterway from its mouth to 51 km downstream. In addition, the Zeran canal is a class III waterway. To make the Vistula or any other river in Poland fully navigable would require enormous financial expenditure, as virtually all the necessary infrastructure would have to be created from scratch.

Summary

This brief outline of the condition of the transport infrastructure in Poland shows up the enormous shortcomings in this area while identifying huge opportunities as demand for transportation services, especially by road and air, continues to increase rapidly. It is a challenge for both government and local authorities as, without an increase in expenditure on the modernisation and development of transport infrastructure, economic growth cannot be maintained.

Part 3

Business Development

29

Investment Strategy

Business Management & Finance (BMF)

Introduction

'In the last ten years Poland has made a major step from being an investor's nightmare to becoming an investor's paradise' – this quote from a veteran businessman specialising in Eastern European ventures, while slightly extreme, sets the tone of this chapter.

Poland has indeed become a country where a traditional style of investor relations now rules. Gone are the days when one could hope to buy enterprises at give-away prices or grab a large market position with a few simple moves. Fortunately, also gone are the times when one could expect the sudden introduction of a new law on taxation or political efforts to stop foreigners from 'taking over' Polish industry. Today, investing in Poland is in many ways more similar to investing in EU countries than one might expect. Nevertheless, there are some particularities that could harm the unaware or allow the knowledgeable to reap additional profits.

So, how would one approach setting out an investment strategy for Polish projects?

Reason for investment

The first and most obvious question to keep clear in one's mind throughout the process is why one is planning to invest in Poland. The main reason is the advantageous combination of cheaper (by EU standards) labour rates with close geographical proximity, allowing for ease of management control and fast transportation. (Compare this to the Far East, where labour is cheaper but lead times for orders and delivery much longer.) This is clearly an advantage once you are already in Poland but what about the costs of closing down or moving existing European facilities? These costs, coupled with associated labour problems, often deter European companies from making such a move. The reasons one should still proceed are the other strategic advantages presented by Poland. These do differ depending on the sector of the economy one is interested in but, in general, as Poland benefits from one of the fastest GDP growth rates in the world, most business sectors will develop there faster than elsewhere in Europe.

In the age of globalisation and falling tariffs, one should seriously look at Poland as an important point on the European or global competition map. What if this company is acquired or this plant opened not by you but by your competitor? Now is the time when the game to gain position and market share is being played.

Finally, one should not take investment decisions in Poland for opportunistic reasons such as 'a company has been offered for sale and it looks cheap, so let's buy it'. As one would expect, opportunities are looked at by hundreds of investors, so if they pass on them there must be a good reason. Also, experience shows that you will eventually have to pay at least a fair market price for what you buy.

Special incentives

The number of opportunities for special treatment of investors by the State Treasury or tax authorities has rapidly declined. Currently, any notable extra benefits for your investment can only be gained by investing in the Special Economic Zones (SEZs). These generally offer up to ten years of corporate taxation holidays and a possible further ten years of half-rated taxation (SEZs were set up for a period of 20 years). The issue of SEZs has become controversial as a result of recent EU accession negotiations. It now seems that there will be only a limited possibility of benefiting from the SEZ scheme: only certain types of investment will qualify and only if they are started by the end of the year 2000.

Special treatment in the case of investments in difficult sectors such as coal mining, steel, shipbuilding etc is also only of general nature (for example, special programmes for industries undergoing employment reduction) and will not be offered for a particular investment project. Polish authorities have learnt that it might be more beneficial to allow an enterprise to fail (eg the Gdansk shipyard) than to create a precedent of government assistance and risk conflict with EU officials.

Influence of EU accession

It has to be said that one of the key reasons for investing in Poland is its forthcoming membership of the EU (estimated to happen in 2002 or 2003). Yet the same EU membership causes significant turmoil in the legislative and government policy domain. The Polish government has found it difficult to keep a firm stance in negotiations with the EU on all issues and decided to defend just a few critical areas. Thus, one will find sectors with a prolonged adjustment mechanism (steel, fuels etc) and others that are already fully open to EU competition. When planning one's investment strategy, one should note the position and possible reaction of EU competitors – they can put forward claims through the European Commission just as effectively as if Poland were already a part of the EU.

Special restrictions

There seem to be very few unusual restrictions on planned investments. There are anti-monopoly requirements, which do not differ greatly from typical EU standards, and permits are required if majority foreign ownership is being acquired in a land-owning company – but these are usually granted without complications.

Certain sectors require licences to operate, eg liquor production, pharmaceuticals gambling etc, but again these usually apply only where one would also expect such requirements in other countries. It is also worth noting that the current government has undertaken a serious drive to limit the number of licensed activities.

Greenfield or acquisition?

The choice between a greenfield investment and an acquisition is one of the most common to be faced with at the start of the process. In most cases the answer is not obvious. The typical disadvantages of acquisitions, most notable in the early days of Polish privatisation (militant trade unions, major lay-offs being required but impossible to implement etc) are now hardly applicable. Experience shows that investors have in general successfully reduced employment to sustainable levels and introduced sensible work practices. Yes, it takes some time and effort but employees do understand and are willing to co-operate to ensure the future of their company.

Acquiring a company (if a suitable one is available) usually allows one to gain a significant share in the market through the capturing of established distribution channels and service networks. It is also a good means of gaining required permits and licences, which otherwise might be difficult to obtain (eg for pharmaceuticals).

On the other hand, greenfields can be established just as fast as in other EU countries. An investor hires whomever he/she wishes and locates a plant in a spot of his/her choosing (maybe within SEZ). The investor is then left with the task of fighting for market share. Sometimes a suitable compromise is the acquisition of an existing company with an old plant and afterwards the building of a new modern facility to which to move production in time. The best of two worlds?

Sources of acquisition targets

Poland is not typical of most post-communist countries, where the source of acquisition targets is limited to the State Treasury. There are, in fact, many different sources of information on interesting companies to buy.

To begin with, the State Treasury has handed over responsibility for a large number of small companies to a fast-acting Privatisation Agency. Local voivodships (provincial governments) also have responsibility for many enterprises that can be contributed in kind to form joint ventures, with an investor putting up his share in cash.

Further good sources are the Mass Privatisation Funds. After spending years restructuring their portfolio of companies, the funds now need to sell these within one to three years. Between them, the funds still own several hundred quite interesting companies.

Finally, there are many conglomerates quoted on the Warsaw Stock Exchange that bought up numerous privatised companies in the early days of reform. Now, under pressure from their shareholders, these conglomerates need to concentrate on their core activities and are thus happy to sell non-core businesses (a good example is Elektrim).

How to win

To begin with, bear in mind the reasons why you would like to invest in Poland. You are looking to buy into a growing economy, as this will provide long-term returns to your shareholders. Thus your business plans and valuations must take account of expected future growth and be geared towards calculating long-term benefits. (Quick, short-term returns are all but gone.)

Do not expect the vendor representing State Treasury to give you special contractual representations or warranties. Poland is a normal country, where hundreds of businesses co-exist. Regulations essential for the development of your business are just as important for others, so it is safe to assume that they will be introduced. Penalties (eg environmental) that can kill your business could also kill hundreds of others, so their application will be avoided. Polish investors know this, take a pragmatic view and thus often win.

Please treat your counterparts with respect. Poland has recently introduced the concept of a civil service and, in various ministries, you can now finally expect to meet high-ranking officials with experience and track record going beyond the last change of government. These individuals have learnt the rules of business over the last ten years and, even if they have not, your competitors will help them see the flaws in your proposal.

Team up with a local source of capital if you want to limit your exposure. There are dozens of financial investors keen to join a strategic investor developing his/her business in Poland. Among these, Polish-based banks will be good partners as they can provide debt and equity capital as well as local market knowledge and influence.

And, finally, seek assistance. There are several large, well-established Polish- and foreign-owned consultancy practices that deal daily with foreign investments in Poland, have contacts with government officials and have already worked out the solutions to most of your potential problems. They will save you a lot of time and money and help you successfully establish a profitable business in Poland.

30

Foreign Investment Regime

Janusz Adamkowski, CMS Cameron McKenna

Historical background

In 1999 Poland celebrated the 10th anniversary of the date when it commenced real political and economic change. The word *real* is worth highlighting since one may think that all developments, including foreign investment in Poland, began then. But this would not be correct.

A careful historian could find that the first references to foreign investment appeared in post-war socialist legislation in 1976, but in fact the first significant invitation issued to foreign investors came in 1982 with the idea of establishing the so-called Polish-Polonian enterprises. The relevant Act of Parliament of 6 July 1982 was mainly addressed to foreign businessmen claiming Polish roots and it created a basis for establishing small and medium-sized operations.

In the mid-1980s, Poland's economy was a catastrophe. A chaotic macro-economic policy was being followed, with market shortages, high inflation and huge foreign debt. It was then that the first real invitation to foreign investors was made through the promulgation of the Act on Companies with Foreign Capital Participation of 23 April 1986. This should probably be considered the effective date of the beginning of foreign direct investments into Poland.

The late 1980s were really a time for pioneers, and the life of the foreign investor was not easy. The regulatory regime and legislative framework were restrictive and very formal. Conditions improved in 1990 and thereafter, when the programme of economic reforms known as the Balcerowicz Plan or 'shock therapy' were introduced.

In 1991, the foreign investment regime was again reformulated and liberalised and the new law, the Act on Companies with Foreign Participation of 14 June 1991, was passed. Numerous amendments have been made to this act over the years, reflecting the steady progress of economic reform in Poland and the adjustments provided in the legislative regime established for foreign investors. This is still a continuous process, supported by milestones such as joining the World Trade Organisation (WTO), joining the OECD in July 1996, joining NATO and the commencement of accession negotiations to the EU.

The perception of Poland being a country of high investment risk was common several years ago, but this has changed and the investment opportunities offered in Poland have been recognised by more and more foreign investors. The Polish government also recognises that foreign capital plays a vital role in the Polish economy.

Foreign investment regime 1999

The Act on Companies with Foreign Participation of 14 June 1991 (the 'Foreign Investment Law' or the 'Act') was an important piece of legislation at the time it was passed. But it is now (as it was then) only one of the elements of the foreign investment regulatory regime, which in fact includes many other legal regulations. The 1991 Act aimed at providing equal conditions of operation for both foreign and domestic investors. As mentioned above, many changes to the Act were introduced over the years to minimise the scope of two-way regulation.

Therefore, if we look into the foreign investment regulatory regime as a whole, we will also need to include a group of other regulations concerning specific areas, including: the acquisition of real estate by foreigners (see Chapter 43 on Property Ownership); foreign exchange control regulations; customs regulations; investments in the financial sector; specific regulations related to selected activities (telecommunications, banking, pensions, gambling, energy, privatisation in general etc). The foreign investment regime is supported by bilateral agreements on avoiding double taxation and on supporting and providing mutual protection of investments.

The Commercial Code plays an important role in any foreign investment performed in Poland, as it regulates the establishment and operation of commercial companies, which are an indispensable instrument for any investor.

Finally, foreign investors will need to abide by and observe the provisions of employment regulations. Immigration regulations do not impact directly on the foreign investment regime but some may apply.

What follows summarises the basic regulations and the key terms subject to which foreign investors may establish and operate their business in Poland. 'Investment' is understood in this paper to mean direct investment and excludes activities beyond the establishment of a permanent base in Poland, ie of a company or representative office.

Foreign Investment Law

Although the Foreign Investment Law in its present form now represents less than 20 per cent of the original act passed in 1991, it still purports to provide the general framework and core regulations for the foreign investment regime.

The Act stipulates that foreign entities are natural persons domiciled abroad, legal persons having their registered seat abroad and business associations established by the persons mentioned above, which lack legal personality and which are formed under the laws of foreign countries. According to the Law, a legal person who holds a registered seat in Poland that is controlled by a foreign party will also be deemed a foreign entity. Control is understood to mean that the foreign entity possesses, directly or indirectly, a majority of votes in the shareholders' meeting or is empowered to appoint or dismiss the majority of members of the management board. Also, companies where more than half of the members of the management board are simultaneously members of the management board or top executives of a foreign entity, or of any other party controlled by the foreign entity, are deemed to be controlled by foreign parties.

Investors may use one of the two available investment vehicles: either a limited liability company or a joint-stock company (see Chapter 37 on Setting up a Company). Both types of corporations are regulated by the Commercial Code. The company can be fully owned by foreign investors or represent a joint venture with Polish investors.

A new Business Activity Act proposed by the government and currently being discussed in parliament is expected to grant foreign investors, subject to reciprocity in the country of origin and except where international treaties may provide otherwise, national treatment with respect to the establishment of business entities in Poland. Additionally, in the absence of reciprocity, the permitted forms of foreign-owned businesses will be expanded to include limited partnerships and branches.

Permits

Requirements to obtain a permit have been removed for certain activities and, at present, a permit issued by the Minister of the State Treasury is only required where the state legal person intends:

- to enter into a contract with a company with foreign participation by which the latter entity will be entitled to: 1) use, for a period longer than six months, the property of a state legal person, be that a separate enterprise, real estate or a part of an enterprise capable of being used for specific business purposes; or 2) by which it will acquire the ownership of such property; or 3) in the circumstances as described in 1) the foreign person would acquire the shares in a company that uses the property of a state legal person, permit is required for the acquisition of shares.

- to take up shares in a company with foreign participation and contribute to its initial share capital a non-monetary contribution including property as described above.

The Minister of the State Treasury will refuse to grant a permit only where entering into above transactions could be detrimental to the country's economic interests, national security, defence or protection of state secrets. The protection of state interests may also prompt the minister to specify the additional conditions to be complied with by the company when granting the permit.

Other than the above mentioned permits, separate licences and permits issued by different administrative authorities may be required by other regulations in order to undertake some economic activities. According to the Law on Economic Activities of 23 December 1988, such activities include, *inter alia*, the prospecting for and extraction of minerals, the manufacture of tobacco products, airport transport and other air services. Other regulations require obtaining a licence for the undertaking of business activities in areas such as insurance, foreign currency dealings, telecommunications or banking.

Capital contribution

The Foreign Investment Law does not contain any special requirements as regards the minimum share capital of the company set up by foreign investors. Therefore, the general rules specified in the Commercial Code apply.

Protection of foreign investors

The Act provides legal protection for foreign entities where such entities have suffered losses resulting from acts of expropriation or implementation of other means causing effects equivalent to expropriation. In such cases, foreign entities are entitled, based on the principle of reciprocity, to compensation up to the amount corresponding to such entity's participation in the assets of the company. The Law stipulates that the foreign entity may apply to the Minister of Finance for the issuance, on behalf of the State Treasury, of a guarantee of payment of such compensation.

The transfer of profits and the repatriation of investments due upon sale or redemption of a shareholding or liquidation are no longer regulated by the Act but have now, in a very complex way, been included in the Foreign Exchange Regulations.

Foreign exchange regulations

The changes made to foreign exchange control regulations over the past few years are also a good example of the continuous development of the business environment in Poland.

In its current form, the Law on Foreign Exchange of 18 December 1998 has more to say to foreign investors than does the Foreign Investment Law. The law has introduced a new concept of residents and non-residents and also free foreign exchange turnover. This freedom is restricted to a certain degree, and both residents and non-residents may be required, under certain circumstances, to apply for a permit. Permits are granted by the president of the National Bank of Poland.

Various forms and acts of foreign exchange have been classified by the new Foreign Exchange Law but, from the foreign investor's point of view, the most interesting is the distinction between current and capital turnover and, within the latter, a clear distinction between direct and portfolio investments. Direct investments encompass: establishing companies; acquiring shares and assets in existing companies that carry rights to at least 10 per cent of the votes at the general meetings of shareholders; acquiring ownership and similar rights; providing financing to companies; obtaining revenue from the sale of shares, rights or property as well as from liquidation. Portfolio investments are dealings on the securities market that provide the investor with up to 10 per cent of the votes at a company's general meeting of shareholders. Over that limit, an investment is deemed to be direct.

The Foreign Exchange Law is supported by a block exemption regulation – a regulation by the Minister of Finance dated 8 January 1999, specifying situations where there is a release from restrictions in foreign exchange turnover.

Representative offices

Foreign companies can also establish a presence in Poland through opening representative offices that are governed by Polish law. According to the Ordinance of the Council of Ministers of 6 February 1976, foreign entities (both natural and legal persons) may set up their representative offices in Poland in the form of a branch office, technical information office or supervisory office. This requires obtaining a permit from the Minister of Economy or other relevant ministers or heads of central administration offices. A branch office may undertake business activities in areas such as foreign trade, transportation, travel services and cultural services. A technical information office is limited to disseminating technical and scientific information on the products of its parent company, whereas a supervisory office supervises the performance of contracts signed with Polish companies. Representative offices may employ both Polish and foreign nationals. Since a branch office is the only type of representative office entitled to undertake business activities, it is subject to tax liabilities in Poland. As mentioned earlier, draft legislation on business activities will eventually regulate this area as well.

Privatisation of state property

The privatisation process in Poland is now well advanced but there are still hundreds of state-owned companies that offer investment opportunities for foreign investors. Privatisation can be implemented via a number of methods.

Since 1990 two basic methods have been used in Poland when privatising state-owned enterprises, ie privatisation through capitalisation and privatisation through liquidation. The former, which is also called indirect privatisation, is implemented through the transformation of a state-owned enterprise into a limited liability company or a joint-stock company, wholly owned by the State Treasury. Shares of this newly created company are then sold to third parties by auction, public offering or negotiations entered into through public invitation. This method of privatisation applies mainly to large companies. Privatisation through liquidation, often called direct privatisation, usually takes place for small and medium-sized companies. Within the framework of this method, the liquidated enterprise or any organised parts of its estate can be sold, contributed to another company or leased for a specified time to a company set up by employees of the liquidated enterprise or other entities. Both methods of privatisation are regulated in the Law on the Commercialisation and Privatisation of State Companies of 30 August 1996.

Another privatisation method was of a mass nature and was basically intended to ensure that Poles were the major beneficiaries of the privatisation process. The process was commenced on December 1994 through the setting up of 15 National Investment Funds (NIFs). The State Treasury then contributed to these funds the shares of state-owned joint-stock companies covered by the Mass Privatisation Programme. According to the Law on National Investment Funds and their Privatisation of 30 April 1993, the task of the funds is to boost the value of the assets of these companies, especially through an increase in the value of their shares. On November 1995, share certificates representing shareholdings in each NIF were made available to all adult Polish citizens in return for a fixed fee. These certificates were last year converted into shares in NIFs after these were admitted to public trading on the Warsaw Stock Exchange. It was hoped that the Mass Privatisation Programme would enhance foreign investment in the participating companies and have a significant impact on the growth of the Polish capital market.

Securities

The main source of law regulating the securities market in Poland is the Law on Public Trading in Securities of 21 August 1997 and the Law on Investment Funds of 28 August 1997.

The Laws define the public trading of securities as an offering, purchase or transfer of rights incorporated in securities issued in series where this is offered, by using mass media or other means, to more than 300 persons or to an addressee who is not identified. The Laws and executive regulations contain a number of exclusions from this general rule. For example, the Laws do not apply to preferential offers of shares to employees under the privatisation legislation, trading in cheques and bills of exchange and trading in deposit certificates and other similar documents issued by banks.

According to the Laws, public trading in securities can only be conducted by brokerage businesses. These, including banks, are subject to licensing by the Securities Commission, which plays the role of central regulator of the securities market in Poland. One of the Commission's tasks is to oversee the observance of rules of fair trading and competition on this market. Brokerage activities can be conducted by foreign parties.

In order for securities to be admitted to trading on the stock exchange, these must be deposited with the National Securities Depositary Office, which is evidenced by inscribed deposit certificates issued by entities running brokerage business, banks or other entities authorised by the Law.

The Laws distinguish between initial and secondary public trading in securities. The latter can be implemented on stock exchanges run by joint-stock companies and covers transactions entered into after securities have been admitted to public trading. At the moment, only one stock exchange operates in Poland, the Warsaw Stock Exchange, opened in April 1991, and the market is only in shares and government bonds.

The introduction of securities into public trading requires following a special procedure set out by the Securities Law. First of all, the Securities Commission's consent is required for the admission of securities. Application for this consent should be made through the brokerage houses and be accompanied by the issuer's submission of a prospectus and other relevant documents required by the Law. Executive regulations stipulate that the contents of such a prospectus should cover information on the issuer's assets, financial and legal position, and on the securities being introduced into public trading. Following the Commission's consent, securities should be deposited with the National Depositary Office, and the issuer must publish the information on the issuance of securities in two national newspapers and make a prospectus available to the public. Any change of details covered by a prospectus should be notified to the Commission and, in some circumstances, also to the information agency indicated by the Commission. In the latter case, such change should also be published in the press. According to the Law, each subsequent issuance of shares by a joint-stock company whose shares have already been admitted to public trading and are publicly traded should be introduced into such trading. The breach of this rule results in the Commission's cancellation of its consent for the admittance of securities to public trading.

In order for securities to be traded on the stock exchange, a resolution must be passed by the Council of the Warsaw Stock Exchange in which it is specified whether securities will be listed on the main market or on the parallel one. Admittance of securities to the former requires following a number of strict requirements, whereas admittance of securities to the latter is less stringent. Securities are introduced into trading on the stock exchange according to the ordinary procedure or through public sale.

The Law imposes a number of restrictions on public trading in securities where significant shareholdings are purchased or sold by investors. For example, anyone who purchases or sells a stake in a joint-stock company listed on the stock exchange and as a result obtains a certain percentage of votes at the general meeting of shareholders should notify this to the Securities Commission, the Anti-monopoly Office and the company concerned. Prior to the notification, it is not permitted to acquire or sell further shares.

Anti-monopoly Law and unfair competition

The basic law applicable to anti-monopoly issues of mergers and acquisitions is the Act on Counteracting Monopoly Practices of 1990 (the 'Anti-monopoly Law'). The main purpose of the Anti-monopoly Law is to ensure the development of competition, protect entrepreneurs from monopolistic practices and protect the interests of consumers. Apart from regulating certain issues relating to mergers and acquisitions, the Anti-monopoly Law also applies to monopolistic practices and the abuse of a dominant position on the market. It is assumed that an entrepreneur occupies a monopolistic position if he/she has no competition on the local or national market. An entrepreneur occupies a dominant position if he/she has no significant competition on the local or national market. It is presumed that a dominant position is one in which the entrepreneur has more than a 40 per cent share of the market.

The Law requires that the Anti-monopoly Office is notified of any intention to merge or transform economic entities, or to establish an entity that could gain a dominant position on the market. The Office has the power to prevent the merger, transformation or establishment if he/she would lead to the relevant entity gaining a dominant position. The Office also has the power to order the division or liquidation of entities that permanently limit competition.

The Office for Protection of Competition and Consumers (the 'Office') is the administrative organ responsible for enforcing the Anti-monopoly Law. The Office is a part of the state administration and is directly answerable to the government. The Office is authorised to issue permits, approvals etc when these are required by law, and can impose fines and other sanctions in case of non-compliance with the Anti-monopoly Law. Any decision of the Office may be appealed by the party of the administrative proceedings to the Anti-monopoly Court, which, as a second instance, may uphold, change or reject such a decision.

The Law on Unfair Competition of 16 April 1993 prohibits acts of unfair competition that endanger or infringe the public interest or the interests of market participants (ie persons carrying on an economic activity, customers and consumers). In particular, prohibited acts include dumping, trade mark infringement, false advertising and misleading comparative advertising, dissemination of false and confusing information and disclosure of business secrets. The Unfair Competition Law provides for civil liability and, for certain types of unfair competition, for criminal liability.

Conclusions

The Accession Agreement with the EU committed Poland to the adjustment of its legal regulations to European standards. A significant part of this work has already been done and there are many areas where Poland has modern and compliant legal regulations. There are many other legal projects currently pending, such as a new Companies Act, to replace the Commercial Code created in 1934.

As mentioned at the beginning of this chapter, the foreign investment regime is the set of various legal regulations that either entirely (eg on the acquisition of real estate by foreigners) or in part contain provisions dedicated to or connected with the business activities of foreign persons and corporations in Poland. Many of these are dealt with in other chapters of this book.

31

Financing with the European Bank for Reconstruction and Development (EBRD)

European Bank for Reconstruction and Development (EBRD)

Introduction

The European Bank for Reconstruction and Development (EBRD) is among the largest foreign investors in Poland. Through its projects, the Bank aims to assist Poland in developing a market economy and works alongside other foreign and domestic investors to achieve this aim. By helping to mitigate project finance risks, the EBRD can help foreign investors achieve commercial success in Poland.

Role of the EBRD

The EBRD was established in 1991 in response to major changes in the political and economic climate in Central and Eastern Europe. Inaugurated less than two years after the fall of the Berlin Wall, the Bank was created to support the transition to market economies in the region following the widespread collapse of communist regimes. Based in London, the EBRD is an international institution with 60 shareholders (58 countries, the EU and the European Investment Bank). Each shareholder is represented on the EBRD's Board of Governors and Board of Directors. The EBRD finances projects using a variety of debt and equity instruments in both the private and public sectors, providing direct funding for financial institutions, infrastructure and other key sectors. Its investments also help to develop skills, to improve the efficiency of markets and to strengthen the institutions that support these markets.

A strength of the EBRD is its in-depth knowledge of its region of operations. As the largest foreign investor in the region's private sector, the EBRD is aware of the problems and the potential of each of its 26 countries of operations. Working closely with private investors, the Bank's staff recognise their concerns about investment in the region and the political and economic uncertainty.

The EBRD operates according to sound banking principles in all of its activities and promotes good business practices. It is careful to ensure that it is 'additional' to the private sector, complementing rather than competing with other private sources of finance.

The EBRD's initial capital base was €10 billion, which was doubled to €20 billion in 1997, allowing the Bank to continue to meet the growing demand for its services and to maintain its commitment to financial self-sustainability.

EBRD financing

The EBRD is keen to encourage co-financiers to take part in its operations – in fact it usually limits its own involvement in private sector projects to 35 per cent of total project cost or capital structure. Apart from private sector companies, the main co-financing partners for the EBRD are commercial banks and other financial institutions. The principal forms of direct financing provided by the EBRD are loans, equity and guarantees. Loans are tailored to meet the particular requirements of the project. The credit risk may be taken entirely by the Bank or partly syndicated to the market. An equity investment may be undertaken in a variety of forms. When the EBRD takes an equity stake, it expects an appropriate return on its investment and will only take a minority position. Guarantees are also provided by the Bank to help borrowers gain access to financing.

Mitigating risk for investment partners

One of the Bank's main advantages is its ability to bear risk, allowing it to extend the boundaries of commercial possibilities in its countries of operations. Where possible, it shares the project risk by acting with other private sector bodies, such as commercial banks and investment funds as well as multilateral lenders. With its AAA credit rating, the EBRD is able to raise funds at the best rates from the international capital markets. By utilising its experience in the region and its advantages as an international financial institution, the EBRD is able to mitigate certain risks, making it an attractive partner. The Bank's participation in a project can help to ensure that the operation is well prepared and implemented. For example, the EBRD will make sure that the project complies with local laws and regulations and that it is financially viable. To help a client attain the required levels of corporate governance and project preparation, the Bank is often able to provide technical assistance funding made available by donor governments.

The EBRD's involvement in a project indicates to the market that the project meets rigorous technical, legal, financial and environmental standards. The Bank is able to structure projects in a way that is likely to attract other financing partners and thereby minimise the risks and costs for the parties involved. One of the main ways of achieving this is by co-financing with private banks, allowing participating banks to benefit from the Bank's preferred creditor status.

The sound management and profitability of a project can be enhanced by the EBRD's presence in an operation. When the Bank takes an equity investment in a company, it uses its influence on the Board to promote good management and to mediate where necessary between local and foreign partners.

A major concern to potential investors is political risk, which, again, the EBRD can help to mitigate. Since all the Bank's countries of operations are represented on the Board of Directors, each member country has the opportunity to object to the approval of any EBRD-financed project. This helps to reduce the threat of any subsequent political risk.

EBRD activities in Poland

As at 31 December 1998, the EBRD had approved 83 investment projects in Poland (excluding projects that have been cancelled), involving direct Bank investment of €1.4 billion. The EBRD's finance helped to mobilise over €5.7 billion of additional investment.

The EBRD has maintained its responsiveness to progress in transition and its 'additionality' through a wide range of initiatives. For example, the Bank has moved across market segments and developed new approaches as the economic transition in Poland has advanced. In particular, the EBRD has adjusted to the transforming Polish market by switching from debt to equity, from Warsaw to the provinces, from foreign-backed joint ventures to Polish companies without foreign shareholders, and from classical bank lending to capital market transactions. It is actively working in the fields of infrastructure, industrial restructuring, and support for small and medium-sized enterprises (SMEs).

Around 87 per cent of EBRD financing has been for private sector operations. One quarter of the Bank's finance has been invested in equity, three quarters in debt. Wholesale lending and equity investments accounted for around 28 per cent of total approvals.

Case study

In June 1997 the EBRD made an equity investment in Hortex, the leading Polish fruit and vegetable processing company. A total of US$28 million was invested by the EBRD in conjunction with the Bank of America for a combined 41 per cent stake in the company. The financing is enabling the company to restructure, modernise and expand its operations in order to improve its profitability. In so doing, the company is enhancing its competitiveness on the domestic market and has been able to expand into markets in the East. The project will also help the company to meet EU requirements in the areas of production, management information and environmental impact.

Key objectives

The EBRD's operational strategy for Poland focuses on the key challenges for the transition to a market economy and emphasises the requirement for a rapid response to new challenges as Poland's transition process moves forward. The Bank is pursuing four operational objectives, as outlined below:

Corporate sector
The EBRD seeks to promote privatisation, restructuring, competition, corporate governance and competent management in sectors where the functioning of markets and the presence and performance of private enterprises must be strengthened. The Bank continues to promote the development of new private enterprises, principally through the equity financing of local enterprises in light manufacturing, consumer products and service sectors. The Bank will continue to participate in the establishment of venture capital funds, in particular provincial-level funds targeting smaller enterprises and cross-border funds that could finance the expansion and integration of Polish businesses on a regional basis.

The Bank is making a special effort to support SMEs through: (a) implementation of the EC-EBRD SME Facility; (b) provision of dedicated credit lines to local banks; (c) continued support to private equity funds; and (d) coordination with bilateral and multilateral institutions.

Financial sector
The EBRD seeks to promote the supply of a broad range of financial structures and products, such as fixed-income securities, asset-backed securities, mortgages, leasing services, insurance products, mutual funds and specialised structured finance. The Bank co-operates closely with local financial institutions to help expand their capacity to provide innovative forms of financing and their ability to compete as the financial sector is deregulated and opened further to foreign entry. The EBRD

continues to make direct investments in local financial institutions, particularly in the co-operative banking sector and in non-bank financial institutions, such as insurance companies, pension funds and consumer finance institutions.

Infrastructure and environment
The EBRD finances infrastructure, municipal and environmental investments and contributes to the increasing use of local currency financing in infrastructure and utilities projects.

The EBRD continues to promote the implementation of energy-saving investments in the private and public sectors by investing in and providing loans to energy service companies. In addition, the Bank will support the rehabilitation of district heating networks by promoting privatisation and restructuring in the sector. The EBRD also seeks to provide financing to industrial companies with the implementation of comprehensive investment programmes aimed at reducing excessive energy consumption.

Additional information

Further information about the EBRD's activities in Poland and its projects with investment partners can be found on the Bank's Website (www.ebrd.com). The site contains the full text of the Bank's key publications, such as the *Annual Report* and *Financing with the EBRD*, which details the Bank's lending requirements. More information about the investment climate in Poland and its latest progress in the transition process can be found in the EBRD's *Transition Report*, published each November.

Contacting the EBRD

Alain Pilloux
Business Group Director, Central Europe
European Bank for Reconstruction and
  Development (EBRD)
One Exchange Square
London EC2A 2JN
United Kingdom
Tel: + 44 20 7338 6521
Fax: + 44 20 7338 7199

Irene Grzybowski
Country Director, Poland
European Bank for
  Reconstruction and
  Development (EBRD)
53 Emili Planter Street
Warsaw Financial Centre
13th Floor, Suite 1300
00–113 Warsaw
Poland
Tel: + 48 22 520 5700
Fax: + 48 22 520 5800

32

Sources of Equity and Debt Finance

Pawel Lipinski, BRE Bank

Introduction

Many domestic firms in Poland lack sufficient equity to accommodate their restructuring needs and to finance investments. The inflow of foreign capital, which increases in lockstep with the Polish privatisation process, helps at least partly to meet the demand for capital. The total value of foreign direct investment in Poland between the early 1990s and the end of 1998 exceeded US$30.8 billion.

The Polish market allows for a number of securitised financing instruments to raise capital and fund investments:

- public issuance of shares;

- private placements;

- public borrowing through the issue of commercial paper or bonds.

Public issuance of stock

The Law on Public Trading of Securities of 21 August 1997 regulates the public trading of securities.

All companies wishing to be listed must submit a prospectus prepared in conformity with certain requirements to the Securities and Exchange Commission. In particular, the prospectus must contain information with respect to the following:

- the issue itself and the issuing company;

- the individuals responsible for the management of the company;

- the description of the company's activities;

- the company's financial data;

- its development prospects.

Companies that wish to access the **main market** of the Warsaw Stock Exchange (WSE) must fulfil certain requirements, including:

- a minimum book value of at least Zl 65 million;
- a minimum share capital of at least Zl 7 million;
- a minimum value of shares to be listed of Zl 40 million;
- at least 500 shareholders holding the shares to be listed;
- a combined pre-tax profit for the last three financial years of at least Zl 16 million and proof of a gross profit made in the last financial year.

Companies approved for public trading must publish periodic reports on a monthly (until July '99), quarterly, semi-annual and annual basis and publicly disclose any event that could materially influence the price or value of securities within 24 hours of such an event.

Smaller companies with a shorter track record can be quoted on the **parallel market**. Although continuing disclosure requirements are identical regardless of whether a company is listed on the primary or on the parallel market, initial listing requirements are easier to meet for a parallel market listing:

- the minimum book value requirement is Zl 22 million;
- the minimum share capital required is Zl 3 million;
- the value of shares to be listed must reach Zl 14 million;
- at least 300 shareholders must hold the shares to be listed;
- the company has to have had a pre-tax profit for the most recent financial year.

A third possibility for raising capital through the stock market exists on the **free market**, where listing requirements are even less demanding than on the parallel market.

By year-end 1998, 183 corporations were listed on the WSE (Figure 32.1 shows the number of WSE débuts 1991–98). During 1998, 57 companies, ie 10 more than in 1997, were newly listed on the exchange. A number of listed companies increased their equity through public issues of new shares. Twenty-five brokerage houses acted as Initial Public Offering (IPO) arrangers and 85 financial institutions as equity underwriters.

Companies that wish to enter the public market but do not qualify for a WSE listing can be quoted on the over-the-counter market (OTC). OTC-listed companies do not have to issue a full prospectus but a shorter memorandum, and the listing and disclosure requirements are less restrictive. At the end of 1998, 24 companies were listed on the OTC market.

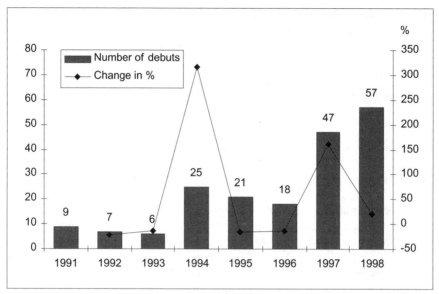

Figure 32.1 Number of débuts on the Warsaw Stock Exchange (WSE)

Private share placements

Private share placements do not guarantee a permanent market valuation for companies nor ensure the liquidity of shares. On the other hand, this source of equity offers some advantageous elements:

- a relatively short time for the raising of capital (from 3 to 6 months);

- low costs in comparison to public issues of shares;

- no listing requirements for the Polish Securities and Exchange Commission;

- no disclosure requirements in either a prospectus or in current and periodic reports;

- the possibility of choosing one's investors and of forming one's own shareholder structure.

Private placements are usually small, reaching up to Zl 10 million. The largest one arranged in 1998 for a utility company from Wroclaw (MPEC) amounted to Zl 72 million and was subscribed by insurance companies. A number of publicly listed companies (eg Prokom, Softbank and Karen) exercised private placements before public trading. Investors comprised corporates, individuals and private-equity funds (Polish Pre-IPO Funds).

Financing through public debt

Polish non-government debt securities include:

- commercial papers;
- municipal bonds;
- corporate bonds;
- certificates of deposits.

Commercial paper

The first commercial paper transactions (CPs) in Poland were executed in 1993–94. At that time, foreign corporations conducting business activities in Poland, such as McDonald's, PepsiCo or Ford, issued most CPs. Since then, a number of Polish companies have issued CPs, particularly companies quoted on the stock exchange (see Figure 32.2). At present, the total number of issuers exceeds 260 companies. The funds raised from the market are used mainly for financing working capital. Additionally, they are used for investment outlays and for bridge financing, before a future share issue can be concluded. In accordance with the new Foreign Exchange Law, the CP market is subject to foreign exchange regulations.

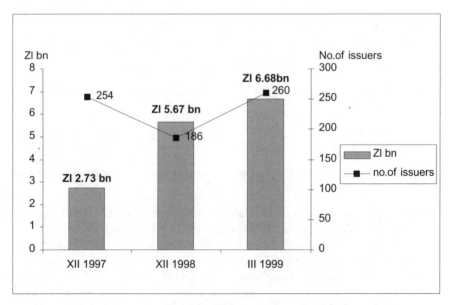

Figure 32.2 Commercial paper (CP) market in Poland

The majority of CPs are issued in the form of promissory notes. Other issues are based on the Act of Bonds (short-term bonds) as well as the Civil Code ('Securities in terms of the Civil Code'). The usual maturity of CPs is three months, although tenors of one or two months are also common, with interest rates based on the respective WIBOR (Warsaw interbank ordinary rate) rates or T-bill yield. Disclosure requirements for issuers are low and not standardised, as the investors do not seek particular information standards. The major investors on the CP market are corporates and banks. Due to legal requirements, insurance companies cannot buy CPs based on promissory notes. Mutual funds cannot invest more than 10 per cent of their assets in non-publicly traded securities. The most active CP arrangers are Bank Handlowy, ING Barings, Pekao S.A., Citibank and BRE Bank.

Municipal bonds

A new law passed in 1995 provides the legal structure for municipal financing and for the introduction of new types of instruments, such as convertibles, income bonds and warrants. These securities can be issued via private placement or through public offerings. All municipal bonds issued so far have been private placements in which the bonds are placed with a small number of institutional investors. At the beginning of 1999, the total volume of bonds issued by cities and municipalities exceeded Zl 600 million. The reform of local governments launched in January 1999 is expected to speed up the development of the municipal bond market.

Corporate bonds

Corporate bonds, including convertible bonds and other bonds, are not very popular in Poland. Companies prefer to take advantage of the CP market, which is more flexible and provides for higher investor demand. Pension funds established in Poland in 1999 as a part of the social security overhaul are likely to prop up the issuance and the demand for longer-term CPs, which yield a higher return than government debt.

Other non-government debt securities

Non-government debt securities include Certificates of Deposits and bank bonds. The main drawback to raising funds through these securities is the obligatory reserve required by the National Bank of Poland (NBP) for the part of the issue that is purchased by non-financial institutions. The new Law on Mortgage Bonds and Mortgage Banks allows mortgage banks to fund their lending through mortgage bonds with longer maturities. These securities will be collateralised and are likely to meet the demand of pension funds. Several domestic and foreign banks have applied to the Banking Supervision Commission for mortgage bank licences. The first one to have received such a licence was the mortgage bank jointly established by BRE Bank and RHEINHYP Rheinische Hypothekenbank.

Financing prospects

Since only a few banks in Poland are in a position to provide large loans to individual borrowers, the prospects for securitised debt financing remain good over the near future, particularly in light of the ongoing financing needs for large investment projects in various sectors of the Polish economy.

33

Structuring Merger and Acquisition Transactions

Business Management & Finance (BMF)

Introduction

For a number of years (until 1998), the Polish capital market was dormant as far as merger and acquisition (M&A) activity was concerned. From 1991, when the Warsaw Stock Exchange (WSE) was re-established, it was rare to see a hostile take-over by a strategic investor. Acquisitions usually took place as a result of a privatisation agreement with the State Treasury or a dedicated capital increase (previously agreed with the management of the targeted company).

During 1998, the Polish capital market changed extensively in this respect, for which there are many reasons. To begin with, the number of companies listed on the WSE has increased dramatically over the last couple of years. At present, companies listed on the WSE are either large, dynamic private enterprises or were originally premium state-owned companies. Usually, companies listed on the WSE are above country average in terms of profitability, growth history and management quality, and that makes them ideal targets for acquisition. Companies listed on the WSE are forced by law to provide investors with regular and accurate financial results, helping investors obtain decent information about the activities of these companies.

During 1998, the Polish capital market went through a number of corrections (including adjusting to the Russian crisis), which made the valuation of companies listed on the WSE attractive for strategic investors looking for a long-term return. In some sectors, like banking, acquisitions were very visible, sometimes hostile and always widely discussed. In many of those deals, banks were targeted by more than one investor and minority investors benefited from sharp price increases driven by competitive bids.

At the same time foreign investors were showing strong interest in establishing operations in Poland, due to increased confidence in the development of the Polish economy, especially after Poland weathered the Russian crisis with no major lasting effects.

Market regulations

The Bill on Public Trading of August 1997 forms the legal framework for M&A activity on the Polish capital market. Precise regulations regarding acquisitions of large stakes were updated at the end of 1998 and now reflect the experience gained during 1998.

This chapter provides some general guidelines for investors investigating acquisition as one of the means for expansion of their business activity in Poland. We have tried to highlight the most important constraints that must be taken into account by someone planning an acquisition in Poland. Opinions presented in this chapter should not be treated as any sort of legal advice or as the basis of any serious investment decision. Every deal should be considered separately and legal advice should always be obtained.

Acquiring a block of shares

Investors wishing to acquire shares in a Polish public company should remember that the acquisition of more than 5 per cent of voting shares must be promptly reported to the Polish Securities and Exchange Commission (SEC) and to the Polish Press Agency. Investors must also report the acquisition of 10 per cent of shares and all purchases resulting in a further increase of more than 2 per cent.

Anybody planning to acquire a strategic stake faces a practical problem in terms of preserving confidentiality, usually a condition of success. The rapid and secret purchase of a large stake may also be difficult as a result of further regulation stating that the purchase of more than 10 per cent of shares within 90 days can only be made through a public offer.

Before such a public offer can be announced, a number of approvals must be obtained:

- In order to acquire shares in a publicly traded company it is important to obtain the approval of the SEC, which must approve acquisitions of shares resulting in control of over 25, 33 or 50 per cent of votes. In theory, the SEC must give approval or rejection within 14 days. In practice, this process can be delayed if some additional information is required. The SEC may only halt the process if it could prove harmful to the Polish economy.

- In order to acquire a strategic stake in a company with significant influence on the competition and the market (as defined by Polish law), permission must be obtained from the Anti-monopoly Office. Such approval is necessary in cases where more than 25, 33 or 50 per cent of shares are purchased. In the case of public companies, the Anti-monopoly Office must give a response within 14 days, while, for companies that are not publicly listed, the process may take longer.

If a targeted company is a bank or insurance company, additional approval must be sought from the Bank Supervision Commission (KNB) or from the Ministry of Finance respectively:

- When buying a stake in a bank, the KNB should be informed of any purchase resulting in gaining control of more than 5 per cent of shares. Buying more than 10, 20, 25, 33, 50, 66 or 75 per cent also requires permission from the KNB. In practice, a newcomer may face serious obstacles in obtaining this permission. Unlike the SEC and the Antimonopoly Office, the KNB has much more flexibility in defining the criteria upon which permission can be granted. The process of licensing may therefore take a bit longer and this should be taken into account when the structure of the transaction is being designed.

- In the case of buying a stake in an insurance company, permission from the Ministry of Finance must be obtained for the purchase of more than 25, 33, 50, 66 or 75 per cent of shares.

Under Polish law, purchases within a period of 90 days of more than 10 per cent of shares in a listed company are only possible through a public offer. In such an offer, the buyer must state the price and number of shares to be purchased. If, as a result of the tender, there are more shares offered for sale than the investor is willing to buy, then proportional reduction is used. The public offer of purchase may be cancelled only in case of a competitive bid being announced. During the period when the offer to buy shares is announced, the buyer is not allowed to make any transactions on the open market (sell or buy shares).

Sometimes transactions are structured in such a way that a strategic investor acts in consort with one or more financial institutions. Buying through a consortium may help to acquire larger packages of shares without being subject to the restrictions applicable in the case of a purchase being made by a single entity. Using a financial investor as a nominee shareholder is sometimes used by investors as a way of avoiding the delay in obtaining the necessary permissions. One must be very careful when structuring transactions with the participation of other entities. Sometimes such action may be construed by regulators as an attempt to bypass legal restrictions and may cause difficulties in obtaining the necessary official approvals. In some cases this could even lead to a violation of law (ie if entities have capital links), which could in turn damage the transaction.

In some cases, and prior to announcing a public offer, the buyer can be successful in reaching a private agreement with shareholders of the company. In such a case, it is important to define the way in which shares will be transferred from one entity to the other. Open market transactions are rarely used in this case. It is possible, however, to execute an off-session block transaction. Again, it must be noted that no more than 10 per cent of shares can be purchased at one time (within 90 days). If a block is larger than 10 per cent, the only way is to announce a public offer, wait 90 days or involve a financial intermediary.

Certain classes of shares (in public companies) are not traded at the stock exchange (if, for instance, these are registered shares with additional voting rights). In such special cases, the SEC is empowered to issue a permit allowing the execution of the sale. Such permits are granted only in very special, well-justified cases.

If an investor, as a result of his transactions, takes control of over 50 per cent of shares of a company, then he must announce a public offer, allowing all other investors to sell their shares in the company. In this respect, regulations governing purchases of large stakes are a little bit more flexible when the buyer is subscribing for new shares, shares bought in an Initial Public Offering (IPO) or from the State Treasury.

The State Treasury as shareholder

In some cases, the State Treasury holds significant blocks of shares. Acquiring those shares may be the key to acquiring control of a company. The State Treasury is subject to numerous restrictions and is only allowed to sell shares according to strictly defined procedures. These procedures may only be amended in exceptional cases, with the approval of the Council of Ministers. One instance that is not governed by standard ministerial procedures is the response to an offer of purchase announced by an investor. As the State Treasury may not be in a position to respond rapidly to such an offer, possible delays should be taken into account in deals where the State Treasury is a shareholder of the targeted company.

The State Treasury also has certain privileges. For instance, it is allowed to publicly conduct the process of the share sale, providing that the block for sale exceeds 10 per cent of shares in the company (the company may also be a publicly listed one). Buying a stake from the State Treasury in a process initiated by its ministry, together with additional purchases on the open market, could be an excellent opportunity to acquire control of a company.

Due diligence

One of the main problems usually faced by investors is the performing of a due diligence process for targeted companies. The problem is of a practical nature and is an important one. Some investors are not prepared to announce an offer of purchase without conducting full due diligence. Starting due diligence usually means that secrecy becomes difficult, thus increasing the risk that information about the merger could leak out. Again, an early announcement of the deal may spoil the transaction. For this reason, investors are often forced to base their investment decision on publicly known data and on limited due diligence. Fortunately the scope of information which is announced by Polish listed companies is fairly comprehensive. In the case of a hostile take-over, investors can only base their decisions on publicly available information.

Once again it should be remembered that every transaction must be separately designed to match specific legal and economic constraints. It is therefore absolutely crucial to obtain support from a brokerage house, and from legal and financial advisors who are familiar with transactions on the public market.

34

Environmental Issues

Robert Adamczyk, W S Atkins Polska

Introduction

The West has often seen Eastern European countries, including Poland, as having serious environmental problems and a lack of institutional regulations. However, this is only partially the case, as environmental regulations are often well developed and, in some instances, the mechanisms employed go far beyond those of certain EU countries. Nevertheless, historic legacies remain, with many Soviet era industrial sites lacking appropriate pollution abatement equipment or being associated with substantial soil or ground-water pollution

Over the past 10 years, significant strides have been made, with environmental issues at the forefront of many industrial investments. In 1998, Poland spent around €2.1 billion, or 1.7 per cent of GDP, on environmental investments. However there is a lack of appropriate infrastructure and this is a major area of investment need and currently presents a potential bottleneck with respect to development. Areas needing specific attention include waste-water treatment, waste management and the ability to deal with contaminated land etc. Therefore, environmental issues need to be carefully considered by every investor operating in Poland.

This is particularly important in the light of Poland's planned entry to the EU, which requires Poland to adopt and implement all of the EU's environmental legislation. Some estimates indicate that Poland will need to invest around €32 billion just to comply with current EU environmental requirements. This presents potential opportunities given the investments needed: for instance, from 2000 Poland will be eligible for EU ISPA (Instrument for Structural Policies for Pre-accession) funding. These funds for environmental investments should be in the region of €200–300 million in addition to what Poland already spends on the environment. Outlined below are some of the key requirements that should be considered by any potential investor in Poland.

Regulatory framework

Institutions

There are several environmental regulatory and enforcement authorities in Poland, including the national, regional and local levels of administration. The key environmental regulators are:

- Ministry of Environmental Protection, Natural Resources and Forestry;

- other environmentally-related ministries, including those of Physical Planning and Construction, Industry, Health & Social Welfare;

- Environmental Departments within voivodship authorities (provincial governments);

- local authorities (*powiat, starostwo, gmina*)

The key environmental enforcement agencies are the state and voivodship Environmental Protection Inspectorates (PIOŚ [now IOŚ] and WIOŚ respectively).

Since the administrative reform of 1998, the majority of environmental permitting activity has been transferred from the voivodship to the *powiat* (*starostwo*) level. The voivodship is still involved in investments deemed hazardous to the environment, as listed in the 'EIA (Environmental Impact Assessment) Ordinance', or if the activity passes a certain threshold (such as amount or type of waste produced for a waste permit). In practice, the *powiat* authorities can be under-resourced in certain areas and hence seek additional back-up from the voivodship environmental departments and Inspectorates.

Key regulations

Since the 1980s Poland has developed extensive environmental legislation in separate environmental laws (acts, executive orders and ordinances), as well as in related fields. Key legislation includes:

- Environmental Protection and Management Act 1980, as amended (most significantly in 1997);

- 1974 Water Law, as amended;

- Waste Act 1997, as amended;

- Physical Planning Act 1994;

- Building Law 1994;

- Other legislation such as that on forests and farming land, nature conservation, highway planning, geology and mining, the State Environmental Protection Inspectorate etc.

There are numerous Executive Acts to each major Act and, as a general rule, environmental standards or threshold values are included in the Executive Acts. Some of the standards that need to be considered include those concerned with:

- ambient air quality;

- emissions from combustion processes with differentiation according to fuel used and between new and old plants; additional process-specific standards are pending;

- water quality;

- surface water standards;

- waste water discharged to surface water and soil;

- noise;

- health & safety standards (worker exposure levels).

As mentioned, some environmental standards are not legally binding but rather used as guidelines by the authorities. These include:

- surface water classification guidelines;

- soil and groundwater clean-up guidelines ('PIOŚ Guidelines').

Permits

Environmental permits are issued under Polish law in the form of administrative decisions deriving their legal effect from the statutory provisions of numerous environmental statutes. Administrative decisions are resolutions of a relevant governmental or self-governmental authority that regulate the rights and obligations of a particular party.

As appropriate to the enterprise, the following are likely to be required:

- air emission permit;

- waste disposal permit;

- waste management permit (licences to operate for entities generating waste);

- water and waste-water permit;

- storm-water permit;

- hazardous waste and material storage permit;

- agricultural and wooded land conversion permit;

- mining concessions.

Fiscal measures

One interesting aspect is the use of fiscal measures. Among these are 'environmental fees' for use of the environment and fines for breaches of permits. The fees, although small for most entities, can reach millions of US dollars for large facilities and serve as a basis of funding for environmental schemes in Poland (through the use of National and Regional Environmental Funds). Fines payable for exceeding limits provided for in permits, as well as, for instance, unauthorised deposition of waste etc, are not tax deductible and can reach high levels. In the past, it was easier in some cases not to have a permit and to pay a higher fine rather than to invest in pollution clean-up equipment. This loophole is being closed, notably with respect to air emissions, where the penalty for not having a valid permit will, from 2000, be increased by 500 per cent (ie five times normal fine level).

Fines are issued as an administrative decision. Air and waste 'environmental fees' are now calculated by each entity on a quarterly and annual basis respectively and paid by the entities in a similar way to tax obligations.

Implementation of environmental regulations

It should be noted that there is no framework legislation for integration of environmental regulations. In consequence, there is still much room for a discretionary approach by the authorities. Furthermore, based on the local environmental situation, each voivodship has the right to impose stricter regional environmental standards and regulations than those provided at the national level. This is potentially a very powerful tool in the hands of the authorities, and has been used, for instance, with respect to air emission permitting for large power plants.

Enforcement of standards is conducted by the Inspectorate, which has the right to access sites and conduct appropriate investigations (including monitoring). The inspectorate activity is focused on major industrial entities but moves are also made to control small facilities. To this effect a list of 80 so-called 'major' polluters was drawn up in the early 1990s. These entities are subject to more frequent inspection and enforcement actions.

The need to adopt the *acquis communautaire* (legal heritage of the EU) will emphasise the need for further changes to Polish environmental legislation. A key issue under discussion is a new framework law that would include provisions for Best Available Techniques (BAT – IPPC Directive requirement), clarification of the EIA approach and access to information. Among issues under discussion are provisions for tradable permits.

Liability issues

Environmental liabilities can result from both past and present operations. It is possible that they may include clean-up of contaminated land, or the need for a new abatement plant in order to meet current and possible future regulatory environmental requirements. Moreover, potential future development constraints need to be considered. The different types of environmental liability are:

- regulatory liability;

- civil liability;

- criminal liability.

Currently, Polish law does not involve the notion of criminal liability for corporate entities. However, administrative liability can be seen as a substitute for criminal liability of corporations. Although Polish environmental law does not refer specifically to liability for groundwater or soil contamination, article 82 of the Environmental Protection Act 1980, as amended, allows the voivodship to issue a clean-up order, in order to bring the site to its 'proper' condition. Although clean-up orders have been rare to date, it is anticipated that such requirements will increase in the future.

Under the Civil Code, if several persons are liable for damage, their liability is joint and several. Under the provision, it is immaterial if damage was caused by an entity that had a permit. Although environmental litigation is still rare in Poland, mechanisms for claims do exist.

The foreign investor

For the foreign investor, environmental issues need to be considered as they can have a direct or indirect financial impact: environmental regulators sometimes perceive any ownership changes as a means of improving environmental performance. The investor will often face environmental issues at three specific points:

- site development: brownfield or greenfield;

- acquisition or merger type transaction;

- operational requirements (day-to-day compliance with regulations).

In the rest of this chapter the first two of these contingencies are reviewed, considering the procedures and some key risks associated with site development and acquisition of an industrial entity in Poland.

Development

Development of existing or new facilities in Poland requires the proposal to go through planning procedures. Depending on the type of activity, an Environmental Impact Assessment will be required as part of the initial planning application (WZiZT) and subsequently to support the building permit application. The need for an EIA is dependent upon whether the investment is judged as presenting significant potential harm or as being harmful to the environment. An investment deemed as potentially significantly harmful requires the approval of the voivodship authorities, while that judged harmful needs the approval of the *powiat authority*.

The EIA process is slightly unusual in Poland and to the European investor it often resembles more of an environmental statement rather than a full EIA. There is a regulatory requirement that all EIAs be prepared by experts recognised by the Minister of the Environment.

Additional issues other than EIA that should be considered at the early stage of making an investment decision are:

- execution of preliminary investigations (asbestos, buried structures etc.);

- technical conditions, notably roads and utilities.

Regulations state the minimum scope of the EIA. Public participation provisions are still of a general nature and in practice remain weak. Nevertheless, local opposition to a project can substantially affect an investment, with NGOs (non-governmental organisations) sensitive to some developments. A more detailed EIA is required before a building permit is issued but sometimes the two can be combined. Planning applications can be made and granted for a site that is not owned by the investor; in practice, obtaining it is seen as a prerequisite for a real estate transaction. If the EIA at this stage is too vague or is not conducted at all, then a risk arises of additional 'investment' obligations imposed by the local authorities during the subsequent building permit application. It is therefore important that the application procedure and the EIA are carefully considered prior to purchasing a site.

In terms of developing brownfield sites, additional issues include heritage and contaminated land. If a proper due diligence has not been conducted, then the EIA may raise planning aspects that could seriously hold up a project. In practice, we have come across investors being substantially delayed by 'unscheduled' archaeological works disposal of contaminated land/structure (including asbestos) or having to deal with potentially listed buildings on site. It should be viewed that the EIA can also significantly affect the quality of the planning decision when received. However, this is often a commercial development issue and thus beyond the scope of this article.

Mergers and acquisitions

For acquisitions, it is the norm for the investor to take on all liability for past pollution. It is possible to structure some deals so as to avoid past regulatory liability, though this may not be possible for land contamination, which may have knock-on effects for the property's value. As a general rule, a new site owner is potentially liable for any necessary clean-up of past pollution.

As there is (thus far) no comprehensive regulation concerning environmental liability in the privatisation process, the seller's and/or purchaser's responsibility for clean-up and control technology is considered on an *ad hoc* basis. It is the norm that the seller (the government) initially carries the environmental liability but this is transferred at the time of sale. Any costs assessed (actual and projected) are either deducted from the purchase price or covered/shared by the seller and purchaser as agreed.

In a number of sales where prior due diligence Environmental Audits were carried out, the following solutions have been adopted:

- adjustments in the purchase price to reflect the purchaser's assumption of responsibility for clean-up;

- transfer of an increased number of shares in return for assuming responsibility for clean-up;

- establishing a contingency fund to cover any unexpected costs of clean-up;

- agreement by the purchaser to commence environmental remediation within a time schedule and the government (the seller) shares the expenses of remediation.

The privatisation process has necessitated the development of specific mechanisms to offset risks to investors. As part of the overall privatisation process, the State Treasury has instituted a statutory requirement for an environmental review of all entities destined for capital privatisation. The State Treasury, which includes a dedicated environmental unit, has developed the practice of using escrow accounts or delayed payment accounts during transactions. These are based on the use of a portion of the transaction value to cover identified liabilities for a specified period of time. Plans exist to further enhance these mechanisms through the amendment of the privatisation and commercialisation legislation, which would allow for the State Treasury to take on liabilities as well as re-establish the use of escrow accounts.

In order to allocate the potential risk of any liabilities in a transaction involving the sale of a company or property, warranties and indemnities have been employed. However, there is still inconclusive case law with respect to the effective use of warranties. It is interesting to note that, unlike in Western Europe, the concept of professional indemnity of the environmental professional is rarely raised in Poland.

Since the focus on environmental liability issues has, to date, been driven mainly by Western investors, little attention has been paid by Polish investors to these issues. It is therefore anticipated that, prior to implementation of formal regulations, routine due diligence Environmental

Audit procedures, established to deal with the environmental concerns of foreign investors, will become the standard.

Environmental Audit

The environmental audit process typically begins with an initial agreement with the client on the scope of the study. This is critical in determining the needs and concerns of the client, and defines the overall content and depth of the ensuing audit. An audit generally involves a significant interaction between the audit team and the senior management and workforce of the enterprise, coupled with an inspection of the sites and facilities involved. An important factor can be the co-operation between the different parts of the due diligence team. It is beneficial if early co-operation is established between the environmental consultant, lawyers and other advisors.

Environmental Audits are usually conducted in a phased approach. The first phase (referred to as the Phase I Audit) consists of a desk study relating to the site's history and use (coupled with site visits and discussions with site personnel), a process and operations review, a documentation review, visits to local authorities etc. This allows for the preliminary identification of environmental risks and possible investment needs. If the conclusion of the Phase I Audit gives some indication of possible contamination, or if the data (eg regarding air monitoring) is not sufficient to make certain judgements, it may be necessary to conduct a Phase II Audit. That might involve intrusive investigations that will include appropriate sampling, analysis and interpretation.

It is important to note that, pursuant to the Mining and Geological Act 1994, a permit must be obtained for all investigatory geological activity. This includes the construction of boreholes for soil and groundwater monitoring. Therefore, a permit should be obtained prior to conducting such site investigation work. Subsequently, the results of the investigation need to be submitted to the authorities. This can create the problem of early 'disclosure' of site contamination to regulators prior to, or during, an acquisition. In practice, alternative methodologies can be employed (such as trial pitting etc). However, this is site specific and warrants careful consideration by the investor and his/her advisors to ensure that the end product meets their requirements. It is important to note that during the EIA process certain Phase II investigations may be required. This type of investigation can lengthen the due diligence process considerably. Plans exist to amend the law to allow for limited investigations without the need of a permit.

Conclusions

Environmental laws and regulations are well established in Poland. There is a general need to assess environmental issues prior to undertaking any significant investments, particularly in the light of Poland's planned entry to the EU. Consequently investors needs to consider the role of environmental due diligence as a means of establishing ways of off-setting some of the environmental risks that the increasing volume of regulation is creating. As part of this risk reduction strategy, the use of warranties, indemnities, insurance, escrow accounts etc needs to be considered. However, in practice, it has been only in the larger, more complex transactions that potential environmental liabilities have influenced the structure of a deal.

In terms of operational and real estate development, there is a need to establish a good working relationship with regulators early on. Early consideration of environmental issues is a key element of creating and building a successful operation in Poland.

35

Business Information Sources

Nick Sljivic, VP International

Introduction

As the decade has progressed, Poland (in line with other Central and Eastern European countries) has seen a marked increase in both the quantity and quality of sources of business information. For those who have not mastered the intricacies of the Polish language, this does not pose an insurmountable hurdle as vast amounts of business information are available in English.

What follows, in no order of preference, details a variety of institutions and organisations that can provide information on the business environment and the facts and figures behind commerce and trade in Poland. Many of the UK sources not only cover Poland but are relevant for the whole of Central and Eastern Europe.

Government sources

The British government has been heavily promoting bilateral trade between Poland and the UK and has instigated many promotional ventures (commissioning reports and organising various trade missions and seminars) over the past few years to highlight opportunities in Poland.

DTI Polish Desk
Kingsgate House
66–74 Victoria Street
London SW1E 6SW
Tel: 020 7215 4812
Fax: 020 7215 8161

The East European Trade Council has a business library in this country and co-operative staff who know the region well. It is worth spending a day browsing through its Polish section, and its bimonthly bulletin details events and information pertaining to the region.

East European Trade Council
Suite 10, Westminster Palace Gardens
Artillery Row
London SW1P 1RL
Tel: 020 7222 7622
Fax: 020 7222 5359

The Commercial Section of the British Embassy in Warsaw is very helpful but usually has only limited specific information available and, due to the large number of enquiries relating to a wide diversity of subjects, lacks the time to deal extensively with individual companies. However, it is a valuable aid in pointing you in the right direction. The British Embassy provides a list of all the UK companies present in the country and very useful advice can be derived from making contact with those UK firms that are already established, and who have gained valuable experience dealing with the laws, culture and business practices of Poland.

British Embassy
Commercial Section
Warsaw Corporate Centre
Emilii Platter
Warsaw
Tel: + 48 22 625 3030
Fax: + 48 22 625 3472
E-mail: ukembwcc@it.com.pl

Polish government sources include the Polish Embassy in London, which should be one of the first ports of call for information. The Polish Inward Investment Agency (PAIZ) produces a wide variety of publications on establishing businesses in Poland and also many industry-specific publications.

Embassy of the Republic of Poland
15 Devonshire Street
London W1N 2AR
Tel: 020 7580 5481
Fax: 020 7323 0195

PAIZ
al Roz 2
00-559 Warsaw
Tel: + 48 22 621 0706
Fax: + 48 22 622 6169

Consultants, lawyers et al

Consultants advising on how to do business in the country are plentiful, both UK-based or Poland-based. All the major management consultancy and law firms are present, plus numerous others, large and small, domestic and international. Many produce business guides of varying degrees of depth and content. Market research firms also abound. If you wish to commission professional organisations to assist you, the British Embassy or the East European Trade Council can provide information on where to find them.

Magazines and journals

English language publications can be divided into those that cover Eastern Europe and those that are specifically focused on Poland. The leading English language business newspaper for Poland is the weekly *Warsaw Business Journal*. Regional publications include *The Economist*'s *Business Central Europe* and *The Wall Street Journal*'s *Central European Economic Review*. The newspaper *Central European Business Weekly* gives comprehensive regional business information, as does the *East European Business Quarterly*.

Warsaw Business Journal
c/o VP International
Redhill House
Chester CH4 8BU
Tel: 01244 681 619
Tel: 01244 681 617
Website: www.vpinternational.com

Business Central Europe
PO Box 14
Harold Hill
Romford RM3 8EQ
Tel: 01708 381 555
Fax: 01708 381 211

Central European Economic Review
PO Box 2845
In de Cramer 37
6401 DH Heerlen
The Netherlands
Tel: + 31 45 576 1222
Fax: + 31 45 571 4722

Central European Business Weekly
c/o VP International
Redhill House
Chester CH4 8BU
Tel: 01244 681 619
Tel: 01244 681 617
Website: www.vpinternational.com

East European Business Quarterly
c/o VP International
Redhill House
Chester CH4 8BU
Tel: 01244 681 619
Tel: 01244 681 617
Website: www.vpinternational.com

Estates News is the definitive monthly publication for the property industry, covering all aspects of the property world (both residential and commercial) in Central and Eastern Europe.

Estates News
Plac Konstytucji 3/103
00-647 Warsaw
Tel/Fax: + 48 22 621 7472

Directories, databases, CD ROMs and mailing lists

The main business databases and directories are produced by organisations such as Hoppenstedt Bonnier, Kompass and Teleadreson. The European Bank for Reconstruction and Development (EBRD) produces the annual *EBRD Directory of Business Information Sources for Central and Eastern Europe and CIS*. Many regions and towns produce their own business directories detailing firms in their areas. Industry-specific directories are produced by most trade associations and chambers of commerce. Mailing lists for the region are available from a wide range of organisations, including those produced by the business database companies themselves and also by organisations that act as list brokers, such as VP International and ABC Direct.

Effective Technology Marketing Ltd
PO Box 171
Grimsby DN35 0TP
Tel: 01472 699 027
Fax: 01472 699 027

Hoppenstedt Bonnier
c/o VP International
Redhill House
Chester CH4 8BU
Tel: 01244 681 619
Tel: 01244 681 617
Website: www.vpinternational.com

Teleadreson
ul Heweliusza 11/1701
Gdansk
Tel: + 48 58 313 421
Fax: + 48 58 313 421

The Internet

Numerous business Internet sites pertaining to the region and to Poland
have sprung up and now offer excellent sources of information for the
price of a phone call. Many English language-based sites have appeared
and content inevitably varies enormously between the different sites.

Business Central Europe	www.bcemag.com
CEEBIZ	www.ceebiz.com
Central Europe Online	www.centraleurope.com
EBRD	www.ebrd.com
Export Hotline	www.exporthotline.com
Internet Securities	www.securities.co.uk
PAIZ	www.paiz.gov.pl
US Government CEE	www.ceebic.com
VP International	www.vpinternational.com

Exhibitions

Visiting or taking part in exhibitions is one of the most effective means
of undertaking market research or finding agents/distributors. The
largest trade fairs held in Poland are in Poznan, but there are also many
regional fairs

Poznan International Trade Fair
Glogowska 14
60-734 Poznan
Tel: + 48 61 866 5870
Fax: + 48 61 866 5827

Conferences

Numerous conferences on every conceivable business topic are regularly organised, including many in Central Europe. Three of the main organisers are Qdos, Euroforum and IBC.

EuroForum
45 Beech Street
London EC2Y 8AD
Tel: 020 7878 6888
Fax: 020 7878 6999

IBC UK Conferences Ltd
Gilmoora House
57–61 Mortimer Street
London W1N 8JX
Tel: 020 7453 2160
Fax: 020 7631 3214

Qdos
37–41 Bedford Row
London WC1 R4JH
Tel: 020 7405 6062
Fax: 020 7404 4725

Publications and reports

Business reports on diverse topics are available at a price. Good ones are worth every penny of the three to four figures that they may cost. The Financial Times Management Reports Division and The Economist Intelligence Unit are two of the leading producers. Various trade associations have commissioned specific reports on their particular sector. Red Square Trading is a specialist market research company that produces comprehensive industry reports on a variety of industries (chemical, pharmaceutical, iron and steel, etc.) The *Central European Automotive Report* covers developments in that sector. *Supermarket* is a weekly publication that covers retailing developments.

FT Newsletters & Management Reports
Maple House, 149 Tottenham Court Rd
London, W1P 9LL
Tel: 0171 896 2222
Fax: 0171 896 2333
Website: www.ft.com

The Economist Intelligence Unit Ltd
PO Box 200
Harold Hill
Romford RM3 8UX
Tel: 0171 830 1007
Fax: 01708 371 850
Website: www.eiu.com

Red Square Trading
c/o VP International
Redhill House
Chester CH4 8BU
Tel: 01244 681 619
Tel: 01244 681 617
Website: www.vpinternational.com

Et al

The EBRD has extensive information, which it offers on a subscription basis; it also offers a personalised research service on the same basis.

EBRD
One Exchange Square
London EC2A 2EH
Tel: 020 7338 6000
Fax: 020 7338 6100
Website: www.ebrd.com

VP International supplies many of the leading publications and reports from Poland (and the region overall), as well as accumulating possibly the most extensive range of business information available on Central Europe at its office in Chester.

VP International
Redhill House
Chester CH4 8BU
Tel: 01244 681 619
Tel: 01244 681 617
Website: www.vpinternational.com

Very occasionally, jewels of information can be found buried in the archives and resources of UK trade associations and local chambers of commerce but most have very limited and/or very dated information. The same applies to the majority of business school libraries. Trade missions organised by some of the chambers, trade associations or the DTI are often a cost-effective means of initially sounding out the Polish market.

36

Trade

Kevin R Smith, AWS Corporate Finance &
Consultancy

Opportunities

Poland is the largest and most active market in Central Europe, with a
population of some 38 million, and GDP growth has been consistently
high, averaging around 5 per cent per annum for a number of years. Alone
of all the countries in the region, Poland's GDP has now climbed back
above that of 1989. Politically and economically stable, it can be considered by many standards to have 'emerged' as a market, although there
remains much growth potential for the foreseeable future.

Risks

The finance of trade with Poland has undergone a number of fundamental
and rapid changes in the last decade. Before the break-up of the Eastern
bloc in 1989 and the disbanding of the Council for Mutual Economic
Assistance (COMECON) in 1991, UK exporters only had to deal with a
very limited number of Foreign Trade Organisations (FTOs) and the
monopolistic state-owned bank responsible for all foreign trade – in
Poland this was Bank Handlowy. Both the FTOs and the state banks were
able to demonstrate a track record of many years and the risk was essentially a sovereign one.

With the emergence of Poland as a separate trading nation came much
more freedom to trade, but potentially much greater risks. The UK
exporter went from dealing with long-established, state-owned organisations in a tightly controlled environment to facing newly established companies and banks with no track record and often very little experience of
international trade or of a market economy. In addition, the legal framework did not initially encourage many foreign companies to enter the
market.

However, as Poland began to accelerate the reforms that were necessary to revitalise the economy, many of the difficulties and risks faced

by a UK company wishing to trade in the country were significantly reduced. Many companies (including small and medium-sized enterprises) have developed a track record, accounts of an ever growing number of internationally active companies are now being audited to Western standards and experience of international trade and of a market economy is being gained ever more quickly. All the larger local banks have become experienced in international banking and, indeed, many are now largely owned, at least in part, by international banking groups.

Prior to the Russian crisis in August 1998, the improving picture meant that finance, especially for trade transactions, had become cheaper and more widely available – this was true throughout the region. While the crisis has had long-term effects on the economies of many of Poland's neighbours, this has not been the case in Poland. Indeed, the perception of risk by the international banking community changed markedly for many countries in the region, but Poland remained virtually unscathed, due to the strength and direction of its economy. This serves as a clear demonstration as to how far Poland has come in refocusing trade from the East to the West and how independent the economy has become.

Foreign trade flows

Poland has become a major trading partner for the UK. In 1998, Britain's exports to Poland amounted to some £1.2 billion, making it the 24th largest export market. Of as much importance is the fact that the Polish economy continues to grow rapidly and, as such, should work its way up the chart, becoming an ever more sizeable market. The value of trade for 1998 was actually marginally lower than in 1997 but this is largely explained by the lower cost of petroleum-related products due to the weakness of the oil price. However, between 1989 and 1997, British exports to Poland increased more than sevenfold and market share has also risen. Table 36.1 provides details of the UK's ten leading categories of exports to Poland in 1998.

Poland continues to attract large amounts of foreign direct investment. Britain is the sixth largest investor, with actual and committed investments of over US$2.5 billion. As companies and the economy grow, both as a result of investment and organically through increased efficiency, their products are reaching an ever wider export market. The quality of the products has improved tremendously, while prices are very competitive on a global basis, largely due to lower labour costs.

During 1998, Poland's exports to Britain amounted to £684 million. Table 36.2 provides details of Poland's ten leading categories of exports to the UK in 1998.

Table 36.1 UK's top ten categories of exports to Poland, 1998

Category	Value (£'000s)
1 Road vehicles	114,463
2 Petroleum, petroleum products and related materials	108,853
3 Electrical machinery, apparatus and appliances/parts	97,988
4 Telecoms, sound recording and reproducing apparatus	87,285
5 Office machines	75,686
6 General industrial machines	72,063
7 Miscellaneous manufactured articles	71,844
8 Medicinal and pharmaceutical products	63,893
9 Essential oils and resins	58,342
10 Specialised machinery for particular industries	56,787
Total exports to Poland from the UK	1,213,416

In order to put this data in context, it is important to consider Poland's other major trading partners. In 1998 total exports worldwide from Poland were in the region of US$9 billion and imports exceeded US$10 billion. The major buyers of Polish goods were Germany, Russia, France, Italy, the USA, the Netherlands and the UK; the major exporters to Poland are those same countries.

Table 36.2 Poland's top ten categories of exports to the UK, 1998

Category	1998 (£'000s)
1 Electrical machinery, apparatus and appliances/parts	71,031
2 Non-ferrous metals	61,267
3 Telecoms, sound recording and reproducing apparatus	52,850
4 Iron and steel	42,693
5 Road vehicles	40,094
6 Articles of apparel and clothing accessories	37,049
7 Paper, paperboard and articles of paper pulp	28,251
8 Coal, coke and briquettes	27,219
9 Metal products	22,545
10 Cork and wood products	20,979
Total exports to the UK from Poland	684,035

As the country's infrastructure is being replaced and updated, improving communication is making the physical aspects of trading with Poland ever easier. This, together with the wide-ranging legislative amendments (especially regarding certification and border controls) required as part of Poland's accession to the EU, is greatly improving the logistical aspects of trading with Poland, and means that the flow of two-way trade with Poland will continue to increase.

Methods of payment

With any transaction, it is important to offer competitive payment methods in order not to jeopardise the sale. However, it is also important not to be pushed into taking risks that are either not fully understood or difficult to assess, as no sale is still better than no payment.

As with any developing country, the first trades in a new market or with a new buyer should normally be conducted using Letters of Credit that are confirmed or discounted by a Western bank. In the early days these could prove quite expensive and difficult to obtain, but most forms of trade credit are now readily available.

It remains a common misconception that the Polish currency (the zloty) is in some form restricted. This is not the case, as the zloty has been fully convertible for some years.

Advance payment

Clearly this is ideal for the exporter but not so good for the buyer and, for that reason, is not that common. However, as payment in advance can avoid the high bank charges imposed on other forms of payment, it can often be worth asking, especially if you have a niche product. However, take care not to lose a sale by insisting on this, as foreign competitors may well be more flexible.

Letters of Credit

The charges associated with issuing a Letter of Credit, together with the fact that the bank may require a deposit of up to 100 per cent, can make them an expensive and not particularly popular option with the buyer. Many of the larger Polish banks are generally considered to be an acceptable payment risk but this should always be investigated before contracts are signed. Once a favourable track record has been established, other payment methods may be considered depending upon individual circumstances.

Bills of exchange and promissory notes

These are often used to finance medium-term credit for larger transactions, using a stream of bills with maturities every six months. The bills often carry a bank aval (guarantee), although this may not be necessary for a few of the largest companies. The exporter can also ask a bank to discount the bills on a non-recourse basis (a forfait), thus ensuring payment and speeding the cash flow. In the early 1990s forfaiting was the main method of financing medium-term trade throughout Central Europe but has declined in importance as other methods have become available.

It is very important to check that the bank guaranteeing any Bills of Exchange is acceptable to a Western bank, as the risk premium and other terms can vary considerably, and some will not be acceptable at all.

Cash against documents

This can be used to ensure that the buyer does not access the goods until they are paid for and can be a compromise solution between buyer and seller.

Open account

Approximately 90 per cent of all trade in the EU is conducted on an open account basis, although many companies have some form of credit insurance. Trade with Poland has not as yet reached this level, but over 60 per cent of imports into the country are already carried out on this basis.

Insurance

Many of the trade insurance companies can insure sales to Poland, although this would typically be part of a whole turnover policy.

Summary

Doing business with Poland has changed almost beyond recognition over the last ten years. Although some aspects remain difficult, these continue to improve and the obvious opportunities for exporting companies in this market should see the amount of trade between Britain and Poland expand further in the coming years.

When entering any market for the first time it pays to be cautious and to seek assistance from someone who knows the market. There can be no doubt that, while risks remain, the balance of risk/reward has moved firmly in the exporter's favour and British companies should ensure that they are not left behind.

Part 4

Building an Organisation

37

Setting Up a Company

Charles Waddell, CMS Cameron McKenna

Introduction

Under the Foreign Investment Law, foreigners may only conduct business in Poland in the form of a limited liability company, a joint stock company or by establishing representative offices in Poland.

The formation procedure for companies is more complex and time consuming than that in Anglo-Saxon jurisdictions and involves both a notary and a registration court examining the Articles of Association (*umowa spółki-*) in the case of a limited liability company, *statut–* in the case of a joint-stock company, to ensure that the provisions of these documents conform with Polish law.

The Foreign Investment Law is about to be superseded by a new 'Business Activities Act'. At the time of writing this chapter, this new law had not completed its passage through Parliament (nor is it expected to enter into force until one year after its enactment), and therefore the final text of the law is not known. The Government's draft law, which has been passed by the Polish Lower House (the *Sejm*), envisages that foreign nationals who have obtained permission to live and work in Poland will have the same rights as Polish citizens regarding undertaking and performing business activities in Poland. Foreign persons would be able to undertake and perform business activities on the same basis as Polish persons. This new law would allow foreign persons to participate in and establish, *inter alia*, Polish partnerships. These provisions are, however, based on the principle of reciprocity such that the rights granted by the new law will only be available to nationals of, and entities established in, states which grant similar rights to Polish persons.

If there is no relevant reciprocity between Poland and the state concerned, then the foreign nationals and entities may only conduct business through limited liability companies, joint stock companies or limited liability partnerships.

The remainder of this chapter is based on the Foreign Investment Law, as this remains the law to date.

Limited liability company (Sp.zo.o)

A Polish limited liability company (Sp.zo.o) is modelled on the German *Gesellschaft mit beschränkter Haftung* (GmbH) and is the equivalent of a British private company. It acquires legal personality upon registration in the commercial register held by the local registration court. As a general rule, the liability of its shareholders is limited to the amount of their respective capital contributions.

A limited liability company may be incorporated by one or more founders. If there is just one founder, that founding entity cannot itself be a limited liability company (or its foreign equivalent) with only one shareholder. Following formation, there is nothing to prevent the founder transferring its share to one shareholder, which is itself a limited liability company with only one shareholder.

The minimum initial share capital for a limited liability company is Zl 4000 (approximately £630). The share capital may be paid up in cash or made up of contributions in kind. Shares paid up in cash must be fully paid up prior to registration of the company in the commercial register. The transfer of in-kind contributions must be assured on the date of the company's registration in the commercial register.

The 'governing bodies' of a limited liability company are the general meeting of shareholders and the management board. An ordinary general meeting must be held within six months of the end of a company's financial year. An extraordinary general meeting must be held if shareholders holding at least 10 per cent of the share capital so request. The decision-making powers of the general meeting are set out in the Polish Commercial Code and in the Articles of Association of the company. All general meetings of the company must be held within Poland. Shareholders may attend personally or by proxy.

The management board is responsible for the day-to-day running of the company and may include one or more members. A general meeting may impose restrictions on the powers of the management board members. There are no residency requirements for foreign management board members in Poland.

Further, a supervisory board must be established when there are more than 50 shareholders in a limited liability company and the share capital exceeds Zl 25,000 otherwise such a board is optional. The supervisory board exercises non-executive powers in relation to the company. It is the company's controlling body and exercises supervision over the company.

Incorporation procedure

The incorporation procedure involves the following:

- the Articles of Association are prepared and executed as a notarial deed;

- the share capital is paid up;

- the governing bodies (the management board and supervisory board, if any) of the company are established;

- the company is registered in the commercial register of the court in the area where the seat of the company is based. The application for registration must be accompanied by specimen signatures of the members of the management board, as well as a list of shareholders and a statement that the share capital is fully paid up and in-kind contributions to the capital have been made.

Joint-stock company (SA)

A Polish joint stock company (SA) is comparable to a German *Aktiengesellschaft* (AG) or a British public limited company. A joint stock company is the only business entity in Poland that is permitted to raise capital by means of a public flotation, (as regulated by the Securities Law 1991 as amended).

The main differences between a limited liability company and a joint stock company are:

- the amount of share capital;

- the fact that a limited liability company cannot offer its shares to the public;

- the fact that only a joint stock company may carry out certain activities such as banking or insurance;

- share certificates are only issued for joint stock companies.

Incorporation procedure

There must be at least three founding shareholders unless the company is founded by national or local government. The share capital must be divided into shares of an equal nominal value. After the company has been entered in the commercial register it is possible for shares to be transferred so that the company has only one shareholder.

Shares

The minimum initial capital for a joint stock company is Zl 100,000 (approximately £16,000). As with limited liability companies, the share capital may be contributed in cash or in kind. If the share capital is contributed in cash, then only 25 per cent needs be paid up prior to registration of the company in the commercial register. A general meeting of company shareholders will decide when the outstanding capital should be paid. In-kind contributions must cover the full share price prior to registration of the company. The value of such in-kind contributions must be verified by a court-appointed auditor. There is no such requirement for an audit to be undertaken for a limited liability company.

A joint stock company can have registered or bearer shares. Bearer shares cannot be issued if the shares are not fully paid up. Shares issued in exchange for in-kind contributions must be registered shares and must remain so for two years.

Preference shares may be issued. The preferential rights attached to these shares could be in relation to voting, dividends or asset distribution on liquidation of the company.

A general meeting of shareholders is the highest form of authority in a joint-stock company.

The management board is responsible for the day-to-day running of the company and may consist of one or more members. There are no residency requirements for foreign members in Poland.

A joint stock company must have either a supervisory board (consisting of at least five members) or a board of auditors.

Written reports

If any of the following are expected to apply, the founders must prepare a written report giving details of the matter:

- the issue of shares for contributions in kind;
- the acquisition in advance of registration of property rights (eg intellectual property, real estate etc);
- the making of payments for services rendered in relation to the incorporation.

This report must justify the transactions and the amount of remuneration involved, and identify the other parties involved. The report must be supported by an opinion from auditors as to whether all the relevant payments were justified. The audits will be appointed by the local registration court from a list kept for this purpose. The report should be supported by original documentation. The auditors can make a written request for any further information they require. The founders must respond to such requests with written answers.

The auditors must provide two copies of their opinion to the registration court, which will in turn provide a certified copy to the founders.

The statute

The statute of a joint stock company must be in the form of a notarised deed and be signed by the founding shareholders. The notarised deed must:

- identify the shareholders and specify the number and type of shares allocated to each of them;

- specify the issue price of the shares and the deadline for payment;

- confirm the election of the first governing bodies;

- if there is a founder's report and auditor's opinion, then the notarised deed(s) must state that each of the prospective shareholders signing the deed(s) is familiar both with the opinion and the contents of the report.

In addition, if capital is to be raised by public subscription, the statute must be published in a national newspaper.

Documents accompanying the application for registration of a joint-stock company

The application for registration must be accompanied by:

- the notarised deed forming the company;

- a declaration signed by all the members of the management board that all payments for shares have been made in accordance with the statute;

- a statement as to the establishment and membership of the governing bodies;

- evidence that the necessary consents have been obtained;

- specimen signatures of the members of the management board, either signed before the court, or authenticated by a notary.

If the capital was raised by public subscription, the following documents must also accompany the application:

- the prospectus;

- the minutes of the 'organisational meeting' (special shareholders' meeting held following a public subscription);

- a list of subscribers, showing the shares allocated to each and the amount of any payments received;

- bank statements evidencing the payments;

- the founder's report and the auditor's opinion (where appropriate);

- the report of the committee elected at the 'organisational meeting'.

Irregularities after registration of a joint-stock company

In the event of irregularities being discovered after registration, the registration court can (either on its own initiative or at the instigation of an interested party) give notice to the company requiring it to correct these irregularities by a deadline set by the court. Failure to comply will lead to a fine or, if the defects are 'materially significant for the continued existence of the company', dissolution. A company of five years' standing cannot, however, be dissolved on the grounds of pre-registration irregularities.

Licences

Generally, a foreign investor does not need to obtain a permit in order to establish a company in Poland. Certain licences are, however, necessary in order to conduct some activities such as the import and export of chemical fuels, trading in weapons, trading in cigarettes and alcohol and the running of pharmacies. There are also separate provisions regulating banking, insurance, financial audit services, international transport, the management of real estate, telecommunication and the provision of brokerage services etc. All of these activities require a licence issued by the appropriate governmental authorities. Permits are also required when a company acquires shares in a Polish state-owned entity.

Under the provisions of the Anti-Monopoly Law, any intention to merge or 'transform' economic entities in order to create an entity that could gain a dominant position in a certain market requires prior notification to be given to the Anti-Monopoly Office.

Property issues

Polish Civil Law recognises several interests in land, namely:

- ownership;
- perpetual usufruct;
- limited property rights ('limited rights in rem') eg mortgages, pledges;
- contractual rights, eg leases.

In order for foreigners to acquire ownership of land or a right of perpetual usufruct in Poland, permission must first be obtained from the Minister of Internal Affairs.

Under the Law of Acquisition of Real Estate by Foreigners, a 'foreigner', in addition to foreign natural persons and legal entities, is defined as a company incorporated in Poland if it is controlled by a natural person without Polish citizenship or a legal entity which has its registered office abroad. Control means a direct or indirect ownership of at least 50 per cent of the Polish subsidiary company's capital. Therefore, if a foreign company establishes a majority-controlled Polish entity, that entity will also need to apply for a permit in order to acquire land.

A permit will also be required if a foreigner acquires a majority share-holding in a Polish company that already owns land. To ease the administrative burden of this requirement, when shares are traded on the stock exchange a Polish company can apply for a general permit rather than a separate permit every time shares change hands.

A foreigner is entitled to lease land without having to obtain a permit. However, Polish law imposes certain restrictions on state entities attempting to dispose of land to foreigners.

The prior consent of the State Treasury is required before a foreigner can acquire shares in a limited liability company or joint stock company which leases assets from the State for a period in excess of 6 months.

Work permits

Any expatriate performing work within the territory of Poland must obtain a work permit.

38

Accounting Policies and Auditing Requirements

KPMG

Accounting policies

Polish accounting standards are governed by the Act on Accounting of 29 September 1994 (the 'Act'). Generally, they comply with the EU IVth and VIIth Directives and with International Accounting Standards (IAS). Polish accounting regulations apply to all persons carrying on business activities, including banks, insurance companies, trading companies and representative offices of foreign companies.

All accounting books and statements must be prepared and maintained in the Polish language and in Polish currency. This does not apply to source documents. Books of accounts and source documents must be retained for a period of five years but annual financial statements must be kept permanently. Accounting records must be maintained in the business' registered office in Poland; if they are kept by third parties and are thus held in another location within Poland, the Tax Office should be informed.

Companies are normally free to adopt any book-keeping system or chart of accounts they wish, as long as they are able to provide all the information necessary for the preparation of the annual balance sheet and monthly and yearly income statements. If the system is computerised, it must comply with certain requirements laid down in the Act.

Accounts should give a true and fair view and be prepared on a going concern basis. Generally, assets will be recognised at the lower of cost and net realisable value.

The financial year, which has to be consistent with the tax year, consists of 12 consecutive months and can commence in any given month. However, if it varies from the calendar year, the Tax Office must be notified. If the company changes its year end, the first accounting period after this is always longer than 12 months.

Depreciation

Depreciation of fixed assets and amortisation of intangibles (patents, licences, brand names etc) is usually calculated on a straight-line basis, by way of varying rates for different items. For accounting purposes, the method and rate of depreciation should be determined based on the expected useful life of the asset; in practice most companies use the rates set for tax purposes, which are defined by the Minister of Finance in a separate decree. Depreciation of machines and equipment is also possible on a reducing balance basis.

In certain circumstances, if technical considerations give sufficient ground, the tax depreciation and amortisation rates may be modified. Intangible assets are typically written off over five years. Costs related to the formation of a joint-stock company and goodwill are amortised, in principle, over a period of five years. Land is not depreciated. Fixed assets under construction are not depreciated until they are capable of being brought into use.

Stock

Stock can be valued using FIFO, LIFO, weighted average cost or actual cost. Periodically, entities must perform stock counts, depending on the type of accounting system in place.

Revaluation of fixed assets

Most fixed assets are subject to statutory revaluations that are decreed from time to time by the Ministry of Finance and are designed to compensate for inflation. Depreciation is then based on the revalued amount. The last revaluation took place at the beginning of 1995. Other upward valuations are not allowed.

Leased assets

The accounting regulations distinguish between 'finance' and 'operating' leases. The classification of leases is made on the basis of specific rules issued by the Ministry of Finance and does not comply with IAS. Assets acquired under a finance lease are capitalised in the lessee's books and depreciated over the period of the lease. The lessor has the right to depreciate assets leased under an operating lease. Accounting for leases is expected to be completely revised so as to comply with IAS.

Accruals

Compared to accounting standards commonly used in other countries, the Polish system offers similar possibilities for creating provisions for losses and costs, as well as writing down the value of stocks or receivables. However, many accruals and provisions justified from an economic perspective and required for accounting purposes may not be fully tax-deductible.

Reserves

Joint-stock companies are obliged to create reserve funds of at least 8 per cent of their after tax profits until the reserve amounts to at least one third of share capital. No such mandatory reserve requirements apply to limited liability companies.

Deferred taxation

The Act on Accounting requires that an entity accounts for deferred taxation where timing differences between the recognition of revenue or expenses for accounting and tax purposes arise. A deferred tax asset is recognised only if it is certain that it will crystallise in the following financial years.

Financial statements and consolidation

The annual financial statements of a company are composed of the balance sheet, income statement, notes and, if the company is obliged to publish its financial statements, a cash flow statement. The reporting formats are laid down in the Act. Financial statements should be supported by a Management Board report commenting on the financial and economic situation of the company.

Groups of companies (normally exceeding three times the size limits for mandatory audit) are required to prepare consolidated financial statements using the equity method. All assets and liabilities of dependent entities are included and associated entities are proportionally consolidated. The ownership percentage and the influence of the parent company on decision-making in related entities determine which consolidation method is applicable. An entity is regarded as dependent if at least 50 per cent of the voting rights are controlled by the parent company. Associated entities are mainly those where the parent controls 20–50 per cent of the voting rights.

Auditing

There is a requirement of statutory audit and publication of the audited financial statements for all joint-stock companies, banks, insurance companies and certain limited liability companies. Limited liability companies requiring an audit are those that, in the preceding year, satisfy any two of the following three size criteria:

- average yearly employment level of more than 50 persons;
- turnover (net of value added tax but including financial income) in excess of €3 million;
- total assets at the balance sheet date in excess of €1 million.

An audit must be carried out prior to the approval of the financial statements by the company's General Assembly and must be performed by an independent chartered accountant who is licensed, on an individual or corporate basis, as an authorised auditor.

Filing

The financial statements, Management Board report, the audit opinion, a certified copy of the acceptance of the financial statements by the company in General Meeting and its decision on the distribution or allocation of profits must be filed in the district Registry Court within 15 days.

The financial statements also have to be filed with the local tax office within ten days of approval by the company in General Meeting but in any event not later than nine months after the financial year has ended.

Reporting requirements for banks, insurance companies, stock exchange quoted companies and those involved in mass privatisation are further regulated by detailed reporting guidelines.

All Polish entities performing economic activities whose employment level is above a specified limit are also obliged to periodically file their financial statements on special forms with the Central Statistical Office.

Note

At the time of going to press, new Acts on Accounting and on Auditing were in the process of being prepared. These are expected to bring Polish accounting and auditing standards more in line with international standards and EU Directives. In particular, it is expected that substantial changes will be made to methods of accounting for leases, mergers and acquisitions, and financial instruments.

39

Fiscal Regime

KPMG

Introduction

The following taxes are those that are encountered most frequently:

- income tax, which is imposed both on legal persons (corporate income tax) and natural persons (personal income tax), with the exception of forestry and agricultural activities;

- 'tax on goods and services', which is the Polish name for value added tax (VAT) and excise tax;

- local taxes and charges;

- stamp fees (duties) and notary fees.

Taxes are regulated by separate acts passed by the Polish parliament. These in turn serve as the basis on which ministerial decrees are published, in most cases by the Minister of Finance. In addition to the decrees, the Ministry of Finance also issues official interpretations of specific regulations.

It should be noted that, at the time of publication, there were already indications that the year 2000 would see substantial reforms of the income tax system and adjustments to VAT.

General rules of taxation

All new businesses commencing their activities are expected to register with the appropriate local tax office and obtain a NIP number (taxpayer identification number). Taxpayers are required to maintain records, which are the basis for the calculation of tax. Businesses are obliged by law to calculate taxes due during the financial year, to make prepayments and also to fulfil certain other fiscal duties. Most returns are filed on a monthly basis.

Taxation system

The Polish taxation system is composed of the following levels:

- **Minister of Finance**, who is responsible for the global supervision of all issues related to the taxation system; within the scope of his responsibility lie all decisions relating to the coherent application of fiscal regulations by local tax authorities;

- **Tax Chambers**, which are hierarchically superior to Tax Offices. Tax Chambers rule on appeals against the decisions of Tax Offices;

- **Tax Offices**, which are tax tribunals authorised to issue administrative decisions with respect to taxpayers within the area of their jurisdiction. Taxes are paid to local Tax Offices.

Taxpayers have the right to lodge appeals against decisions issued by Tax Offices. If a taxpayer also questions the verdict of the Tax Chamber, the taxpayer has the right to lodge an appeal with the Supreme Administrative Court (NSA).

Corporate income tax

All companies that are established in Poland are liable for corporate income tax on their worldwide income. Income that is taxed abroad is either exempt from tax in Poland (in accordance with relevant double taxation treaties) or is subject to taxation in line with the provisions of those treaties. Where no treaty applies, Poland will allow a credit for any foreign tax paid.

Foreign companies are only taxed on revenue from Polish sources.

The corporate income tax rate for 1999 is 34 per cent. This is expected to be reduced gradually to 22 per cent. In the absence of a specific choice, the financial (fiscal) year is the calendar year but companies are free to choose any other year end.

Calculation of the tax base

Corporate income tax is levied on revenues from which the costs incurred in generating those revenues have been deducted. Certain expenses are specifically non-deductible, for example:

- representation and advertising expenses (other than media advertising) in excess of 0.25 per cent of revenue;

- provisions for bad debts, unless the debtor is bankrupt or the debt cannot be collected despite court procedures having been followed;

- interest on overdue taxes;

- fines and indemnities arising out of faulty goods and services.

The amount of taxable income may also be reduced by brought forward losses. For losses arising in fiscal years beginning on or after 1 January 1999, up to 50 per cent may be off-set in any one of the next five years. Previously, only one third of a loss could be offset in one of the next three years.

Presently, a taxpayer can also claim investment tax relief (a form of accelerated depreciation) but this benefit is being phased out; certain conditions must be met in order to qualify for this investment relief. Additionally, in the year following the investment relief, a 'premium' of one half of the relief claimed in the previous year may be deducted.

Companies setting up within Special Economic Zones (SEZs) are offered possible corporate income tax exemptions for up to ten years. During the remaining period of the SEZ's operating life, companies may be exempt from 50 per cent of corporate income tax. However, permits for carrying on business activity in the SEZs will only be issued by the zone management itself until the end of 2000, due to pressure from the EU. In 2001, permits will only be issued for SEZs situated in communities where the unemployment rate is more than 50 per cent above the Polish average unemployment rate (the current unemployment rate is approximately 12 per cent). From 1 January 2002, permits will only be issued by the Minister of Economy in consultation with the Minister of Finance.

The Tax Law allows donations (eg scientific, technical, educational, cultural) to be deducted, up to 10–15 per cent of pre-tax income before donations.

Since 1 January 1996 it has been possible for Polish companies to form fiscal groups, and file one tax return off-setting profits and losses within the group. However, the regulations are restrictive, and in practice limit the development of this form of business operation.

Thin capitalisation rules have come into force from 1 January 1999, limiting the deductibility of interest on loans and credits from certain related parties both in Poland and off-shore. The debt–equity ratio is 3:1.

The Tax Law lays down specific transfer pricing provisions in line with OECD regulations. These regulations govern transactions between related parties in circumstances where the taxpayer renders services on terms clearly in favour of the other party. The regulations also apply when the taxpayer manages his/her business so as not to disclose revenues or discloses them at a level below that which should be expected. In either of these two cases, the tax authorities have the right to determine the amount of tax payable.

Taxation of foreign companies

Foreign companies deriving income from Poland, subject to Double Tax Treaties, may be taxed on the basis of a deemed tax base if their accounting records do not comply with Polish standards but their liability is calculated using normal corporate tax rates.

Withholding tax of 20 per cent is levied on the following payments to a non-resident taxpayer:

● dividends and other distributions from Polish companies;

● interest;

● copyright royalties, payments relating to trade marks or know-how and income arising from the sale of such rights, and licence fees.

These rates can be reduced by double tax treaties agreed between Poland and other nations.

Personal income tax

Individuals who are permanent residents of Poland or who remain in the country for more than 183 days in a calendar year are subject to Polish tax on their worldwide income. Other persons are taxed only on income from Polish sources. This 'limited tax liability' also extends to foreign persons who are living in Poland temporarily and are employed either by companies with foreign participation, or by branches and other representative offices of foreign companies and banks. Polish-sourced income also includes remuneration paid abroad in respect of employment duties performed in Poland.

The following sources of income are exempt from personal taxation:

● interest on deposit and current accounts;

● reimbursement of moving expenses and relocation allowances (up to 200 per cent of the remuneration for the month in which an employee is transferred);

● per diem allowances and other reimbursed expenses up to certain limits;

● provision of accommodation by an employer when an employee works outside his/her place of permanent residence (up to three times the minimum wage for the previous December per month).

Taxable income may be decreased by the amount of certain donations, up to 10–15 per cent of pre-tax income, and of compulsory social security payments (paid in Poland). Within specified limits, expenditure on new houses or renovation expenses may also be deducted, but this benefit is being phased out.

Tax is levied on an individual's total income (with the exception of income earned from dividends, interest on loans and proceeds from real estate sales). The rates for 1999 are as follows:

Taxable income	Tax payable
Up to Zl 29,626	19 per cent less Zl 394,80
Zl 29,624–59,248	Zl 5233.76 + 30 per cent over Zl 29,624
Over Zl 59,248	Zl 14,120.96 + 40 per cent over Zl 59,248

Income from dividends from Polish companies and interest on loans is taxed at a flat rate of 20 per cent and is not added to earnings from other sources. This also applies to earnings from the sales of real estate, where the flat tax rate is 10 per cent of the sale price. Persons with limited tax liability are subject to a flat rate tax of 20 per cent on director's fees, service fees and certain other income.

Social security (ZUS)

In 1999 the social security system underwent major reform. The system now consists of three 'Pillars', to which payments are made, the first and second being obligatory.

Social security contributions in 1999 are 36.59 per cent of an employee's gross salary, with 18.71 per cent borne by the employee and 17.88 per cent by the employer. This covers retirement and disability pensions, and illness and accident insurance. Once an employee's salary exceeds 30 times the average wage predicted for the current year (Zl 50,000 at present) no further contributions to the pension and disability funds are made. In addition, obligatory health insurance of 7.5 per cent of the gross salary is paid by Polish citizens; this is deductible from the monthly amount withheld for personal income tax.

Social security authorities do not impose ZUS contributions on payments made by foreign companies to expatriates *seconded* to Polish companies on the basis of their foreign employment contracts.

Furthermore, ZUS contributions are not payable on fees paid to members of the management boards of Polish companies. This is in keeping with the general rule of the Polish social security system, ie that social security premiums are to be calculated on the amount of remuneration obtained as a result of employment on the basis of a Polish employment contract (or, in certain circumstances, personal service and agency contracts).

VAT and excise tax

VAT

The 'tax on goods and services' (the Polish name for VAT) is charged on sales and supplies of goods (raw materials, supplies, goods for resale, products and fixed assets) and services by registered businesses in Poland, and on the import and export of goods and services into Poland.

Businesses are entitled to deduct the VAT they are charged on inputs ('input tax') from the VAT that they charge their customers ('output tax'). The net amount of output VAT is paid by the seller of the goods or services to the Tax Office. If the input tax exceeds output tax, the company may carry forward the excess and offset it against its VAT liability in succeeding periods. In certain circumstances, when there is a permanent excess of input tax, the excess is refunded to the business by the Tax Office.

The main difference between the Polish and EU VAT systems is the treatment of cross-border services. VAT applies on all services physically performed in the territory of Poland regardless of the nationalities of the buyer and seller. Services provided in the territory of Poland by a non-VAT-registered foreign person are subject to a reverse charge by the Polish recipient; unlike in the EU, however, the reverse-charged VAT is irrecoverable.

An export of services is a service provided by the taxpayer outside Poland, although certain services performed in Poland are treated in the same way. These can be subject to a zero rate of VAT. Most services performed in Poland for a foreign recipient will, however, be subject to normal VAT; the foreign entity cannot make a claim for a direct refund but, if it is registered for Polish VAT, it may be able to offset this as normal input VAT. Exports of services are normally only deemed to be completed when the invoice is paid by the customer.

Businesses are required to register for VAT when their turnover exceeds PLN 80,000.

Most sales of goods and services to individuals who are not carrying on business activities have to be recorded on special fiscal cash registers.

There are three separate rates of VAT: 22, 7 and 0 per cent, plus certain other transitional rates. The general rate of VAT imposed is 22 per cent. The 7 per cent rate applies to the sale of fertilisers, fodder and machines for the agricultural and forestry sectors, appliances for health care, processed food articles, musical scores, children's articles, communal services, certain construction materials, transportation tourism and leisure services. The 0 per cent rate of VAT applies to exported goods and services and certain other specialised services, mostly related to international transport services.

In addition, the law provides specific exemptions from VAT for certain goods and services, including:

● banking and financial services;

● products of the meat, fish and poultry industries, and agricultural activities (this exemption is expected to be abolished in the near future);

● services rendered relating to the postal service, housing and education;

● culture, arts, health care and sports.

A taxpayer who makes VAT exempt sales cannot recover the input VAT relating to such sales.

The liability for VAT normally arises at the earlier of: the moment the sales invoice is issued; or seven days after the goods are delivered; or the services are rendered. A VAT liability should be paid on or before submitting the monthly VAT declaration to the Tax Office, which is due on the 25th of the following month. Prepayments of over 50 per cent also trigger a VAT liability. Special rules apply for some types of services.

Excise tax

Excise tax is imposed at the manufacturing or import stage. The tax is calculated as either a percentage of the manufacturing sales price of the goods or as a percentage of the customs value of the goods sold.

Excise tax is imposed on selected goods, including: alcoholic beverages, tobacco products, engine oils and fuels, cars, sailing and motor yachts, certain electronic equipment, perfumes and the production and import of plastic wrappings.

Local taxes and charges

Among the different taxes and charges imposed by local authorities (eg cities, communes), the most important are those levied on real estate and transportation equipment. The tax on real estate is currently very low compared with the market value of property (especially in urban areas) and will be replaced by a system based on market rental values.

Stamp fees and notary fees

Stamp fees are charged on applications, permits and certificates issued on the request of third parties and for administrative activities undertaken on the basis of a third party's request.

Stamp duty applies on most civil law contracts that are not subject to VAT, including the sale of shares and property rights (2 per cent), the sale of real estate (5 per cent) and the granting of loans by non-banks (2 per cent). It also applies on increases in share capital (2–0.1 per cent).

Fees in private notary offices may differ. General rules lay down the maximum levels for fees, frequently based on the value of an agreement. The fee, however, may not be more than Zl 5000.

40

Trade Finance

*Anna Bartnicka-Jodko and Andrzej Oleś,
BRE Bank*

Introduction

Over the last three years, Polish foreign trade turnover and main streams
of exports and imports have grown substantially, as shown in Table 40.1.

Table 40.1 Polish foreign trade turnover, by main streams (US$ million)

	1996	**1997**	**1998**
Total exports	24,439.8	25,751.3	28,228.9
of which:			
– to OECD	18,775.9	19,204.2	22,261.7
– to EU	16,195.6	16,526.5	19,269.8
Total imports	37,136.7	42,307.5	47,053.6
of which:			
– from OECD	29,511.3	34,022.9	38,564.7
– from EU	23,738.0	26,998.2	31,027.3
Total trade balance	–12,696.9	–16,556.2	–18,824.7
of which:			
– with OECD	–10,735.4	–14,818.7	–16,303.0
– with EU	–7,542.4	–10,471.7	–11,757.5

The increase in Poland's foreign trade turnover has led to Polish banks
becoming more involved in the settlements of import-export transactions and to Polish importers requiring increased financing for such
transactions.

At present, approximately 30 of the 84 commercial banks operating in
Poland offer financing of foreign trade transactions at different levels of spe-
cialisation. The list of institutions specialised in trade finance includes some
Polish banks, which had traditionally serviced the foreign trade sector (eg
Bank Handlowy, BRE Bank, Bank Pekao), foreign banks' branches and affil-
iates, and a majority of foreign-owned Polish banks. These banks have

access to a wide network of foreign correspondent banks, which facilitates the handling of documentary operation transactions and shortens settlement periods. Thus, exporters and importers can choose trade finance products to suit their particular needs from quite a spectrum of banks.

Import and export financing

The forms of financing offered by Polish banks specialised in financial servicing of foreign trade transactions do not differ in principle from those offered by international financial institutions. However, the full use of the different trade-financing products remains low when compared to Poland's foreign trade volume and structure. The main reason for this seems to be an insufficient level of knowledge of the instruments available for the financing of commercial transactions, particularly among newly established and privately owned corporate entities.

The banks' terms and conditions for trade finance services that are made available to customers and potential users may in some cases influence the choice of product, especially for newly established entities. Some companies, novice in the field of trade finance, may prefer to accept simple and perceivably inexpensive payment terms rather than enter into negotiations with banks on issues of risk, fees, interest rates etc.

With the relaxation of foreign exchange regulations, trading on open account terms has become a frequently used and simple technique, offered at limited banking fees and ancillary costs, especially for transactions involving parties in Western Europe who themselves already had long-established trade relations. Different collection procedures have been in place, most typically Bills of Exchange with accompanying shipping documents to be sent to the buyer's bank and documents to be released against acceptance/payment of the bill.

Although these classic and straightforward payment terms represent the bulk of settlements of Poland's foreign trade, the Polish banking community is ready and able to offer more sophisticated products to satisfy particular import and export financing needs.

Trade finance products

Letters of Credit

The use of Documentary Letters of Credit (L/Cs) is common practice, both for settlement purposes as well as for short- and medium-term financing. L/Cs are of many different types, including:

- At Sight L/Cs and Deferred Payment L/Cs;
- L/Cs available on acceptance;

- Transferable L/Cs;

- Back-to-back L/Cs;

- L/Cs with a Red Clause.

Cash deposits remain a primary form of collateral but are increasingly being replaced by other types of collateral such as Promissory Notes, pledges on stocks and Bill of Lading (B/L) endorsements. Those customers with long-standing trading experience in particular markets may enjoy pre-agreed limits for L/C transactions granted by banks, with no collateral required. Secured and unsecured credit lines that may be utilised in the form of documentary credits are also available both for banks and customers active in international trade.

Discounting of drafts under Acceptance L/Cs and discounting of receivables under Deferred Payment L/Cs are products that are promoted to exporters and are being offered as post-shipment financing. This is subject to the bank's judgement of existing credit risk and its assessment of the exporter's reputation and credit standing.

Depending on the bank's strategy with respect to its own portfolio of receivables, its know-how in settlements and financing of foreign trade transactions, such negotiable instruments (Bank Acceptances) may be held until maturity or sold without recourse on the international secondary market.

Bank Loans

Transaction bank loans secured by the assignment of proceeds from the L/C can take the form of both post-shipment or of pre-shipment financing. In addition to the evaluation of credit risk and open credit lines, additional collaterals, usually in the form of exporters' Promissory Notes, are required.

Discounting Promissory Notes or Bills of Exchange is contingent on the creditworthiness of both the drawer and the acceptor of the Bill of Exchange, or its payee, as well as on the maturity date of the bill. This, in general, does not exceed 90 days but could go up to 180 days.

Factoring

There are principally two companies in Poland specialising in factoring that belong to the international factoring network. These are POLFACTOR, founded jointly by BRE Bank and Intermarket Factoring of Vienna, and Handlowy-Heller, founded jointly by Bank Handlowy and VB-Heller Bank. Both companies provide a full range of factoring services. Transactions are effected on the basis of limits for particular customers (exporters and importers), set up bilaterally by the factoring companies.

Guarantees

Bank guarantees offer the beneficiary bank an irrevocable and usually unconditional on-demand obligation to pay a guaranteed sum. Guarantees are frequently used by exporters in the form of tender guarantees, performance guarantees and advance payment guarantees. Guarantees are also used by importers who seek a buyer's credit with a payment guarantee.

Since the main banks in Poland have access to a wide network of correspondent banks, the issuance of a direct guarantee or indirect counter-guarantee for a foreign guarantor frequently facilitates trade with countries posing high economic and political risk.

As is the case with other banking products that create an irrevocable bank commitment, the issuance of a guarantee is subject to the presentation of a commercial agreement and to adequate collateral being provided.

Supporting instruments

Forward transactions that protect exporters and importers from exchange rate fluctuations are offered by most Polish banks.

Insurance against commercial and political risk in short-term commercial transactions (no longer than 180 days) is available from KUKE.[1] Short-term commercial risk coverage is offered on a whole turnover basis, and relates essentially to business with developed market economies. Indemnity is provided against a buyer's default resulting from insolvency or protracted payment default. Coverage for up to 100 per cent of the loss is available.

The assignment of an insurance policy to a bank may constitute adequate collateral for a credit being granted for the financing of export transactions.

[1] KUKE – Export Credit Insurance Corporation. This majority state-owned corporation is empowered to cover both commercial and non-commercial country risk and to engage in reinsurance activities. Initially, the corporation restricted its activities to insuring short-term commercial risk. Following supplementary legislation passed in 1994, KUKE now offers medium-long term and political risk coverage as well.

41

Import and Export

KPMG

Introduction

A completely overhauled Polish customs regime was brought in on 1 January 1998 with the enactment of a new Customs Code, broadly modelled on the EU Customs Code. There are, however, significant differences between these two codes, which, combined with high duty rates on certain items and an unsophisticated and bureaucratic approach sometimes adopted by the Customs Office, can create significant pitfalls for importers and exporters.

One area that often causes difficulties is the requirement for importers and exporters to be Polish individuals or companies. This creates many problems for multi-national enterprises, particularly in respect of cross-border supply-and-install contracts, leasing and commission-based structures.

In addition to the import of goods for free circulation, the following are the most commonly encountered customs regimes:

- transit;

- bonded warehouse;

- Customs Free Zone;

- inward processing;

- temporary importation;

- outward processing.

Customs duties are levied on imports only; the old export duties that existed under the communist regime have been abolished. There are two types of duty that can be levied specifically on imports of goods (in addition to VAT and excise duty, which are levied on imported goods on a similar basis to domestic transactions):

- **customs duty**, which has variable rates depending on the type of goods and their origin;

- **import levies**, which are imposed on certain agricultural goods. The list of goods covered and the applicable rates vary from time to time depending on market conditions.

Importation procedure

The basic customs document is the Single Administrative Document (SAD), which is very similar to that used in the EU. The procedure itself is generally bureaucratic and paper driven, although computerisation of border crossings is taking place slowly. Simplified procedures do exist for large regular importers. Customs agents also operate and are permitted to handle the importation procedure on behalf of an importer of goods.

In order to secure the payment of import duties, Customs Offices have the power to seize goods or accept guarantees such as bank guarantees, Bills of Exchange or government bonds.

Valuation of goods

The basis for the assessment of customs duty is the customs value. The valuation principles are closely modelled on the GATT/WTO valuation provisions. The customs value of goods is comprised of the transaction value (the last purchase), increased by any other costs up to the Polish border, such as transport and insurance, commissions, packaging and various licence fees relating to the purchase of goods etc. Unlike in the EU, a valuation based on the first sale for export is not permitted.

In calculating the VAT payable on the import, the appropriate rate is applied to the customs valuation, increased by the duty payable and any excise tax.

Duty rates and origin

The Polish customs tariff consists of nine-digit codes that are based on the harmonised OECD customs tariff (CN). Each code is allocated a number of different rates, depending on the origin of the goods.

The origin rules are similar to those in most developed countries and focus on the place of the substantive manufacture of the goods rather than on the nationality of the seller. Special rules exist in the Accession Treaty concluded between Poland and the EU in respect of goods processed in the EU.

Polish rates are high compared to the EU but are on a downward trend. Preferential rates apply to goods with their origin in the EU (most but not all goods are subject to 0 per cent), EFTA, CEFTA, the Baltic States and Israel. It is worth noting that there are no preferential rates for goods originating in the USA, the Far East and the CIS. Without a certificate of origin, lower rates cannot apply.

Duty exemptions

There are a number of exemptions within the Customs Code, but the most important for business are the following:

- **Contributions in kind**: Customs Duty can be waived on certain assets contributed by a foreign shareholder to a local company in exchange for shares. The local company should not dispose of the goods within three years.

- **Temporary importation**: Goods can be imported for a specific period of time (normally up to two years) with a full or partial exemption from Customs Duty.

- **Inward processing**: This allows the processing of foreign-owned goods in Poland and their re-exportation without an obligation to pay Customs Duty.

- **Outward processing**: This allows the processing of Polish-owned goods abroad and their re-importation to Poland with a full or partial exemption from Customs Duty.

- **Samples and advertising materials**: Models, samples and other items of no commercial value brought into Poland by businesses for publicity purposes can be exempted from Customs Duty. An exemption also applies to items brought in by the organisers of and participants in commercial fairs and exhibitions, including food and beverages to be used for marketing purposes.

It should be noted, however, that an exemption from Customs Duty does not automatically give rise to an exemption from the VAT payable on the importation of goods.

Special procedures

Bonded warehouses

A bonded warehouse is a separate part of the customs territory of Poland, where businesses may store and prepare goods for sale. Until the goods leave the warehouse, no Customs Duty or VAT is payable.

A bonded warehouse may be public (available for use by a third party) or private (used exclusively by the operator). Goods may be stored for an indefinite period, but security must be deposited for the Customs Duty and VAT on the goods.

Customs Free Zones

A Customs Free Zone is also not part of the customs territory of Poland. Polish legislation is less restrictive than that of the EU in that it allows more scope for the establishment of a 'private' zone, ie one that is operated exclusively by an individual entity for its own purposes in a place of its designation.

It is possible to process goods within Customs Free Zones.

Exportation of goods

No export duty applies to exported goods. An exporter is entitled to apply the zero VAT rate to such sales. It is important to note, however, that the zero rating is conditional on the exporter having proof (in the form of export documents) that the goods have left Poland.

Note

Poland introduced a system of VAT refunds for tourists in September 1999. Purchases must be made from an authorised retailer and exceed Zl 200.

42

Intellectual Property

Marek Rosinski and Paulina Kieszkowska,
CMS Cameron McKenna

Introduction

Poland is currently negotiating its membership of the EU. The protection of intellectual property (IP) rights is one of the central issues to the negotiations. The first steps of integration, ie legislation screening, have proved that Poland has quite a modern and EU-coherent intellectual property legal system. On the basis of the Association Agreement between Poland and the EU, Poland must harmonise its laws with European regulations. Currently, work is pending on the new Industrial Property Law, which would include all IP rights except copyright. The new law should bring all IP regulations into harmony with EU regulations.

Poland is also a party to all important international conventions regarding the protection of intellectual property rights.

Types of intellectual property rights

Currently, Poland protects all categories of IP exclusive rights: copyright (including software, industrial designs and databases) and neighbouring rights, patents, utility models, designs, trademarks and topography of semi-conductor products.

The holders of all IP rights described above have similar remedies in case of a breach of their rights, *inter alia* the right to demand the cessation of infringement, payment of damages and return of the unjust enrichment. Such a claim may be protected by a temporary order issued by the court. The holder of the IP right may also demand the publication of a statement of apology. In the case of patents, utility models, trademarks and copyright, the law also provides for criminal liability for the infringement of rights.

Know-how is not subject to any specific legislation, but may be protected contractually on the basis of civil law and unfair competition law, as well as under the TRIPS (Trade-related aspects of Intellectual Property Rights) agreement (1994).

Patents

The Law

Patents are protected by the Law on Inventions (1972) (revised text, Official Journal 1993 No. 26, poz.117, as amended). Following the changes to the economic system in Poland, the Law on Inventions was significantly revised in 1992–93. Poland is a party to the Paris Convention on the Protection of Industrial Property (Stockholm Act 1967), as well as TRIPS.

Subject of protection

The Law on Inventions protects inventions that can be patented. Inventions are defined as technical solutions that do not clearly derive from common technical knowledge and that have practical use.

Patents are granted only for 'new' inventions, ie inventions that were not presented to the public before the priority date of application. The Law provides for statutory exclusions from patent protection. Its *ratio* is not to protect knowledge which should be publicly available (scientific principles and discoveries; new animal breeds and plant varieties; treatment of diseases). Furthermore, the Law excludes the protection of inventions the use of which is contrary to law or against the interest of public order.

A patent, as a certificate of ownership of an invention, is granted by the Patent Office upon an application containing a description of the invention. A patent grants the exclusive right to use the invention professionally and commercially for 20 years. The protection of a registered patent is limited to the territory of Poland.

The priority date starts from the date of filing the application or presenting the patent at an exhibition (subject to filing the application within six months). Foreign applications may also be granted priority on the basis of the Paris Convention on the Protection of Industrial Property (Stockholm Act 1967).

Entitled party

The creator of an invention is the owner of the rights thereto. Inventions created by employees are owned by the employer unless an agreement between them provides otherwise.

Utility models and designs

Models

Utility models are protected by the Law on Inventions (1972) (revised text, Official Journal 1993 No. 26, poz.117, as amended) and the Paris Convention on the Protection of Industrial Property (Stockholm Act 1967), as well as TRIPS.

Utility models are defined as new and useful solutions that refer to the shaping, structuring or method of combining for use of an already existing object. They are protected for an initial five-year term, which is renewable for an additional five-year period. The protection of a registered utility model is limited to the territory of Poland.

The provisions on protection exclusions, the definition of the scope of the utility model rights, the list of the type of rights, the priority definition and the entitled party rights are analogous to the ones listed above in the case of patents.

Designs

The right to a design is defined in the Regulation of the Council of Ministers on the protection of designs (1963) (Official Journal 1963, No. 8, item 45). A design is a new aesthetic form of an object, which may amount to a new shape, surface features, lines, colour or design, which characterise the object in an original way, and which may be applied for industrial production. Designs are registered in the Patent Office for a period of five years, renewable for another five-year period. The protection of a registered design is limited to the territory of Poland.

All other protection aspects are regulated in the Law on Inventions analogously.

Trademarks

The Law

Trademarks are protected by the Trademark Law (1985, Official Journal of 1985, No. 5, item 17, with amendments). Poland is a party to the Paris Convention on the Protection of Industrial Property (Stockholm Act), as well as TRIPS, the Madrid Agreement on the International Registration of Trademarks (1989) and the Madrid Agreement for Counteracting False and Deceptive Indications of the Origin of Goods (Hague Act 1925).

Subject of protection

A trademark must indicate the origin of goods and services of an enterprise and distinguish them from other goods and services. The Trademark Law therefore makes trademark registration conditional upon a product having distinguishing characteristics. A trademark cannot contain any geographical indications (unless agreed by the proper authorities), national symbols or awards. It cannot be registered if it is similar to any trademark previously applied for, registered or commonly known. A trademark indicating services that may only be provided on the basis of a concession or licence may only be registered in favour of a company that has obtained such concessions or licences.

A trademark may take different forms: verbal, verbal-graphic, graphic, 3D and sound. Verbal trademarks, in order to be distinguishable, cannot be based only on Polish common language words, unless their combination is original and has acquired a secondary registerability, ie has been used for the identification of goods or services and is already distinguished by the public as such.

Trademarks are registered by the Patent Office. The term of registration is ten years from the date the application is filed. It may be prolonged for another ten years. The protection of the trademark starts from the date the application is filed, although it is conditional upon registration. The protection of a registered trademark is limited to the territory of Poland. The Trademark Law also protects commonly known trademarks. Priority of registration is granted to the first application filed in the Patent Office or filed internationally on the basis of the Madrid Agreement on the International Registration of Trademarks.

Copyright and neighbouring rights

The Law

Copyrights and neighbouring rights are protected by the Law on Copyright and Neighbouring Rights (1994) (Official Journal 1994, No. 24, item 83, with amendments). Poland is a party to the Bern Convention on Copyright Protection (Paris Act 1971) and the Rome Convention on Neighbouring Rights, Phonograph Producers' Rights and Television Broadcasting Rights (1961), and TRIPS.

Subject of protection

In Poland, as in most other jurisdictions, any manifestation of individual creative activity, irrespective of its form, value, designation or manner of expression, is considered a 'work' and is subject to the protective provisions of copyright law.

Polish law therefore sets out a defined (but non-exhaustive) list of works over which copyright protection can be exercised. Although the categorisation may vary from jurisdiction to jurisdiction, Polish law follows international norms. Thus, as well as written and musical material, computer software and industrial designs, the law will also protect 'derived' works, such as translations, adaptations or alterations. Furthermore, collections, anthologies, selections and databases are all covered by copyright legislation, even though they may contain otherwise unprotected material, provided that the particular selection, layout or composition can be considered 'creative'.

Polish copyright protects both the personal and economic rights of the author. Economic rights consist of the exclusive right to use a work and dispose of its use throughout all areas of exploitation, and to receive remuneration. Moral rights are protected eternally and cannot be waived or transferred. Economic rights, subject to the exceptions provided by law, expire 50 years after the author's death. If the author is unknown, and if the copyright *ex lege* is owned by a person other than the author (for instance, the employer), the 50-year limit runs from the first publication.

Audio-visual works

The Law has a separate section regarding the protection of audio-visual works. Under its provisions, the producer *ex lege* owns the rights to the audio-visual work. The producer must pay royalties to a group of co-authors of the audio-visual work and those royalties must be proportional to the revenues from cinema distribution, lending, renting and public reproduction of the audio-visual work. Erroneously, the royalty payment obligation does not include television broadcasting.

Software

The protection of software provisions is based on the EU Directive 91/250/EEC of 14 May 1991, relating to the legal protection of computer programs, and provides for the protection of all forms of its expression (documentation of the project, designs). Ideas are not protected. By virtue of law, the employer is the owner of software created by an employee. Liability for software defects is narrowly defined.

Neighbouring rights

Neighbouring rights include the performers' rights, phono- and videogram producers' rights, as well as broadcasting station rights, of which only performers are granted moral rights. The law provides a closed catalogue of neighbouring rights. The scope of their protection is narrower than the protection of copyrights.

Topography of semi-conductor products

The Law

The topography of semi-conductor products is protected on the basis of the Law on the Protection of the Topography of Semi-conductor Products (1992) (Official Journal of 1992, No. 100, item 498). Poland is a party to the TRIPS Agreement. The Polish law is based on the EU Directive 87/54/EEC of 16 December 1986 on the legal protection of the topography of semi-conductor products.

Subject of protection

The topography is defined as a series of elements, of which at least one is active, irrespective of the form of fixation, representing the pattern of layers. The right to the topography depends on registration by the Patent Office. Registration is granted only for original topographies, for ten years from the end of the year of its first introduction to the market, or from the end of the year of its application to the Patent Office.

Property Ownership

Steven Shone, CMS Cameron McKenna

Introduction

The real estate market in Poland has developed dramatically since the fall of Communism. The law on property has developed less dramatically. While some changes in the law relating to mortgages have improved the prospects for the development of a normal property lending market, other reforms are still awaited. This is not as sorry a situation as it may appear. Poland had a functioning modern Civil Code immediately before World War II. During the communist era the Code was not updated to reflect the modern world of real estate investment. This still leaves Poland in a much better position than some other emerging markets.

Types of title

There are three forms of property title that may be registered in Poland; *wlasnosc, uzytkowanie* and *uzytkowanie wieczyste.*

Wlasnosc or 'ownership' equates to freehold or fee simple title. Outside the cities, subject to permit issues (see below), it is often possible to acquire freehold land for development. Polish agriculture was never collectivised and most land in the countryside is in private hands. Because the average Polish farm is so small, however, much effort and care is required in assembling sites, especially as Polish law does not provide for land options. Conditional preliminary agreements to purchase are often used as substitutes for options.

In the cities, and especially in Warsaw, it is more difficult to acquire freehold sites. Much of the land in cities, and most of the land in Warsaw, was expropriated under decrees passed immediately after World War II. Much of that expropriated land is now vested in the democratic city authorities that were created by the Law on Self-Government of 8 March 1990.

Deficiencies in the system of funding for local authorities have created a situation in which these authorities are sometimes reluctant to sell land outright. They often prefer either to contribute freeholds to joint venture companies in which they are shareholders, or to grant *uzytkowanie wieczyste* interests, retaining the freehold reversion.

The joint venture approach was attacked by the Local Public Economy Act or Utilities Act of 20 December 1996, which seems to have been intended to prevent local governments from carrying on purely commercial activities. However, it was so poorly drafted that local authorities and their private sector partners have found no difficulty in circumventing it.

Uzytkowanie

The *uzytkowanie* or 'usufruct' will be familiar to anyone who has conducted real estate business in a Civil Law jurisdiction. Based on a Roman Law concept, it allows the use of a piece of land and the enjoyment of the literal or metaphorical fruits thereof by the usufructee. It is unlikely often to be of interest to commercial investors because it is not assignable. In some circumstances it may be useful to vest such a title in a special-purpose company so that it can – in effect – be transferred by the sale of shares. Usually, it would be easier and safer to buy a freehold or *uzytkowanie wieczyste* title.

Uzytkowanie wieczyste

The *uzytkowanie wieczyste* or 'right of perpetual usufruct' (RPU) is a form of title to land peculiar to Poland. 'Perpetual usufruct' is a perfectly accurate translation of a misleading name. The RPU is neither perpetual nor a usufruct. Despite the grandiose and inaccurate name, an RPU is closer to a common law ground lease than to any Civil Law concept.

An RPU may only be created in relation to freehold land owned by state or local authorities. Once granted, RPUs can usually be freely traded, depending on their specific provisions. Usually the local authority has a pre-emptive right to recover the land if the usufructee sells while the land is still unimproved.

The agreement creating an RPU should specify the commencement and completion dates of the development works to be carried out on the site, the types of buildings and facilities to be constructed and the maintenance obligations. If these obligations are not satisfied, the RPU may be terminated.

RPUs may be granted for terms of from 40 to 99 years in return for an initial capital payment or premium of up to 25 per cent of the undeveloped value of the land. An annual rent is due, usually 3 per cent of such value. A higher rent may be specified in the deed creating the RPU. In cases where the land is to have certain public uses, the rent may be lower, typically 1 per cent.

If an RPU is granted on developed land, than the usufructee should pay the full value of the buildings. Interestingly, the usufructee is the outright owner of buildings on the land. The annual rent can be reviewed not more than once a year. There is a valuation procedure to deal with this.

The possibility of such frequent reviews of what is essentially a ground rent introduces unwelcome uncertainty. However, in the economic conditions in Poland since the fall of Communism, many property developers have preferred to acquire RPU interests rather than freeholds. Annual rent of 3 per cent of undeveloped value is a fairly small price to pay to avoid the necessity of financing 75 per cent of the site value.

The law gives the usufructee a right to review the RPU on expiry. If an extension is not granted, the usufructee is entitled to compensation for the value of the buildings reverting to the freeholder. However, the valuation procedures are less than clear. Given that the first RPUs have not yet expired, there are no precedents for what happens in such a situation.

One assumes that the motivation for local authorities to have granted so many RPUs was political, rather than economic. Local authorities would usually have made a better financial return by selling freeholds and investing the additional 75 per cent of the price in other ways. Perhaps local authorities feared that funding from central government would be reduced if they reported large 'privatisation' proceeds. Private individuals holding RPUs are now entitled to acquire the freehold reversion. Furthermore, under the Property Management Act of 1997, a freeholder of land subject to an RPU may sell only to its usufructee.

Many developments in post-communist Poland have been financed and executed on sites held under RPU title. The title can be registered, a mortgage taken against it and it is (usually) fully transferable. Financial institutions seem to have had little trouble in accepting RPUs, rather than freeholds, as security.

Registration of title

Poland has two land registers. The first, the *rejestr gruntow* (Land Register) contains details of the location, area and designated use of the property (this is similar to the French *cadastre*). Indeed, there are proposals to make the system more closely resemble that in France, and then to base an *ad valorem* property tax on that register.

The Land Register is maintained by the land-surveying department of the relevant local authority. Plots are mapped on public plans and identified by unique plot numbers.

In theory, this is a public service. In practice, however, there are some elements of 'regulation'. For example, investors from Common Law countries are often shocked by the requirement in some cases for permission to be obtained to divide their land into smaller plots. This seems to them a blatant violation of their rights to deal freely with their own property.

Sales of part are delayed by this, and it creates problems for developers assembling sites with a view to sub-selling component parts of the project. In fairness to Poland, such regulations exist in other Civil Law countries, where the State often takes a more aggressive role in economic life than Anglo-Saxons would find comfortable. However, bureaucratic delays, and the occasional attempt to extort bribes to avoid such delays, seem to be the main consequences of the system.

The second land register is the *Ksiega Wieczysta* (Land and Mortgage Register). In this register, the owners and mortgagees of land are identified and details of easements, mortgages and other encumbrances are recorded. The plots comprising the land holding in question are identified by reference to the Land Register, whereas the *Ksiega Wieczysta* itself deals with the legal description of the land and its associated rights and encumbrances.

The register books are physical and are kept in the local Land Register Court. Given Poland's exciting history, lawyers may need considerable linguistic skill to inspect them, as entries can be in Polish, German or Russian. While the registers are public and therefore open to personal inspection by prospective purchasers, copies of the entries may be obtained only by the registered owner. If the file is being worked on by a Land Register Court judge, it will simply be unavailable and even a physical inspection will be impossible.

Inconveniently, there is no system of official searches of the register, and no 'protection period' during which it is 'frozen' to allow a purchaser or mortgagee to be entered into it. This means that there is a risk of entries being made between the dates on which the purchaser inspects the register and applies to be entered as the new owner.

This problem is addressed in many ingenious ways by Polish lawyers and notaries. These days, closings often involve junior employees of the purchaser's law firm being stationed in the Land Register Court with mobile telephones to confirm that the registers are unchanged at the time of purchase.

Leases

The lease is the key to the creation of a real estate investment. Real estate investors hope to buy an income stream and/or capital growth, not bricks and mortar. Yet leases are regarded as lowly and insignificant documents in many Polish law firms and handed to junior people to be negotiated. There are no standard forms in use, save those developed by individual real estate companies or major law firms. Every day, incredible errors are made.

This is doubly dangerous for the international developer or investor, as the 'default' forms of lease provided for by the Civil Code are poorly adapted to the conditions of a modern property market. If not carefully modified to institutional requirements, they fall far short of a 'triple net' or 'FRI' lease.

Landlords are restricted to using one of the two types of lease known to Polish law. They and their lawyers cannot devise new forms. Only the Polish parliament can amend the law to create new types of lease. This is not so far a legislative priority in a country where the problem is little understood. Poland's legislators face many demands on their time as the country readies itself for entry to the EU. As real estate law is expressly excluded from the Treaty of Rome, such issues are unlikely to come under legislative scrutiny for some years.

While lawyers cannot create new types of lease, they can and do erect impressive legal superstructures on the foundations of those that exist. If this work is done carefully, it is possible to create Polish leases that are institutionally acceptable. Until the last two years, any such statement was purely theoretical. Now that Poland has the beginnings of an institutional property market, it is finally possible to say that institutions with demanding requirements have bought investments based upon Polish 'triple net' leases. However, it is also true that – such is the lack of understanding of institutional requirements in the Polish market – it is hard to find such investments among the many developments created in the post-communist era.

There are two types of Polish lease, called respectively *dzierzawa* and *najem*. Some write these as 'lease' and 'tenancy' in English, as if this distinction imparted any useful information. It does not, and the Polish names are used throughout this chapter.

Dzierzawa

The *dzierzawa* is a form of lease capable of being granted for a fixed term of up to 30 years. It was designed mainly for use in agricultural tenancies. Some authorities believe that the maximum term may be extended by the device of including a right to a further term in the initial lease, or by granting 'serial leases'. These are sometimes called 'thirty plus thirty' leases in Polish real estate circles, and some people think that, as they then give a reasonably long term, they form a useful basis for real estate investment. They do not.

Whether or not the 'thirty plus thirty' device works, a *dzierzawa* is subject to insuperable objections as a basis for a property investment. It creates only contractual rights between the parties, not rights in the property itself. While it may be noted on the register of the superior title, it cannot be registered as a separate property interest, nor can it be mortgaged. It may be possible to assign it, depending on its contractual terms, but the assignment is like that of any other contract.

If unmodified, the *dzierzawa* imposes substantial obligations on the landlord. However, since the *najem* is the type of lease more often used for occupational tenants, it is more relevant to discuss the possibility of modification to institutional requirements in that context.

Najem

The *najem* is a lease designed for occupational users such as tenants of houses, apartments, shops and offices. Again, it is a purely contractual right, not an interest in land. The maximum fixed term for such a lease is ten years. A *najem* can only safely be used for the purpose for which it was intended, as an occupational lease.

Just as the 'thirty plus thirty' *dzierzawa* has its supporters, there is a school of opinion in favour of the 'ten plus ten' *najem*. Investors from countries where longer occupational leases are common may favour attempting to extend the life of the leases in their development. This device has been quite widely used, and may work, especially if backed up by penalties on the tenant and by guarantees from a substantial parent company in the case of default. However, most occupational leases in Poland have terms of from five to seven years. In the current market, a ten-year lease would be considered quite long.

The normal Civil Code provisions relating to a *najem* are very far from the institutional norm of 'triple net'. If specific provisions to the contrary are not negotiated, the landlord will have substantial obligations in relation to repairs, maintenance and services. There are some mandatory provisions of the Civil Code that cannot be overridden by the wishes of the parties as expressed in the contract. For example, a tenant will always be able to terminate a lease on health and safety grounds. A landlord with 'Legionnaires' Disease' in his air-conditioning system, for example, would find it difficult to prevent a tenant from terminating his lease. In these cases, prudent landlords include provisions in the lease allowing notice periods and 'cure periods' sufficient to allow such problems to be rectified.

For the most part, however, the qualities of a 'triple net' lease can be replicated in a Polish *najem*. Given that institutional investors are only just arriving to set standards, it is not surprising that there is still a widespread lack of understanding of the 'triple net' concept.

Time, experience, and the failure of landlords to sell their investments to institutions because of their lawyers' mistakes, are gradually educating the market and the advisors who serve it.

Mortgages

A *hipoteka* (mortgage) is a limited right in property. It must be created by a written agreement in the form of a notarial deed. This must identify the property on which it is to be secured and comprise all the essential terms of the loan. A *hipoteka* must be registered in the *Ksiega Wieczyste* to be effective. A subsequent purchaser of the land will be bound by a *hipoteka* as it is a right in property.

The *hipoteka* may be of two different kinds: *Hipoteka zwykla* ('simple mortgage') and *hipoteka kaucyjna* ('capped mortgage'). *Hipoteka zwykla* secures the principal debt together with the interest accruing on such debt pursuant to the agreement. *Hipoteka kaucyjna* provides for a cap for the amount secured. The principal debt, accrued interest and other claims may not exceed the capped amount.

Important changes to the Polish mortgage law were introduced on 1 January, 1998. The position of mortgagees was considerably improved and a *hipoteka* now confers security comparable to that given by mortgages in many other jurisdictions. However, many potential lenders worry about two issues in relation to Polish mortgages. Firstly there is the question of the statutory lien enjoyed by the Polish authorities in relation to unpaid taxes and social security contributions. While this is not an insuperable problem, it has certainly inhibited lending and prevented a proper market from developing. The 1992 Law on Mortgage Securities and Mortgage Banks, modelled on German legislation, promises to relieve this problem somewhat, as mortgages to such institutions will be true first charges, not subject to the statutory lien. Mortgages to other banks, companies or private individuals will still suffer from the present problem, so that there will be a two-tier market.

The second problem is with enforcement. The Polish courts have no recent track record in enforcement, but it is generally expected that it would usually be slow and difficult. The enforcement of a *hipoteka* requires an 'enforcement title'. This may be a court order, arbitration award or a voluntary submission to enforcement executed by the debtor in the form of a notarial deed. Concerns about the time a court would take can therefore be alleviated by using either arbitration provisions or by voluntary submission to enforcement. However, it is understandably difficult to persuade a borrower that he/she must submit to enforcement without the right to challenge it, merely because the lender is concerned about the effectiveness of the Polish courts.

A court is obliged to issue an enforcement order within three working days of due presentation of the enforcement title. The enforcement of a claim secured by a mortgage involves a forced sale of the encumbered property. The proceeds from the sale of such a property are then paid to the claimants according to the priority of their claims.

The sale of the property must be announced at least one month in advance in accordance with a statutory procedure. The sale is made by public tender supervised by a judge.

A similar procedure is followed during a sale of a property in the case of insolvency, unless a committee of creditors approves a private treaty sale outside the usual procedures. However, the proceeds from such a sale are then transferred to the bankruptcy estate and creditors are paid out according to the priority of their claims.

Permits to acquire land

In order for foreigners to acquire a freehold or RPU (or to acquire shares in a company holding a freehold or RPU) in Poland, permission must first be obtained from the Ministry of Internal Affairs and Administration, which will consult with other ministries if the land is considered to be of importance. There are some minor exceptions but these generally have little effect on significant projects or investments.

It is important to note the definition of 'foreigner' for the purposes of land acquisition. Under the Law on Acquisition of Real Estate by Foreigners, in addition to foreign individuals and corporations, a Polish company will also be considered a 'foreigner' if it is controlled by an individual person who is not a Polish citizen or a legal entity with its registered office abroad. 'Control' is defined as having direct or indirect ownership of at least 50 per cent of the Polish subsidiary company's capital. Therefore, if a foreign company establishes a majority-controlled Polish entity, that entity will also need to apply for a permit in order to acquire land.

Permission for acquisition of land by foreigners is generally forthcoming and is not viewed as a particular impediment to property investment. It is usually more in the nature of an administrative hurdle.

Restitution claims

Many business people looking to do real estate business in Poland are concerned about potential restitution claims. This is more of a political than a legal issue. Numerous draft laws have been proposed to deal with claims of the former owners of land expropriated by the Communists. To date only a minor piece of legislation returning to the Jewish community land used for synagogues or other community purposes has been passed.

Claims for 'reprivatisation' (as it is more commonly called in Poland) that have succeeded to date were founded on administrative irregularities in the original expropriation proceedings. The Communist authorities did not always trouble themselves to follow their own rules. There is no current legal basis for the reprivatisation of land that was properly expropriated in accordance with the legal procedures in force.

All the plausible drafts of a reprivatisation law have in common the principle that former owners will generally be compensated in some way, rather than having their ownership restored. In the absence of a law to resolve the situation once and for all, it is quite common for former owners or their descendants to try to capitalise on the situation by approaching developers or investors for money to 'buy out' their interests. Often the basis for such claims is very flimsy.

This is an issue that needs to be considered and cleared up on a site-by-site basis, but it is rarely an obstacle to investment.

Estate agents

The Property Management Act 1994 now regulates the activities of estate agents in Poland. This act defines the process followed in order to conclude agreements on the purchase of property or a lease. All practitioners must be licensed, and since the foreign surveyors of the international companies rarely have the language skills to pass the necessary examinations, they must co-operate with or employ Polish professionals. To date there are few licensed agents.

It should be noted that, as in many European jurisdictions, estate agents take fees from both seller and purchaser, and from both landlord and tenant. This can lead to misunderstanding when clients come from countries where this does not happen and believe that they are receiving independent advice. Some firms, including most of the well-known international names, do act only for one side or the other, and do give impartial advice. A prudent client would check on this issue before giving instructions, and buyers or tenants should check what fees, if any, are expected of them before they make any commitment to buy or lease.

The market

The property market has made progress in the years since the fall of Communism. There is now a large supply of modern Class A office space in the centre of Warsaw. There is a smaller supply of good-quality suburban space and lesser-class, cheaper, but still modern and functional space.

Outside Warsaw, the office market has still to develop. As the companies that established themselves in the capital city look to open regional centres, and as local Polish companies develop, the demand for such space can be expected to increase. Some attempts have already been made to meet it.

Throughout Poland, retail centres are springing up. Mostly, these are simple combinations of supermarkets, DIY stores and a few boutiques but there are also some developments in the pipeline more worthy of the name 'shopping centre'. Chains of petrol stations, often associated with fast food and small retail facilities, have opened all over the country.

Disposable income for leisure purposes is surprisingly high. This is a society where most people spend much less than is typical in Western Europe on their housing, and where few consumers have the opportunity or the inclination to take on debt. Poland has a very young population and this adds to the demand for leisure and entertainment facilities. Most of the world's major multiplex cinema operators are competing for suitable sites, quite often in retail developments. Other leisure operators are trying to develop such leisure facilities as bowling.

The health and fitness craze has still not caught on, but some developers hope to catch that wave by providing sports clubs and gyms now, before most Poles know that they want them.

The warehouse and industrial sectors have also seen some progress and, indeed, one of the very first acquisitions of a Polish development by an institutional investor was a warehousing and industrial park. Much is still lacking in this respect, especially in places other than Warsaw, and these markets remain to be tapped.

Poland is an interesting, challenging but worthwhile place for real estate developers, investors and lenders to do business. As in any market, it is vitally important to learn to understand the local business culture and to take advice from those familiar with the country, whether good local partners or good local professionals.

The author acknowledges the assistance received in writing this chapter from Barbara Olejniczak, Jolanta Nowakowska-Zimoch, Malgorzata Pietrzak-Paciorek, Maciej Lichy and Pawel Debowski in the Real Estate and Construction Department of CMS Cameron McKenna Sp. zo.o.

44

Employment Law

Marek Wroniak, CMS Cameron McKenna

Introduction

The rules governing the relationship between the employer and the employee in Poland are contained in a number of laws. The primary law is the Labour Code of 1974, as amended and as supplemented by decrees issued by the Minister of Labour and the Council of Ministers. There are other important laws, such as those governing trade unions, redundancy, unemployment etc.

The provisions of the contract of employment and of any other act forming the contract of employment (such as an appointment, election or nomination) must comply with the Labour Code. Any provisions of contracts less favourable to the employee than those provided for in the Labour Code are deemed null and void, and are replaced by the appropriate provisions of the Labour Code.

The Labour Code applies not only to Polish employees and Polish employers (including companies incorporated in Poland with foreign participation) but also to Polish employees and foreign employers operating in Poland, unless the individuals involved are governed by special rules under international treaties.

Employment contracts

Different kinds of employment contract

According to the Labour Code, there are three types of employment contract: for a definite period, for an indefinite period and for the completion of a specific task. Each of the contracts may be preceded by a contract for a trial period, not longer than three months.

Contracts must in principle be concluded in writing. If for some reason the contract of employment has not been concluded in writing, the employer is required to confirm within seven days the terms and conditions of the contract. The employment contract must state the parties involved, the kind of job to be performed and the employee's duties, the date the employee starts the employment, the place of employment and the employee's remuneration. The contract may have a provision confirming the employee's obligation to comply with legal provisions regarding discipline, order, safety and hygiene.

Termination of employment contract

Under the Labour Code each party may, at any time, terminate an employment contract concluded for a trial period or indefinite period of time. The termination of a contract of employment takes effect after the lapse of the period of notice.

The termination of a contract of employment concluded for a definite period of time can be terminated only if that contract was concluded for a period longer than six months and if the parties to the contract provided for a two-week notice period. A contract concluded for a definite period shorter than six months cannot be terminated by notice.

An employment contract may be terminated by one of the following:

- by an agreement reached between the parties;

- by a notice given by one of the parties, maintaining the prescribed length of notice;

- without maintaining the prescribed length of notice in consequence of a waiver provided by one of the parties;

- by the natural lapse of the period for which it was concluded.

The easiest means of dissolving a contract of employment is to terminate it by an agreement reached between the parties. This almost totally eliminates the possibility of a subsequent dispute.

Termination of employment contract with notice
According to article 36 of the Labour Code, the notice period required to terminate an employment contract concluded for an indefinite period of time is as follows:

- two weeks: if an employee has been employed for less than six months with the current employer;

- one month: if an employee has been employed for longer than six months but less than three years with the current employer;

- three months: if an employee has been employed for longer than three years with the current employer.

The notice of dissolution of an employment contract concluded for an indefinite period of time must be fair, ie there is to be some important reason justifying the decision of the employer. The Labour Code does not specify any list of such reasons. It may be, for instance, that the employee has systematically failed to perform the duties specified in the employment contract. The employer must be prepared to prove that the dismissal is fair, in case the notice of termination is questioned by the employee.

A contract of employment concluded for a trial period of time may be terminated with the following notice period:

- three days: if the trial period is less than two weeks;

- one week: if the trial period is longer than two weeks;

- two weeks: if the trial period is three months.

Employment contracts drawn for the completion of a specific task may be terminated before their expiry date by giving a two-week period of notice, but only in the event of liquidation or bankruptcy of the employer.

Termination procedure is as follows. Notice to terminate the employment contract should be given in writing.

The termination procedure involves notification to an appropriate trade union of the intention to give notice of termination of a contract of employment concluded for an indefinite period (this procedure does not have to be followed if the employee is not a member of a trade union). The trade union has certain rights of objection but cannot prevent the termination once all the required procedures have been followed. It is important to note that the notice cannot be issued unless and until these procedural steps have been taken. The employer is not required to follow this procedure in the case of liquidation or bankruptcy.

A number of **restrictions** apply to the employer's ability to terminate a contract of employment: for example, if the employee is near the age of retirement or is on sick leave. In addition, there are a number of categories of individuals who have special protection under the law and persons in these categories can only be dismissed, if at all, with the consent of certain bodies (eg pregnant women, officials of the trade union operating at the employer's company). Persons benefiting from such protection may still be dismissed for fault. Restrictions on dismissal will cease to apply in the case of bankruptcy or liquidation of the employer.

Wrongful termination with notice has consequences for the employer. If a contract of employment for an indefinite period is found to have been terminated unjustifiably or in a way contrary to the procedural provisions relating to termination of contracts of employment, the court – on the demand of the employee – is empowered to nullify the notice of termination. If the contract has already been terminated, the court may require that the employee be reinstated in his/her job with the same working conditions and with any outstanding wages to be paid to the employee for not more than two months (full payment is granted only to individuals under special protection). Alternatively the court may order that compensation be paid of an amount equal to the length of the notice period not more than three months remuneration of the employee.

If a contract concluded for a definite or trial period has been wrongly terminated, the employee shall be entitled to compensation only.

Termination of employment contract without notice
An employer may terminate an employment contract without giving notice in the case of serious misconduct by the employee, incompetence, prolonged absence for medical reasons or certain other cases.

Misconduct is understood to mean failure by the employee to comply with the duties incumbent on him/her under the Labour Code. For example, the employee may have seriously violated the basic duties of employees (have been absent from work without providing a reason, arrived at work drunk or drunk alcohol at work, abused social insurance) or violated the internal work by-laws, rules of the business or employment contract. The employer cannot terminate the contract more than one month after becoming aware of the fault. There are certain justifiable reasons for an employee's absence that cannot be used as the basis for a termination.

Where termination is to take place without notice, the employer must notify the appropriate trade union of the proposed termination and of the reasons. The trade union has three days in which to state its objections.

Wrongful termination without notice can have consequences for the employer. An employee who has had his/her contract of employment terminated without notice in violation of the provisions of the Labour Code is entitled to be reinstated on the same terms and conditions or to receive compensation. The compensation cannot be higher than the remuneration for the notice period in cases of a contract concluded for a definite period of three months remuneration. In cases where the employee is reinstated he is entitled to the remuneration for the period of being unemployed if this does not exceed three months. The Labour Court will decide whether the employer must reinstate or compensate the employee.

When the employee ends his/her duties, the employer must provide a work certificate stating his/her length of service, duties, qualifications, the reasons for the termination of his/her contract, and the level of salary reached.

If the employer fails to provide the employee with his/her work certificate at the end of the employment period, resulting in the employee being unable to get another job, then the employee is entitled to compensation for the period that he/she is unemployed, amounting to a maximum of six weeks remuneration.

Redundancy

A separate law exists dealing with redundancy, the Law of 28 December 1989. Redundancy is considered to be justifiable when an employer wishes to reduce the labour force for economic, organisational or technological reasons, and when, within a three-month period, a company of under 1000 employees plans to reduce its workforce by over 10 per cent or when a company of over 1000 employees plans to reduce its workforce by over 100 people. Where the employer is not able to satisfy the numerical conditions, then the same procedures apply as are set out above under 'Termination of employment contract' (with some modifications) and the employees are entitled to severance pay as outlined below.

The provisions of this law also apply in the event of liquidation or bankruptcy of the employer.

Procedure

At least 45 days before notices of termination are to be issued, company management must give written notification of its intention to the appropriate trade union(s). The trade union(s) must also be supplied with the reasons for termination and the number of employees to be dismissed.

Upon receipt of the notification, the trade union may request information regarding the economic and financial situation of the employer and details of future employment. The trade union is entitled to submit proposals to reduce the number of terminations within 14 days. Company management then has seven days to notify staff of its views on these proposals.

Within 30 days of the notification to the trade union, the union and company management should come to an agreement for the basis and timing of the terminations. If there is more than one trade union in the company, such agreement should be reached with all trade unions. If it is impossible to reach agreement, the basis for the redundancies would then be determined by the manager or the employer.

At least 45 days before notices of termination are to be issued, the employer must inform the local labour authorities in writing of its intention to reduce its labour force.

Severance pay

An employee who is made redundant is entitled to severance pay equal to:

- one month's salary: if the employee has worked for less than 10 years;
- two month's salary: if the employee has worked for longer than 10 years but less than 20 years;
- three month's salary: if the employee has worked 20 years or more.

The severance pay cannot exceed 15 times the minimum remuneration as mentioned below.

Remuneration

Remuneration must be paid in Polish zlotys, and must be paid in return for duties actually performed. The minimum remuneration for employees working on a full-time basis is Zl 528 month as of 1 January 1999. The minimum remuneration level is revised on a quarterly basis by the Minister of Labour. Each employee receives remuneration in proportion either to a fixed hourly rate or to a fixed monthly minimum, and is paid every month.

Each employer must issue employees with a copy of the company's remuneration by-laws.

Working hours

Working hours, as set by the Labour Code, may not exceed 8 hours per day and 42 hours per week. How working hours are allocated is determined by the internal regulations of each company.

Work performed in excess of these working hours constitutes overtime. Employees are entitled to receive additional remuneration for overtime. The Labour Code establishes a maximum amount of overtime per employee: 4 hours a day and 150 hours a year. The employee receives increased remuneration at the rate of 50 per cent extra ('time and a half') for the first two hours of overtime and 100 per cent extra for subsequent hours ('double time'), as well as for working overtime at night, on Sundays and on holidays.

Employees occupying independent or executive posts may be required to work in excess of normal working hours without the right to additional remuneration.

Night hours begin at 9pm and end at 7am. For night work, an employee is entitled to obtain 20 per cent extra remuneration calculated on the basis of the minimum remuneration.

Sundays and official holidays are not working days. If an employee works on these days they should have a day off in lieu.

Holidays

An employee is entitled to paid holidays and special holidays granted in specific circumstances. The number of paid holiday days is based on length of service. The calculation of paid holiday entitlement must (with a few exceptions) take account of the employee's period of service not only in his/her current job, but also in his/her previous jobs.

An employee is entitled to the following paid holidays:

- 18 days: after one year's service;

- 20 days: after six years' service;

- 26 days: after ten years' service.

The period of employment on which the length of holidays depends includes a period of education, assuming that the employee has graduated from school or university not more than six years ago.

Employees are also granted other kinds of leave. Examples include maternity leave and leave granted for special events, such as marriage, the birth of a child, and the death of a spouse, child or parent.

Employment law relating to directors

A director of a company or enterprise may be a member of the management board of the company. In this case, he/she will be appointed by the appropriate body of the company, such as the shareholders' meeting or the supervisory board. Such an appointment may be for an indefinite period of time, though he/she may be recalled (dismissed) at any time. An employment relationship may arise from the appointment.

However, the employment relationship requires the agreement of an employment contract with the director. An employment contract with a director is constructed according to the rules of the Labour Code.

Dismissal from the management board does not constitute termination of an employment contract. Employment contracts with directors usually provide for a confidentiality clause and a non-competition clause (in many cases, this may be by separate agreement). A director of the company need not necessarily be appointed as a member of the management board and, if this is the case, his/her employment is based only on an employment contract.

Employment of foreign citizens

The employment in Poland of foreign citizens is conditional upon a permit issued by the regional labour office, a special visa issued by the Polish consulate or embassy and a work permit issued by the regional labour office. The above mentioned documents are valid for one year, but they may be prolonged.

A foreign citizen may be a member of a company's management board or supervisory board, and if he does not undertake any employment, the above mentioned conditions and documents are not needed.

Trade unions

The freedom to organise trade unions is established by the Law on Trade Unions of 23 May 1991. Under this law the minimum number of people needed to establish a trade union organisation is ten. Unions are authorised to act in the following ways:

- give opinions on matters concerning the interests of all the staff;
- supervise the conditions of safety in the workplace;
- determine the division of the social and housing fund;
- give opinions on matters relating to individual employees;
- issue opinions in the case of termination of contracts of employment concluded for indefinite periods (see above).

Employees who are officials of the trade union receive special protection in respect of their employment contracts. Their employment contracts may not be terminated except in situations determined by law. The employer has an obligation to provide the trade unions with working space as well as equipment.

In many cases, the trade unions and the employers conclude collective agreements that set out the obligations of employers and employees, as well as the rights of the trade unions in the company.

Labour costs

Social security contributions

All employees are covered by social security. Contributions are calculated on the basis of an employee's cash income and in-kind benefits. Changes to the social security system became effective on 1 January 1999. The new social security system is based on the three 'Pillars' (see Chapter 47 on Pensions). The employer participates in the First and the Second Pillars.

The **First Pillar** of the reformed social security system consists of four funds. The funds that constitute the First Pillar are the retirement fund, the pension fund, the illness fund and the accident fund. A premium is collected for the Social Security Office (ZUS) from both the employer and employee. The premium is now divided as follows:

- retirement fund: 19.52 per cent (the employee and employer each pay 9.76 per cent);
- pension fund: 13 per cent (the employee and employer each pay 6.50 per cent);

- illness fund: 2.45 per cent (is paid only by the employee);

- accident fund: 2.03 per cent (in 1999 and, from 2000, 0.40–8.12 per cent, depending on the safety conditions of the company); paid only by the employer.

When a person's income from all sources of employment exceeds 30 times the average national monthly salary (it is announced once a year in the country's budget), the employer and the employee cease to pay premiums for retirement and pension funds.

The **Second Pillar** is constituted by a number of open pension funds, the employee choosing which one of the funds to contribute to. The part of the premium paid for the Second Pillar amounts to 9 per cent of the employee's remuneration and is transferred by ZUS from the premium paid to the retirement fund (in the First Pillar).

Apart from the above the employer covers additional social security contributions:

- 3 per cent is allocated to the Labour Fund;

- 0.15 per cent is allocated to the Guaranteed Remuneration Fund for Employees.

An additional contribution of 7 per cent may be imposed on companies in which working conditions have deteriorated. Such a contribution would be imposed by the Social Insurance Office at the request of the local labour inspector and of the regional sanitary inspector.

Contributions are also paid with regard to **foreign employees** working in Poland, though foreign employees may apply to the Ministry of Labour for an exemption from payment.

Each employer must register its employees with the local Social Security Office (ZUS). The payment of contributions and filing of clearing declarations by an employer must take place by the 15th day of the month following the payment of the salary to the employee.

Where the company uses the services of **independent contractors**, the social security contribution allocated to the Social Insurance Fund is as follows:

- both parties pay the premium for the retirement fund of 19.52 per cent (each pays 9.76 per cent) and the premium for the pension fund of 13 per cent (each pays 6.50 per cent);

- the illness fund premium is paid only by the contractor;

- the accident fund premium is paid by the client company if the service is conducted at its seat.

The above contributions are due only where the relevant contract has been concluded for a period of at least 15 days, or where several contracts with the same company for shorter periods of time last at least 15 days when considered jointly. In the latter case, no contributions are required when the period between the end of one contract and the beginning of another is at least 60 days.

There are separate rules concerning contributions to the Social Insurance Fund for those who are **self-employed**.

An employer's **failure to comply** with provisions on social security contributions may entail a fine of up to Zl 5000.

Social assistance fund

All companies employing more than 20 people must have a social assistance fund, which is intended to provide financial resources for 'social activities' and for the maintenance of the enterprise's social facilities. 'Social activities' are understood to be free or partly paid for services provided by employers in the area of recreation, culture and education, sports, financial aid and aid in kind. The term also covers financial aid, both repayable and non-repayable, for housing purposes.

Benefits from the fund may be provided to employees and their families, previous employees who have become pensioners and their families, and other individuals to whom the company has awarded the right to enjoy social benefits financed by the fund. The obligation for an employer to have a fund does not mean that every employee is entitled to enjoy benefits from it. The right to these benefits, as well as their scope, depends upon the general, family and financial situation of an employee.

Typical forms of aid will include financial assistance and aid in kind for the poor (eg to purchase clothing), subsidies for children's holidays and recreation, leisure and sports activities etc.

Detailed rules on the use of a fund's resources, as well as the principles and conditions under which these resources may be used, are defined in the by-laws agreed by the employer with the company's trade unions. Where such unions do not exist, the by-laws are agreed with an employee elected to represent staff interests.

Non-compliance with the provisions of the law, such as failing to create a fund, may result in the company's management being fined by the labour inspector an amount up to Zl 5000.

State Rehabilitation Fund for the Disabled

Companies employing over 25 people, at least six per cent of which are *not* disabled, must make monthly payments to the State Rehabilitation Fund for the Disabled. These payments are not tax deductible for employers.

Benefits due during temporary incapacity to work

Where an employee is temporarily incapable of working, he/she shall retain the right to:

- 80 per cent of his/her remuneration (unless the employer makes higher provision): where incapacity for work is due to illness or to isolation because of a contagious disease;

- 100 per cent of his/her remuneration: where incapacity for work is due to an accident at work, an accident while travelling to or from work, an occupational disease or disease during pregnancy.

Remuneration is paid for each day of incapacity for work, including rest days. It is not due when an employee has no right to sickness benefit. For a period of incapacity to work that lasts longer than 35 days per calendar year, an employee is entitled to receive sickness benefit from the social security system.

Disability or retirement severance pay

An employee who satisfies the conditions entitling him/her to receive a disability or retirement pension, and whose employment relationship expires in connection with a disability or retirement, is entitled to cash severance pay equal to one month's remuneration.

Death benefit

Death benefit is payable to the deceased employee's spouse and dependants (children up to 18 years, or 25 years if they are students) when an employee dies during employment or while receiving benefits following termination of employment due to incapacity to work by reason of illness. The amount of the benefit is dependent on the employment period with a given employer and is calculated as follows:

- one month's remuneration: where employment was less than 10 years;

- three months' remuneration: where employment was longer than 10 years;

- six months' remuneration: where employment was longer than 15 years.

Death benefit is equally divided between all entitled members of the employee's family. Death benefit will not be payable by an employer when he/she has provided life insurance cover for employees. The family of the deceased employee is entitled to insurance compensation of value at least equal to the value of the usual death benefit, as outlined above.

45

Recruitment and Compensation

Korn/Ferry International

Trends in the labour market

In 1990 a substantial breakthrough took place in the labour market situation in Poland. The departure from the principles of a centrally planned economy resulted in the rejection of the fiction of full employment that had been present in official ideology throughout the whole post-war period, and in the transformation of hidden unemployment (up to 50 per cent, depending on the sector) into overt unemployment.

The numerous changes in laws on employment that were adopted during the 1990s provided an institutional and legal framework for the changes taking place on the labour market. The most important direction for these changes was to shift the overall responsibility for employment from the state to individuals, thus making people fully responsible for their existence as participants in the labour market.

The most characteristic trends of the Polish labour market in the 1990s were as follows:

- The number of employees in state-owned companies substantially decreased. The privatisation processes and the emergence of new greenfield businesses resulted in substantial changes in labour market structure. While in the early 1990s almost 60 per cent of the working population was employed in the public sector, the proportion has now decreased to less than 30 per cent.

- The changes in the structure of labour that began a few years ago have not yet been completed. In fact, they are only half-way there, as many public sector companies have not yet undergone privatisation. (The agricultural sector, with its outdated employment structure, is a problem in itself.) The newly created businesses in the private sector do not usually reflect the employment structure that could be expected of a privately owned firm. This is mainly because most family (or privately) owned firms are not very developed in terms of labour management. In more mature economies, economic development automatically leads to more effective employment structures; this has not yet been the case in Poland.

- The market-oriented reforms have seen the emergence of massive unemployment. The unemployment rate, which increased most during the first stage of market reforms (up to 16 per cent in 1995), has now decreased again (to 10 per cent in 1998).

- Regardless of whether unemployment rises or falls, major differences continue to exist between individual social groups on account of gender, education, age and regions. Generally, men, youths, those with high mobility and those with high professional qualifications are not threatened by unemployment.

- Professional qualifications are one of the most important factors influencing one's success in the labour market. Those with university degrees are the most likely to find well-paid employment.

- The regional accessibility of qualified labour differs in individual areas. The more advanced the economic development of the region, the more available highly qualified labour and managerial skills are.

At the turn of the millennium, developments on the Polish labour market will depend on:

- demographic pressure;

- economic growth;

- restructuring of public sector industry (ie coal, steel etc);

- changes in the social security system.

The above, combined with improving educational systems leading to an increase in the quality of professional skills, as well as the growing mobility of employees, could form the foundation for the sustained transformation of the labour force in Poland. In the longer run, the increased efficiency of Polish human resources will contribute to Poland's successful accession to the EU.

Trends in the managerial market

A typical feature of the managerial market in Poland is the inadequate number of executives at middle management level. Individuals who have several years' experience at this level within the organisational structure of a company try to achieve a senior management position as quickly as possible. This tends to cause a managerial 'competency crisis' and is often a serious hindrance for companies in their everyday operations.

Job hopping is another important element in the Polish managerial market. Before 1990, Polish managers used to change companies relatively rarely, though they often worked for more than one employer at a time in order to supplement their incomes. After 1990, despite better job opportunities (increasing numbers of Western companies began entering the Polish market), job hopping became quite frequent, especially at the beginning of the decade. These frequent changes resulted in a high demand for qualified managers. Multi-national companies dealing in the capital market in Poland were prepared to offer much better salaries and more opportunities for promotion. Employers fought over potential employees.

The market structure is currently much more stable: the supply of managerial skills and professional expertise has increased and the expectations of managers have undergone revision. Managers in Poland are becoming increasingly dedicated to the companies they manage or co-manage, and now strive to achieve success by implementing defined strategies, realising that it is only in this way that they will be able to be in a competitive position in the labour market in the long term. Finally, job hopping has been limited by the stabilisation of the market, as compensation levels have become more standardised.

Highly qualified managers plan their professional careers just as they would make investment decisions, seeing their experience and expertise as capital to be strategically invested. That is why, when talking to a potential future employer, managers try to understand as fully as possible the scale and commitment of the company's investment plans in Poland (high investment levels and dedicated financial resources are seen as a risk minimisation element). One of the first questions asked by a senior executive when offered a CEO position in a company of which he knows little would relate to the company's strategic plans in Poland, its level of planned investments, the role of the Polish business within the company's international structure etc. The Polish managerial market is becoming more and more competitive for employers. Intensified capital investments by multinational companies, as well as the restructuring of local enterprises, have caused a significant increase in the number of available job opportunities for highly qualified managers and a gradual, but systematic, increase in managerial expectations.

Managers expect to be given the ability to make decisions and to have opportunities for professional development. Management in Poland is becoming better educated than ever and has more extensive professional experience, and naturally expects new job opportunities to bring an increase in their level of responsibility and decision-making. Managers feel they are prepared not only to initiate the implementation process for a business strategy, but also they often see their professional career as an opportunity to participate in the development of new business. Strategic planning has become one of the most sought after components of a job description.

Professional qualifications

Typical professional career development and the formal educational requirements for management in Poland differ greatly from what is considered usual in 'Western' countries. An understanding of the specific character of the Polish managerial market is often a condition of success in finding the right person for a position.

Managers in Poland are generally very well educated. A considerable majority have a university degree, often complemented by additional postgraduate studies or programmes that are specific to business, such as an MBA or a business course offered by local universities. Managers have command of foreign languages, although usually of only one. The most popular is English; German and French are less frequent. The use of several languages is primarily characteristic of the younger generation.

Due to the specific character of the investment process in Poland, some qualifications are now more common than others. The managerial market includes many candidates with experience of top financial positions, although it remains difficult, within this professional group, to find individuals who, as well as being able to implement reporting systems or management information systems, would also have expertise in dealing with major investments, and cash management and control. Individuals with such formal experience are therefore the most highly prized professionals.

Sales directors constitute a large professional group. The Polish market is such that employers can expect to find sales executives with up to ten years of experience. However, the considerable majority of sales managers are people who are doers rather than strategists; until recently, sales strategies were defined by European headquarters, and sales managers co-ordinated the execution of pre-established business objectives. Finding a person with experience in independently building sales strategies therefore requires particular methods of approaching this professional group.

Marketing managers are becoming a large professional group, yet the scale of their professional experience is usually a period of no more than six to seven years. Marketing directors in Poland rarely have experience in designing new products, but are well able to build the remaining elements of a strategy and of operational activities within the field of marketing.

One of the most neglected management functions in the fervour of change and economic growth is that of human resources (HR). Only a small number of managers in this field have achieved board member status and, as a result, it is still difficult to expect them to have a strategic focus on HR management. Similarly to marketing, the HR field is dominated by young professionals and this function will have to mature before the availability of quality human resources management increases. Today, the search for a high-calibre HR director with expertise in strategic planning requires the use of executive search, and the pool of best-qualified individuals from which to choose will not exceed 60 names.

A completely new, emerging profession is that of operations (production and logistics) and quality control management. The modern production industry is the youngest sector of the Polish employment market, which is why, regardless of the popularity of engineering-related education, it is still difficult to find candidates with the required professional experience in this field. Technical studies were very popular in Poland before 1990, yet the objectives faced by operations managers in previous years rarely included such parameters as efficiency, productivity, cost efficiency or quality – those professionals who are able to meet these challenges are therefore especially valuable.

Finding the right person for a CEO position will often require an open mind in approaching the candidate's professional career development before 1990 and a willingness to accept that it is still difficult to find general managers with ten years of experience.

An attentive observer of the trends and tendencies in the managerial market in Poland will easily observe the increase in market potential: in a few years' time, managers in Poland will be a serious threat to managers in the West.

Compensation

The level and structure of managerial compensation in Poland is beginning to reflect Western standards. Apart from a stable, annual base salary, now increasingly on a par with that of Western managers, a compensation package will often include elements such as an annual bonus, an insurance package (life insurance and insurance against accidents), as well as social benefits (medical care, pension fund, membership in sports clubs, etc). Managers in Poland also expect the use of a company car, a mobile phone and a computer as necessary tools of their trade.

Compensation levels are often increasingly linked to results. An annual compensation package will now most likely be complemented by a 'mobile' element, usually a bonus at 10–30 per cent of the annual salary or stock options. Stock options are becoming a frequently used tool for motivating and rewarding management in Poland, such compensation becoming more and more popular both in Polish and foreign listed companies. Stock option programmes are aimed at increasing the level of commitment of managers, as well as tying the employee to the company (a employee may only repurchase particular parts of the stock option package at a set date).

There are also numerous, though less popular, financial and non-financial benefits specific to individual organisations to help them achieve an edge in the recruitment market. Such elements include housing loans (or

guarantees for bank loans) and financing tuition (such as MBA programmes) abroad.

While negotiating changes in their professional career, managers in
Poland pay special attention to the value of the whole compensation package. Candidates for managerial positions first evaluate the value of their
current compensation package, taking into consideration all of its elements. Due to progressive stabilisation of compensation levels at the managerial level, candidates are often willing to accept minor salary raises in
return for more favourable non-financial or mobile elements.

46

Management Development

Andrew Murray, British Council, and Nick Sljivic, VP International

Introduction

There is a huge need for management training of all types in Poland. After decades of a command-led economy, Polish managers were left generally ill-equipped to deal with the onslaught of market forces, having never been exposed to, or trained in, modern management principles. All aspects of management development are seeing enormous expansion in Poland, aiding managers in improving the depth and breadth of their skills. An empirical observation is that young Polish managers have an overwhelming desire to better themselves (in terms of job prospects and remuneration) by gaining recognised management qualifications.

Management education is a very new phenomenon in Poland, only introduced in the past few years as an academic and practical discipline. Pre-1990, under the socialist political and economic system, there were no formal management courses leading to any internationally recognised qualifications. During this period, courses were available at Polish universities in subjects such as accountancy, economics and international trade. However, these were highly theoretical in their content and, due to the closed nature of society and education, totally lacking in exposure to modern international management thinking or practice. In addition, they were mainly oriented to conducting business with COMECON countries. Management training organisations that existed in Poland at that time were operated by state-run companies or were state-owned organisations. There were no private training companies and no MBA programmes.

Once Poland became open to international influences at the start of the 1990s, it became apparent that there were enormous shortcomings in Polish management. For example, pre-1990, sales and marketing were virtually non-existent as professions, financial management largely consisted of book-keeping and audit and the use of IT lagged far behind that of the West. As a consequence, a large proportion of Polish managers have had limited exposure to, and a poorer grasp of, business fundamentals when compared to Western European managers of a similar age and experience.

There is now, in consequence, an increasing awareness of the need for more and better-quality management. Much of the stimulus for improvement in all management areas began with the arrival of international companies bringing their own standards and practices. In general there is a huge difference between the investment that international companies earmark for their staff and that offered by Polish firms. International companies have a far greater appreciation of, and invest far more in, management training than traditional domestic companies.

Types of management education

The provision of management development services comes in numerous and various guises. Types of management education in Poland can be categorised as follows:

- internal courses;

- external training not leading to a qualification;

- training leading to qualifications eg in accountancy and banking;

- undergraduate business degrees;

- MBA programmes.

The commitment to management training and the format it takes very much depends on the individual company. Decisions on training expenditure depend on a combination of factors, including:

- local company policies;

- international company policies;

- company requirements;

- management's appreciation of staff training;

- management's awareness of training options;

- company's financial standing;

- available budgets;

- pressure from individuals within the company.

Many national and international training companies have become established in Poland, covering every aspect of the business spectrum. The large accountancy companies offer a wide range of training courses, innumerable IT training companies now exist and a large number of organisations now offer courses that lead to professional management certificates. For example, there are numerous organisations offering courses, both distance learning and part time, that lead to accountancy qualifications such as ACMA, ACCA and CIMA.

The rise of MBA programmes

One particular aspect of management education that has burgeoned in recent years has been that of the supply of, and demand for, MBA programmes. There are now over 40 domestic MBA programmes, as well as numerous international ones (full time, part time and distance learning), being promoted in Poland.

There is growing awareness of course availability and also of the benefits of acquiring an MBA qualification as a means of furthering a career. Therefore, demand at all business schools in Poland is growing year on year, as is the interest in full-time overseas programmes and international distance learning programmes, such as those offered by the University of Chicago in Barcelona and IFM (The Manchester Business School–University of Wales finance-oriented MBA).

The first business schools appeared in Poland in the early 1990s. Most were established with assistance from Western business schools and from international government and private donations. On the whole, most Polish MBA courses are regarded as inferior to international programmes but many are now gaining in status, most notably those in Warsaw, such as the Warsaw School of Economics' MBAs, offering various programmes in conjunction with well-respected international partners such as the Universities of Minnesota, Calgary and Quebec.

The British government's Know-How Fund recognised the importance of management education for the successful transition to a market economy and provided significant support to develop regional business schools. These were not solely for MBA programmes, but for the provision of practical management courses for the local business community. The reasons for a regional focus were a combination of the disproportionate attention paid to the economic development of Warsaw and the recognition of the economic importance of the regions. In 1990, four business schools were established, linked to UK management institutions (Lodz, Gdansk, Poznan and Lublin) and a further three Polish institutions have been supported since 1996 (Szczecin, Bialystok and Wroclaw).

International business language training

The demand for foreign language courses for business has grown at an enormous rate as international companies have become established and

Poland increases its links with the West. Overwhelmingly, the most popular language is English, followed by German and Russian. The number of
language schools has exploded over the past several years, offering every
combination of languages and specialisations. There are now an estimated
150–200 language courses available in Warsaw alone. The British Council
(one of the leading providers of English language courses) estimates that
over 80 per cent of private language school students are from the business
community.

The future

The demand for management education will continue to increase, as will
appreciation of the benefits to individuals and organisations of having
staff that are adequately trained and have had the opportunity to develop
their management competencies fully.

There is an opportunity for many more specialist training organisations
to provide services in Poland as the economy becomes ever more sophisticated. The most obvious route for a new entrant would be via some form
of partnership with one of the many existing institutions. These now have
the requisite experience and links with the business community but would
benefit from the assistance of training companies that have proven international track records in management development.

47

Pensions

Iain Batty and Nicholas Donnithorne,
CMS Cameron McKenna

Introduction

Pension provision, both state and non-state, has been the subject of far-reaching reforms in Poland, with the final stages to be implemented by the end of 1999. The reforms are largely based on the World Bank 'three-pillar' model. The first pillar is a revised, unfunded state pension arrangement. The second pillar is a mandatory private sector defined-contribution arrangement. The third pillar is designed as a voluntary arrangement based on occupational, employer-sponsored pension schemes.

The reforms have also ensured that the new pension provisions are fully integrated into the social security system in Poland. With overall social security contributions at 45 per cent of salaries, employers are taking an increased interest in the pension reforms, in particular in assessing whether they should provide some form of third pillar arrangement for their employees. Investors are also studying the market with interest. With a relatively high population at about 38 million people and many billions of dollars expected to enter the private pension funds each year, there are potential opportunities for providing services in one or both of the two private pillars.

Whereas, previously, the employer was responsible for paying the employee's social security contributions in their entirety, under the revised system, while the overall cost of labour remains the same, the employee now pays approximately 50 per cent of these contributions. About two thirds of the social security contributions are directed to the Pillar One funds, made up from both employer and employee contributions, and about one-fifth of them are directed to Pillar Two from the employee's portion of the contributions.

Pillar One

The state-funded Pillar One is financed on a pay-as-you-go basis and is funded from a proportion of the social security contributions. Employees are supposed to contribute to the social security fund (except those in certain specified occupations such as policemen or farmers) and are entitled to receive benefits. Under the recent reforms every employee has an individual account and the contributions received are used to create notional capital for pension benefits. Pillar One pension benefits are payable on retirement from age 62 for both men and women. When the decision to retire has been made, the notional capital attributable to that individual is calculated against their future life expectancy to produce a monthly pension.

The Pillar One fund additionally guarantees a minimum pension and supplements the pensions of those individuals whose benefits would otherwise be less than 28 per cent of net average earnings to this level. Approximately 10 per cent of pensioners currently receive such supplements.

Pillar Two

The Pillar Two funds started collecting contributions from April 1999. There are in effect two legal entities involved: the pension fund is simply a vehicle for the collection of assets held on behalf of members; all managerial and administrative functions in relation to the fund are controlled by the pension fund society that governs it. The pension fund society must be a joint-stock company and must be capitalised to a minimum level of €4 million. Additionally, the assets of the fund must be held by a depository.

It is mandatory for all those in employment who were under 30 on 1 January 1999 to join a Pillar Two fund by the end of September 1999. Those that have not joined will be randomly allocated to a fund by the social security agency. For those in employment aged 30–50, joining a fund is voluntary, though, once the decision to participate in Pillar Two is taken, it is irrevocable. The contribution to the fund is 9 per cent of wages for those earning less than 250 per cent of the national average earnings. For those who earn more than this ceiling, contributions are only payable up to this level.

Since the funds are accumulation vehicles only, they have no role in the actual provision of retirement benefits. At retirement, a transfer payment will have to be taken to a dedicated pension annuity company of the member's choice. Although the relevant annuity law has yet to be passed, the member will have an option as to the type of annuity that he/she purchases, and what type of guarantees are included.

To date, 21 funds and governing societies have been licensed to operate. They have all had to overcome significant legal hurdles and licensing procedures. Members of the governing bodies of the pension fund societies have had to fulfil exacting requirements in terms of technical and professional expertise. The licence applications have been scrutinised extensively by the regulatory body, which has often requested considerable additional information from applicants.

There are very detailed regulations concerning the investment of pension fund assets. Broadly, once the necessary regulation is passed at least 95 per cent of the funds must be invested domestically within 18 separate investment classes. In most cases there is a maximum percentage of the funds' value that may be invested in a particular class.

Subject to the requisite regulation being passed a maximum of 5 per cent of the value of a fund may be invested abroad but, again, only in certain specified classes of investment. The pension fund society must undertake all domestic asset management itself but the management of fund assets invested abroad may be delegated to asset managers with their registered offices in the relevant country.

The effect of the Pillar Two system on employers is limited. The only significant impact is that they have to forward the appropriate contribution in respect of their employees to the social security agency, which is responsible for transmitting these to the funds.

From the point of view of the investor, there are some opportunities in this market. It would still be possible to apply for licences to establish a pension fund and pension fund society but, by the time these had been obtained, most members would have been signed up by other funds. Therefore, the opportunity at this stage lies with buying into the established market. There are high capital requirements to meet in order to establish a pensions operation and, because of the individual nature of the product, a requirement for a large and well-organised distribution network. Analysts are forecasting wide-scale mergers and acquisitions in this overcrowded market. It has only been possible to sign members up to funds in the last few months but already there appear to be clear winners and losers. Moving into the market at this stage will eliminate the uncertainty that existed for those funds that were established at the outset, but it will only be for the investor with deep pockets. The rewards, however, can be significant. The permissible charging structure is a front end charge on contributions received and an annual management fee. The key to survival in this market is attracting and retaining a large number of members.

Opportunities also clearly exist for service providers. It is expected that several billion dollars a year will be paid into the new funds and the requirements for depositories, transfer agents, consultants and other service providers will grow with the funds.

Pillar Three

It is hoped that the first two pillars of the pension system should enable the majority of workers to achieve a pension that will meet their basic needs during retirement. However, for those who feel they wish to make additional provision for their retirement, they may have a third option, if their employer sponsors a pension programme.

Unlike Pillar One and Pillar Two contributions, which are paid to the social security agency and relevant pension fund and are paid from pre-tax income, Pillar Three contributions are paid from post-tax income. However, benefits derived from Pillars One and Two are subject to tax, while those from a Pillar Three source are not. For all three pillars, during the accumulation period, all investment growth is rolled up free of tax.

A Pillar Three scheme may take one of four forms. The employer may establish its own tailor-made, defined-contribution fund governed by an employee pension fund society; or take out group insurance for employees with a joint-stock life insurance company; or pay employee contributions to an open investment fund; or pay employee contributions to a mutual insurance company. While it is legally possible to establish a Pillar Three scheme, at the time of writing no schemes have been established as most employers are waiting for the proposed amendments to this law to be passed by parliament.

It is widely believed that the option for employers to enter into an arrangement with a mutual insurer is not really viable. There are several reasons for this, although the main one is that the regulations governing mutual insurance companies are unclear and imprecise. As to the other options, it is calculated that, for employers of more than 1000 employees, the long-term cost savings alone may tend to favour the establishment of an individual fund, although the initial start up costs can be extensive. For employers of less than 1000 employees, this option may be cost-effective if they enter into a joint arrangement with one or more employers. Unlike an individual employer fund, the start-up costs for an arrangement with a life insurance company or an investment fund are likely to be much lower. However, ongoing costs may be higher.

With massive competition for qualified and experienced employees, it is thought that many employers will be prepared to provide Pillar Three arrangements. The lack of tax relief on contributions is a drawback but both the employer and the employee will benefit from relief from social security contributions. Because of the high level at which these are set, such relief may, along with the obvious benefits of attraction and retention of employees, prove attractive enough to convince an employer to create a Pillar Three scheme.

48

Dispute Resolution

Pawel Pietkiewicz, Neil Aitken and Charles Spragge, CMS Cameron McKenna

Introduction

The two principal means for the resolution of commercial disputes in Poland are the Polish court system and (domestic and international) arbitration under the Code of Civil Procedure 1964.

Essentially, the judicial system in Poland consists of three levels of state courts – district, provincial and appellate – and of the national Supreme Court, which hears cassation applications from the provincial and appellate courts acting as courts of second instance. Hearings must generally be conducted in public, although a court can sit in closed session for exceptional cases involving, for instance, state or trade secrets. There are detailed rules covering pleadings, evidence, judgements, appeals, enforcement and costs. Judges are appointed by the president of the Republic on the recommendation of the minister of justice, who in turn acts on the advice of the National Chamber of Judicature.

Domestic and international arbitration is governed by the Code of Civil Procedure of 1964. There are several permanent arbitration bodies in Poland, of which the most prominent is the Arbitration Court at the National Chamber of Commerce in Warsaw.

Besides judges and state criminal prosecutors, there are three other types of general lawyers in Poland: advocates, *radca prawny* (who are the nearest equivalent to English commercial solicitors) and notaries public.

This articles describes:

- the civil courts of Poland;

- the Polish arbitration regime;

- certain Polish arbitration bodies;

- the organisation of the Polish legal professions.

Although the stirrings of interest in the techniques of alternative dispute resolution (ADR), such as conciliation and mediation, are becoming evident, for the present there is little sign that these techniques will be widely adopted in Poland in the immediate future.

Civil courts

Structure

Justice is administered through the state courts and the national Supreme Court. The structure and jurisdiction of the state courts is set out in the Code of Civil Procedure 1964 and in the Act on the Structure of the State Courts. There are three levels of state law courts: district, provincial and appellate. Within each level, there are distinct divisions for civil and criminal cases. There are also specialised courts for commercial law, labour law, social insurance and family law disputes. There are ten regional appellate courts in the major cities, and these hear appeals from the provincial courts. The Supreme Court in Warsaw hears cassation applications (described below) from the provincial and appellate courts acting as a court of second instance.

First instance

As a general rule, an action should be started in the relevant first instance court for the area in which either the defendant resides or (if it is a firm) has its registered office. If the claim concerns a commercial agreement, an action can also be started in the court for the region in which the agreement was to be performed. The first instance court in which proceedings are properly begun will retain a residual jurisdiction.

Procedure

Polish law requires all court hearings to be conducted in public, although a court may exceptionally decide to sit in closed session to avoid the disclosure of, for example, state or trade secrets. The parties also have a limited opportunity to request a closed hearing in cases where the requesting party can show sufficient reason. This sometimes happens in family proceedings, for example. But it is not clear how willing a court would be to sit in closed session simply to preserve the confidentiality of an arbitration procedure whose award it had been asked to set aside.

Pleadings

Polish pleadings are less formal than in England and set out allegations of both fact and law. The pleadings also refer to and attach the evidence on which the parties rely.

Civil proceedings are started when the claimant files the plea, which is similar to the English statement of claim. The chairman of the court examines the plea to check that it meets all the requirements: for example, whether the registration fee has been paid, and whether the legal demand and the grounds for it are defined precisely enough. If the court decides that there are no grounds for rejecting the statement of claim, it examines its own competence and decides whether or not the proceedings should continue. The chairman fixes a date for trial and orders a copy of the statement of claim to be delivered to the defendant.

Generally speaking, a defendant does not have to make any written reply to the statement of claim, unless the dispute is a commercial one – although in complex cases the court can order a written defence – and may not have to attend any hearing or participate in the trial process in any way. Although a claimant is entitled to respond to a defendant's reply to the claim in advance of the hearing, in practice the claimant's response is usually dealt with during the trial.

Evidence

There is no equivalent in Poland of the common law obligation of discovery that requires the parties to disclose to each other all the relevant documents in their possession. Rather, the disclosure of documentary and other evidence is at the discretion of the chairman of the court, who is responsible for preparing the case for trial. At an early stage, the chairman will question the parties to sharpen the issues in dispute between them.

The court may request to see any document but it may not force the party to present such a document (the only exceptions are for labour and family disputes). Written witness statements are not used and evidence is given orally to the court at the hearing.

At trial, witnesses may be questioned by the parties and by the court, which in a commercial case usually consists of a single judge. Evidence may be given under oath, and witnesses may be prosecuted under the criminal code if they give dishonest evidence to the court. Witnesses do, however, have a limited right of silence if there is a danger of self-incrimination or if their evidence might reveal state secrets. Exceptionally, contradictory witness evidence will be dealt with by confrontation: the relevant witnesses are summoned to appear before the trial judge and confront each other about their conflicting evidence. This process has a good record of producing agreement and often results in one party abandoning his/her version of events. If specialised evidence is needed, expert witnesses are appointed by the court and not by the parties. The court will also decide whether the expert should give evidence orally or in writing.

All court hearings are minuted by the judge's clerk, usually in handwritten note form. The minutes cover all oral evidence, submissions, decisions and orders of the court. Consistent with the principle that it is the court, and not the parties, that controls the action, the proceedings are closed by the court once it considers that it has sufficient evidence upon which to reach a judgement.

Judgements

Usually, judgement follows immediately after the close of proceedings and is given in writing. In complex cases, however, judgement may be adjourned for up to two weeks. The parties can request the court to produce a written version of its oral judgement, which should contain the court's detailed reasoning. But the request for a reasoned judgement must be made within a week of the judgement. The court will also produce a written judgement if there is an appeal.

Appeals

There are three types of appeal: appeal, cassation and complaint.

Appeal
There is an automatic right of appeal against a court judgement, subject only to the limitation rules. An appeal will be determined on the basis of the evidence produced at the trial hearing. If an appeal is allowed, the appellate court may change the original judgement or, if it rules that the original proceedings were invalid, it can annul the judgement and refer the case back to the court of first instance.

Appeals must normally be made within two weeks of the appellant having received a reasoned judgement or three weeks if he/she did not ask for such a judgement. The appeal papers are lodged with the court against whose judgement the party intends to appeal. The respondent may answer the points of appeal by submitting a written reply directly to the relevant appellate tribunal within two weeks of the appellant's papers being lodged. The reply may refer to new facts and evidence. However, a respondent is under no obligation to answer the appellant's case.

The quorum of all the appellate tribunals is three professional judges. The appeal is heard by the provincial court if the judgement of the district court is heard and by the appellate court if the judgement of the provincial court is appealed. Subject to limited exceptions under the Code of Civil Procedure 1964, their judgement will be immediately enforceable.

Cassation
A litigant can in certain circumstances make a cassation application to the Supreme Court to annul the decision of a provincial court or appellate court acting as a court of second instance. The Supreme Court hears cassation applications from provincial and appellate courts of appeal only on

points of law or on the basis that there was some prejudicial procedural irregularity during the case.

The appellant must lodge detailed grounds of cassation within a month of the provincial appellate court's judgement. The respondent then has two weeks in which to reply. Once all relevant materials have been lodged, the appellate court will send the case papers to the Supreme Court. It can either confirm the judgement or overturn it wholly or in part. If the Supreme Court takes the second course, then the district or provincial court must re-examine its judgement in the light of the Supreme Court findings.

Complaint

Anyone involved in a case, from parties to witnesses, can raise a complaint in relation to certain procedural faults committed by the court. The complaint must be lodged with the court in which the irregularity is alleged to have occurred within a week of its occurrence. The court of the second instance, that is the provincial or appellate court, will generally hear the complaint in closed session.

Enforcement

The enforcement of court judgements and orders is dealt with by the relevant court's execution officer. This official takes all the necessary steps to enforce a court's judgement. If necessary, the execution officer can be assisted in his/her duties by the police.

Costs of litigation

The losing party is usually ordered to pay the winner's costs. However, the court has a discretion to make no costs order at all, or to order that a losing party pays only part of the costs. Costs can include court charges, the fees of legal representatives and other general expenses. But there is a ceiling on how much someone can recover. In effect, legal expenses that exceed the amount assessed as the reasonable cost of instructing a local lawyer will be irrecoverable.

Speed of litigation

The Polish courts are struggling to deal with a growing case backlog. This is partly due to a lack of technical equipment – judges' clerks still take all notes by hand, for example – and partly due also to the difficulty of recruiting and keeping good judges.

Judges

Judges are appointed by the president of the Republic on the recommendation of the minister of justice, who in turn acts on the advice of the

National Chamber of Judicature. The National Chamber of Judicature consists of the judges of the Supreme Court and the minister of justice. Each member has a single vote in the selection of nominees. The president can decline or accept the National Chamber's candidates but cannot superimpose his own choice. It is reported that, to date, the president has always accepted the National Chamber's nominations. The National Chamber of Judicature also recommends appointments to the Supreme Court. Both these courts include eminent legal academics as well as senior professional judges among their members.

The independence of the judiciary is guaranteed by the constitution and judges may not accept any other office or engage in any activity incompatible with their judicial role. They are also barred from accepting appointment as arbitrators and must even resign their judicial office, for example, if their spouse begins work as an advocate in private practice in the territory of the court where the judge is appointed.

Arbitration

Arbitration in Poland is governed by the Code of Civil Procedure 1964: key points are listed below. Many of the provisions of the Code of Civil Procedure are similar to those of the UNCITRAL Model Law on International Commercial Arbitration. Conciliation and alternative dispute resolution services are rarely used. So far, Polish parties have been slow to use arbitration for their domestic trade disputes; the Arbitration Court at the National Chamber of Commerce had only just over 100 domestic arbitral references in 1998.

A new arbitration act based on the UNCITRAL Model Law is in the pipeline. The legislation has been delayed partly because arbitral reform is of low political priority. However, when it does finally reach the statute book, the new act is unlikely to be confined to international disputes.

Under the present regime, there is a preliminary issue that has to be decided before a dispute can legitimately go to arbitration. Only disputes involving what are called patrimonial rights – that is, property rights including monetary claims and intellectual property rights (but excluding alimony and labour relations disputes) – can be resolved by arbitration. However, the dividing line between patrimonial and non-patrimonial rights is not always clear.

Key points in the Code of Civil Procedure 1964 are:

- the Code sets out the formal requirements for a valid arbitration agreement;

- state courts must decline jurisdiction in a dispute governed by a valid arbitration clause;

- arbitrators can be challenged or removed by a state court; the court has a discretion to allow the challenge to be held in camera;

- the parties to an arbitration are jointly and severally liable for an arbitrator's fees and expenses;

- in the absence of any choice by the parties as to the procedure to be adopted by the tribunal, the tribunal may choose its own procedure for the arbitration; the tribunal is in any event to undertake a thorough examination of the case before it;

- an arbitral tribunal has no inherent powers to compel the production of witnesses or evidence;

- the Code specifies the form in which an award must be made and requires that the reasons for the award are given;

- the arbitrators of an *ad hoc* tribunal held in Poland must, after the award has been served on the parties, deliver all the case records and the original copy of the award to the relevant local court; the awards of arbitrations conducted by the Polish permanent arbitration institutions are held by the institutions themselves;

- the decisions of the arbitral tribunal on fact or law cannot be appealed and the Code gives the decisions the same status as public court judgements;

- a court may, in principle, refuse to declare a Polish arbitral award enforceable if it is considered to be contrary to the legal order in the Republic of Poland or the principles of social community life; this public order type provision is rarely relied on now by the courts;

- in certain limited circumstances, a domestic arbitral award can be set aside; the parties have one month from the service of the award to bring proceedings to set it aside.

Enforcement of foreign arbitral awards

Poland is a signatory to the New York Convention on the Recognition and Enforcement of Foreign Arbitral Awards 1958 and to the Geneva European Convention on International Arbitration 1961. Enforcement of a foreign award can only be refused by the Polish courts on limited grounds.

Permanent arbitration bodies

There are approximately 20 private permanent arbitration tribunals operating in Poland. The best known are the Arbitration Court at the National Chamber of Commerce and the International Court of Arbitration for Marine and Inland Navigation.

Arbitration Court at the National Chamber of Commerce

The Arbitration Court at the National Chamber of Commerce traces its modern origins back to 1950. It remains the most internationally prominent of the arbitral bodies. The court's secretariat is based in Warsaw. As well as administering institutional, international and domestic arbitrations, it also offers a conciliation service. The court operates on the basis of three different arbitration rules, applicable to domestic disputes, international disputes and an *ad hoc* arbitration administered by the court.

The court maintains a list of foreign and Polish arbitrators who are suitable for appointment either to international or to domestic tribunals. Foreign parties are free to nominate arbitrators that are not included on the court's approved list. However, if the arbitration is to be held in Poland, the individual chosen must meet certain statutory requirements. Currently the Arbitration Court is in the process of drafting its new rules which may come into effect in the year 2000.

International Court of Arbitration for Marine and Inland Navigation

Based in Gdynia, the International Court of Arbitration for Maritime and Inland Navigation is a by-product of the split litigation system adopted by the command economies of Eastern Europe. The court was established under an agreement reached in 1959 by the Polish, East German and Czechoslovak chambers of foreign trade.

As its name suggests, the court was given exclusive jurisdiction over disputes between the trading entities of the three states arising from any civil law relationship concerned with maritime and inland navigation. In addition, parties of other nationalities were able to submit their shipping disputes to the court's jurisdiction.

Following the withdrawal of the East German chamber's participation in the court in 1990, the general collapse of CMEA in 1991 and the division of the Czechoslovak state in 1993, the court has seen its caseload shrink significantly. It maintains its full secretariat, though, and receives the occasional reference. Nevertheless, it is likely to be absorbed by its more powerful cousin, the Arbitration Court at the National Chamber of Commerce in Warsaw.

Organisation of legal professions

In Poland the legal profession comprises judges, state criminal prosecutors and three types of general lawyer: advocates, *radca prawny* and notaries public.

Advocates

Advocates are Poland's nearest equivalents to English barristers. However, they do not enjoy the same near-exclusive right of audience before any court. Nor do they rely entirely on work referred to them by other lawyers. As well as representing clients in court, advocates can give clients general legal advice and may draft documents. Advocates are not allowed to advertise their services and can only practise as self-employed practitioners. They have no legal immunity, either in respect of the advice they give or of their conduct as legal representatives in court.

Polish advocates working for foreign law firms in Poland do so on a consultancy basis and local advocates are either sole traders or working in association with others. They jealously guard their self-employed status as a mark of their traditional independence from the state. Polish advocates must have a law degree, undergo a period of apprenticeship and then pass the bar examination in order to qualify for this professional rank.

Radca Prawny

Traditionally *radca prawny* were the in-house lawyers for state-owned enterprises and foreign trading houses. They now most closely resemble English commercial solicitors.

Not only do they give legal advice and represent clients in court (save in criminal or family matters), they also constitute the majority of qualified lawyers working in the Polish offices of the international law firms. They are generally required to be an employee or to be a shareholder in a limited partnership. Only *radca prawny* who are shareholders in a partnership are able to advise and represent private clients. For this reason, it is expected that many law firms will convert to partnership.

After acquiring a degree in law, *radca prawny* must undertake a set period of legal practice experience before being eligible to sit their regulatory body's professional entrance examination. Their professional conduct will thereafter be regulated by their particular regional professional association, which maintains a list of its members.

Notaries public

This is the smallest of the three branches of the profession. It consists of government-licensed notaries who, as well as giving legal advice, are the only lawyers authorised to notarise documents. They may also complete notarised forms and draw up legal documents. They have no legal immunity in respect of their legal work.

The fees of notaries are fixed by the ministry of justice and notaries have their own professional associations called 'notarial chambers' (*izba notarialna*).

Notaries must work as assistant notaries for two years after acquiring their law degrees before they become eligible to take their professional examinations. If successful, and subject to finding appropriate employment, they can be appointed notaries.

Appendices

Appendix 1

City Guides

Ernst & Young

DOING BUSINESS IN WARSAW

Business centre of Poland

Warsaw, the capital of Poland and located in the central part of the country, is the country's largest city, inhabited by 1.6 million people with another 0.5 million living in the surrounding areas. Warsaw has the highest population density (142 people/m^2) and the lowest unemployment rate (7.3 per cent). Warsaw is not only the capital of finance and business, but also of Polish culture, science and entertainment.

The city is also the capital of the largest and richest province of the country, the voivodship of Mazowieckie, which covers an area of 35,597 km^2. The province, which has a population of over 5 million (13.1 per cent of the total population of Poland), is divided into 38 districts and 325 *gminas*, ie basic administrative units.

Currently, the major problems for the city are decrepit housing and the poor state of municipal infrastructure. However, it should be noted that Warsaw benefits from the fastest economic development among Polish cities and that the living standards in the capital are rising fast every year.

Industry and Trade

The Mazowieckie province has 8444 public sector enterprises employing 1,640,441 people. One third of these companies provide educational and municipal services, while over 600,000 employees work in public transport and communications.

Private firms, which number almost 400,000, provide employment for about 1,300,000 people. Companies dealing in trade and services account for 40 per cent of the total number of firms and employ 376,000 people. There are also 54,200 manufacturing enterprises employing 370,000 workers.

Financial services

Warsaw is the headquarters for over 20 banks operating in Poland. They operate about 500 transaction points in the province and provide standard services in both Polish and foreign currencies. However, some restrictions are still in force as far as foreign currencies are concerned. A number of foreign banks also have branches in Warsaw (Creditanstalt, Raiffeisen Centrobank, Vereinsbank, Westdeutsche Landesbank, Dresdner Bank, Credit Lyonnais, Société Générale, Citibank, Deutsche Bank).

Over 300 ATM cash points in the city accept VISA, Mastercard, Cirrus, American Express, Eurocheque, Diner's Club and a few other cards. Credit card payments are accepted at over 8000 points of sale all over Warsaw.

Insurance companies operate an extensive network in Warsaw. You can insure your premises at 157 transaction points or buy a life insurance policy at 80. A number of leasing companies carry on business in the city.

Foreign money may be exchanged for Polish zlotys in numerous exchange booths (Kantors), usually providing better exchange rates than banks.

Trade fairs

Over one hundred trade fairs and exhibitions are held in Warsaw every year. Most of them take place in the Palace of Culture and Science or at the Mokotow exhibition centre. However, the capital still lacks a modern exhibition centre to meet the growing demand from trade organisations.

Foreign investments

Warsaw is the most attractive Polish city for foreign investors, recording the highest level of foreign investments in Poland. The city attracts large hypermarket chains, leading financial holdings, hotel chains, construction companies and manufacturing firms. The value of foreign investments has already exceeded US$5 billion, of which US$870 million came from Daewoo (automobile manufacture, electronics and insurance activities). Other large investors are France Telecom, PepsiCo, Citibank, JP Morgan, Thompson MultiMedia and Procter & Gamble.

Mass media

Inhabitants of Warsaw are able to watch all the major TV stations (including TVP I/II, Polsat, TVN, Nasza Telewizja and WOT, a local station) and to tune in to about two dozen radio stations. Over 500,000 people have cable TV in their homes. Satellite TV is also very popular in Warsaw, especially two recently launched digital stations (Wizja TV and Cyfra+).

All the national daily newspapers and most Polish magazines are edited in Warsaw. The major national daily newspaper, *gazeta Wyborcza*, has a regional edition, *Gazeta Stoleczna*, with a circulation of 130,000 copies. *Zycie Warszawy*, the most popular local paper, sells 25,000 copies daily.

Advertising costs in the Polish media can be illustrated by the following example: a 30-second prime time commercial costs Zl 60,000 on national TVP, or Zl 2000 on local WOT. A full-size b/w advertisement costs Zl 50,000 in the *gazeta Wyborcza* or Zl 14,250 in the local paper.

Office space, apartments, land

Office space

The capital still lacks sufficient office space of the highest quality ('A' class) to meet the high demand from Polish and international companies. Considerable investment earmarked for the construction of modern office buildings and centres is expected to result in a fast-increasing supply of office space (by over 100,000 m^2/year) and declining prices.

The average rent for 'A' and 'B' class office space varies between US$35 and US$50/m^2/month, but can go as high as US$80/$m^2$. Usually, rental agreements for office space are concluded for at least one year.

Apartments for rent

The scarcity of good-quality apartments makes it difficult to find a reasonably priced one quickly. Currently, monthly rates for a 70 m^2 apartment start at US$2000. Cheap, small flats of poor quality can be found for prices as low as US$250 per month. Most apartments are located in the centre, in Saska Kepa or Gorny Mokotow.

Real estate agents can assist you in finding an appropriate apartment. You are also advised to review the classified sections in *Zycie Warszawy* or *Gazeta Stoleczna* or to place an ad yourself.

When renting an apartment, the standard practice is to pay a deposit amounting to one month's rent, and then pay the rent on a monthly basis, sometimes in US dollars.

Land for industrial purposes

Warsaw still has a fair amount of scarcely used and completely unused land waiting for investors. Current rent levels for industrial land vary between US$2 and US$30/m^2, depending on the location and the planned activity.

Employment and education

Employment

Warsaw enjoys the highest concentration of employees with higher education among Polish cities. Still, it may be quite difficult to find all the specialists you need, due to the high demand for qualified technicians and managers.

The average monthly salary is about US$500 gross – again, the highest in Poland. This figure, however, should be treated as a rough indication only and, for many positions, higher salaries are expected. The level of salary depends very much upon the size of the company and the composition of the whole remuneration package. The availability of well-trained and experienced people is growing steadily in every category but it may be difficult to find an English or German-speaking book-keeper, for instance.

Education

Warsaw has several institutes of higher education, including the University of Warsaw (50,000 students), the Polytechnic (20,000 students), the Warsaw School of Economics, the Agricultural Faculty and the Catholic School. Apart from these public institutes, Warsaw also has 34 private high schools. Altogether, more than 100,000 students study in the capital.

Tourist attractions, sports and recreation

Among the many public places embellishing the city, the Old Town with its beautiful Marketplace is a focal point. The Historical Museum of the City of Warsaw is located on the Market Square. The Royal Castle, the carefully reconstructed seat of the Polish Kings, is also nearby.

Among the 20 or so theatres in the city, the National Theatre, an enormous building on Theatre Square with magnificent interiors, is the most spectacular. The nearby Jablonowski Palace is undergoing renovation and, once it is completed, this architectural masterpiece will bring back the previous splendour of the square.

The Palace of Culture and Science is a great but under-rated tourist attraction: this is one of the tallest buildings in Poland and from the top (paid entrance) you can enjoy the best view of the city.

The greatest Polish museum, the National Museum (3 Jerozolimskie Ave), is another point of interest in Warsaw. Apart from its valuable collections of Polish art, the museum is proud of its fine collections from ancient Egypt, Syria and Cyprus.

Galleries and antique shops where interesting Polish artworks as well as old furniture may be found are common on Krakowskie Przedmiescie St and in the Old Town.

Sports and Recreation

Many sports can be practised in Warsaw and its surroundings, including tennis, swimming, horse riding, squash, bowling, skating, parachuting and even rowing on the Vistula. Some 50 km from the city there is an artificial lake, Zegrzynski Zalew, ideal for water sports on warm days.

Warsaw has two beautiful parks that are certainly worth a visit: the Palace in Wilanow, the splendid Baroque residence of Jan III Sobieski, and the beautiful Lazienki Park, dating from the 18th century, with numerous palaces.

The Kampinos National Park located just outside the city is excellent for hiking. Zelazowa Wola, the birthplace of Frederick Chopin, is located 70km west of Warsaw.

Medical and emergency services

Tourists and business travellers should call 999 for an ambulance. Free medical care is available to those covered by the Polish social security system. Bi-lateral social security agreements have been concluded with a number of European countries, but it is advisable to rely on private clinics, at least for the treatment of minor ailments. The following hospitals are recommended:

- Hospital of the Ministry of Health and Social Welfare, 18 Emilii Plater St; this is a private hospital where government officials and foreign diplomats are treated;

- Banacha Hospital, 1 Banacha St.

- Children's Health Center, 20 Dzieci Polskich Ave;

- Litewska Hospital, 24 Marszalkowska St; treats children.

Pharmacies can be found all over Warsaw. 24-hour pharmacies are located on the top floor of the Central Station and in the Domy Towarowe Centrum complex.

Telecommunications and postal services

Telecommunications

Local or international calls can be made from public phones, which are dispersed all over the city, using a magnetic card or – rarely – tokens.

For international connections, call the national Polish telecom, TP SA, or dial AT&T Direct (tel: 0-800 111 11 11), Canada Direct (tel: 0-800 111

41 18), MCI WorldPhone (tel: 0-800 111 21 22) or Sprint Global One (tel: 0-800 111 31 15/77).

There are four 'internet cafes' in Warsaw, the best one being Casablanca at 4/6 Krakowskie Przedmiescie St.

Mobile phones

Four mobile telephone networks operate in Warsaw. There is one analogue NMI 450 system operated by CENTERTEL, two GSM 900 networks called ERA GSM and PLUS GSM, and the recent IDEA network using the DCS (GSM) 1800 standard. The analogue network covers almost the whole country, but connections outside Poland are possible with only a few countries. In Warsaw, connections may be difficult in peak hours. On the other hand, IDEA covers only the major urban areas of Poland, but provides relatively cheaper connections of high quality. All networks are widely available through numerous dealers. It is also possible to rent a mobile phone from the many sales outlets located in the city.

Postal services

The central post office, located at 31/33 Swietokrzyska St, is open 24 hours and provides all normal postal services, packages, PO boxes, phones, faxes and bill payments. Telegrams can also be sent from here, or set up over the phone by calling 905. Other post offices are located all over Warsaw.

Transport

Mass transit

Regular daytime transport runs from about 5.00 to 23.00, depending on the line (Warsaw's metro closes around 23.30). All metro, tram and bus lines run on a ticket punch system. Unlike in some other Polish cities, tickets are not available from bus drivers. A ticket costs Zl 2, while a monthly pass is Zl 50.

Airport

Aeroplanes from abroad land at the Okecie airport, 20 km from the centre of the city. Airport–City express buses, which call at the major hotels, as well as regular buses and taxi cabs, are available at the airport.

Traffic in the city

Traffic in Warsaw is getting heavier, with more and more city dwellers owning cars. While the number of cars has now exceeded 70 per 100 inhabitants, there has been no corresponding development of city roads for years. You may find it difficult to get through downtown, especially during peak hours, ie between 7.00 and 10.00 or between 15.00 and 18.00. It is therefore recommended to take a tram or metro rather than go by car.

Taxis

Most cabs have a Zl 3.60 initial charge. The official Warsaw rate went up to Zl 1.60 per km recently and the maximum rate is Zl 2.00 per km. Rates go up by half after 22.00 and on weekends. Taxis from the airport, train station, the Old Town and hotels could overcharge you, so probably the best option is to call for a cab to pick you up (no additional charge). Some generally reliable companies are MPT, Sawa Taxi (tel: 644 44 44), Volfra Taxi, Merc Taxi (tel: 677 77 77).

Car rental companies

A number of car rental companies offer a vast range of vehicles for rent. These include:

- ANN, Okecie Airport (tel: + 48 22 650 32 62);
- AVIS, Okecie Airport (tel: + 48 22 650 48 72);
- HERTZ (tel: 0-800 1-HERTZ);
- Europcar (tel: + 48 22 644 47 90);
- Intercar (tel: + 48 22 625 45 94).

Rail links

Getting around Poland is often accomplished faster and more easily by train. In Warsaw, most trains depart from the Central Station (*Dworzec Centralny*) located at the corner of Jerozolimskie Ave. and Jana Pawla II Ave. Tickets are available in the station itself, or at Orbis tourist offices for no additional charge.

Hotels and restaurants

Hotels

Warsaw still has, at present, relatively few first-class and standard hotels, though there are a number of oustanding hotels in the city centre.

Deluxe (*****) hotels:

- Hotel Bristol, the most prestigious in the city, situated on the famous Royal Way, 42/44 Krakowskie Przedmiescie St. Single room: US$290–310;

- Sheraton Warsaw Hotel & Towers, 2 Prusa St. Single room: US$255–335;

- Hotel Victoria Intercontinental, 11 Krolewska St. Single room: DM380–480;

- Marriott Hotel, 65/79 Jerozolimskie St.

Superior first class (****) hotels:

- Hotel Forum, 24/16 Nowogrodzka St. Single room: DM275;

- Hotel Mercure Fryderyk Chopin, 22 Jana Pawla II Ave. Single room: US$185;

- Hotel Holiday Inn Warszawa, 48/54 Zlota St. Single room: US$209–238.

Prices for a single room in a first-class, three-star hotel vary between Zl 120 and Zl 300 per night.

Restaurants

Apart from hotel restaurants, Warsaw has many quality restaurants, offering both Polish and international cuisine. Most of them accept credit cards. They include, among others:

Polish:

- Bazyliszek, 3/9 Old Town Square;

- Dom Polski, 11 Francuska St;

- Fukier, 27 Old Town Square;

- Garret, 55/73 Marszalkowska St (upstairs);

- Karczma Gessler, 21/21A Old Town Square;

- Mibella Grill Bar, 56 Kasprowicza St;

- Yesterday, 2/4 Szkolna St.

American and Tex-Mex:

- Alamo Steak House, 119 Jerozolimskie St;

- Blue Cactus, 11 Zajaczkowska St;

- El Popo, 27 Senatorska St;

- London Steak House, 42 Jerozolimskie St;
- TGI Friday's, 29 Jana Pawla II Ave (new Atrium Bldg.).

Asian:

- Bliss, 3 Boczna St;
- Las (Korean cuisine), 43 Niepodleglosci Ave;
- Maharaja Thai (Thai cuisine), 13 Szeroki Dunaj St;
- Tsubame (Japanese cuisine), 16 Foksal St;
- Tybet Himalaje (Tibetan cuisine), 39 Mokotowska St.

European:

- Adler (Austrian & German cuisine), 69 Mokotowska St;
- Belvedere, Lazienki Park Orangery;
- Cafe Kredens (Italian cuisine), 36 Przemyslowa St;
- Casa Valdemar (Spanish cuisine), 7/9 Piekna St;
- Chianti (Italian cuisine), 17 Foksal St;
- Flik (International and Polish cuisine), 43 Pulawska St;
- La Bohème, 1 Teatralny Square (National Theatre);
- Montmartre (French cuisine), 7 Nowy Swiat St;
- Qchnia Artystyczna, Ujazdowski Castle, 6 Ujazdowskie Ave;
- Rabarbar, 9/11 Wierzbowa St;
- Santorini (Greek cuisine), 7 Egipska St;
- U Szwejka, 1 Konstytucji Square.

Night clubs, casinos

Warsaw has three major casinos:

- Casinos Poland – Warsaw's high-energy, high-stakes casino at the Marriott Hotel, 65/79 Jerozolimskie St;
- Orbis Casino at Hotel Victoria, 11 Królewska St;
- Queen's Casino in the Palace of Culture, 1 Plac Defilad.

A passport is required to enter Warsaw's casinos and dress codes are in force.

DOING BUSINESS IN GDANSK

The 'Solidarity' port

Gdansk, the capital city of the province of Pomerania, is located on the Baltic Coast close to the mouth of the Vistula River.

With a population of over 460,000 inhabitants, Gdansk is the sixth biggest city in Poland. The earliest reference to the city was in the year 997, in the Roman work *Vita Sancti Adalberti*, which describes Bishop Wojciech (Adalbert) of Prague's mission to Prussia to spread Christianity. Gdansk is geographically very close to two other cities, Sopot and Gdynia. Because of their close links, the three cities are treated as one conurbation with 760,000 inhabitants, referred to as Trojmiasto (Tri-City).

At various times in its long history, Gdansk has been part of different nations, so the influence of various cultures has made Gdansk a unique city. After World War II, Gdansk was traditionally recognised as the centre of resistance against the communist regime. Its workers, including those of the Gdansk Shipyard, organised numerous strikes to gain economic and political freedoms. In August 1980, the first free trade union in Eastern Europe, Solidarnosk (Solidarity), was established in Gdansk. Finally, strikes by Solidarity led to the first free elections in Poland post-war. The resulting Solidarity-led government implemented a radical reform programme aimed at putting Poland on the path to a market economy.

Industry and trade

Throughout its thousand years of existence, the economy of this port city has always been inseparably tied to trade. Gdansk is the biggest Baltic port after Gothenburg and is uniquely positioned as the largest non-freezing port in Eastern Europe. A 17 m deep fairway allows the largest vessels sailing the Baltic Sea to make use of the Gdansk port facilities.

Gdansk's other important industries are ship building, food processing, fuel and chemicals. The largest companies (in alphabetical order) in Gdansk are:

- Baltic Malt (malt production);
- Dr Oetker (food processing);
- Eaton Controls (automotive);
- Fazer (confectionery);
- Fosfory (mineral fertilisers);
- GE Capital Services (financial);

- GPRD (road construction);

- Mackowy (food processing);

- Mostostal (building contractors);

- Olicom (information technology);

- Olvit (food processing);

- Rafineria Gdanska (refinery);

- Stocznia Gdanska (shipyard);

- Stocznia Remontowa (ship repairs).

Useful addresses and telephone numbers

Department of Economic Policy
Tel: + 48 58 302 24 69
(For inquiries regarding investment opportunities)

Real Estate Marketing Office
Tel: + 48 58 302 30 41
(For inquiries regarding the purchase of public owned real estate)

Pomeranian Provincial Office
21/27 Okopowa Street, 80–810 Gdansk
Tel: + 48 58 307 76 44

Gdansk City Council,
8/12 Nowe Ogrody Street, 80–803 Gdansk

Gdansk Chamber of Commerce
ul Dlugi Targ 39/40
Tel: + 48 58 301 13 25

Regional Development Agency
ul Piwna 36/39
Tel: + 48 58 346 32 31

Gdansk Pomeranian Development Agency Co.
ul Piwna 36/39
Tel: + 48 58 308 43 19

'Solidarnosk' Economic Foundation
ul Waly Piastowskie 24
Tel: + 48 58 308 43 19

Hotels

Holiday Inn
ul Waly Piastowskie 1
Tel: + 48 58 307 43 66

Hotel Hanza
ul Tokarska 6
Tel: + 48 58 305 34 27

Hotel Szydlowski
ul Grunwaldzka 114
Tel: + 48 58 341 82 11

Hotel Posejdon
ul Kapliczna 30
Tel: + 48 58 553 18 03

Hotel Marina
ul Jelitkowska 20
Tel: + 48 58 553 20 79

Hotel Heweliusz
ul Heweliusza 22
Tel: + 48 58 301 56 31

Hotel Novotel
ul Pszenna 1
Tel: + 48 58 301 56 11

Hotel Europa
al Niepodleglosci 466 Sopot
Tel: + 48 58 551 44 90

Zhong Hua Hotel
al Wojska Polskiego 1 Sopot
Tel: + 48 58 550 20 20

Grand Hotel
ul Powstancow Warszawy 12/14 Sopot
Tel: + 48 58 551 00 41

Hotel Gdynia
ul. Armii Krajowej 7 Gdynia
Tel: + 48 58 620 66 61

Restaurants

Pod Lososiem
ul Szeroka 52/54
Tel: + 48 58 301 76 52

Tawerna
ul Powroznicza 19/20
Tel: + 48 58 301 41 14

TGI Friday's
ul Waly Piastowskie 1
Tel: + 48 58 306 39 47

U Szkota
ul Chlebnicka 9/12
Tel: + 48 58 305 49 47

La Gondola
ul Portowa 8 Gdynia
Tel: + 48 58 620 59 23

Marco Polo
ul Slaska 21, Gdynia
Tel: + 48 58 628 64 68

Moon
ul Slaska 27, Gdynia
Tel: + 48 58 661 26 64

Balzac
ul 3 Maja 7, Sopot
Tel: + 48 58 551 77 00

Irena
ul Chopina 36, Sopot
Tel: + 48 58 551 20 73

Rozmaryn
ul Ogrodowa 8, Sopot
Tel: + 48 58 551 11 04

Villa Hestia
ul Wladyslawa IV 3/5, Sopot
Tel: + 48 58 551 21 00

DOING BUSINESS IN KATOWICE

Silesian crossroads

Katowice (population 353,000) is the capital of the Silesian voivodship created on 1 January 1999 following the merger of the Katowice, Czestochowa and Bielsko-Biala voivodships. Although the smallest in Poland in terms of square area (just 12,000 km^2), the voivodship has a population of 4.9 million. Katowice is situated in the central part of the Silesian region, which, in turn, is close to the Czech and Slovakian borders. This makes Katowice part of one of the largest consumer and capital investment markets in Central Europe. Historically, the region was known to be at the crossroads of the ancient European trade routes from west to east and from north to south.

Katowice is also the scientific and cultural centre of a region that is one of the most industrialised in Poland. Having been accorded the status of town only in 1865, Katowice is therefore one of the youngest of the largest Polish cities. Its rapid development was mainly due to the region's abundant natural resources and well-developed communication infrastructure.

The administration of Katowice is two tiered: as it is the capital of the region, it is the seat of the central government representative, who bears the title Voivode. Katowice, as a city, has its own local civic administrative structure, independent of the regional government.

Trade and industry

The economy was traditionally dependent on coal mining and metallurgy, the very industries currently undergoing far reaching technological restructuring as well transformation in terms of both organisation and ownership. The local economy now includes automobile, machine, chemical, food processing and textile industries. For many years, the region has been attracting a number of foreign investors, with Fiat Auto, ABB, Saint Gobain, TRW, Henkel, Unilever and Heineken among the earliest.

The economy of the voivodship depends on its 323,000 companies, which employ over 3 million people. Of all Polish companies, 13 per cent are located in the Silesian voivodship, employing 21 per cent of the national workforce: every fifth Polish worker is employed in Silesia.

The Katowice Special Economic Zone (KSSE), established for a period of 20 years and covering over 830 hectares, has already attracted some 25 companies, the biggest being General Motors, Delphi, Roca, Isuzu Motors, Lear Corporation and Agora.

Employment and education

One of the main advantages of the region is a very well-educated work-force, with a strongly rooted work ethic and entrepreneurial skills. These qualities have made Silesia a leading low-risk destination for capital investment. There are 20 higher education institutions, the oldest and largest being the Academy of Economics, the Silesian Polytechnic, the Silesian University and the Silesian Medical Academy.

The region's high level of economic development is reflected in one of the lowest unemployment rates in Poland.

Financial services

Katowice can boast of a well-developed network of banks and brokerage houses. In addition to the national banks, many international banks are also located here: Raiffeisen Centrobank, Citibank, Deutsche Bank, BNB–Dresdner Bank, Bank Austria Creditanstalt and Credit Lyonnais.

Trade fairs

The Katowice International Fair (MTK) organises around 30 events every year, of which almost half are on an international scale. This places MTK in second place in Poland after the Poznan International Fair.

The only World Trade Center office in southern Poland is located in Katowice.

Tourism, recreation and sports

Katowice also offers plenty of leisure time activities. There are several the-atres, three concert halls, a symphony orchestra, two opera houses, 36 museums and almost 900 libraries.

The biggest concert, exhibition and sports centre in Poland is also located right in the centre of Katowice. The Provincial Park of Culture and Recreation located on the outskirts of Katowice and, spreading over 600 hectares, is a real oasis and includes a fun fair, a zoo, a national sports stadium, a planetarium and astronomical observation dome, a swimming pool, rose gardens and a Scansen Museum.

Infrastructure

The cost of rent and maintenance of office space is comparable to other big Polish cities, but is lower than in Warsaw, the Polish capital.

The main road and rail links joining Poland with the rest of Europe run through the city and its suburbs. Transport and communication outside the Katowice conurbation is not a problem – a weekend in the mountains can start on Friday. Within the Katowice area, though, a boom in car ownership hinders mobility, despite an efficient tram and bus network. The need for capital investment in this area is still great.

The local international airport is in Pyrzowice, 30 km from Katowice. Also not too far away, in Gliwice, is the duty-free land port, which connects the Gliwice canal with the river Oder, which, in turn, links it with the seaports of Szczecin and Swinoujscie.

Useful addresses and telephone numbers

Provincial Administration Office
ul. Jagiellonska 25, 40-032 Katowice
Tel: + 48 32 255 46 93

Governor
Tel: + 48 32 255 40 37

City Council
ul Mlynska 4, 40–098 Katowice
Tel: + 48 32 253 80 11

Mayor
Tel: + 48 32 253 81 33

City Promotion and Foreign Relations Office
Tel: + 48 32 253 87 50

Foreign Relations Department
ul Rynek 13
Tel: + 48 32 253 83 31

Directory information
Tel: + 48 32 913

Chamber of Commerce
ul Bytkowska 1b,
Tel: + 48 32 254 03 58/58 77 33

Katowicka Specjalna Strefa Ekonomiczna
ul Lompy 13,
Tel: + 48 32 251 07 36/251 09 58

Silesian Development Agency
ul Wita Stwosza 31,
Tel: + 48 32 257 95 19/257 95 20

Katowice Fairs Centre
ul Bytkowska 1b,
Tel: + 48 32 59 60 61/204 246 2

LOT Polish Airlines
Tel: + 48 32 206 24 60/206 29 53

Hotels

Hotel Orbis 'Warszawa'
Al Rozdzienskiego 16
Tel: + 48 32 200 44 44/200 44 54

Hotel Silesia
ul Piotra Skargi 2
Tel: + 48 32 59 62 11/253 75 84

Hotel Noma Residence
Kobior-Promnice
Tel: + 48 32 219 46 78/219 40 63

Hotel Silvia
ul Gliwicka 1, Gliwice
Tel: + 48 32 234 83 16

Restaurants

Restauracja Chopin
ul Kosciuszki 169
Tel: + 48 32 257 15 75

Restauracja Orientalna A-Dong
ul Matejki 3
Tel: + 48 32 58 66 62

Restauracja Wloska Divertimento
ul Krakowska 5, Myslowice
Tel: + 48 32 222 24 59

Restauracja Czerwona Oberza
ul Wita Stwosza 5
Tel: + 48 32 251 60 30

Restauracja Lazurowa Oberza
ul Katowicka 44
Tel: 0501 419 573

Pub Bourbon
ul Basztowa 7, Gliwice
Tel: + 48 32 331 41 01

DOING BUSINESS IN LODZ

Youthful dynamism

The name of the city of Lodz, although difficult to pronounce for a foreigner, has a simple meaning in Polish – 'boat'. In fact, Lodz is located on a small river called Lodka, which means 'small boat'.

Lodz, the second largest city of Poland (with over 800,000 inhabitants), is also one of the country's most important industrial, academic and cultural centres. The rapid changes experienced in recent years visibly suit the city's youthful, dynamic and entrepreneurial population. After some quiet years thanks to Poland's central planners Lodz is now on a fast track to becoming – if not a 'promised land', as it was referred to in a famous novel by Nobel Prize winner Wladyslaw Reymont – a most interesting place for doing business at the turn of the 20th century, just as it was one hundred years ago.

The capital of the Lodzkie region (population 2.7 million), it is located almost in the very geographical centre of Poland. All the voivodship towns (provincial capitals) are located within 350 km of Lodz, while there are six European capital cities – Berlin, Vienna, Prague, Bratislava, Minsk and Vilnius – less than 500 km away.

Trade and industry

Lodz used to be an important centre of the textile industry (Wolczanka SA, Prochnik SA, Wi-MA SA) but is now less dependent on this sector. In addition to a plethora of textile and clothing businesses there are many companies operating in such diverse fields as medical equipment (FAMED 1), pharmaceuticals (Polska Grupa Farmaceutyczna SA), chemicals (ORGANIKA SA, ATLAS SC), engineering (ABB Elta Sp.zo.o, ELESTER SA, Lozamet Sp.zo.o), food processing (AGROS-OPTIMA SA), home appliances (Bosch-Siemens), and cosmetics (POLLENA-EWA SA, LOKI, Kolastyna).

Although diversified services are developing extremely fast in Lodz, as in other Polish cities, industry remains the foremost job creator, accounting for some 60 per cent of total urban employment.

The 1990s have seen a rapid development of trade and services in Lodz. The unique, 5 km long Piotrkowska Street, which is one of the best-known shopping streets in Poland, has been turned into a promenade area. Alongside numerous restaurants offering Polish, Italian, French, Chinese, as well as Turkish and Vietnamese, cuisine, there are also about a hundred pubs, where thousands of people come to relax. Lodz is often referred to as Poland's pub capital. Piotrkowska Street also has many galleries and antiques boutiques, where interesting articles of Polish art, as well as old furniture, can sometimes be found at bargain prices.

Nearby, you will find the splendid palaces of the 19th-century industrial tycoons of Lodz, who incarnated the city's entrepreneurial spirit (for instance, the former Herbst's Palace in Ksiezy Mlyn).

A modern exhibition centre, EXPO-Lodz, suitably located and easily accessible, has made the city one of the most important exhibition centres in Poland.

Education

Lodz has several institutes of higher education, including the University, with 20,000 students, the Technical University (10,000 students), and the Film, TV and Theatre School, which can boast of a few famous graduates: Roman Polanski, Andrzej Wajda and Jerzy Skolimowski.

The textile-based industrial structure and tradition of the city is reflected, too, in the educational system, with the Fabric and Clothing Faculty at the Academy of Arts, and the Textile Engineering Faculty at the Technical University.

Regarding the proportion of the population with university education, the Lodzkie voivodship ranks seventh in Poland, and the supply of well-trained and experienced people continues to grow steadily.

Financial services

Twenty-four domestic and foreign banks, including Bank Creditanstalt SA, Citibank and Raiffeisen Centrobank SA, have head offices or branches in Lodz. Most banks provide standard services in both foreign currencies and the Polish zloty. Almost all the insurance companies operating in Poland are present in Lodz.

Foreign investment

According to the *Map of Investment Risk* report, produced by the Institute of Market Economy Research, large cities are the most attractive destinations for investments in Poland and Lodz is ranked in the top A group.

Foreign companies have invested over US$600 million in Lodz and a further US$1 billion is planned for the near future. ABB, AIG Lincoln, HD Lee Company Inc, Amcor, Coca-Cola, Gillette, Shell, BP, Aral, Statoil, PepsiCo, Metro AG, McDonald's, Rossmann, Billa, VF Corporation, Kyoungbang, Cacao Callbaut, Legler, Boco, East-West Spinning, Carly Gry, Coats Viyella Plc, Dyrup and Bosch-Siemens are some of these foreign investors.

Infrastructure

An ambitious plan to build 2600 km of modern highways in Poland by the year 2010 has been launched. Two of the most important routes, East–West and North–South, will intersect some 15 km from the centre of Lodz, placing the city in the very centre of Poland's road transportation network. Two major train stations and two smaller ones offer numerous railway connections from Lodz. It takes two hours to get to Warsaw, four hours to Poznan, five hours to Berlin and three hours to Katowice. The frequent Warsaw–Lodz air link, inaugurated in April 1999, will get you to Warsaw in 35 minutes.

The abundance of scarcely used or unused land in Lodz makes real estate prices decidedly lower than in Warsaw. However, Lodz does not offer, at present, many modern hotel facilities.

Austria, Mexico and Lithuania are represented in Lodz through honorary consuls, and 'twin city' co-operation agreements have been signed, among others, with Lyon, Stuttgart, Chemnitz and Tampere. Co-operation in certain areas such as culture, education and local administration is particularly high.

Tourism, recreation and sports

Eight theatres, including one of the best opera houses in Poland, offer a variety of entertainments. The bi-annual Dance Festival is gaining in both prestige and popularity, while the Lodz Orchestra performs concerts on a regular basis.

The Jewish cemetery at Baluty, the largest in Europe, 42 hectares with 180,000 graves, is a moving sight.

Among the many public parks that embellish the city, special mention should be made of the large Park of Culture and Recreation, with its zoological and botanical gardens, as well of the Lagiewniki forest. Two artificial lakes, Sulejowski and Jeziorsko, some 50 km from the city, are ideal for water sports on warm days.

Useful addresses and telephone numbers

Provincial Administration Office
ul Piotrkowska 104, Lodz   Tel: + 48 42 632 90 40
Governor (Mr Michal Kasinski)   Tel: + 48 42 633 17 60
Department of Economic Policy   Tel: + 48 42 632 99 53

City Council
ul Piotrkowska 104, Lodz   Tel: + 48 42 638 40 00
Mayor (Tadeusz Matusiak)   Tel: + 48 42 638 41 15
Department of the City Strategy   Tel: + 48 42 638 44 42
City Promotion and Foreign Relations Section   Tel: + 48 42 638 40 20
Investor Services Section   Tel: + 48 42 638 44 37

Chamber of Commerce and Industry
ul Tuwima 30
Tel: + 48 42 633 03 49/633 51 35

Fairs Co-ordinator
ul Stefanowskiego 30
Tel: + 48 42 637 29 34

Cultural Information Centre
ul Zamenhofa 1/3
Tel: + 48 42 633 92 21

Lotnisko Lublinek – Airport
Tel: + 48 42 687 07 01

LOT Airlines
ul Piotrkowska 122
Tel: + 48 42 633 48 15/633 48 77

Radio Taxi
Tel: + 48 42 919/650 50 50/640 04 00/636 36 36/640 01 00

DHL International Poland
Pl. Pokoju 2a
Tel: + 48 42 630 61 06

UPS United Parcel Service
ul Traugutta 21/23
Tel: + 48 42 656 87 98

Pocztex, parcel and other post office services
ul Tuwima 38
Tel: + 48 42 633 09 36/633 94 52

Directory information
Tel: + 48 42 913

Hotels

Hotel Grand
ul Piotrkowska 72
Tel: + 48 42 633 99 20

Hotel Centrum
ul Kilinskiego 59/63
Tel: + 48 42 632 86 40

Hotel Swiatowit
Al Kosciuszki 68
Tel: + 48 42 636 36 37

Restaurants

Esplanada, Polish cuisine
ul Piotrkowska 100
Tel: + 48 42 630 59 89

Lyon, French restaurant
ul Piotrkowska 103/105
Tel: + 48 42 632 37 77

Savoy, Polish and French cuisine
ul Traugutta 6
Tel: + 48 42 632 15 42

Centrum, Polish and French cuisine
ul Kilinskiego 59/63
Tel: + 48 42 633 92 96

Nad Lodka, traditional Polish cuisine
Al Wlokniarzy 151
Tel: + 48 42 651 49 75

Akropol, Greek taverna
ul Traugutta 9
Tel: + 48 42 632 04 15

Dworek Restaurant
ul Rogowska 24
Tel: + 48 42 659 76 40

Irish pub
ul Piotrkowska 77
Tel: + 48 42 630 23 88

Portobello Pub
Pl Komuny Paryskiej 6
Tel: + 48 42 639 77 90

DOING BUSINESS IN POZNAN

Right at the heart of Europe

Poznan is the capital city of Wielkopolska, the second largest voivodship in Poland, spreading over a large area in the western part of the country. The Wielkopolska province, which has a population of 3.5 million, was created following the consolidation of the five former provinces of Poznan, Leszno, Kalisz, Konin and Pila. It covers almost 30,000 km^2 and has the third highest output among Polish provinces. Compared to other parts of the country, this province is more urbanised and its inhabitants are regarded as being particularly entrepreneurial, hard working and open to new ideas. In the last few decades, Poznan and the surrounding areas have developed into one of the most prosperous parts of the country, with a highly developed system of banking and trade. This has made Poznan highly attractive to foreign investors. The constant inflow of foreign capital into the region has contributed to the rapid development of the city's infrastructure and a falling unemployment rate.

With a population of 600,000, Poznan is one of the largest cities in Poland. Founded in the 13th century and built on the river Warta, Poznan, along with Wroclaw, is a major centre for business, industry and finance in western Poland. A prosperous and fast developing city, it enjoys a convenient location close to the German border, half way between Berlin and Warsaw. Poznan truly lies right at the heart of Europe.

Trade and industry

The thriving local economy comprises 65,596 registered businesses as at the end of 1998. Out of these, 690 were state-owned enterprises and 1557 were operating as companies with foreign participation. The public sector accounts for 184 companies, while 12,773 companies and partnerships make up the private sector. The most important industries in the Poznan area are the following:

- maritime industry (H. Cegielski-Poznan SA);

- electrical engineering (Centra/Excide SA);

- chemical and biochemical industries (GlaxoWellcome Poznan S.A., BEIERSDORF-Lechia SA);

- food processing (Goplana/Nestle, Wrigley Poland Sp.zo.o, Lech Browary Wielkopolski SA, CPC Amino Sp.zo.o);

- transportation/logistics and automobile industry (Raben Logistics Sp.zo.o, Volkswagen Poznan Sp.zo.o);

- Telecommunications (Alcatel Teletra SA).

Poznan's economic strengths include its convenient location, long-standing tradition of good workmanship and international contacts (especially with Germany), well-developed services, as well as an educated and skilled workforce.

Trade fairs

Poznan is a city of fairs with long histories, the most prominent of them the Poznan International Fair. This is the most important international event of this kind in Poland, dating back 70 years. The number of fairs in Poznan has grown over time, to reach 24 per year.

Infrastructure

Getting to and around Poznan is relatively easy. The city has a wide network of public transport (trams, fast tram, buses) and taxis. It also has railway and air connections to major Polish and several European cities.

The costs of living and office space prices are comparable to other major Polish cities but below those of Warsaw. Clean streets with extensive green areas ensure pleasant surroundings.

Poznan is also a centre for music and theatre, holding the well-known Wieniawski Violin Festival, the Jazz Fair and the Malta Street Theatre Festival.

Useful addresses and telephone numbers

Provincial Administration Office
al Niepodleglosci 16/18   Tel: + 48 61 854 10 71
Governor (Mr Maciej Musial)   Tel: + 48 61 851 55 66
Department of Regional Development   Tel: + 48 61 852 55 21

County Offce
ul Jackowskiego 18/20   Tel: + 48 61 841 05 02

City Council
Poznan City Hall
pl Kolegiacki 17   Tel: + 48 61 852 72 81/
                                                        878 52 00
City Council Office   Tel: + 48 61 852 41 60
Mayor (Mr Ryszard Grobelny)   Tel: + 48 61 852 21 68
Foreign Relations Department   Tel: + 48 61 851 67 65
Department of Information and Development   Tel: + 48 61 852 19 47

Telephone directory information
Tel: + 48 61 913

Chamber of Commerce and Industry
ul Glogowska 26
Tel: + 48 61 864 07 54

City Information Centre
ul Ratajczaka 44
Tel: + 48 61 851 96 45

WCT, IATA Agency
ul Dabrowskiego 5
Tel: + 48 61 848 13 42

LOT Polish Airlines
ul sw Marcin 69
Tel: + 48 61 852 28 47

Radio Taxi
Tel: + 48 61 919, 951/821 62 16/851 95 19/851 55 15/848 04 80/821 92 19

Emergency services (toll free)

Ambulance Tel: 999, **Police** Tel: 997, **Fire Brigade** Tel: 998

Pocztex, parcel and other post office services
ul Kosciuszki 77
Tel: + 48 61 869 75 41

CERTUS, Private Hospital (24-hours)
ul Grunwaldzka 156
Tel: + 48 61 867 58 51

Malta Ski – all-year skiing centre
ul Wiankowa 2
Tel: + 48 61 879 411

Poznan Fairs Centre
ul Glogowska 14
Tel: + 48 61 869 25 92

Hotels

Hotel Orbis Merkury
ul Roosevelta 20
Tel: + 48 61 855 80 00, 855 89 55

Hotel Meridian
ul Litewska
Tel: + 48 61 847 15 64, 847 34 41

Hotel Orbis Poznan
pl Andersa 1
Tel: + 48 61 833 20 81, 833 29 61

Restaurants

Bambus, Chinese restaurant
Stary Rynek 64/65
Tel: + 48 61 853 06 58

Estella, Italian restaurant
ul Garbary 41
Tel: + 48 61 852 34 10

Kresowa, Eastern European cuisine
Stary Rynek 3
Tel: + 48 61 853 12 91

Mexican Grill
ul 27 Grudnia 19
Tel: + 48 61 852 05 23

Oczy Czornyje, Russian restaurant
ul Marcinkowskiego 24
Tel: + 48 61 852 54 75

Valpolicella, Italian restaurant
ul Wroclawska 7
Tel: + 48 61 855 71 91

Le Magnolia, French restaurant
ul Glogowska 40
Tel: + 48 61 864 14 07

Pod Psem, restaurant with local cuisine
ul Garbary 54
Tel: + 48 61 851 99 70

DOING BUSINESS IN SZCZECIN

Economic advantage

Administrative reform carried out on 1 January 1999 made Szczecin the capital of the newly established West Pomeranian voivodship. This voivodship, which covers an area of over 22,900 km, is the fifth largest among the 16 new provinces and includes 61 cities and towns, accounting for 7 per cent of the total number in Poland. Its 1.7 million population, amounting to 4.5 per cent of the total population of the country, makes it the 11th most populated region. The West Pomeranian voivodship is composed of 20 district authorities and 114 communes.

Western Pomerania is regarded as a very attractive region for investments. The thriving economic climate stimulates international co-operation, while the convenient geographical location attracts many foreign investors. Western Pomerania, which shares a border with Germany, has become a lively centre of cross-border trade.

This geographical location is an unquestionable advantage for the city. Situated at the mouth of the Odra river, 12 km from the Polish-German border and 55 km from the Baltic Sea, Szczecin combines with the adjacent city of Swinoujscie to make up the biggest port area on the Baltic Sea. Its relative proximity to major cities such as Berlin (130 km), Warsaw (516 km), Prague (around 500 km), Stockholm (454 km) and Copenhagen (274 km) makes it an important international transportation junction. Szczecin is also the meeting point of transit roads that connect Western Europe with the Baltic countries and Scandinavia with the south of the continent.

With a population of some 420,000, Szczecin counts among the seven largest cities in Poland and is an important centre of industry, trade and culture in Western Pomerania. With its borders adjoining the EU, its traditional port functions and broad international contacts, Szczecin is in a particularly advantageous situation as far as economic development is concerned.

Industry and trade

At the end of 1998, 139,000 companies were registered in Szczecin. Of these, 36.9 per cent were dealing in trade and ship repairs, 10.7 per cent in construction and the remaining 52.4 per cent were classified as others. The majority of the companies in the last group specialise in financial services and real estate.

The economic potential of the West Pomeranian region has been historically influenced by the port and related activities. The largest employer is the Szczecin Shipyard. Sea-based industries include fishing, fish processing, shipbuilding and ship repair, sea and coastal transport, tourism and recreation. Today, some 25,000 people work in sea-based industries: 13,000 in the shipping industry, 9000 in sea transport and 1500 in fishing. Other major industries include energy, chemicals, food processing and beverages.

Polska Zegluga Morska (Polish Steamship Company) is the largest ship owner in the region, specialising in cargo transportation. Unity Line Sp.zo.o is the owner of the 'Polonia' ferry to Ystad. There are five Polska Zegluga Baltycka (Baltic Steamship Company) ferries that ply regularly between Poland and Denmark, as well as Norway and Sweden. Szczecin, therefore, has direct connections with large Scandinavian cities. Polska Zegluga Baltycka is also the owner of the modern passenger terminal in Swinoujscie.

Many Szczecin shipyards and companies provide services to the shipping industry. For example, the 'Flying shipyard' is considered to be the only such repair service in the world. Two ship repair yards, 'Gryfia' and 'Parnica' have the highest output in Europe, while the shipbuilding yard 'Stocznia Szczecinska' SA is the fifth largest in the world. The Szczecin Shipyard, a modern industrial group, earns 40 per cent of its profits from the sale of ships.

The top five West Pomeranian companies are as follows: Szczecin Shipyard SA, 'Police' Chemical Plants in Police, 'Zalom' Cable Manufacturer, Superfish W. i J. Struzyna in Ustronie Morskie and Drobimex-Heintz Sp.zo.o in Szczecin.

Foreign investment

Szczecin is also the centre of the Pomeranian Euro-region. The geopolitical location of the city stimulates new business, making it one of the more popular Polish destinations for foreign investment. Szczecin has qualified, together with Warszawa, Katowice, Krakow and Poznan, to be part of the group 'A' cities – that is, the cities most attractive to investors.

The number of foreign companies in the West Pomeranian region is growing steadily, with some 2000 companies established by the end of 1997. The average participation level of foreign capital in companies is 75 per cent, similar to the Polish average. The main sources of foreign capital are Germany (56.6 per cent), Sweden (10.8 per cent), Denmark (6.1 per cent), and the Netherlands (3.3 per cent). The main sectors of investments include trade and ship repairs (29.5 per cent) and manufacturing (27.3 per cent). About 8.6 per cent of foreign capital is invested in construction, transport and telecommunications. Foreign investors have only a minority of shares in most cases, while most (54 per cent) of the foreign companies are small, on average employing five people. Only 2 per cent of foreign investors are represented in companies that employ between

101 to 250 people. The biggest foreign investors are the Swedwood Group, which owns over 98 per cent of the shares in Szczecinski Przemysl Drzewny SA, and Bitburger Brauerei, which owns 100 per cent of the shares in Bosman Browar Szczecin SA.

Employment

The unemployment rate in Szczecin has gradually decreased over time, from 7.4 per cent in 1992 to 4 per cent in 1998. The situation looks completely different in the overall West Pomeranian region, where unemployment is a major problem. The unemployment rate in the region was 13.1 per cent in mid-1998, while the national average was 9.8 per cent. The whole voivodship has the lowest proportion of unemployed youth: around 25 per cent of all the registered unemployed.

Trade fairs

Szczecin is an attractive place for trade fairs, with several annual fairs gaining in popularity. At present, Miedzynarodowe Targi Szczecinskie is the largest organiser of fairs in Western Pomerania, having organised, up to December 1997, 50 large fairs, with the participation of 7081 companies and some 560,000 visitors. Companies from Germany, Sweden, Denmark, the Czech Republic and Slovenia were among the many exhibitors.

The location of the city and its proximity to 14 border crossings help foster international contacts. Szczecin, which is an excellent economic base for serving the EU market, is also a bridge to the East.

Tourist attractions, sports and recreation

The extremely varied Western Pomeranian landscape is one of the most interesting in Poland, especially in the region of the Wolin National Park. Cliffs several metres high, wide beaches and rare species of animals and birds (aurochs, eagles) attract many tourists to this region. The region's many lakes (eg Szwajcaria Polczynska) constitute a paradise for fishermen, while abundant forests provide for good hunting. The especially picturesque regions of Karsibor and Kurowskie Blota, along Lake Swidwie, are bird reserves. In Kolczewo, on Wolin Island (about 15 km east of Miedzyzdroje), you can find excellent golf courses, visited by golfers from Germany, Scandinavia and the UK. The region is also famous for horseriding stables, while there are many sea and river harbours for water sport enthusiasts. One of the many attractions for tourists visiting Western Pomerania is the annual Viking Festival.

Useful addressses and telephone numbers

City Hall
pl Armii Krajowej 1
Tel: + 48 91 424 53 00

Voivod's Office
ul Waly Chrobrego 4
Tel: + 48 91 434 24 13

Passport Office
ul Waly Chrobrego 4
Tel: + 48 91 430 37 39

Euroregion Pomerania
al Wojska Polskiego 164, 71–335 Szczecin
Tel: + 48 91 486 08 15, fax: + 48 91 486 08 11

World Trade Centre Szczecin – Promotion Office
al Wojska Polskiego 164
Tel: + 48 91 484 78 31

General Consulate of the Federal Republic of Germany
ul Krolowej Korony Polskiej 31
Tel: + 48 91 22 52 12/22 52 13
Fax: + 48 91 22 51 33

General Consulate of Denmark
al Niepodleglosci 17
Tel: + 48 91 488 89 84

Polish Airlines LOT
al Wyzwolenia 17
Tel: + 48 91 433 99 26 domestic flights
Tel: + 48 91 433 50 58 international flights

Polish Trains PKP information
Tel: + 48 91 935
Tel: + 48 91 934 arrival info
Tel: + 48 91 933 departure info

Taxis

Auto Taxi 919, Euro Taxi 434 34 34, Taxi Radio 487 58 75

Banks

Bank Pekao SA Grupa Pekao SA
ul Grodzka 9
Tel: + 48 91 434 03 87

Bank PKO B.P.
al Niepodleglosci 40
Tel: + 48 91 488 23 05

Deutsche Bank
Plac Rodla 8, Pazim Centre
Tel: + 48 91 359 58 77

Hypo Bank
ul Konski Kierat 13
Tel: + 48 91 488 00 46

Hotels

Radisson SAS
Plac Rodla 10
Tel: + 48 91 359 55 95

Park
ul Plantowa 1
Tel: + 48 91 434 00 50

Panorama
ul Radosna 60
Tel: + 48 91 460 76 07

Neptun
ul Matejki 18
Tel. + 48 91 488 38 83

Restaurants

Avanti
al Jednosci Narodowej 43
Tel: + 48 91 434 64 10

Café Europa
pl Rodla 10
Tel: + 48 91 359 55 95

Renaissance
pl Rodla 10
Tel: + 48 91 359 55 95

Virga
al Wojska Polskiego 245
Tel: + 48 91 452 63 74
– night club

Imperium
ul Boh Warszawy 34/35
Tel: + 48 91 433 29 45

Quo Vadis
pl Rodla 10
Tel: + 48 91 359 55 95

Pubs

Rezonans
al Jednosci Narodowej 43
Tel: + 48 91 434 64 10

Irish Pub Dubline
ul Kaszubska 57

'Okeh' American Food
ul Piastow 1
Tel: + 48 91 484 36 18

Copernicus
pl Rodla 10
Tel: + 48 91 359 55 95

Theatres and Concert Halls

Philharmonic
pl Armii Krajowej 1
Tel: + 48 91 224 723

Opera and Operetta
ul Korsarzy 34
Tel: + 48 91 489 03 40

Polish Theatre
ul Swarozyca 5
Tel: + 48 91 433 00 75

Museums and galleries

National Museum
ul Staromlynska 27
Tel: + 48 91 433 60 70

Gallery of Art 'Kierat-2'
ul Malopolska 5
Tel: + 48 91 434 21 04

DOING BUSINESS IN WROCLAW

'Europolis'

Companies interested in penetrating Eastern European markets often set up businesses in Poland, the most stable economy in the region. The majority of such companies choose Warsaw, but for those who do not like the bustle of crowded cities, there is a tempting alternative, Wroclaw (pronounced Vrotswav). Located approximately 160 km from the nearest frontier crossing point to Germany and about 120 km from the Czech border, the economic, scientific and cultural potential of the city has earned it the title of a 'Europolis': a European centre. In 1997, Wroclaw, with three other Polish cities, was awarded the right to use the flag of the EU.

Wroclaw, which was part of Prussia for around 200 years, is also known under its German name Breslau. Wroclaw is a border city where Polish, Czech, Austrian and German cultures have intermingled over the centuries. This multi-cultural character, which makes Wroclaw unique, is gaining in importance with the removal of trade barriers and the unification of Europe.

Located at the intersection of historical routes from north to south and from east to west, Wroclaw is a major transportation centre in this part of the continent.

Today, Wroclaw's urban area covers 293 km², with a population of 642,000, the fourth largest in Poland. For many centuries the city has been regarded as the capital of the Lower Silesia region, which has a population of 4 million. This land, steeped in history, is now a region with significant economic resources and a substantial consumer market.

Industry and trade

Wroclaw has nearly 7500 production plants, including over 600 large factories. The city's industries employ approximately 60,000 people, 28 per cent of the region's workforce. The private sector, which owns 98.8 per cent of the region's industrial plants, accounts for only 42 per cent of the total industry volume, because some of the largest manufacturers have not yet undergone privatisation. The machine tool industry accounts for the largest share of overall industrial output (30 per cent).

In June 1998, Wroclaw had 78,600 registered business entities, of which 77,700 were privately owned. Twenty thousand new businesses were created over the last three years.

Three of the 15 Special Economic Zones (SEZs) are located in Lower Silesia. Companies, both foreign and Polish, investing in these zones are accorded favourable tax regimes, under certain conditions (these are currently under review by the government).

Foreign investments

Foreign investments in Wroclaw have grown rapidly since 1990, with 1200 registered joint venture companies at the present time. The local authorities, fully realising the positive impact of foreign investment on the regional economy, are particularly helpful, which makes life very much easier for foreign companies investing in Wroclaw or the Lower Silesia region.

Most of the foreign investors (accounting for over US$28 million) are British in origin, with Cadbury Schweppes, Cussons Group Ltd and British Vita ranking among the top ten. The US comes second, with 31 firms, including Coca-Cola, McDonald's, Cargill, General Bottlers and American Retail System, which have injected US$18 million into the regional economy.

A total of 345 German companies have invested over US$10 million in Wroclaw province, the largest ones being Siemens, Viessmann, Mercedes and the Volkswagen Group.

Sweden, represented by companies such as ABB, IKEA, Volvo, Wabco, Alfa Laval Agri and SCA Monlycke, has also made significant investments in the region. ABB, which acquired 70 per cent of the Dolmel Company, is particularly important for the Wroclaw economy.

Altogether, companies from over 40 countries in Europe, America, Asia and Africa are present in the region. Eleven firms from the former Soviet Union, with investments totalling US$1.8 million, are also located here.

Distribution networks are being developed by foreign investment (Makro Cash & Carry, Billa, Hit, Geant, Tesco, Korona, Carrefour and ECE).

Financial services

Businesses in Wroclaw can choose from among the 30 regional and national banks, as well as six foreign banks: Citibank SA (USA), Creditanstalt SA and Raiffeisen Centrobank SA (Austria), Hypo-Bank SA, Deutsche and Dresdner Bank (Germany) and Société Générale SA (France). The major Polish banks operating in Wroclaw are Bank Zachodni SA, Bank Handlowy SA, Bank PKO BP, Bank Pekao SA, Bank Rozwoju Eksportu and Bank Slaski.

Trade fairs

Wroclaw is the venue for 14 business fairs (the majority of them international).

Employment and education

The unemployment rate in the Wroclaw area is 4.2 per cent.

Wroclaw is also one of the major university centres in Poland, with nine state and five private universities, totalling over 80,000 students.

Infrastructure and real estate

The international airport of Strachowice, located at a distance of 6km from the city centre and 4km from the A4 expressway, ensures connections to Warsaw, Frankfurt/Main, Düsseldorf, Copenhagen and Vienna.

The national operator TP SA and four cellular phone operators provide telecommunication services. Private telecommunication services are just taking off, while there is also easy access to satellite and data transmission networks.

Real estate prices (including land) continue to be lower than in Western European countries. In Wroclaw, the purchase price of an apartment is US\$550–850/m^2, and land prices are 20 times less. Rental price for class 'A' office space, usually situated in the Old Town area, ranges from US\$20 to 25 m^2. Class 'B' or 'C' office space, usually located outside the city centre, is priced between US\$7 and 15/m^2. Other locations in the region are much cheaper.

Tourist attractions, sport and recreation

Wroclaw, which enjoys a picturesque location on the Odra river, is called 'the city of a hundred bridges', because of the many bridges over the Odra's tributaries and numerous canals which cross the area. This places Wroclaw in fourth place in Europe in the bridge league, behind Venice, St Petersburg and Amsterdam.

There are plenty of green parks and green areas within the city, while the whole Lower Silesia region is excellent for skiing, hiking, climbing, biking, horse riding, bird watching or car racing.

Wroclaw is the one of the major cultural centres of Poland. The city and the region are the venues for famous theatre performances, movie events, painting exhibitions, etc.

But, above all, the most valuable asset of Wroclaw is its open minded and friendly people. They give the city a unique atmosphere, encouraging visitors to come back again and again.

Useful addresses and telephone numbers

Municipality of Wroclaw – City Promotion and Foreign Relations Office
ul Sukiennice 9
Tel: + 48 71 40 74 65

Ministry of State Treasury – Regional Office
ul Powstancow Slaskich 5
Tel/Fax: + 48 71 361 96 99

Passport Office (Foreigners Department)
pl Powstancow Warszawy 1
Tel: + 48 71 40 65 31

Provincial Labour Office
pl Powstancow Warszawy 1
Tel: + 48 71 40 69 58

Provincial Department of Civil Matters
pl Powstancow Warszawy 1
Tel: + 48 71 40 69 53

Hotels

Dwor Polski
ul Kielbanicza 2
Tel/Fax: + 48 71 372 34 15/372 34 19

Wroclaw
ul Powstancow Slaskich 7
Tel: + 48 71 372 44 66

Maria Magdalena
ul sw Marii Magdaleny 2
Tel: + 48 71 341 08 98 Fax: + 48 71 341 09 20

Exbud
ul Kielbasnicza 24
Tel: + 48 71 3723649

Novotel
ul Wyscigowa 35
Tel: + 48 71 362 87 85 Fax: + 48 71 339 80 75

Restaurants

Academia Brasserie (French)
ul Kuznicza 65/66
Tel: + 48 71 343 45 29

Artzat
ul Malarska 16
Tel: + 48 71 372 37 66

Casablanca
ul Wlodkowica 8a
Tel: + 48 71 344 78 17

Karczma Lwowska
Rynek 4
Tel: + 48 71 343 98 87

Spiz – Mini Brewery
Rynek Ratusz 2
Tel: + 48 71 344 52 67

Trattoria La Scala
Rynek 38
Tel: + 48 71 372 53 94

Pizza Hut
Rynek 48
Tel: + 48 71 343 80 48

Splendido
ul Swidnicka 53
Tel/Fax: + 48 71 343 95 55

Appendix 2

Chambers of Commerce and Business Associations

Compiled by the British Polish Chamber of Commerce

International Bodies

American Chamber of Commerce in Poland (AmCham)

The American Chamber of Commerce in Poland (AmCham) was established in 1991. The Chamber has grown rapidly since then and in 1999 membership exceeded 320 firms. AmCham represents over US$9.2 billion in paid-in or committed funds in Poland.

AmCham is a voluntary organisation; its activities are funded entirely from its membership. The Chamber is a member of the world-wide network of AmChams and the European Council of American Chambers of Commerce (ECACC).

Benefits of membership

- monthly meetings: guest speakers from the highest levels of Polish government, US administration and interpersonal financial institutions address the membership on current issues;

- 'Business Mixers': held monthly, provide an informal setting for members to get to know each other better and discuss business issues;

- government relations: AmCham represents the views of its membership before the Polish and US governments;

- committees: the following committees are active in the Chamber: Human Resources, Pharmaceutical, Energy, Telecommunications, Marketing, Tax, Real Estate and Agriculture;

- workshops/seminars: sponsored by committees on a variety of topics;

- social events: AmCham sponsors a July 4th Picnic, annual golf tournament and other social events;

- *American Investor*: 11 issues per year cover the latest changes in the business environment;

- annual membership directory: the place to find who's who in the American and international business community in Poland, along with a detailed description in both Polish and English.

Membership
AmCham has two types of membership:

- company: open to companies that are incorporated in the USA, or partially owned by US legal entities; international companies with a presence in both the USA and Poland are eligible for corporate membership. Annual membership is US$1000.

- individual: available to any US citizen who is engaged in business in Poland, providing his/her company or employer is not eligible for company membership. Annual membership is US$500.

Embassy of the Kingdom of the Netherlands

ul Chocimska 6
00-791 Warsaw
Poland
Tel: + 48 22 849 23 51/52
Fax: + 48 22 848 83 45
E-mail: nlgovwar@ikp.pl
President: Mr J J de Viser – Ambassador

European Public Policy Advisers (EPPA) Polish Office

EPPA Poland
ul Marszalkowska 82
Suite 516a
00-517 Warsaw
Poland
Tel: + 48 22 622 1269/623 6702
Fax/Tel: + 48 22 623 6702
E-mail: eppapol@medianet.com.pl
Director: Sawomir Witek
Established: 1991 (Polish Office)

EPPA UK
European Public Policy Advisers Ltd
12–14 Denman Street
London W1V 7RN

United Kingdom
Tel: + 44 20 7439 3929
Fax: + 44 20 7734 2380
Chairman: Jeremy Kane
Director: Liz Spencer

EPPA is a pan-European, independent, political marketing consultancy. It has built a reputation for integrity and reliability over 12 years by focusing on its clients' needs and investing in understanding their objectives and markets. EPPA's three practices cover Public Policy Management, Political Communications and International Trade. Together these provide a fully integrated range of services, tailor-made to the needs of each client.

The consultancy adds value by enabling clients to develop and deliver strategies that secure sustainable competitive advantage. EPPA provides a wide range of analytic tools, capable of taking full account of public trends, legislative and regulatory developments, trade negotiations and other public factors affecting clients' objectives.

EPPA helps clients assess and manage cost-effectively a wide range of commercial activities. These include: inward investment and privatisation; mergers and acquisitions and competition issues; regulatory compliance; corporate reputation and relationship building. It assists in developing government–business partnerships, policy analysis and formation, and timely inputs into legislation. EPPA can support clients' risk assessment, management and communication, as well as cost–benefit analyses. It works with clients to plan and implement fully integrated political communication programmes to support each client's specific objectives.

With offices in every EU country and the main Central and East European states, EPPA provides clients with pan-European reach and culturally sensitive delivery of services managed and run by the client's own EPPA team.

In addition, EPPA offers a range of electronically based information services and tools for measuring the effectiveness of external relations activity.

Forum of European Union Chambers of Commerce

The European Union Chambers Forum is an association of European Union Chambers in Poland (British, Danish, Finnish, French, German, Greek, Italian). Its objectives are to facilitate the dialogue between EU investors in Poland and to support the entrance of Poland into the EU in the shortest possible time.

The Forum's Chairman for 1999 is Cristiano Pinzauti, president of Wang Global and vice president of the Italian Chamber. The Forum's vice chairmen are Barbara Stachowiak-Kowalska, director of the British Chamber, and Robert Kamionowski, attorney-at-law and board member of the Danish Chamber.

The Forum's key activities recently have included organising working breakfasts with key personalities, such as the prime minister, the deputy prime ministers, various ministers and the president of the National Bank of Poland, as well as operational meetings with directors of various Polish institutions.

Future plans are to extend existing activities, in particular by increasing the number of operational meetings, to foster co-operation with the Polish authorities on issues pertaining to the accession of Poland to the EU and to continue championing the needs of EU investors in Poland.

French Chamber of Commerce

ul Krucza 16/22
00-526 Warsaw
Tel: + 48 22 622 30 05/622 30 15
Fax: + 48 22 622 30 24
E-mail: ccifp-affaires@zigzag.pl
President: Jean Caillot
Established: 1994

Italian Chamber of Industry and Commerce in Poland

ul Trebacka 4
00-074 Warsaw
Poland
Tel: + 48 22 630 9761/630 9760
Fax: + 48 22 828 9781/827 4673
E-mail: rbali@ikp.pl
President: Massimo Cupello Castagna, President of Ferrero Poland
Established: 1996

The Italian Chamber of Industry and Commerce in Poland was established in 1996 at the initiative of large Italian investors such as Fiat, Ferrero and SM Enterprises in order to represent the interests of Italian companies to the Polish authorities, central agencies and local administration. Its main objectives are:

- representation of members to the Polish authorities;

- establishing permanent contacts with Polish central and local administration;

- participating in a triangle commission with government, trade unions and employers associations;

- stimulating co-operation between Italian investors and Polish entrepreneurs;

- creation of transnational businesses with investors from Central European countries;

- face-to-face meetings with counterparts from the EU, as well as from the Far East;

- legal support to aid co-operation between investors and companies;

- consulting in relation to investment activity on the third market;

- regional meetings with investors of Central European countries.

The Chamber co-operates with parliamentary commissions by providing opinions to members on new draft regulations concerning the economy as a whole and in particular matters such as visa policy, customs regulations, property ownership by foreigners, corporate taxation and the promotion of small and medium-sized enterprises.

It offers many useful services for members and associates, including the transmission of legal/economic information of interest to employers and investors active in Poland, the organisation of seminars, putting members in touch with reputable consulting companies and lobbying by hosting business breakfasts with VIPs. These meetings provide an opportunity for members to present their own opinions or questions to the Polish authorities.

The Chamber also offers members plenty of discounts and privileges, especially for airlines, hotels and country clubs (Alitalia, for example, grants members substantial discounts).

It publishes its own bulletin with, for example, reports of Chamber events and other relevant information about its activities.

The Chamber is a founder of the Forum of the European Union Chambers of Commerce. Members can therefore participate in important social events organised for foreign investors in Poland.

National bodies

British Polish Chamber of Commerce

Head Office
ul Zimna 2/1
00-138 Warsaw
Poland
Tel: + 48 22 654 59 71–76
Fax: + 48 22 654 16 75
E-mail: bpcc@bpcc.org.pl
Web site: http://www.bpcc.org.pl
Contact: Teresa Polubiec, Personal Assistant
E-mail: teresa@bpcc.org.pl
Established: 1992

Established in 1992, the BPCC now has over 400 corporate members. The majority of members represent British and international companies but a natural and positive development is the growing number of Polish companies that are joining the Chamber. The BPCC's Patrons are: Allied Irish Bank; Cameron McKenna; British Airways; Polish Airlines LOT; PricewaterhouseCoopers; Wielkopolski Bank Kredytowy SA.

It is active throughout Poland and in the UK, with branch offices and a regular programme of events in Gdansk, Katowice, Krakow, Poznan, Warsaw, Wroclaw and London. Events, ranging from conferences, workshops and seminars to business drinks, breakfast briefings and dinner discussions, provide members with a forum to exchange ideas, make new contacts and meet prominent politicians and officials of the British, Polish and European governments, as well as other opinion leaders. There is also a social programme for members and their families, with family fun days, quiz evenings, an annual dinner dance and concerts.

The BPCC produces two invaluable publications: an annual bi-lingual Membership Directory and a bi-monthly newsletter, *Contact*. The 5000 copies of *Contact* are distributed to members and key business organisations and through hotel chains and airlines. Selected extracts can be viewed on the BPCC Web site.

Close co-operation with other business development organisations, including British Chambers of Commerce Europe-wide, the British Embassy, the Forum of EU Chambers, British Trade International and the Polish Embassy in the UK, gives BPCC members a formidable infrastructure within which to succeed and grow. To assist members in accessing vital data it runs an Information Centre, based in Warsaw but linked globally through the Internet.

Foreign Investors' Chamber of Industry and Commerce

ul Krakowskie Przedmiescie 47/51
00-071 Warsaw
Poland
Tel: + 48 22 826 22 34/828 78 89/826 18 22
Fax: + 48 22 826 85 93
E-mail: biuro@iphiz.com.pl
Web site: http://www.iphiz.com.pl
President: Stefan Lewandowski
Contact person: Maria Andrzej Falinski, Managing Director
Established: 19 June 1989

The Chamber was established in 1989 as the first independent organisation for the business community, associating joint ventures and operating in all industrial sectors. It includes large companies such as ABB, Daewoo, ING Bank and Procter & Gamble among its members, as well as medium-sized and small enterprises, all of which enjoy the same rights and privileges within the organisation.

As a self-governing, non-political and democratic organisation, the Chamber has gained a meaningful position during the ten years of its existence. The community of foreign investors considers it a valuable representative that defends its interests, while the state authorities have recognised it as an important partner contributing to the creation of favourable conditions for foreign investment in Poland.

On an everyday basis, the Chamber runs specialised courses and training activities, produces its own publications for members and assists in resolving numerous business, organisational and legal issues.

Gdynia Wool Chamber

The Gdynia Wool Chamber is the Association for the Textile and Clothing Industry. It is located in Gdynia and was founded in 1965 at the initiative of Polish wool industry and wool trading companies to represent member companies in their dealings with government institutions and national and international organisations. In particular, it acts as a consultative body on economic and legislative matters with respect to the textiles field.

The Chamber is also a member of the Committee of Wool Textile Industries – Interlaine of the EU and hosts the offices of the Woolmark Company (formerly the International Wool Secretariat), which together operate promotional campaigns in Poland, leading to the licensing of the Woolmark label.

The Association participates in the work of joint committees of Interlaine and Euratex. Currently, there are about 100 firms associated with the Gdynia Wool Chamber, which is considering membership of the International Apparel Federation headquartered in London.

Industry, Trade and Finance Association of Poland

4 Trebacka Street
00-074 Warsaw
Poland
Tel: + 48 22 630 96 90/630 96 37
Fax: + 48 22 826 00 10
E-mail: lewiatan@elektron.pl
Web site: www.polindustry.org.pl
General Director: Kazimierz Jaszczyk
Established: 15 October 1997

The Industry, Trade and Finance Association of Poland is an organisation operating on the basis of the Association Act of 7 April 1989. It is an association of 150 managers of the largest and best-known Polish companies (ordinary members) and of 100 companies managed by these executives (supportive members). The association represents 15 per cent of the Polish economy and its membership forms a core structure around which thousands of medium-sized and small enterprises operate. All member companies conform to European standards and will actively participate in the accession process to the EU.

The Association's objective is to support the economic development of the Polish state in order to achieve sustained and orderly growth and enable Polish companies to compete successfully on world markets. In order to meet these objectives, the Association is committed to promoting and supporting activities in the following areas:

- privatisation of the economy;

- integration with the EU;

- establishment of a pro-development tax system;

- balancing of the state budget;

- concentration of domestic capital;

- export development;

- security of business operations, including protection against unfair competition;

- demonopolisation of the economy.

Mazovian Small Business Chamber

27 Smocza str
01-048 Warsaw
Poland
Tel: + 48 22 838 32 11/838 01 72
Fax: + 48 22 838 35 53
E-mail: izbarimp@fund.org.pl
President: Leszek Janowki
Established: 1929

The Chamber is an organisation of economic self-government representing over 50,000 firms, guilds, craft co-operatives and joint-stock companies. It provides modern consultancy and marketing services for both domestic and foreign companies, legal and financial advice, as well as marketing, taxation and other professional training courses. Since 1992 it has run a computer database to promote Polish products and services. It matches domestic and international partnerships, sends trade missions abroad, hosts trade missions from foreign countries and helps businesses find partners. The Chamber promotes Polish products at international fairs and exhibitions in many countries, represents Polish small and medium-sized enterprises and craft firms at all international events and participates in conferences and seminars devoted to their problems.

The Chamber offers assistance in a wide range of business topics: the tax department gives information about current tax regulations and interpretation, and provides tax training. It is also able to help with meetings, conferences, consultations, lectures, shows and other similar events, and in conjunction with its Small Business Foundation it runs an annual All-Polish Economic Small Business Forum. It organises the participation of Polish entrepreneurs in the yearly International Small Business Congress. The Chamber's newspaper is entitled *Small Business Handicraft*.

National Chamber of Fashion/Polish Centre of Fashion Promotion

The Chamber was founded in 1994 and is currently housed in the fully restored 19th-century classical building in the centre of Lodz (well known as the location of Ludwik Gayer's first mechanical spinning and weaving mill), which used to be known as the Polish Manchester. The building was restored and adapted to its present use with the help of funds allocated by the Phare programme of the EU. The main responsibility of the Centre is the promotion of the Polish textile and apparel industry and all aspects of textile design. The building comprises a purpose-designed 300-seat showroom with stage and catwalk, including atelier and audio-visual presentation facilities.

The Chamber co-ordinates many national activities related to the dissemination of fashion trends, and organises seminars and visits to famous fashion centres, exhibitions and fairs. It integrates activities related to industrial design by means of its Apparel Designers Club, which organises fashion design competitions, promoting young designers in Poland and abroad. It also co-operates with private design houses and tertiary educational design establishments in the country. The Chamber is planning to join the International Apparel Federation (IAF).

Polish Agency for Foreign Investment (PAIZ)

Polish Agency for Foreign Investment
al Roz 2
00-559 Warsaw
Poland
Tel: + 48 22 629 57 17/621 62 61

Fax: + 48 22 621 84 27
E-mail: post@paiz.gov.pl
Web site: http://www.paiz.gov.pl
Established: 1992

PAIZ was established in 1992 to promote Poland's investment opportunities and to encourage foreign companies to choose Poland as their preferred investment location. At the 8th Annual Convention of Investment Promotion Agencies in Chicago in September 1997, PAIZ was named European Investment Promotion Agency of the Year.

It helps businesses considering investment in Poland by:

- providing information, advice and guidance to foreign investors;

- facilitating the initial stages of their investment process;

- providing legal, technical and financial information;

- assisting foreign investors in identifying potential business partners;

- maintaining a link between foreign investors and the appropriate government and local authorities.

The Agency is a joint-stock company, wholly owned by the State Treasury. Its role is that of an intermediary serving individual and corporate foreign investors.

Through maintaining an on-going dialogue with the Polish authorities PAIZ constantly strives to improve the local environment for foreign investment, and ensure that potential investors have access to key players in the Polish market.

Polish Agency for Regional Development

4a Zurawia St.,
00-503 Warsaw
Poland
Tel: + 48 22 693 54 53/693 56 53/629 28 88/629 28 89
Fax: + 48 22 693 54 06/627 22 46
E-mail: parr@pagi.pl
Web site: http://www.bmb.com.pl/parr
General Director: Dr Marek Kozak
Contact Person: Robert Szewczyk, Specialist on Regional Policy
Established: 1993

The Polish Agency for Regional Development (PARR) is a State Treasury foundation established by the Polish government in 1993 in order to support regional development in Poland and, more particularly:

- to stimulate and support economic initiatives as well as cultural, social, administrative and organisational objectives in underdeveloped regions, in areas that require development or transformation of infrastructure, and those threatened with high unemployment;

- to promote the spread of information, advisory services and training programmes, as well as market-related and technical material on all aspects of regional development;

- to set up and participate in the establishment of financial institutions for regional development;

- to provide financial and other support to organisations facilitating change in the economic structure of regions.

The Polish Agency for Regional Development co-operates with state organisations and other institutions, including regional development agencies, that deal with the problems of regional development and structural unemployment. It is responsible for the implementation of aid programmes in several regions, selected by the Polish government: Lodz, Katowice, Walbrzych, Rzeszow, Suwalki, Olsztyn, Krosno, Nowy Sacz, Piotrkow Trybunalski, Sieradz, Loma, Zamooa, Koszalin, Elbaag, Opole, Krakow and Zielona Gora.

The Polish Agency for Regional Development implements and administers – among others – the following programmes:

- Phare-STRUDER (regarding equity capital and provision of guarantees);

- Phare-RAPID;

- Phare-STRUDER 2;

- Phare-INRED;

- Aid Programme for small and medium-sized enterprises for replacement of assets destroyed in the 1997 flood;

- Dialogue and Development programme for capitals of 33 provinces that on 1 January 1999 lose their status;

- PSPR (Polish-Swiss Regional Programme).

Polish Business Roundtable

ul Klonowa 6,
00-591 Warsaw
Poland
Tel: + 48 22 848 3933
Fax: + 48 22 646 1829

E-mail: rada@prb.pl
President: Ms Henryka Bochniarz
Established: 30 May 1992

The Polish Business Roundtable is an association of entrepreneurs that represents companies with leading capital and economic positions and aids in the identification of development opportunities in Poland.

The decision to establish the Roundtable was taken at a gathering of entrepreneurs in Warsaw in April 1992, attended by several dozen chief executive officers of the largest Polish and foreign companies in the country.

The key objectives and current tasks of the Roundtable are defined in the form of policy resolutions adopted annually by the general assembly of members. As a rule, these activities are aimed at implementing the key economic principles advocated by the Association.

The Roundtable advocates unrestricted economic activity, perceived as a civil right, free from limitations such as licences and concessions, and based on the invariability of the fundamental legal standards that govern business activity. It promotes private ownership and a free market, and affirms that the public sector should be significantly reduced and state intervention in the economy kept at a minimum. The Roundtable believes that economic entities must be enabled to associate freely.

The Polish Business Roundtable is headed by its president, Henryka Bochniarz. The executive board consists of the following:

- Aleksander Gudzowaty;

- Jan Kulczyk;

- Zbigniew Niemczycki;

- Janusz Palikot;

- Tomasz Sielicki;

- Witold Zaraska.

With the same address and president is the Polish Confederation of Private Employers, established 7 January 1999.

Polish Chamber of Commerce for Electronics and Telecommunications

28/30 Barska str
02-315 Warsaw
Poland
Tel: + 48 22 822 46 63/823 25 15
Fax: + 48 22 822 69 08

E-mail: kigeit@kigeit.com.pl
Executive Chairman: Stefan Kaminski
Established: February 1993

The Polish Chamber of Commerce for Electronics and Telecommunications (KIGEiT) is an independent organisation of economic entities involved in the manufacture, export, import, trade, services and R&D work in the area of electronics. The entities are registered in Poland and have a track record of a meaningful presence in the Polish market. KIGEiT was founded in November 1992 and officially registered in February 1993. In most countries, chambers of commerce are regional organisations. Poland, however, has developed a specific variety of sectoral chambers, which are associations of all national businesses active in the same economic sector.

Presently, the Chamber has 160 companies affiliated, of which 130 are private and 30 state-owned. Most of these have 50–200 employees and are involved in the following activities:

- manufacture 65 per cent;

- trade 19 per cent;

- services 16 per cent;

Understanding 'electronics' in its broadest sense to include the technology of processing and transmitting information, members have a wide range of activities, including:

- consumer electronics (radio and television sets, video equipment, tape recorders, gramophones, records, dictaphones);

- telecommunications equipment;

- office and computer equipment;

- electronic components;

- wide range of services in the scope of electronics and telecommunication.

Members are represented by the Chamber in the following way:

- representation and defence of the economic interests of corporate affiliates, particularly in relation to the state authorities;

- initiatives for new legislative amendments (updates) and evaluation of legislative acts, including tax and custom duty measures as they apply to electronics;

- assessment of the practical application of legal regulations affecting the pursuit of business by KIGEiT members;

- co-operation in the creation of economic and legal conditions advantageous to the activity of the electronics industry market in Poland and their development;

- creation of a system of technical and commercial information among KIGEiT members;

- working against dishonest competition and advertising, and unfair trading and dealing, particularly in the use of dumping techniques and in ensuring that producers (importers) maintain a high quality of equipment and service;

- protection of the interests of consumers by generating demand for high-quality Polish goods supplied with certificates and service guarantees;

- preparation of the Polish market and electronics industry for integration with the EU;

- assisting in dispute resolution and conciliation.

The Chamber's services to members are:

- running statistical databases on the electronic market and industry in Poland, providing economic and marketing analysis for members of KIGEiT (via the Electronic Market Institute);

- advancement of the development of professional education in electronics with the co-operation of educational bodies;

- training courses for KIGEiT members (importers);

- preparing co-operation meetings between representatives of Polish and international electronics businesses;

- organisation of meetings and conferences to promote the electronics sector.

Chamber promotional activities include:

- patronage of electronics fairs;

- the magazine *The Bank of Offers and Co-operation*;

- publishing (*Chamber Information Bulletin* published quarterly as a supplement to *Electronics*).

Co-operation and sharing of commercial information involves:

- co-operation with similar organisations and with the main bodies of the state and administrative authorities;

- technical and commercial co-operation in order to use the productive and distributive potential of KIGEiT members in an optimum way;

- co-operation with consumer bodies, particularly regarding disputes on economic activities, including complaints about electronic equipment;

- advising the government on customs tariffs, based on the proposals of KIGEiT members;

- research on the restructuring of the electronics industry, carried out in conjunction with the Ministry of Trade and Industry;

- co-operation with the Ministry of Posts and Telecommunications.

Polish Chamber of Commerce of Importers, Exporters and Co-operation

ul sw. Marcin 80/82
61-809 Poznan
Poland
Tel: + 48 61 851 78 48/851 78 49
Fax: + 48 61 851 78 28
E-mail: pigieik@optimus.poznan.pl and pigieikinfo@pig.org.pl
Web site: http://www.pig.org.pl
President of the Board: Henryk Judkowiak
Contact: Justyna Mlickaal, Legal Advisor
Established: 11 October 1995

The Polish Chamber of Commerce of Importers, Exporters and Cooperation's activities include:

- organising trade meetings between Polish and foreign companies, contacting partners, helping businesses co-operate, matching investors and companies, suppliers of machines, equipment and technologies;

- providing legal, economic and banking services;

- representing the interests of member companies involved in importation, exportation, international and local co-operation;

- collecting information from provinces, cities and community authorities of the Wielkopolska region on possibilities of investments in their area;

- organising business meetings and fair participation for members;

- helping members develop local and foreign trade and commercial contacts;

- supporting members' economic initiatives;

- originating projects and legislation and giving opinions on these;

- protecting the interests of members against dishonest competition and fraudulent partners;

- providing consulting and advisory services;

- operating an Economic Information System database;

- preparing economic trips and missions abroad.

The Polish Textile Chamber

The Polish Textile Chamber is located in Lodz and was founded in 1993 on the initiative of certain textile companies – with the aim of representing the textile industry in dealings with Polish central and regional government. The Chamber has as associates over 100 companies and some research institutes. During the course of its existence the Chamber has been involved in the following activities:

- fighting against unfair practices in the import of textiles into the Polish market (analysis of losses to the Polish economy and ways of preventing dishonest competition to the domestic industry);

- studying and preparing proposals to the government regarding customs tariffs;

- submitting to the government a set of proposals for strategies for the development of the textile industry;

- preparing periodic reports for the government on the state of the textile industry, co-operating with the voivodship local authorities in local textile industry development;

- participating in the preparation of consultative material for negotiations on the entry of Poland into the EU.

Regional bodies

Chamber of Commerce and Industry in Krakow

ul Florianska 3, 31–019 Krakow and
skr pocztowa 45, 30-960 Krakow
Poland
Tel: + 48 12 422 13 74/422 89 07
Fax: + 48 12 422 91 38/422 55 67
E-mail: biuro@iph. krakow.pl
Web site: http://www.iph. krakow.pl
President: Tomasz Szczypinski

The Chamber of Commerce and Industry in Krakow is a self-governing business institution, first established in 1850 as an official representative of manufacturers, merchants and craftsmen.

Its main mission is to act on behalf of its member companies, as well as the local business community, in order to create an environment conducive to the development of private enterprises and the market economy, and to promote high ethical standards in business activity.

It has over 250 member companies, among which are the largest and best-known companies, banks, foundations and small enterprises in the area.
The Chamber offers:

- business information (register of business entities, Infodata enquiry agency);

- matching of companies (print-outs of address lists, organisation of business meetings);

- legalisation of foreign trade documents;

- trade missions, business trips to fairs and exhibitions;

- training, seminars, courses (Krakow Business School);

- Regional Office of the Euro Info Correspondence Centre is attached to the Chamber.

Lodz Chamber of Industry and Commerce

30 Tuwima str
90-002 Lodz
Poland
Tel: + 48 22 630 66 64/633 03 49
E-mail: liph@liph.com.pl
Web site: http://liph.com.pl
Director: Anna Strzechowska
Deputy Director: Teresa Zdunek
Established: 1990

The aims and activities of the Chamber include:

- representing and protecting the business interests of its members in relation to the state administration and regional authorities;

- offering opinions on governmental bills and legal regulations on behalf of economic units associated with the Chamber;

- creating and propagating ethical principles and 'fair deal' behaviour, in particular elaborating and improving the rules on fair play and fair competition;

- contributing to the development of economic life and supporting members' business initiatives;

- promoting professional development and improving personnel qualifications in collaboration with appropriate educational institutions;

- organising and creating opportunities to solve disputes by means of conciliation and arbitration;

- offering opinions pertaining to general and recognised practices in business activity;

- providing information on corporate business organisations and giving opinions on economic development within the area of the Chamber's activities;

- collecting data and information on business organisations operating within the Lodz region;

- promoting businesses and assisting in the establishment of business relations with domestic and foreign partners;

- providing assistance to Members of the Chamber in solving the economic, organisational and legal issues connected with their business activities;

- appointing experts to ascertain facts, pass opinions and submit experts' reports on business activities of economic units associated with the Chamber.

Wielkopolska Chamber of Commerce and Industry

26 Glogowska Str
P.O. Box 50
60-734 Poznan
Poland
Tel: + 48 61 866 41 54/866 17 28
Fax: + 48 61 866 14 28/866 41 58
E-mail: wip-h@wip-h.poznan.pl
Web site: http://www.wip-h.poznan.pl
President: Wojciech Kruk, Manager Foreign Markets
Established: October 1989

Registered in October 1989 to continue the traditions of the Chamber of Commerce and Industry that existed in Poznan before the Second World War, the Wielkopolska Chamber of Commerce and Industry is an institution of the region's economic self-government body, created by its members. The group comprises over 500 members, the majority medium-sized and small private companies.

The main task of the Chamber is to facilitate business contacts and to bring together potential business partners, both domestic and foreign. Other activities include the dissemination of economic and legal information, organising special training courses, arranging trade missions and delegations as well as receiving such missions from abroad, and organising participation in international trade fairs and exhibitions. The Chamber can also provide details of knowledgeable contacts in local government and other authorities. In December 1994, the Chamber appointed a permanent economic mediation court.

The Chamber has co-founded several business-oriented schools in Poznan, including the Wielkopolska Business School, the Higher School of Management and Banking and the Secretarial Training School. Maintaining relations with numerous similar organisations, both in Poland and abroad, the Chamber has signed 19 agreements of co-operation with foreign chambers.

The Chamber's members have access to international sources of economic information: the Enterprise, Exprom, BRE and BC-Net systems.

The Chamber's structure includes specialised departments for: Domestic Trade; Banking and Finance; Techniques and Technologies. The staff of the Chamber are qualified to conduct trade discussions and negotiations in several languages – English, German, French and Russian.

Radom Chamber of Industry and Commerce

ul Traugutta 53
26-600 Radom
Poland
Tel: + 48 48 363 05 20/363 05 01
Tel/Fax: + 48 48 363 35 37
E-mail: radom@rip-h.radom.pl
Web site: http://www.rip-h.radom.pl
President: Zdzislaw Gregorczyk
Contact person: Tomasz Staniszewski, Secretary
Established: 21 June 1991

The Chamber is an organisation of a local nature, covering the area of Radom province. It is active both in Poland and abroad and has over 180 members representing the most important firms in the province.

The main aims of Chamber are:

- representation of members to local government, state administration, national and international governments;

- participation in public consultations and delegation of representatives to the advisory departments of the local government and state administrative bodies;

- organisation of trade fairs, exhibitions, meetings and promotions, both in Poland and abroad;

- collection and dissemination of information on Polish and foreign firms and on a variety of technologies and products;

- consulting in the field of civil, commercial and duty law; business consulting;

- collection and dissemination of information on crediting and business financing (foreign credits, guarantees);
- management of publishing and advertising activities;
- provision of professional training for members at the national level;
- co-operation with Chamber of Commerce and Industry at the national level and with societies of similar interests;
- supplying information on its website.

Appendix 3

Contributors' Addresses

Agro Business Consult Ltd (ABC)
Zurawia 22
00-515 Warsaw
Poland
Tel: + 48 22 629 1072
Fax: + 48 22 622 0667
E-mail: abc@abcpoland.com.pl

AWS Corporate Finance Consultancy
Copper Fields
Harlequin Lane
Crowborough
East Sussex TN6 1HU
United Kingdom
Tel: + 44 1278 445 151
Fax: + 44 1892 667891
E-mail: AWSCONSULT@aol.com

BOC Distribution Services Sp.zo.o
ul Sokalowska 10
05-090 Raszyn
Warsaw
Poland
Tel: + 48 22 720 1274
Fax: + 48 22 720 1274
Contact: Lesley Brett, General Director

Brandstorm International
Mieroslawskiego 2b
01-527 Warsaw
Poland
Tel: + 48 22 39 24 69/601 330 576
Fax: + 48 22 628 17 28
E-mail: jsenft@brandstorm.net

BRE Bank SA
ul Senatorska 18
00-082 Warsaw
Poland
Tel: + 48 22 829 0000
Fax: + 48 22 829 0080

British Council
al Jerozolimskie 59
00697 Warsaw
Poland
Tel: + 48 22 695 5900
Fax: + 48 22 621 9955
E-mail: bc.warsaw@britcoun.org.pl
Internet: www.britcounc.org/poland

British Embassy
Warsaw Corporate Centre
28 ul Emilii Platter
00-688 Warsaw
Poland
Tel: + 48 22 625 3030
Fax: + 48 22 625 3472
E-mail: ukembwcc@it.com.pl

British Polish Chamber of Commerce (BPCC)
ul Zimna 2 m 1
00-138 Warsaw
Poland
Tel: + 48 22 654 5971–5
Fax: + 48 22 654 1675

Business Management & Finance SA (BMF)
ul Dworkowa 3
00-784 Warsaw
Poland
Tel: + 48 22 646 8989
Fax: + 48 22 646 9798
E-mail: office@bmf.com.pl

CMS Cameron McKenna Sp.zo.o
Warsaw Financial Centre
53 ul Emilii Platter
00-113 Warsaw
Poland
Tel: + 48 22 520 5555
Fax: + 48 22 520 5556
E-mail: office@cmck.com

Contact
Magazine of the British Polish Chamber of Commerce
ul Zimna 2 m 1
00-138 Warsaw
Poland
Tel: + 48 22 654 5971/73
Fax: + 48 22 654 1675
E-mail: esf@bpcc.org.pl
Internet: www.bpcc.org.pl
Contact: Ewa Swietochowska-Filipek

Ernst & Young
ul Sienna 39
00-121 Warsaw
Poland
Tel: + 48 22 528 7777
Fax: + 48 22 528 7778

European Bank for Reconstruction and Development (EBRD)
One Exchange Square
London EC2A 2JN
United Kingdom
Tel: + 44 20 7338 6198
Tel: + 44 20 7338 6159

Healey & Baker
Sienna Centre
ul Sienna 73
00-833 Warsaw
Poland
Tel: + 48 22 820 20 20
Fax: +48 22 820 20 21

ICL Poland Sp.zo.o
ul Leszno 21
01-199 Warsaw
Poland
Tel: + 48 22 631 0566
Fax: + 48 22 632 0979

International Apparel Consultancy
3 Albemarle
Wimbledon Parkside
London SW19 5NP
United Kingdom
Tel/Fax: + 44 20 8788 2609

Korn/Ferry International
ul J Hoene-Wronskiego 7
00-434 Warsaw
Poland
Tel: + 48 22 622 2829
Fax: + 48 22 622 2838

KPMG Polska Audyt Sp.zo.o
Centrum LIM Ixp
al Jerozolimskie 65/79
00-697 Warsaw
Poland
Tel: + 48 22 630 7236
Fax: + 48 22 830 0796
E-mail: office@kpmg.pl

Office of the Committee for European Integration
al Ujazdowskie 9
00-918 Warsaw
Poland
Tel: + 48 22 694 6756
Fax: + 48 22 694 7226
E-mail: arkadiusz–michonski@mail.ukie.gov.pl
Internet: www.ibspan.waw.pl/ukie

Ove Arup
Warsaw
Poland
Tel: + 48 22 622 2925
Fax: + 48 22 622 2932
E-mail: richard.thurlow@arup.com

Danuta Pilecka
Health Economist, Economic and Management Consultant
PO Box 1
05-420 Jozefow
Poland
Tel/Fax: + 48 22 789 2137
E-mail: danapil@ikp.atm.com.pl
Internet: www.atm.com.pl/~danapil

VP International
Red Hill House
Hope Street
Chester CH4 8BU
United Kingdom
Tel: + 44 1244 681 619
Fax: + 44 1244 681 617
E-mail: nicksljivic@saqnet.co.uk

Warsaw Business Journal
New World Publishing
ul Sloneczna 29
00-789 Warsaw
Poland
Tel: + 48 22 646 2801
Fax: + 48 22 646 0576
E-mail: thom@wbj.pl

W S Atkins Polska Sp.zo.o
ul Marszalkowska 82
00-517 Warsaw
Poland
Tel: + 48 22 623 6340/621 9150
Fax: + 48 22 623 6341
E-mail: adamczyk@wsatkins.com.pl
Contact: Robert Adamczyk, Head of Environmental Department; Chris Moore, Associate Director, Inward Investment Team

Appendix 4

Sources of Further Information

United Kingdom contacts

Association of British Chambers of Commerce (ABCC)
4 Westwood House
Westwood Business Park
Coventry CV4 8HS
United Kingdom
Tel: + 44 24 7669 4484
Fax: + 44 24 7669 5844

British Council
10 Spring Gardens
London SW1A 2BN
United Kingdom
Tel: + 44 20 7930 8466
Fax: + 44 20 7839 6347

British Invisibles
Windsor House
39 King Street
London EC2 8DQ
United Kingdom
Tel: + 44 20 7600 1198
Fax: + 44 20 7606 4248

City Network for East-West Trade (CeeNet)
Warnford Court
Throgmorton Street
London EC2N 2AT
United Kingdom
Tel: + 44 20 7638 9299
Fax: + 44 20 7588 8555

Confederation of British Industry (CBI)
Centre Point
103 New Oxford Street
London WC1A 1DU
United Kingdom
Tel: + 44 20 7379 7400
Fax: + 44 20 7240 1578

Customs and Excise
Dorset House
Stamford Street
London SE1 9PY
United Kingdom
Tel: + 44 20 7202 4687
Fax: + 44 20 7202 4131

Department for International Development
The Know How Fund
Central and South Eastern Europe Department
Room J1/6A
24 Whitehall
London SW1A 2ED
United Kingdom
Tel: + 44 20 7210 0029/65
Fax: + 44 20 7210 0030

Department of Trade and Industry initiatives:

Polish Country Desk
Kingsgate House
66–74 Victoria Street
London SW1E 6SW
United Kingdom
Tel: + 44 20 7215 4735
Fax: + 44 20 7215 4743
Website: www.dti.gov.uk/ots/centeuro

DTI Export Publications
Admail 528
London SW1W 8YT
United Kingdom
Tel: + 44 20 7510 0171
Fax: + 44 20 7510 0197

East European Trade Council (EETC)
Suite 10
Westminster Palace Gardens
Artillery Row
London SW1P 1RL
United Kingdom
Tel: + 44 20 7222 7622
Fax: + 44 20 7222 5359

Export Market Information Centre (EMIC)
Department of Trade and Industry
1st Floor
Kingsgate House
66–74 Victoria Street
London SW1E 6SW
United Kingdom
Tel: + 44 20 7215 5444/5
Fax: + 44 20 7215 4231

World Aid Section
Department of Trade and Industry
Kingsgate House
66–74 Victoria Street
London SW1E 6SW
United Kingdom
Tel: + 44 20 7215 6157
Fax: + 44 20 7215 4231

Embassy of the Republic of Poland – London
Commercial Counsellor's Office
15 Devonshire Street
London W1N 2AR
United Kingdom
Tel: + 44 20 7580 5481
Tel: + 44 20 7323 0195

European Bank for Reconstruction and Development (EBRD)
One Exchange Square
London EC2A 2EH
United Kingdom
Tel: + 44 20 7338 6000
Fax: + 44 20 7338 7892

European Investment Bank
London Office
68 Pall Mall
London SW1Y 5ES
United Kingdom
Tel: + 44 20 7343 1200
Fax: + 44 20 7930 9929

The International Finance Corporation
European Office
4 Millbank
London SW1P 3JA
United Kingdom
Tel: + 44 20 7222 7711
Fax: + 44 20 7976 8323

London Chamber of Commerce and Industry
69 Cannon Street
London EC4N 5AB
United Kingdom
Tel: + 44 20 7248 4444
Fax: + 44 20 7489 0391

Technical Help to Exporters
British Standards Institute
389 Chiswick High Road
London W4 4AL
United Kingdom
Tel: + 44 20 8996 9000
Fax: + 44 20 8996 7400

Poland contacts

PAIZ
al Roz 2
00-559 Warsaw
Poland
Tel: + 48 22 621 0706
Fax: + 48 22 622 6169

British Embassy
Commercial Section
Warsaw Corporate Centre
Emilii Platter
Warsaw
Poland
Tel: + 48 22 625 3030
Fax: + 48 22 625 3472

Embassy of the United States of America
al Jerozomolinskie 56c
00-803 Warsaw
Poland
Tel: + 48 22 625 4374
Fax: + 48 22 621 6327

Chambers of Commerce

American Chamber of Commerce in Poland
ul Swietokrzyska 36/6
00-116 Warsaw
Poland
Tel/Fax: + 48 22 622 5525/620 2698

British Chamber of Commerce in Poland
ul Krolewska 27a m 379
00-060 Warsaw
Poland
Tel: + 48 22 27 72 81 (–89)
Fax: + 48 22 27 72 81

British Polish Chamber of Commerce
ul Zimna 2 m 1
00-138 Warsaw
Poland
Tel: + 48 22 654 59 71/73
Fax: + 48 22 654 1675
Website: www.bpcc.org.pl

Danish-Polish Chamber of Commerce
ul Rakowiecka 19
02-517 Warsaw
Poland
Tel: + 48 22 49 74 14
Fax: + 48 22 49 92 39

French Chamber of Commerce
ul Senatorska 38
00-095 Warsaw
Poland
Tel: + 48 22 26 62 71(–4) ext 103
Fax: + 48 22 27 74 27

Polish-German Chamber of Commerce
ul Miodowa 14
P.O. Box 439
00-950 Warsaw
Poland
Tel: + 48 22 635 3353
Fax: + 48 22 635 8106

Swedish-Polish Chamber of Commerce
ul Jasna 12
00-013 Warsaw
Poland
Tel: + 48 22 26 7201
Fax: + 48 22 26 0101

Chamber of Commerce of Construction and Technological Services Exporters
ul Wierzbowa 9/11
00-094 Warsaw
Poland
Tel/Fax: + 48 22 27 39 24

Chamber of Commerce of Electrical Engineering
ul Pozaryskiego 28
04-703 Warsaw
Poland
Tel: + 48 22 12 00 21
Fax: + 48 22 12 75 35

Chamber of Commerce of Exporters and Importers
ul Bema 65
01-244 Warsaw
Poland
Tel/Fax: + 48 22 632 6872

Chamber of Commerce of Folk and Artistic Craftsmanship 'Cepelia'
ul Chmielna 8
00-950 Warsaw
Poland
Tel: + 48 22 26 60 31/26 46 53
Fax: + 48 22 26 36 62

Foreign Investors Chamber of Industry & Commerce
ul Krakowskie Przedmiescie 47/51
00-071 Warsaw
Poland
Tel: + 48 22 27 22 34
Fax: + 48 22 26 85 93

National Chamber of Commerce
ul Trebacka 4
00-074 Warsaw
Poland
Tel: + 48 22 630 9609
Fax: + 48 22 827 9478

Polish Chamber of Commerce, Poznan Division
al Niepodleglosci 2
61-874 Poznan
Poland
Tel: + 48 61 53 29 28
Fax: + 48 61 52 16 70

Polish Chamber of Commerce, Torun Division
Aleje 500 lecia 31
87-100 Torun
Poland
Tel: + 48 56 24 511

Polish Chamber of Commerce
ul Trabacka 4
00-916 Warsaw
Poland
Tel: + 48 22 27 94 78
Fax: + 48 22 2746 73

Polish Chamber of Commerce of Electronics
ul Barska 28/30
02-315 Warsaw
Poland
Tel: + 48 22 22 46 63
Fax: + 48 22 22 69 08

Polish Chamber of Chemical Industry
ul Zurawia 6/12
00-926 Warsaw
Poland
Tel: + 48 22 628 2051 ext 224/225
Fax: + 48 22 625 3178

Polish Pharmacy Chamber of Commerce
ul Czarnieckiego 48
01-548 Warsaw
Poland
Tel/Fax: + 48 22 39 20 80

Small Business Chamber
ul Smocza 27
01-048 Warsaw
Poland
Tel: + 48 22 38 32 11
Fax: + 48 22 38 3553

Business & Investment Organisations

Business Center Club
Plac Zelaznej Bramy 2
00-136 Warsaw
Poland
Tel: + 48 22 625 3037
Fax: + 48 22 621 8420

Foundation for Polish Exports
ul Krolewska 27
00-060 Warsaw
Poland
Tel: + 48 22 27 68 10
Fax: + 48 22 27 68 10

The Market Information Center of Foreign Trade in Warsaw
ul Krucza 38/42
00-512 Warsaw
Poland
Tel: + 48 22 628 2728
Tel/Fax: + 48 22 628 8680/629 1222

Polish Business Advisory Service
al Niepodleglosci 186
00-608 Warsaw
Poland
Tel: + 48 22 625 9781
Fax: + 48 22 625 9880

Polish Foundation
ul Astronomow 3
01-450 Warsaw
Poland
Tel/Fax: + 48 22 37 32 37 ext 303

PROMASZ
Bureau for Studies and Economic Consulting
ul Barbary 1
00-686 Warsaw
Poland
Tel: + 48 22 628 3159
Fax: + 48 22 629 2616

UNIDO Industrial Cooperation and Investment Promotion Service
Aleje Niepodleglosci 186
00-608 Warsaw
Poland
Tel: + 48 22 625 9467/625 9186
Fax: + 48 22 625 8970
Int'l Tel/Fax: + 48 39 12 17 72

TWIG Data Bank
ul Mazowiecka 13
00-052 Warsaw
Poland
Tel: + 48 22 27 53 15/26 76 32
Fax: + 48 22 27 51 51

Government contacts

Ministry of the Economy
pl Trzech Krzyży 5
00-507 Warsaw
Poland
Tel: + 48 22 693 5000
Fax: + 48 22 628 6808

Ministry of Environmental Protection, Natural Resources and Forestry
Wawelska 52/54
00-922 Warsaw
Poland
Tel: + 48 22 825 0001

Ministry of Food and Agriculture
ul Wspolna 30
00-930 Warsaw
Poland
Tel: + 48 22 628 0570
Fax: + 48 22 629 5599
Website: www.minrol.gov.pl/bprasowe/index.html

Index

Index of Advertisers